全国高等院校英语本科专业规划教材
本书获扬州大学教材出版基金资助

英美文学:阅读与批评
English and American Literature: Reading and Criticism

张小平 编著

苏州大学出版社

图书在版编目(CIP)数据

英美文学:阅读与批评 / 张小平编著. —苏州: 苏州大学出版社, 2015.9 (2023.1重印)
全国高等院校英语本科专业规划教材
ISBN 978-7-5672-1463-7

Ⅰ. ①英… Ⅱ. ①张… Ⅲ. ①英语-阅读教学-高等学校-教材②英国文学-文学研究③文学研究-美国 Ⅳ. ①H319.4:I

中国版本图书馆 CIP 数据核字(2015)第 198167 号

书　　名:	英美文学:阅读与批评
	English and American Literature: Reading and Criticism
作　　者:	张小平　编著
责任编辑:	金莉莉
策　　划:	汤定军
装帧设计:	刘　俊
出版发行:	苏州大学出版社(Soochow University Press)
社　　址:	苏州市十梓街1号　邮编: 215006
印　　装:	广东虎彩云印刷有限公司
网　　址:	www.sudapress.com
E - mail:	tangdingjun@suda.edu.cn
邮购热线:	0512-67480030
销售热线:	0512-65225020
开　　本:	700mm×1000mm　1/16　印张: 25.5　字数: 499千
版　　次:	2015年9月第1版
印　　次:	2023年1月第2次印刷
书　　号:	ISBN 978-7-5672-1463-7
定　　价:	75.00元

凡购本社图书发现印装错误,请与本社联系调换。服务热线: 0512-65225020

前　言

　　文学是一种社会生活方式。研究表明，在人类步入文明时代之前，文学就以号子、歌唱、神话原始形式成为社会生活的一部分。没有文学润泽的人生是干涸的，没有文学滋养的社会则是不可思议的。文学是一面镜子，它映照着社会的方方面面，以其涉及面之广博、思想和知识之深奥、观察之细腻与多维、语言之优美与形象为人们提供了浏览、阅读、把玩、品味、赏析、研究多层次的需求，因此，马克思称它是"百科全书"。阅读文学作品，人的心灵便多了一双想象的翅膀，人生五味，世间百态，万千感受，尽在其中。游弋在或庄重典雅，或诙谐幽默，或寓意丰厚，或辛辣尖刻，或俏皮夸张，或亦庄亦谐的文学作品中，感受文学作品的思想美、语言美、形象美、气韵美、意境美，既提高文学素养，陶冶情操，又增长知识，锻炼思维。研读英美文学不仅具有上述收获，更可以了解英美社会的风土人情，增强对英语语言的感悟。

　　当前，我国高等院校英语专业和一些非英语专业都开设有相关的英美文学阅读和文学欣赏课程，可供选择的英美文学教材和读物种类繁多，有文学史、文学选读或者二者合一的文学史及文学选读，它们各具特点，各有不同侧重点。但是，根据作者多年的教学经验来看，读史也好，选读作品也罢，没有一定的与之相应的文学批评知识，学生很难把握文学作品的实质，更难领略经典作品带给人们的真、善、美的启迪和熏陶。本书旨在引领读者用文学批评的基本方法，结合英美文学中的精华篇章，学会如何研读英美文学宝库中的经典文学作品。本书力图以规范的语言、浅显流畅的文句，向读者介绍英语文学的主要形式——诗歌、小说和戏剧的基本要素及其发展的基本脉络，在此基础上，遴选了英美文学史上近60位重要作家的多部经典作品，旨在帮助读者加深对文学本质、文学流派和文学风格的了解和认识，力求选材上具有新意。

　　诗歌是文学的最早形式，在中国有世界最早的诗歌集《诗经》以及《萨格尔》、《江格尔》、《布洛陀》、《苗族古歌》等史诗；在两河流域有《吉尔伽美什》；在印度有《摩诃婆罗多》和《罗摩衍那》；在欧洲有《荷马史诗》；而英国文学的源头则是公元8世纪的史诗《贝尔沃夫》。因此，本书作者有意识地把诗歌放在第一部分。小说从它诞生伊始，便吸引了广大的读者群，并逐渐成为文学的主体，拥有最重量级的地位，同时也成为电影编剧的主要脚本，因此,本书作者把它放在第二部分,并占有较多篇幅。戏剧作为不可忽视的文学艺术形式,成为本书第三部分的探讨内容。这样的结构安排考虑到了历史和逻辑的统一,也考虑到了突出重要部分的内容,希望起到纲领分明、量体裁衣的效果。

本书可作为高校英语专业和非英语专业学生的英美文学课程的教学用书和参考书,可供广大英语教师、英美文学爱好者以及具有一定英语水平的自学者选用作为阅读材料,也为英语专业毕业生写作英语论文时提供格式、术语的参考。全书分为三个部分,共十七章,融文学批评与文学名作欣赏为一体,在文学批评讲解的同时,贯穿了文学作品的欣赏和研究。文学批评部分贯穿于文学作品的赏析中,并在每一章后面附有文学批评的理论"小贴士"。文学作品部分除了经典选文外,还精心设计了相关的阅读思考题。此外,本书还附有作家的生平及创作介绍、文学论文写作时的文献格式和方法、文学术语词汇表、文学批评基本理论。如果作为教材,文学鉴赏理论部分可由教师把握,作家介绍则供学生参考;课堂教学应以启发式和讨论式的教学方法为主,师生互动,注重培养学生的理性思辨能力和理解分析能力,让学生在获得理论指导的同时又能得到文本分析的实践,有效地提高学生的文学欣赏水平和英文写作的能力。

本书在编写过程中得到了扬州大学的俞洪亮教授、秦旭教授、于建华教授、王金铨教授、周领顺教授、王莎烈教授等有关领导与老师的大力支持,趁此书附梓之机,谨向他们表示由衷的感谢。

美国特拉华大学英语系主任 Stephen Bernhardt 教授在百忙之中审阅了本书的初稿,并提出了许多进一步修改的宝贵意见;美国诺维奇大学第一副校长黄桂友教授、厦门大学杨仁敬教授和詹树魁教授、吉林大学胡铁生教授、苏州大学贾冠杰教授一直关心和支持本书的撰写工作,他们提供了不少帮助;作者任教过的学生也对本书的编写提出了许多尽管稚嫩但有意义的修改意见。此书得以顺利出版,也凝聚了他们的劳作,作者在这里致以真诚的谢意。

本书在编写过程中参考了大量中外出版的文学批评理论、英美文学史和英美文学作品选读方面的书籍,注释和思考题部分也参照了一些有关的书籍,在参考文献部分均一一列出,在此向原作者深表感谢。

由于作者个人某些局限,书中讹误、缺点和疏漏之处在所难免,诚望专家和同行不吝赐教,以便再版时订正。

张小平

2015 年春于扬州笃行楼

Contents

Part One　Poetry　/ 001

● 1. **Reading a Poem**　/ 002
　　　The Lake Isle of Innisfree (1892)　/ 004
　Lyric Poetry　/ 007
　　　A Red, Red Rose (1796)　/ 008
　Narrative Poetry　/ 009
　　　"Out, Out—" (1916)　/ 009
　Dramatic Poetry　/ 011
　　　My Last Duchess (1842)　/ 011
　[Reading Critically] Can a Poem Be Paraphrased?　/ 014

● 2. **Listening to a Voice**　/ 014
　Tone　/ 014
　　　To a Locomotive in Winter (1881)　/ 015
　　　I Like to See It Lap the Miles (about 1862)　/ 016
　The Person in the Poem　/ 017
　　　Hawk Roosting (1960)　/ 017
　　　I Wandered Lonely as a Cloud (1807)　/ 018
　Irony　/ 020
　　　The Chimney Sweeper (1789)　/ 021
　[Reading Critically] Paying Attention to the Obvious　/ 022

● 3. **Words**　/ 023
　Literal Meaning　/ 023
　　　This Is Just to Say (1934)　/ 023
　　　Sonnet 18 (1609)　/ 024
　　　Aftermath (1873)　/ 025
　Allusion　/ 026
　Connotations　/ 026
　　　London (1794)　/ 027
　　　Fire and Ice (1923)　/ 029
　　　Break, Break, Break (1842)　/ 029
　[Reading Critically] The Ways a Poem Suggests　/ 030

● 4. **Imagery and Symbol**　/ 031

In a Station of the Metro (1916) / 032
Analyzing Images / 032
The Winter Evening Settles Down (1917) / 033
She Walks in Beauty (1815) / 034
Spring and All (1923) / 035
The Red Wheelbarrow (1923) / 036
Dreams (about 1932) / 036
Symbol / 037
The Lightning Is a Yellow Fork (about 1870) / 038
Allegory / 039
Anecdote of the Jar (1923) / 040
The Road Not Taken (1916) / 041
Poem (1934) / 042
Bright Star! Would I Were Steadfast as Thou Art (1819) / 042
[Reading Critically] How to Read a Symbol / 043

● 5. **Figures of Speech** / 044
Speaking Figuratively / 044
The Eagle (1851) / 045
The Flea (1633) / 046
Metaphor and Simile / 047
Flower in the Crannied Wall (1869) / 048
To See a World in a Grain of Sand (about 1803) / 048
It Dropped So Low—in My Regard (about 1863) / 049
Other Figures of Speech / 049
The Silken Tent (1942) / 051
The Tyger (1794) / 051
The Sick Rose (1794) / 053
[Reading Critically] How Metaphors Enlarge a Poem's Meaning / 053

● 6. **Sound** / 054
Alliteration / 054
Assonance / 055
The Splendor Falls on Castle Walls (1850) / 055
Rime / 056
Desert Places (1936) / 057
Rhythm / 058
Meter / 059
Verse Form / 062
Stanza Form / 063
The Descent of Winter (Section 10/30) (1934) / 064

Beat! Beat! Drums! (1861)　/ 064
Dream Boogle (1951)　/ 065
She Dwelt Among the Untrodden Ways (1800)　/ 066
[Reading Critically] What Is Poetry?　/ 066

Part Two　Fiction　/ 069

Fables, Parables, and Tales　/ 070
Short Stories　/ 071
Long Stories and Novels　/ 072

1. Plot　/ 076
Pride and Prejudice (1813) (Chapters 1 and 58)　/ 078
Tess of the d'Urbervilles (1891) (XXXIV)　/ 085
[Reading Critically] What's the Plot?　/ 093

2. Character　/ 094
The Jilting of Granny Weatherall (1930)　/ 097
Everyday Use (1973)　/ 106
[Reading Critically] How Does Character Create Action?　/ 113

3. Setting　/ 114
The Storm (1898)　/ 116
To Build a Fire (1910)　/ 120
[Reading Critically] How Do Time and Place Set a Story?　/ 133

4. Point of View　/ 133
A Rose for Emily (1931)　/ 137
The Tell-Tale Heart (1843,1850)　/ 145
[Reading Critically] How Does Point of View Shape a Story?　/ 149

5. Tone and Style　/ 150
A Clean, Well-Lighted Place (1933)　/ 154
Barn Burning (1939)　/ 158
[Reading Critically] Be Style Conscious　/ 173

6. Symbol　/ 173
The Chrysanthemums (1938)　/ 176
Odour of Chrysanthemums (1911,1914)　/ 185
[Reading Critically] Recognizing Symbols　/ 201

7. Theme　/ 202
The Open Boat (1897)　/ 205
The Garden Party (1922)　/ 224
[Reading Critically] Stating the Theme　/ 236

8. Evaluating a Story / 237
  Eveline (1914) / 242
  Catch-22 (1961) / 246

Part Three Drama / 256

1. Reading a Play / 257
  A Play in Its Elements / 259
  Dialogue / 260
  Story / 261
  Character / 263
  Action / 264
    Desire under the Elms (1924) / 265
  [Reading Critically] Conflict Resolution / 271

2. Dramatic Types / 272
  Tragedy / 272
  Comedy / 274
  Tragicomedy and Theatre of the Absurd / 276
    Hamlet (1601) / 278
    The Importance of Being Earnest (1895) / 287
  [Reading Critically] Breaking the Language Barrier / 293

3. The Development of Drama / 294
  English Drama in the 20th Century / 295
  American Drama in the 20th Century / 296
    Rosencrantz and Guildenstern Are Dead (1966) / 299
    The Death of a Salesman (1949) / 327
  [Reading Critically] Critical Performance / 340

Appendixes / 342
  Appendix 1. Writers Presented in This Book / 342
  Appendix 2. Reference Guide for Citations / 370
  Appendix 3. Glossary of Literary Terms / 375
  Appendix 4. Critical Approaches to Literature / 393

Bibliography / 399

Part One   Poetry

Things that are true expressed in words that are beautiful.

—Dante

What is poetry? Pressed for an answer, Robert Frost made a classic reply: "Poetry is the kind of thing poets write." In all likelihood, Frost was not trying merely to evade the question but to chide his questioners into thinking for himself. A trouble with definitions is that they may stop thinking. If Frost had said, "Poetry is a rhythmical composition of words expressing an attitude, designed to surprise and delight, and to arouse an emotional response", the questioners might be content to learn the truth about poetry. In fact, he would have learned nothing, or not so much as he might learn by continuing to wonder, for Frost also made another try at a definition: "A poem is an idea caught in the act of dawning."

The nature of poetry eludes simple definitions. In this respect it is rather like jazz. Asked after one of his concerts, "What is jazz?" Louis Armstrong replied, "Man, if you gotta ask, you'll never know." Definitions will be of little help at first if we are to know poetry and respond to it. We have to go to it, and are willing to see and hear. For this reason, you are asked in reading this book not to be in any hurry to decide what poetry is like, but instead to study poems and to let them grow in your mind. At the end of our discussions of poetry, the problem of definition will be taken up again.

Perhaps you already have friendship, or at least a fair acquaintance, with some of the great English-speaking poets of all time. What this part of the present book provides is an introduction to the study of poetry. It tries to help you look at a poem closely, to offer you a wider and more accurate vocabulary with which to express what poems say to you. It will suggest ways to judge for yourself the poems you read. It may set forth some poems new to you.

A frequent objection is that poetry ought not to be studied at all. In this view, a poem is either a series of gorgeous noises to be funneled through one ear and out the other without being allowed to trouble the mind, or an experience so holy that to analyze it in a classroom is as cruel and mechanical as dissecting a hummingbird. To the first view, it might be countered that a good poem has something to say that is well worth listening to. To the second view, it might be argued that poems are much less perishable than hummingbirds, and luckily we can study them in flight. The risk of a poem's dying from observation is not nearly so great as the risk of not really seeing it at all. It is doubtful that any excellent poem has ever vanished from human memory because people have read it too closely.

Good poetry is something that readers can care about. In fact, an ancient persuasion of humankind is that the hearing of a poem, as well as the making of a poem, can be a religious act. Poetry, in speech and song, was part of classic Greek drama, which for the playwright, actor and spectator alike was a holy day ceremony. The Greeks' belief that a poet writes a poem only by supernatural assistance is clear from the invocations to the Muse that begins the *Iliad* and the *Odyssey* and from the opinion of Socrates (in Plato's *Ion*) that a poet has no powers of invention until divinely inspired. Among the ancient Celts, poets were regarded as magicians and priests, and whoever insulted one of them might expect to receive a curse in rime potent enough to afflict him with boils and to curdle the milk of his cows. Such identifications between the poet and the magician are less common these days, although we know that poetry is involved in the primitive white-magic of children, who bring themselves good luck in a game with the charm "Roll, roll, Tootsie-roll!/Roll the marble in the hole!" and who warn against a hex while jumping along a sidewalk: "Step on a crack,/Break your mother's back."

To read a poem, we have to be willing to offer it responses besides a logical understanding. Whether we attribute the effect of a poem to a divine spirit or to the reactions of our glands and cortexes, we have to take the reading of poetry seriously (not solemnly), if only because—as some of the poems in this book may demonstrate—few other efforts can repay us so generously, both in wisdom and in joy. If, as we hope you will do, you sometimes browse in the book for fun, you may be annoyed to see so many questions following the poems. Should you feel this way, try reading with a slip of paper to cover up the questions. You will then—if the Muse should inspire you—have paper in hand to write a poem.

1. Reading a Poem

How do you read a poem? The literal-minded might say, "Just let your eye light on it"; but there is more to poetry than meets the eye. What Shakespeare called "the mind's eye" also plays a part. Many a reader who has no trouble understanding and enjoying prose finds poetry difficult. This is to be expected. At first glance, a poem usually will make some sense and give some pleasure, but it may not yield everything at once. Sometimes it only hints at meaning still to come if we will keep after it. Poetry is not to be galloped over like the daily news: A poem differs from most proses in that it is to be read slowly, carefully, and attentively. Not all poems are difficult, of course, and some can be understood and enjoyed on first seeing. But good poems yield more if read twice; and the best poems—after ten, twenty, or a hundred readings—still go on yielding.

Approaching a thing written in lines and surrounded with white space, we need not expect it to be a poem just because it is verse. (Any composition in lines of more or less regular rhythm, usually ending in rimes, is verse.) Here, for instance, is a specimen of verse that few will call poetry:

> *Thirty days hath September,*
> *April, June, and November;*
> *All the rest have thirty-one*
> *Excepting February alone,*
> *To which we twenty-eight assign*
> *Till leap year makes it twenty-nine.*

To a higher degree than that classic memory-tickler, poetry appeals to the mind and arouses feelings. Poetry may state facts, and more important, it makes imaginative statements that we may value even if its facts are incorrect. Coleridge's error in placing a star within the horns of the crescent moon in "The Rime of the Ancient Mariner" does not stop the passage from being good poetry, though it is faulty astronomy. According to the poet, Gerard Manley Hopkins, poetry is "to be heard for its own sake and interest even over and above its interest of meaning". There are other elements in a poem besides plain prose sense: sounds, images, rhythms, and figures of speech. These may strike us and please us even before we ask, "But what does it all mean?"

This is a truth not readily grasped by anyone who regards a poem as a kind of puzzle written in secret code with a message slyly concealed. The effect of a poem (one's whole mental and emotional response to it) consists in much more than simply a message. By its musical qualities, by its suggestions, it can work on the readers' unconsciousness. T. S. Eliot put it well when he said in *The Use of Poetry and the Use of Criticism* that the prose sense of a poem is chiefly useful in keeping the reader's mind "diverted and quiet, while the poem does its work upon him". Eliot went on to liken the meaning of a poem to the bit of meat a burglar brings along to throw to the family dog. What is the work of a poem? It is to touch us, to stir us, to make us glad, and possibly even to tell us something.

How to set about reading a poem? Here are a few suggestions.

To begin with, read the poem once straight through, with no particular expectations; read open-mindedly. Let yourself experience whatever you find, without worrying about the large general and important ideas the poem contains (if indeed it contains any). Don't dwell on a troublesome word or difficult passage—just push on. Some of the difficulties may seem smaller when you read the poem for a second time; at least, they will have become parts of a whole for you.

On the second reading, read for the exact sense of all the words; if there are words you don't understand, look them up in a dictionary. Dwell on any difficult parts as long as you need to.

If you read the poem silently to yourself, sound its words in your mind. (This is a technique that will get you nowhere in a speed-reading course, but it may help the poem to do its work on you.) Better still, read the poem aloud, or hear someone else read it. You may discover meanings you did not perceive in it before. Even if you are no actor, to decide how to speak a poem can be an excellent method of getting to understand it. Some poems, like bells, seem heavy till heard. Listen while reading the following lines from Alexander Pope's *Dunciad*. Attacking the minor poet James Ralph, who had sung the praises of a mistress named Cynthia, Pope makes the Goddess of Dullness exclaim: "Silence, ye wolves! while Ralph to Cynthia howls, /And makes night hideous—answer him, ye owls!" When *ye owls* slide together and become *yowls*, poor Ralph's serenade is turned into the nightly outcry of a cat.

Try to paraphrase the poem as a whole, or perhaps just the more difficult lines. In paraphrasing, we put into our own words what we understand the poem to say, restating ideas that seem essential, coming out and stating what the poem may only suggest. This may sound like a heartless thing to do to a poem, but good poems can stand it. In fact, to compare a poem to its paraphrase is a good way to see the distance between poetry and prose. In making a paraphrase, we generally work through a poem or a passage line by line. The statement that results may take as many words as the original, if not more. A paraphrase, then, is ampler than a summary, a brief condensation of gist, main idea, or story.

Here is a poem worth considering line by line. The poet writes of an island in a lake in the west of Ireland, in a region where he spent many summers as a boy.

The Lake Isle of Innisfree (1892)

William Butler Yeats

I will arise and go now, and go to Innisfree,
And a small cabin build there, of clay and wattles made:
Nine bean-rows will I have there, a hive for the honey-bee,

And live alone in the bee-loud glade.

And I shall have some peace there, for peace comes dropping slow,
Dropping from the veils of the morning to where the cricket sings;
There midnight's all a glimmer, and noon a purple glow,
And evening full of the linnet's wings.

I will arise and go now, for always night and day
I hear lake water lapping with low sounds by the shore;
While I stand on the roadway, or on the pavements gray,
I hear it in the deep heart's core.

Though relatively simple, this poem is far from simple-minded. We need to absorb it slowly and thoughtfully. At the start, for most of us, it raises problems: What are *wattles*, from which the speaker's dream-cabin is to be made? We might guess, but in this case it will help to consult a dictionary: They are "poles interwoven with sticks or branches, formerly used in building as frameworks to support walls or roofs". Evidently, this getaway house will be built in an old-fashioned way: It won't be a prefabricated log cabin or A-frame house, nothing modern or citified. The phrase *bee-loud glade* certainly is not commonplace language of the sort we find on a cornflakes package, but right away, we can understand it, at least partially: It is a place loud with bees. What is a *glade*? Experience might tell us that it is an open space in woods, but if that word stops us, we can look it up. The *linnet* is a creature with wings—a songbird of the finch family, although we do not see it frequently in our life. But even if we do not make a special trip to the dictionary to find *linnet*, we probably recognize that the word means "bird", and the line makes sense to us.

A paraphrase of the whole poem might go something like this: "I'm going to get up now, go to Innisfree, build a cabin, plant beans, keep bees, and live peacefully by myself amid nature and beautiful light. I want to, because I can not forget the sound of that lake water. When I'm in the city, a gray and dingy place, I seem to hear it deep inside me."

These dull remarks, roughly faithful to what Yeats is saying, seem a long way from poetry. Nevertheless, they make certain things clear. For one, they spell out what the poet merely hints at in his choice of the word *gray*: that he finds the city dull and depressing. He stresses the word; instead of saying *gray* pavements, in the usual word order, he turns the phrase around and makes *gray* stand at the end of the line, where it rimes with *day* and so takes extra emphasis. The grayness of the city therefore seems important to the poem, and the paraphrase tries to make its meaning obvious.

Whenever you paraphrase, you stick your neck out. You affirm what the poem gives you to understand. And making a paraphrase can help you see the central thought of the poem, its theme. Theme is not the same as subject, the main topic, whatever the poem is "about". Not all poems clearly assert a proposition, but many do; some even declare their themes in their opening lines. In Yeats' poem, the subject is the lake isle of Innisfree, or a wish to retreat to it. But the theme is, "I yearn for an ideal place where I will find perfect peace and happiness." Themes can be stated variously, depending on what you believe most matters in the poem. Taking a different view of the poem, placing more weight on the speaker's wish to escape the city, you might instead state the theme: "This city is getting me down—I want to get back to nature." But after taking a second look at that statement, you might want to sharpen it. After all, this Innisfree seems a special, particular place, where the natural world means more to the poet than just any old trees and birds he might see in a park. Perhaps a stronger statement of theme, one closer to what matters most in the poem, might be: "I want to quit the city for my heaven on earth." That, of course, is saying in an obvious way what Yeats says more subtly, more memorably.

A paraphrase, of course, never tells all that a poem contains; nor will every reader agree that a particular paraphrase is accurate. We all make our own interpretations; and sometimes the total meaning of a poem evades even the poet who wrote it. Asked to explain his difficult *Sordello*, Robert Browning replied that when he had written the poem only God and he knew what it meant. Still, to analyze a poem as if we could be certain of its meaning is, in general, more fruitful than to proceed as if no certainty could ever be had. The latter approach is likely to end in complete subjectivity: the attitude of the reader who says, "Yeats's 'The Lake Isle of Innisfree' is really about the lost island of Atlantis. It is, because I think it is. How can you prove me wrong?" Interpretations can not be proven "wrong". A more fruitful question might be, "What can we understand from the poem's very words?"

All of us bring personal associations to the poems we read. "The Lake Isle of Innisfree" might give you special pleasure if you have ever vacationed on a small island or on the shore of a lake. Such associations are inevitable, even to be welcomed, as long as they don't interfere with our reading the words on the page. We need to distinguish irrelevant responses from those the poem calls for. The reader who can not understand "The Lake Isle of Innisfree" because she is afraid of bees is not reading a poem by Yeats, but one of her own inventions.

Now and again we meet a poem—perhaps startling and memorable—into which the method of paraphrase won't take us far. Some portion of any deep poem resists explanation, but certain poems resist it almost entirely. Many poems of religious mystics seem closer to dream than waking. So do poems that purport to record drug experiences, such as Coleridge's "Kubla Khan", as well as poems that embody some private system of beliefs, such as Blake's "The Sick Rose", or the same poet's lines from *Jerusalem*, "For a Tear is an Intellectual thing,/And a Sigh is the Sword of an Angel King." So do nonsense poems, translations of primitive folk songs, and surreal poems. ①

Such poetry may move us and give pleasure (although not, perhaps, the pleasure of mental understanding). We do it no harm by trying to paraphrase it, though we may fail. Whether logically clear or strangely opaque, good poems appeal to the intelligence and do not shrink from it.

So far, we have taken for granted that poetry differs from prose; yet all our strategies for reading poetry—plowing straight on through and then going back, isolating difficulties, trying to paraphrase, reading aloud, using a dictionary—are no different from those we might employ in unraveling a complicated piece of prose. Poetry, after all, is similar to prose in most respects. At the very least, it is written in the same language. Like prose, poetry shares knowledge with us. It tells us, for instance, of a beautiful island in Lake Gill, County Sligo, Ireland, of how one man feels toward it. Maybe the poet knows no more about Innisfree than a writer of a travel guidebook knows. And yet Yeats' poem indicates a kind of knowledge that tourist guidebooks do not ordinarily reveal: That the human heart can yearn for peace and happiness that the lake isle of Innisfree with its "low sounds by the shore" can echo and reecho in memory forever.

Lyric Poetry

Originally, as its Greek name suggests, a **lyric** was a poem sung to the music of a lyre. This earlier meaning—a poem made for singing—is still current today, when we use lyrics to mean the words of a popular song. But the kind of printed poem we now call a lyric is usually something else, for over the past five hundred years, the nature of lyric poetry has changed greatly. Ever since the rise of the printing press in the 15th century, poets have written less often for singers, more often for readers. In general, this tendency has made lyric poems contain less word-music and more thought—and perhaps more complicated feelings.

---

① The French poet Andre Breton (founder of Surrealism, a movement in art and writing) declared that a higher reality exists, which to mortal eyes looks absurd. To mirror that reality, surrealist poets are fond of bizarre and dreamlike objects such as soluble fish and white-haired revolvers.

Here is a rough definition of lyric as it is written today: a short poem expressing the thoughts and feelings of a single speaker. Often a poet will write a lyric in the first person (e.g. "I will arise and go now, and go to Innisfree"), but not always. Instead, a lyric might describe an object or recall an experience without the speaker's ever bringing himself or herself into it.

Perhaps some people still expect a lyric to be an outburst of feeling, somewhat resembling a song, at least containing musical elements such as rime, rhythm, or sound effects. Such expectations are fulfilled in "The Lake Isle of Innisfree", that impassioned lyric full of language rich in sound (as you will hear if you'll read it aloud). In practice, though, many contemporary poets write short poems in which they voice opinions or complicated feelings—poems that no reader would dream of singing. Most people would call such poems lyrics, too.

But in the sense in which we use it, lyric will usually apply to a kind of poem you can easily recognize. Here, for instance, is a lyric.

A Red, Red Rose (1796)

Robert Burns

O my luve's① like a red, red rose,
    That's newly sprung in June;
O my luve's like the melodie,
    That's sweetly played in tune②.

As fair art thou, my bonie lass,
    So deep in luve am I;
And I will luve thee still, my dear,
    Till a'③ the seas gang dry.

Till a' the seas gang dry, my dear,
    And the rocks melt wi'④ the sun;
And I will luve thee still, my dear,
    While the sands o' life shall run.

And fare thee weel⑤, my only luve,

---

① luve: love, here referring to the young man's sweetheart
② in tune: harmoniously
③ a': all
④ wi': with
⑤ fare thee weel: farewell to you

And fare thee weel a while;
And I will come again, my luve,
Tho' it were then thousand mile!

Study Questions:
1. What does the speaker compare his love to in Stanza 1?
2. How does the speaker express his lasting love for his girl?
3. How far away will the speaker leave his girl?
4. What figure of speech does the poet use in this love poem?
5. The poem has been highly praised and sung as a love song. Give some reasons for its popularity.

Narrative Poetry

A lyric sometimes relates an incident, or draws a scene, yet it does not usually relate a series of events. That happens in a **narrative poem**, one whose main purpose is to tell a story.

In Western literature, narrative poetry dates back to the Babylonian *Epic of Gilgamesh* (composed before 2000 B. C.) and Homer's epics *Iliad* and *Odyssey* (composed before 700 B. C.). It may well have originated much earlier. In England and Scotland, storytelling poems have long been popular; in the late Middle Ages, ballads—or storytelling songs—circulated widely. Some survive in our day, and folksingers sometimes perform them.

Evidently the art of narrative poetry invites the skills of a writer of fiction: the ability to draw characters and settings briefly, to engage attention, to shape a plot. Needless to say, it calls for all the skills of a poet besides. Here is a narrative poem. How would you paraphrase the story it tells?

"Out, Out—" (1916)[1]

Robert Frost

The buzz-saw snarled and rattled in the yard
And made dust and dropped stove-length sticks of wood,
Sweet-scented stuff when the breeze drew across it.
And from there those that lifted eyes could count

---

[1] The title of this poem echoes the words of Shakespeare's Macbeth on receiving news that his queen is dead: "Out, out, brief candle! / Life's but a walking shadow, a poor player/ That struts and frets his hour upon the stage/ And then is heard no more. It is a tale/ Told by an idiot, full of sound and fury, / Signifying nothing" (*Macbeth* V, v, 23 –28).

Five mountain ranges one behind the other
Under the sunset far into Vermont.
And the saw snarled and rattled, snarled and rattled,
As it ran light, or had to bear a load.
And nothing happened: day was all but done.
Call it a day, I wish they might have said
To please the boy by giving him the half hour
That a boy counts so much when saved from work.
His sister stood beside them in her apron
To tell them "Supper". At the word, the saw,
As if to prove saws knew what supper meant,
Leaped out at the boy's hand, or seemed to leap—
He must have given the hand. However it was,
Neither refused the meeting. But the hand!
The boy's first outcry was a rueful laugh,
As he swung toward them holding up the hand
Half in appeal, but half as if to keep
The life from spilling. Then the boy saw all—
Since he was old enough to know, big boy
Doing a man's work, though a child at heart—
He saw all spoiled. "Don't let him cut my hand off—
The doctor, when he comes. Don't let him, sister!"
So. But the hand was gone already.
The doctor put him in the dark of ether.
He lay and puffed his lips out with his breath.
And then—the watcher at his pulse took fright.
No one believed. They listened at his heart.
Little—less—nothing!—and that ended it.
No more to build on there. And they, since they
Were not the one dead, turned to their affairs.

Study Questions:

1. How does Frost make the buzz-saw appear sinister?

2. How does he make the buzz-saw seem, in another way, like a friend?

3. What do you make of the people who surround the boy—the "they" of the poem? Who might they be? Do they seem to you concerned and compassionate, cruel, indifferent, or what?

4. What does Frost's reference to *Macbeth* contribute to your understanding of "Out, Out—"?

5. How would you state the theme of Frost's poem?

Dramatic Poetry

A third kind of poetry is **dramatic poetry**, which presents the voice of an imaginary character (or characters) speaking directly, without any additional narration by the author. A dramatic poem, according to T. S. Eliot, does not consist of "what the poet would say in his own person, but only what he can say within the limits of one imaginary character addressing another imaginary character". Strictly speaking, the term dramatic poetry describes any verse written for the stage (and until a few centuries ago most playwrights, like Shakespeare and Molière, wrote their plays mainly in verse). But the term most often refers to the **dramatic monologue**, a poem written as a speech made by a character (other than the author) at some decisive moment. A dramatic monologue is usually addressed by the speaker to some other characters who remain silent. If the listener replies, the poem becomes a dialogue in which the story unfolds in the conversation between two speakers.

The Victorian poet Robert Browning, who developed the form of the dramatic monologue, liked to put words in the mouths of characters who were conspicuously nasty, weak, reckless, or crazy; see, for instance, Browning's "Soliloquy of the Spanish Cloister" in which the speaker is an obsessively proud and jealous monk. The dramatic monologue has been a popular form among American poets, including Edwin Arlington Robinson, Robert Frost, Ezra Pound, Randall Jarrell, and Sylvia Plath. The most famous dramatic monologue ever written is probably Browning's "My Last Duchess" in which the poet creates a Renaissance Italian Duke whose words reveal more about himself than the aristocratic speaker intends.

My Last Duchess (1842)
Ferrara[①]

Robert Browning

That's my last Duchess painted on the wall,
Looking as if she were alive. I call
That piece a wonder, now; Frà Pandolf's[②] hands
Worked busily a day, and there she stands.
Will't please you sit and look at her? I said
"Frà Pandolf" by design, for never read

---

① Ferrara: a city in northern Italy (it is the scene). Browning may have modeled his speaker after Alonzo, Duke of Ferrara (1533—1598).
② Frà Pandolf: fictitious name of an artist

Strangers like you that pictured countenance,①
The depth and passion of its earnest glance,②
But to myself they turned (since none puts by
The curtain I have drawn for you, but I)③
And seemed as they would ask me, if they durst④,
How such a glance came there; so, not the first
Are you to turn and ask thus. Sir, 'twas not
Her husband's presence only, called that spot
Of joy⑤ into the Duchess' cheek; perhaps is
Frà Pandolf chanced to say, "Her mantle laps⑥
Over my lady's wrist too much," or "Paint
Must never hope to reproduce the faint
Half-flush that dies along her throat."⑦ Such stuff⑧
Was courtesy, she thought, and cause enough
For calling up that spot of joy. She had
A heart—how shall I say?—too soon made glad,
Too easily impressed; she liked whate'er
She looked on, and her looks went everywhere.
Sir, 'twas all one!⑨ My favor at her breast⑩,
The dropping of the daylight in the West,
The bough of cherries some officious⑪ fool
Broke in the orchard for her, the white mule
She rode with round the terrace—all and each

---

① for never read/Strangers like you that pictured countenance: for strangers like you never looked at that face in the picture

② The depth and passion of its earnest glance: the deep feelings showed on her face as she glanced in earnest

③ since none puts by/The curtain I have drawn for you, but I: since none but I have the right to draw the curtain behind which the portrait is hung

④ durst: dare

⑤ 'twas not/Her husband's presence only, called that spot/Of joy: It was not only her husband's presence that caused that blush to appear

⑥ laps: wraps round

⑦ the faint/Half-blush that dies along her throat: the dim reddish blush that gradually disappears along her throat

⑧ Such stuff: such foolish words

⑨ 'twas all one: all the following things meant the same to her

⑩ My favor at her breast: the gift I gave her which she wore at her breast

⑪ officious: over-zealous

        Would draw from her alike the approving speech,
        Or blush, at least. She thanked men—good①! but thanked
        Somehow—I know not how—as if she ranked
        My gift of a nine-hundred-year-old name②
        With anybody's gift. Who'd stoop to blame
        This sort of trifling? Even had you skill
        In speech—which I have not—to make your will
        Quite clear to such an one③, and say "Just this
        Or that in you disgusts me; here you miss,
        Or there exceed the mark"—and if she let
        Herself be lessoned so, nor plainly set
        Her wits to yours, forsooth, and made excuse—
        E'en then would be some stooping; and I choose
        Never to stoop. Oh, sir, she smiled, no doubt,
        Whene'er I passed her; but who passed without
        Much the same smile? This grew; I gave commands;
        Then all smiles stopped together④. There she stands⑤
        As if alive. Will't please you rise? We'll meet
        The company below, then. I repeat,
        The Count your master's known munificence⑥
        Is ample warrant that no just pretense
        Of mine for dowry will be disallowed;
        Though his fair daughter's self, as I avowed
        At starting, is my object. Nay, we'll go
        Together down, sir. Notice Neptune⑦, though,
        Taming a sea-horse, thought a rarity,
        Which Claus of Innsbruck⑧ cast in bronze for me!

---

① good: a parenthetical remark spoken by the Duke
② My gift of a nine-hundred-year-old name: the title of the Duchess which I gave her
③ such an one: referring to the Duchess
④ Then all smiles stopped together: Then she died
⑤ There she stands: referring to the portrait on the wall
⑥ munificence: bountifulness
⑦ Neptune: referring to the statue of Neptune, the Greek sea-god, which the Duke is showing to the envoy as they are going downstairs to meet the people there
⑧ Claus of Innsbruck: fictitious name of an artist

Study Questions:

1. Who is the Duke addressing? What is this person's business in Ferrara?

2. What is the Duke's opinion of his last Duchess's personality? Do we see her character differently?

3. If the Duke was unhappy with the Duchess's behavior, why didn't he make his displeasure known? Cite a specific passage to explain his reticence.

4. How much do we know about the fate of the last Duchess? Would it help our more understanding of the poem?

5. Does Browning imply any connection between the Duke's art collection and his attitude toward his wife?

[Reading Critically]

Can a Poem Be Paraphrased?

Since the full meaning of a poem is so completely wedded to its exact wording, some people maintain that no poem can be truly paraphrased. As we have discussed earlier in the chapter, however, such an opinion misses the point of paraphrasing. A paraphrase does not attempt to re-create the full effect of a poem; it only tries to map out clearly the key images, actions, and ideas. A map is no substitute for a landscape, but a good map often helps us find our way through the landscape without getting lost.

2. Listening to a Voice

Tone

Like tone of voice, **tone** in literature often conveys an attitude toward the person addressed. Like the manner of a person, the manner of a poem may be friendly or belligerent toward its readers, condescending or respectful. Again like the tone of voice, the tone of a poem may tell us how the speaker feels about himself or herself: cocksure or humble, sad or glad. But when we usually ask, "What is the tone of a poem?" we mean, "What attitude does the poet take toward a theme or a subject?" Is the poet being affectionate, hostile, earnest, playful, sarcastic, or what? We may never be able to know, of course, the poet's personal feelings. All we need to know is how to feel when we read the poem.

Strictly speaking, **tone** is not an attitude; it is whatever in the poem makes an attitude clear to us: the choice of certain words instead of others, the picking out of certain details. In A. E. Housman's "Loveliest of Trees", for example, the poet communicates his admiration for a cherry tree's beauty by singling out for attention its white blossoms; had he wanted to show his dislike for the tree, he might have concentrated on its broken branches, birdlime, or snails. Rightly to perceive the tone of a poem, we need to read the poem carefully, paying attention to whatever suggestions we find in it.

Here are two poems. Read them carefully and try to find the differences of the two poems in tone.

To a Locomotive in Winter (1881)
Walt Whitman

Thee for my recitative,
Thee in the driving storm even as now, the snow, the winter-day declining,
Thee in thy panoply①, thy measur'd dual throbbing and thy beat convulsive,
Thy black cylindric body, golden brass and silvery steel,
Thy ponderous side-bars, parallel and connecting rods, gyrating, chuttling at thy sides,
Thy metrical, now swelling pant and roar, now tapering in the distance,
Thy great protruding head-light fix'd in front,
Thy long, pale, floating vapor-pennants, tinged with delicate purple,
The dense and murky clouds out-belching from thy smoke-stack,
Thy knitted frame, thy springs and valves, the tremulous twinkle of thy wheels,
Thy train of cars behind, obedient, merrily following,
Through gale or calm, now swift, now slack, yet steadily careering;
Type of the modern—emblem of motion and power—pulse of the continent.
For once come serve the Muse and merge in verse, even as here I see thee,
With storm and buffeting gusts of wind and falling snow,
By day thy warning ringing bell to sound its note,
By night thy silent signal lamps to swing.
Fierce-throated beauty!
Roll through my chant with all thy lawless music, thy swinging lamps at night,
Thy madly-whistled laughter, echoing, rumbling like an earthquake, rousing all,
Law of thyself complete, thine own track firmly holding,
(No sweetness debonair of tearful harp or glib piano thine,)
Thy trills of shrieks by rocks and hills return'd,
Lauch'd o'er the prairies wide, across the lakes,
To the free skies unpent and glad and strong.

---

① panoply: suit of armor

I Like to See It Lap the Miles (about 1862)①

Emily Dickinson

I like to see it lap the Miles—
And lick the Valleys up—
And stop to feed itself at Tanks—
And then—prodigious step

Around a Pile of Mountains—
And supercilious peer
In Shanties—by the sides of Roads—
And then a Quarry pare

To fit its Ribs
And crawl between
Complaining all the while
In horrid—hooting stanza—
Then chase itself down Hill—

And neigh like Boanerges—
Then—punctual as a Star
Stop—docile and omnipotent
At its own stable door—

Study Questions:

1. What differences in tone do you find between Whitman's and Dickinson's poems? Point out in each poem whatever contributes to these differences.

2. In Whitman's opening line, what is "a recitative"? What other specialized terms from the vocabulary of music and poetry does each poem contain? How do they help underscore Whitman's theme?

3. "Boanerges" in Dickinson's last stanza means "sons of thunder", a name given by Jesus to the disciples John and James (see Mark 3:17). How far should the readers work out the particulars of this comparison? Does it make the tone of the poem serious?

4. Poets and songwriters probably have regarded the locomotive with more affection than they have shown most other machines. What do these two poems tell you about locomotives that you

---

① Parentheses around a date that follows a poem title indicate the poem's date of composition, when it was composed much earlier than its first publication date.

would not be likely to find in a technical book on railroading?

The Person in the Poem

The tone of a poem, we said, is like the tone of voice in that both communicate feelings. Still, this comparison raised a question, when we read a poem, whose "voice" speaks to us?

"The poet's" is one possible answer; and in the case of many a poem, that answer may be right. Usually we can be sure that the poet speaks of her or his very own book, and of her or his own experiences. In order to read a poem, we seldom need to read a poet's biography; but in truth there are certain poems whose full effect depends upon our knowing at least a fact or two or the poet's life.

When the poet says "I", we may want to assume that he or she is making a personal statement. But reflect: do all poems have to be personal? In other poems, the speaker is obviously a persona, or fictitious character: not the poet, but the poet's creation. As a grown man, William Blake, a skilled professional engraver, wrote a poem in the voice of a boy, an illiterate chimney sweeper. No literary law decrees that the speaker in a poem even has to be human; sometimes the poem is spoken by a bird, a canoe, or something else outside of human world. Good poems have been uttered by clouds, pebbles, clocks, and cats.

Here is a poem spoken by a hawk, a dramatic monologue that expressed the animal's thoughts and attitudes in a way consciously designed to emphasize how different its worldview is from a human perspective.

Hawk Roosting (1960)
Ted Hughes

I sit in the top of the wood, my eyes closed.
Inaction, no falsifying① dream
Between my hooked head and hooked feet:
Or in sleep rehearse perfect kills and eat.

The convenience of the high trees!
The air's buoyancy② and the sun's ray
Are of advantage to me;
And the earth's face upward for my inspection.

---

① falsifying: fraudulently altering
② buoyancy: power of supporting a body so that it floats in a liquid

My feet are locked upon the rough bark①.
It took the whole of Creation
To produce my foot, my each feather:
Now I hold Creation in my foot

Or fly up, and revolve it all slowly—
I kill where I please because it is all mine.
There is no sophistry② in my body:
My manners are tearing off heads—

The allotment of death.
For the one path of my flight is direct
Through the bones of the living.
No arguments assert my right:

The sun is behind me.
Nothing has changed since I began.
My eye has permitted no change.
I am going to keep things like this.

Study Questions:

1. Find three observations the hawk makes about its world that a human would probably not make. What do these remarks tell us about the bird's character?

2. In what ways does Ted Hughes create an unrealistic portrayal of the hawk's true mental powers? What statements in the poem would an actual hawk be unlikely to make? Do these passages add anything to the poem's impact? What would be lost if they were omitted?

In a famous definition, William Wordsworth calls poetry "the spontaneous overflow of powerful feelings … recollected in tranquility". But in the case of the following poem, Wordsworth's feelings were not all his; they did not just overflow spontaneously; and the process of tranquil recollection had to go on for years.

I Wandered Lonely as a Cloud (1807)
William Wordsworth

I wandered lonely as a cloud
That floats on high o'er vales and hills,

---

① bark: tough outer skin of tree-trunks
② sophistry: a false argument

When all at once I saw a crowd,
A host, of① golden daffodils,
Beside the lake, beneath the trees,
Fluttering and dancing in the breeze.

Continuous② as the stars that shine
And twinkle on the milky way,
They stretched in never-ending line
Along the margin of a bay:
Ten thousand saw I at a glance,
Tossing their heads in sprightly③ dance.

The waves beside them danced; but they
Out-did the sparkling waves in glee;
A poet could not but be gay,
In such a jocund company;
I gazed—and gazed—but little thought
What wealth the show to me had brought:

For oft, when on my couch I lie
In vacant or in pensive mood④,
They flash upon that inward eye
Which is the bliss of solitude⑤;
And then my heart with pleasure fills,
And dances with the daffodils.

Study Questions:

1. Why is the poet deeply impressed by the daffodils? How does the poet employ personification to describe the beauty of the daffodils?
2. How does the poet express his appreciation of memory in the poem?
3. What kind of mood does the poet reveal in the last stanza?
4. What is the effect of the poet taking the first person in his poem?

---

① A host, of: a large number of
② Continuous: Extending without break
③ sprightly: lively, full of energy
④ In vacant or in pensive mood: In a mood in which the mind is devoid of any thought or in a deeply thoughtful mood
⑤ They flash upon that inward eye/ Which is the bliss of solitude: When alone, Wordsworth recalls the beautiful scene, which gives him great happiness

5. What philosophical and mystical thoughts does the poet reveal in the poem?

Irony

To see a distinction between the poet and the words of a fictitious character—between Robert Browning and "My Last Duchess"—is to be aware of **irony**: a manner of speaking that implies a discrepancy. If the mask says one thing and we sense that the writer is in fact saying something else, the writer has adopted an ironic point of view. No finer illustration exists in English than Jonathan Swift's "A Modest Proposal", an essay in which Swift speaks as an earnest, humorless citizen who sets forth his reasonable plan to aid the Irish poor. The plan is so monstrous that no sane reader can assent to it: The poor are to sell their children as meat for the tables of their landlords. From behind his false-face, Swift is actually recommending not cannibalism but love and Christian charity.

A poem is often made complicated and more interesting by another kind of irony. **Verbal irony** occurs whenever words say one thing but mean something else, usually the opposite. The word "love" means "hate" here: "I just love to stay home and do my hair on a Saturday night!" If the verbal irony is conspicuously bitter, heavy-handed, and mocking, it is **sarcasm**: "Oh, he's the biggest spender in the world, all right!" (The sarcasm, if that statement were spoken, would be underscored by the speaker's tone of voice.)

Dramatic irony, like verbal irony, contains an element of contrast, but it usually refers to a situation in a play wherein a character, whose knowledge is limited, says, does, or encounters something of greater significance than he or she knows. We, the spectators, realize the meaning of this speech or action, for the playwright has afforded us superior knowledge. In Sophocles' *King Oedipus*, when Oedipus vows to punish whoever has brought down a plague upon the city of Thebes, we know—as he does not—that the man he would punish is himself. Superior knowledge can be enjoyed not only by spectators in a theater but by readers of poetry as well. In *Paradise Lost*, we know in advance that Adam will fall into temptation, and we recognize his overconfidence when he neglects a warning. The situation of Oedipus contains also cosmic irony, or irony of fate: some Fate with a grim sense of humor seems cruelly to trick a human being. Cosmic irony clearly exists in poems in which Fate or the Fates are personified and seen as hostile, as in Thomas Hardy's "The Convergence of the Twain".

To sum up: The effect of irony depends upon the readers' noticing some incongruity or discrepancy between two things. In verbal irony, there is a contrast between the speaker's words and meaning; in an **ironic point of view**, between the writer's attitude and what is spoken by a fictitious character; in dramatic irony, between the limited knowledge of a character and the fuller knowledge of the reader or spectator; in **cosmic**

irony, between a character's aspiration and the treatment he or she receives at the hands of Fate. Although, in the work of an inept poet, irony can be crude and obvious sarcasm, it is invaluable to a poet of more complicated mind, who imagines more than one perspective.

Read the following poem, and understand the tone and irony in the poem.

The Chimney Sweeper (1789)
William Blake

When my mother died I was very young,
And my father sold me while yet my tongue
Could scarcely cry "'weep! 'weep! 'weep! 'weep!"①
So your chimneys I sweep, and in soot I sleep.

There's little Tom Dacre, who cried when his head,
That curled like a lamb's back, was shaved: so I said
"Hush, Tom! never mind it, for when your head's bare
You know that the soot cannot spoil your white hair."

And so he was quiet, and that very night,
As Tom was a-sleeping, he had such a sight!
That thousands of sweepers, Dick, Joe, Ned, and Jack,
Were all of them locked up in coffins of black.

And by came an Angel who had a bright key,
And he opened the coffins and set them all free;
Then down a green plain leaping, laughing, they run,
And wash in a river, and shine in the sun.

Then naked and white, all their bags left behind,
They rise upon clouds and sport in the wind;
And the Angel told Tom, if he'd be a good boy,
He'd have God for his father, and never want joy.

And so Tom awoke; and we rose in the dark,
And got with our bags and our brushes to work.
Though the morning was cold, Tom was happy and warm;
So if all do their duty they need not fear harm.

---

① The child's lisping attempt at the chimney sweeper's street cry, "Sweep! Sweep!"

Study Questions:

1. What does Blake's poem reveal about conditions of life in London of his day?

2. Sum up your impressions of the speaker's character. What does he say and do that displays it to us?

3. What pun do you find in Line 3? Is its effect comic or serious?

4. In Tom Dacre's dream (Lines 11–20), what wishes come true? Do you understand them to be the wishes of the chimney sweeper, of the poet, or of both?

5. In the last line, what is ironic in the speaker's assurance that the dutiful "need not fear harm"? What irony is there in his urging all to "do their duty"? (Who have failed in their duty to "him"?)

6. What is the tone of Blake's poem? Angry? Hopeful? Sorrowful? Compassionate? (Don't feel obliged to sum it up in a single word.)

[Reading Critically]

Paying Attention to the Obvious

If the tone is a speaker's attitude toward his or her material, then to understand the tone of a poem, we need mostly just to listen—as we might listen to a real conversation. The key is to hear not only what is being said but also how it is being said. Does the speaker sound noticeably surprised, angry, nostalgic, tender, or expectant? A common mistake in analyzing poetry is to discuss subtle points of interpretation before you fully understand the obvious features of a poem.

In critical writing it almost never hurts to begin by asking obvious questions:

1. Does the speaker reveal any obvious emotion or attitude about the subject or the setting of the poem?

2. If there is an implied listener to the poem, how does the speaker address them? Is there anything obviously unusual about the tone?

3. Is there any obvious difference between the reaction of the speaker to what is happening in the poem and your own honest reaction? If the gap between the two reactions is large (as it is in Robert Browning's "My Last Duchess", for instance), what does it suggest?

4. If the difference between your honest reaction and the speaker's is enormous, is the poem in some way ironic?

3. Words

Literal Meaning

In reading a poem, some people assume that its words can be skipped over rapidly, and they try to leap at once to the poem's general theme. It is as if they fear being thought clods unless they can find huge ideas in the poem (whether or not there are any). Such readers often ignore the literal meanings of words: the ordinary, matter-of-fact sense to be found in a dictionary.

Consider the following poem and see what you make of it.

This Is Just to Say (1934)
William Carlos Williams

I have eaten

the plums

that were in

the icebox

and which

you were probably

saving

for breakfast

Forgive me

they were delicious

so sweet

and so cold

Some readers distrust a poem so simple and candid. They think, "What's wrong with me? There has to be more to it than this!" But poems seldom are puzzles in need of solutions. We can begin by accepting the poet's statements, without suspecting the poet of trying to hoodwink us. On later reflection, of course, we might possibly decide that the poet is playfully teasing or being ironic; but Williams gives us no reason to think that. There seems no need to look beyond the literal sense of his words, no profit in speculating that the plums symbolize worldly joys and that the icebox stands for the universe. Clearly, a reader who held such a grand theory would have overlooked (in eagerness to find a significant idea) the plain truth that the poet makes clear to us: that ice-cold plums are a joy to taste.

To be sure, Williams' small poem is simpler than most poems are; and yet in reading any poem, no matter how complicated it is, you will do well to reach slowly and reluctantly for a theory to explain it by. To find the general theme of a poem, you first need to pay attention to its words. Poets often strive for words that point to physical details and solid objects. They may do so even when speaking of an abstract idea.

If a poem reads daffodils instead of *plant life*, *diaper years* instead of *infancy*, we call its diction, or choice of words, concrete rather than abstract. Concrete words refer to what we can immediately perceive with our senses, or particular individuals who belong to those general classes. Abstract words express ideas or concepts: *love*, *time*, and *truth*. In abstracting, we leave out some characteristics found in each individual, and instead observe a quality common to many.

Ezra Pound gave a famous piece of advice to his fellow poets: "Go in fear of abstractions." This is not to say that a poet cannot employ abstract words, nor that all poems have to be about physical things. Much of T. S. Eliot's *Four Quartets* is concerned with time, eternity, history, language, reality, and other things that cannot be physically handled. But Eliot, however high he may soar for a larger view, keeps returning to earth. He makes us aware of things.

Here are two poems. Please detect its literal meaning and its connotations.

Sonnet 18 (1609)
William Shakespeare

Shall I compare thee to a summer's day?
Thou art① more lovely and more temperate②.
Rough winds do shake the darling buds of May,
And summer's lease③ hath all too short a date.
Sometime④ too hot the eye of heaven⑤ shines,
And often is his gold complexion dimm'd;

---

① art: are
② temperate: moderate
③ summer's lease: A lease is a written agreement, made according to law, by which the use of a building or a piece of land is given by its owner to somebody for a certain time in return for rent. Here summer is personified as a tenant holding a "lease" for a short term and time is holding that "lease" like some kind of eternal landlord.
④ sometime: sometimes
⑤ the eye of heaven: the Sun

And every fair from fair sometime declines①,
By chance, or nature's changing course, untrimm'd②;
But thy eternal summer shall not fade,
Nor lose possession of that fair thou ow'st③,
Nor shall Death brag thou wander'st in his shade④,
When in eternal line to time thou grow'st⑤.
So long as men can breathe or eyes can see,
So long lives this, and this gives life to thee.

Study Questions:

1. In Shakespearean sonnet, to what does Shakespeare compare "thou"? How do you think the poet answers the question he puts forth in the first line?

2. What makes the poet think that "thou" can be more beautiful than summer and immortal?

3. Sum up in your own words the message of Shakespeare's poem. In stating its theme, did you have to read the poem for literal meanings, figurative comparisons, or both?

Aftermath (1873)
Henry Wadsworth Longfellow

When the summer fields are mown,
When the birds are fledged and flown,
And the dry leaves strew the path;
With the falling of the snow,
With the cawing of the crow,
Once again the fields we mow
And gather in the aftermath.

Not the sweet, new grass with flowers
In this harvesting of ours;
Not the upland clover bloom;
But the rowen mixed with weeds,
Tangled tufts from marsh and meads,

---

① And every fair from fair sometime declines: And the beauty of every beautiful thing will fade at some future time

② untrimm'd: stripped of beauty

③ ow'st: own

④ Nor shall Death brag thou wander'st in his shade: Death shall not brag that you will go to the underworld

⑤ When in eternal lines to time thou grow'st: When you and the eternal time are one and the same

Where the poppy drops its seeds
In the silence and the gloom.

Study Questions:

1. How does the etymology and meaning of "aftermath" help explain this poem? (Look the word up in your dictionary.)

2. What is the meaning of "fledged" (Line 2) and "rowen" (Line 11)?

3. Once you understand the literal meaning of the poem, do you think that Longfellow intended any further significance to it?

Allusion

An **allusion** is an indirect reference to any person, place, or thing—fictitious, historical, or actual. Sometimes, to understand an allusion in a poem, we have to find out something we did not know before. But usually the poet asks of us only common knowledge, he assumes that we will understand his allusions in his poem and perhaps even catch its meaning.

Allusions not only enrich the meaning of a poem, they also save space. Often in reading a poem you will meet a name you do not recognize, on which the meaning of a line (or a whole poem) seems to depend. When you venture out on your own in reading poems, you may find yourself needlessly perplexed unless you look up such names, the way you look up any other words. Unless the name is one that the poet made up, you will probably find it in one of the larger desk dictionaries, such as Webster's *New Collegiate Dictionary*, *The American Heritage Dictionary*, or *Webster's II*. If you do not solve your problem there, try an encyclopedia, a world atlas, *The New Century Cyclopedia of Names*, or *Brewer's Dictionary of Phrase & Fable*. Some allusions are quotations from other poems. Partly it is just one poet's delight in repeating another poet's verbal home runs, but well-chosen allusions also pack an extra wallop of meaning into a poem.

Connotations

Every word has at least one **denotation**: a meaning as defined in a dictionary. But the English language has many a common word with so many denotations that a reader may need to think twice to see what it means in a specific context. A word also has **connotations**: overtones or suggestions of additional meaning that it gains from all the contexts in which we have met in the past. The word "skeleton", according to a dictionary, denotes "the bony framework of a human being or a vertebrate animal, which supports the flesh and protects the organs". But by its associations, the word can arouse thoughts of war, of disease and death, or (possibly) of one's plans to go to medical school.

In imaginative writing, connotation is crucial. Consider Romeo's assertion that Juliet "is the sun", surely even a lovesick boy cannot mean that his sweet heart is "the incandescent body of gases about which the earth and other planets revolve" (a dictionary definition). He means, of course, that he thrives in her sight, that he feels warm in her presence or even at the thought of her, that she illumines his world and is the center of his universe. Because in the mind of the hearer these and other suggestions are brought into play, Romeo's statement, literally absurd, makes excellent sense.

Here is a famous poem written by William Blake. You can see the differences between connotations and denotations of a word.

London (1794)
William Blake

I wander through each chartered street,
Near where the chartered Thames does flow,
And mark in every face I meet
Marks of weakness, marks of woe.

In every cry of every man,
In every infant's cry of fear,
In every voice, in every ban,
The mind-forged manacles I hear.

How the chimney-sweeper's cry
Every black'ning church appalls
And the hapless soldier's sigh
Runs in blood down palace walls.

But most through midnight streets I hear
How the youthful harlot's curse
Blasts the new born infant's tear
And blights with plagues the marriage hearse.

Here are only a few of the possible meanings of three of Blake's words:

- *chartered* (Lines 1, 2)
DENOTATIONS: Established by a charter (a written grant or a certificate of incorporation); leased or hired.

CONNOTATIONS: Defined, limited, restricted, channeled, mapped, bound by law; bought and sold (like a slave or an inanimate object); *Magna Carta*; charters given to crown colonies by the King.

Other words in the poem with similar connotations: *Ban*, which can denote (1) a legal prohibition; (2) a churchman's curse or malediction; (3) in medieval times, an order summoning a king's vassals to fight for him. *Manacles*, or shackles, restrain movement. *Chimney-sweeper*, *soldier*, and *harlot* are all hirelings.

Interpretation of the lines: The street has had mapped out for it the direction in which it must go; the Thames has had laid down to it the course it must follow. Street and river are channeled, imprisoned, enslaved (like every inhabitant of London).

- *Black' ning* (Line 10)

DENOTATION: Becoming black.

CONNOTATIONS: The darkening of something once light, the defilement of something once clean, the deepening of guilt, the gathering of darkness at the approach of night.

Other words in the poem with similar connotations: Objects becoming marked or smudged (*marks of weakness*, *marks of woe* in the faces of passers-by; bloodied walls of a palace; marriage blighted with plagues); the word *appalls* (denoting not only "to overcome with horror" but "to make pale" and also "to cast a pall or shroud over"); midnight streets.

Interpretation of the line: Literally, every London church grows black from soot and hires a chimney-sweeper (a small boy) to help clean it. But Blake suggests too that by profiting from the suffering of the child laborer, the church is soiling its original purity.

- *Blasts*, *blights* (Lines 15–16)

DENOTATIONS: Both blast and blight mean "to cause to wither" or "to ruin and destroy". Both are terms from horticulture. Frost blasts a bud and kills it; disease blights a growing plant.

CONNOTATIONS: Sickness and death; gardens shriveled and dying; gusts of wind and the ravages of insects; things blown to pieces or rotted and warped.

Other words in the poem with similar connotations: Faces marked with weakness and woe; the child becomes a chimney-sweeper; the soldier killed by war; blackening church and bloodied palace; young girl turned harlot; wedding carriage transformed into a hearse.

Interpretations of the lines: Literally, the harlot spreads the plague of syphilis, which, carried into marriage, can cause a baby to be born blind. In a larger and more meaningful sense, Blake sees the prostitution of even one young girl corrupting the entire institution of matrimony and endangering every child.

Some of these connotations are more to the point than others; the reader of a poem nearly always has the problem of distinguishing relevant associations from irrelevant ones. We need to read a poem in its entirety and, when a word leaves us in doubt, look for other things in the poem to corroborate or refute what we think it means. Relatively simple and direct in its statement, Blake's account of his stroll through the city at night becomes an indictment of a whole social and religious order. The indictment could hardly be this effective if it were "mathematically plain". Its every word restricted to one denotation clearly spelled out.

Here are two poems. Read them and make sure what these poems say, please.

Fire and Ice (1923)
Robert Frost

  Some say the world will end in fire,
  Some say in ice.
  From what I've tasted of desire
  I hold with those who favor fire.
  But if it had to perish twice,
  I think I know enough of hate
  To say that for destruction ice
  Is also great
  And would suffice.

Study Questions:
1. To whom does Frost refer in Lines 1 and 2?
2. What connotations of "fire" and "ice" contribute to the richness of Frost's comparison?

Break, Break, Break (1842)
Alfred, Lord Tennyson

  Break, break, break,
   On thy cold grey stones, O Sea!
  And I would① that my tongue could utter
   The thoughts that arise in me.

   O, well for the fisherman's boy,

---

① would: wish

>   That he shouts with his sister at play!
>   O, well for the sailor lad,
>   That he sings in his boat on the bay!
>
>   And the stately ships go on
>   To their haven① under the hill;
>   But O for the touch of a vanished hand,
>   And the sound of a voice that is still!②
>
>   Break, break, break,
>   At the foot of thy crags, O Sea!
>   But the tender grace of a day that is dead
>   Will never come back to me.

Study Questions:

1. What kind of feeling does the first line of the poem express?
2. What does the poet describe the joyful brother and sister and the singing sailor and the stately ships?
3. What kind of day will never return to the speaker?
4. Why does the poet describe the stones as "cold" and "gray"?
5. What musical elements can you find in the poem?

[Reading Critically]

The Ways a Poem Suggests

Although a poem may contain images and ideas, it is made up of words. Language is the medium of poetry, and the exact wording of a successful poem is the chief source of its power. Poems suggest some messages so clearly through imagery, tone, and diction that they do not need to declare them overtly. Poetry is a special way of speaking that requires a special way of listening. Poetry does not merely speak to the analytical parts of our minds but to the wholeness of our humanity. A good poem invites us to become fully alive and respond with our intuition, imagination emotions, and intelligence. It even speaks to our physical bodies through sound, rhythm, and sensory imagery.

Since poems speak to us so completely, they often convey their meaning indirectly. An image may express something so clearly that the poem does not need to repeat it

---

① haven: harbour
② a vanished hand, / And the sound of a voice that is still: the hand and the voices of Arthur Hallam

explicitly. In this sense, poems operate no differently from daily life.

In reading about a poem, listen carefully to everything it is telling you. Note anything important to the story or situation of the poem that we have to infer for ourselves. When journalists write a news story, they always try to cover the "five W's" in their opening paragraph—who, what, where, when, why. These may be worthwhile questions to ask about a poem. If one or more of them is missing, how does that affect our understanding of the poem?

1. *Who?* Who is the speaker or central figure of the poem?

2. *What?* What is being seen or presented? Does the poem ever suddenly change its subject?

3. *Where?* Where is the poem set? Does the setting so clearly suggest something important that the rest of the poem does not need to repeat the message?

4. *When?* When does the poem take place? If a poet explicitly states a time of day or time of year, it is very likely that the when of the poem is important.

5. *Why?* If the poem describes some dramatic action but does not tell us why it is being performed, perhaps the author wants us to ponder the situation carefully.

You don't have to answer all the questions, but it will help to ask them, remember, it is almost as important to know what a poem is not telling us as what it does.

4. Imagery and Symbol

Though the term "image" suggests a thing seen, when speaking of images in poetry we generally mean a word or sequence of words that refers to any sensory experience. Often this experience is a sight (visual imagery), but it may be a sound (auditory imagery) or a touch (tactile imagery, as a perception of roughness or smoothness). It may be an odor or a taste or perhaps a bodily sensation such as pain, the prickling of goose-flesh, the quenching of thirst, or the perception of something cold.

To render the abstract in concrete terms is what poets often try to do; in this attempt, an image can be valuable. An image may occur in a single word, a phrase, a sentence, or, as in this case, an entire short poem. To speak of the imagery of a poem—all its images taken together—is often more useful than to speak of separate images.

Does an image cause a reader to experience a sensual impression? Not quite. Read the following poem and detect what images in it present to you.

In a Station of the Metro (1916)
Ezra Pound

The apparition of these faces in the crowd;
Petals on a wet, black bough.

Pound said he wrote this poem to convey an experience: emerging one day from a train in the Paris subway (metro), he beheld "suddenly a beautiful face, and then another and another". In this final version of this poem, each line contains an image, which, like a picture, may take the place of a thousand words.

Reading the word "petals", no one literally sees petals; but the occasion is given for imagining them. The image asks to be seen with the mind's eye. And although "In a Station of the Metro" records what Ezra Pound saw, it is of course not necessary for a poet to actually have lived through a sensory experience in order to write it.

It is tempting to think of imagery as mere decoration, particularly when we read Keats, who fills his poems with an abundance of sights, sounds, odors, and tastes. But a successful image is not just a dab of paint or a flashy bauble. Indeed, some literary critics look for much of the meaning of a poem in its imagery, wherein they expect to see the mind of the poet more truly revealed than in whatever the poet explicitly claims to believe. Though Shakespeare's Theseus (in *A Midsummer Night's Dream*) accuses poets of being concerned with "airy nothings". poets are usually very much concerned with what is in front of them. This concern is of use to us. Perhaps we need a poet occasionally to remind us that even the coffee we absentmindedly sip comes in (as Yeats put it) a "heavy spillable cup".

Analyzing Images

To help you analyze how the **imagery** of a poem works, here is a simple exercise: Make a short list of the poem's key images. Be sure to write down the images in the order they appear in the poem, because the sequence of images is often as important as the images themselves. (For example, a poem whose images move from *sunlight* to *darkness* might well signify something different from one that begins with *darkness* and concludes with *sunlight*.) Remember that not all images are visual. Images can draw on any or all of the five senses. In jotting down images, don't omit key adjectives or other qualifying words. Those words are often your best clues to a poem's tone or perspective.

Let's try this method on a short poem. An initial list of images in Robert Bly's "Driving to Town Late to Mail a Letter" might look something like this:

cold and snowy night
deserted main street
mailbox door—cold iron
snowy night (speaker loves its privacy)
speaker drives around (to waste time)

Did we forget anything? Yes, the title! Always look to a poem's title for guidance. Bly's title, for instance, contains several crucial images. Let's add them to the top of the list:

driving (to town)
at night
a letter (to be mailed)

Looking at our list, we see how the images provide an outline of the poem's story. We also see how Bly begins the poem without allowing us initially to understand how his speaker views the situation. Is driving to town late on a snowy evening a positive, negative, or neutral experience? By noting where (in Line 4) the speaker reveals a subjective response to an image ("There is a privacy I love in this snowy night"), we also begin to grasp the overall emotional structure of the poem. We might also note on our list how the poem begins and ends with the same image (driving), but uses it for different effects at the two places. At the beginning the speaker is driving for the practical purpose of mailing a letter but at the end merely for the pure pleasure of it.

After adding a few notes on our list to capture these insights, we are ready to begin writing our paper. Without realizing it, we have already worked out a rough outline of our paper—all on a single sheet of paper or a few inches of computer screen.

Here are five poems, read them and learn to analyze how the imagery in these poems works.

The Winter Evening Settles Down (1917)
T. S. Eliot

The winter evening settles down
With smell of steaks in passageways.
Six o'clock.
The burnt-out ends of smoky days.
And now a gusty shower wraps
The grimy scraps

Of withered leaves about your feet
And newspapers from vacant lots;
The showers beat
On broken blinds and chimney-pots,
And at the corner of the street
A lonely cab-horse steams and stamps.

And then the lighting of the lamps.

Study Questions:

1. What mood is evoked by the images in Eliot's poem?
2. What kind of city neighborhood has the poet chosen to describe? How can you tell?

She Walks in Beauty (1815)

George Gordon Byron

She walks into beauty, like the night
    Of cloudless climes① and starry skies;
And all that's the best of dark and bright
    Meet in her aspect② and her eyes;
Thus mellowed to this tender light
    Which heaven to gaudy day denies.

One shade the more, one ray the less,
    Had half impaired them nameless grace
Which waves in every raven tress③
    Or softly lightens o'er her face;
Where thoughts serenely sweet express
    How pure, how dear their dwelling places④

And on that cheek, and o'er that brow,
    So soft, so calm, yet eloquent,
The smiles that win, the tints that glow,
    But tell of days in goodness spent,
A mind at peace with all below,

---

① clime: climate
② aspect: face, appearance
③ raven tress: long black hair
④ their dwelling places: her mind

A heart whose love is innocent!

Study Questions:

1. What images does the poet take to describe the lady's beauty? And from what aspects does the poet represent the lady's beauty?

2. What does the poet want to reveal at last by describing the beauty of the lady?

Spring and All (1923)
William Carlos Williams

By the road to the contagious① hospital
under the surge of the blue
mottled clouds driven from the
Northeast—a cold wind. Beyond, the
waste of broad, muddy fields
brown with dried weeds, standing and fallen

patches of standing water
the scattering of tall trees

All along the road the reddish
purplish, forked, upstanding, twiggy
stuff of bushes and small trees
with dead, brown leaves under them
leafless vine—

Lifeless in appearance, sluggish②
dazed spring approaches—

They enter the new world naked,
cold, uncertain of all
save that they enter. All about them
the cold, familiar wind—

Now the grass, tomorrow
the stiff curl of wild carrots leaf

One by one objects are defined—

---

① contagious: (of a disease) transmitted in this way
② sluggish: inert, slow moving

It quickens: clarity, outline of leaf
But now the stark dignity of
Entrance—Still, the profound change
has come upon them: rooted, they
grip down and begin to awaken

Study Questions:

1. What things are described in the poem as *cold* and *dead*, and *lifeless*?

2. Which aspect of spring does the poem emphasize? And how does the poet suggest that the beginning of life is not an easy process?

The Red Wheelbarrow (1923)
William Carlos Williams

So much depends

upon

a red wheel

barrow

glazed with rain

water

beside the white

chickens

Study Questions:

1. What kinds of images does the poet exhibit? Do you think it is effective for the poet to express his purpose?

2. Why might the objects in the poem be very important? Can you be sure? Explain.

Dreams (about 1932)
Langston Hughes

Hold fast to dreams

For if dreams die

Life is a broken-winged bird

That cannot fly.

Hold fast to dreams

For when dreams go

Life is a barren field
Frozen with snow

Study Questions:
1. What images does the poet employ to describe the life once we lose our dreams?
2. Why must we stick to our dreams?

Symbol

The national flag is supposed to bestir our patriotic feelings. Such a flag is a **symbol**: a visible object that suggests some further meaning in addition to itself. In literature, a symbol might be the word *flag* or every description of flag in an entire novel, story, play, or poem.

A flag may be called a **conventional symbol**, since it can have a conventional or customary effect on us. Conventional symbols are also part of the language of poetry, as we know when we meet the red rose, emblem of love, in a lyric, or the Christian cross in the devotional poems of George Herbert. More often, however, symbols in literature have no conventional, long-established meaning, but particular meanings of their own. In Melville's novel *Moby Dick*, to take an example, whatever we associate with the great white whale is not attached unmistakably to white whales by custom. Though Melville tells us that men have long regarded whales with awe and relates Moby Dick to the celebrated fish that swallowed Jonah, the readers' response is to one particular whale, the creature of Herman Melville. Only the experience of reading the novel in its entirety can give Moby Dick his particular meaning.

We should say meanings, for it is a good thing Melville made Moby Dick a whale, a creature large enough to contain all that critics have found in him. A symbol in literature, if not conventional, has more than just one meaning. In "The Raven" by Edgar Allan Poe, the appearance of a strange black bird in the narrator's study is sinister; and indeed, if we take the poem seriously, we may even respond with a sympathetic shiver of dread. Does the bird mean death, fate, melancholy, the loss of a loved one, knowledge in the service of evil? All these, perhaps. Like any well-chosen symbol, Poe's raven sets going within the readers an unending train of feelings and associations.

We miss the value of a symbol, however, if we think it can mean absolutely anything we wish. If a poet has any control over our reactions, the poem will guide our responses in a certain direction. Let's read Emily Dickinson's poem, and try to understand what a symbol means in a poem.

The Lightning Is a Yellow Fork (about 1870)

Emily Dickinson

> The Lightning is a yellow Fork
> From Tables in the sky
> By inadvertent fingers dropt
> The awful Cutlery
>
> Of mansions never quite disclosed
> And never quite concealed
> The Apparatus of the Dark
> To ignorance revealed.

If the lightning is a fork, then who are the fingers that drop it, the table from which it slips, the household to which it belongs? The poem implies this question without giving an answer. An obvious answer is "God", but can we be sure? We wonder, too, about these partially lighted mansions: If our vision were clearer, what would we behold?

"But how am I supposed to know a symbol when I see one?" For a reader, such a question perhaps visits your mind. The best approach is to read poems closely, taking comfort in the likelihood that it is better not to notice symbols at all than to find significance in every literal stone and huge meanings in every thing. In looking for the symbols in a poem, pick out all the references to concrete objects—newspapers, black cats, twisted pins. Consider these with special care. Notice any that the poet emphasizes by detailed description, by repetition, or by placing it at the very beginning or end of the poem. Remember to ask: What is the poem about? What does it add up to? If, when the poem is paraphrased, the paraphrase depends primarily upon the meaning of certain concrete objects, these richly suggestive objects may be the symbols.

A symbol is not an abstraction. Such terms as *truth*, *death*, *love*, and *justice* cannot work as symbols (unless personified, as in the traditional figure of Justice holding a scale). Most often, a symbol is something we can see in the mind's eye: a newspaper, a lightening bolt, a gesture of nodding goodbye.

In narratives, a well-developed character, who speaks much dialogue and is not the least bit mysterious, is usually not a symbol. But watch out for an executioner in a black hood; a character, named for a biblical prophet, who does little but utters a prophecy; a trio of old women who resemble the Three Fates. (It has been argued, with good reason, that Milton's fully rounded character of Satan in *Paradise Lost* is a symbol embodying evil and human pride, but a narrower definition of symbol is more frequently useful.) A symbol may be a part of a person's body (the baleful eye of the murder victim in Poe's story "The Tell-Tale Heart") or a look, a voice, or a mannerism.

A symbol usually is not the second term of a metaphor. In the line "The Lightning is a yellow Fork", the symbol is the lightning, not the fork.

Sometimes a symbol addresses a sense other than sight: the sound of a mysterious harp at the end of Chekhov's play *The Cherry Orchard*; or, in William Faulkner's tale "A Rose for Emily", the odor of decay that surrounds the house of the last survivor of a town's leading family—suggesting not only physical dissolution but also the decay of a social order. A symbol is a special kind of image, for it exceeds the usual image in the richness of its connotations.

Holding a narrower definition than that used in this book, some readers of poetry prefer to say that a symbol is always a concrete object, never an act. They would deny the label "symbol" to Ahab's breaking his tobacco pipe before setting out to pursue Moby Dick (suggesting, perhaps, his determination to allow no pleasure to distract him from the chase) or to any large motion (as Ahab's whole quest). This distinction, while confining, does have the merit of sparing one from seeing all motion to be possibly symbolic. Some would call Ahab's gestures not a symbol but a symbolic act.

To sum up, a symbol radiates hints or casts long shadows. We are unable to say it "stands for" or "represents" a meaning. It evokes, it suggests, it manifests. It demands no single necessary interpretation, such as the interpretation a driver gives to a red traffic light. Rather, like Emily Dickinson's lightning bolt, it points toward an indefinite meaning, which may lie in part beyond the reach of words.

Allegory

If we read of a ship, its captain, its sailors, and the rough seas, and we realize we are reading about a commonwealth and how its rulers and workers keep it going even in difficult times, then we are reading an allegory. Closely akin to symbolism, **allegory** is a description—usually narrative—in which person, places, and things are employed in a continuous and consistent system of equivalents.

Although more strictly limited in its suggestions than symbolism, allegory need not be thought to be inferior. Few poems continue to interest readers more than Dante's allegorical *Divine Comedy*. Usually, the meanings of an allegory are plainly labeled or thinly disguised. In John Bunyan's allegorical narrative *The Pilgrim's Progress*, it is clear that the hero Christian, on his journey through places with such pointed names as Vanity Fair, the Valley of the Shadow of Death, and the Doubting Castle, is the soul, traveling the road of life on the way toward Heaven.

An allegory, when carefully built, is systematic. It makes one principal comparison, the working out of whose details may lead to further comparisons, then still further comparisons: Christian, thrown by Giant Despair into the dungeon of the Doubting Castle, escapes by means of a key called Promise. Such a complicated design may take great length to unfold, as in Spenser's *Faerie Queen*.

Whether an object in literature is a symbol, part of an allegory, or no such thing at all, it has at least one sure meaning. Moby Dick is first a whale and the *Boston Evening Transcript* is a newspaper. Besides deriving a multitude of intangible suggestions from the title symbol in Eliot's long poem *The Waste Land*, its readers cannot fail to carry away a sense of the land's physical appearance: a river choked with sandwich papers and cigarette ends, London Bridge "under the brown fog of a winter dawn". A virtue of *The Pilgrim's Progress* is that its walking abstractions are no mere abstractions but are also human: Giant Despair is a henpecked husband. The most vital element of a literary work may pass us by, unless before seeking further depths in a thing, we look to the thing itself.

Read the following poems and try to understand what symbols in them suggest.

Anecdote of the Jar (1923)

Wallace Stevens

I placed a jar in Tennessee,
And round it was, upon a hill,
It made the slovenly wilderness
Surround that hill.

The wilderness rose up to it,
And sprawled around, no longer wild.
The jar was round upon the ground
And tall and of a port in air.

It took dominion① everywhere.
The jar was gray and bare.
It did not give of bird or bush,
Like nothing else in Tennessee.

Study Questions:

1. What does the jar in the poem symbolize? Why does the speaker place it on top of a hill?
2. The jar is "round" and "of a port in air", meaning that it has a stately importance. What

---

① dominion: ruling power

effect does it have on surroundings when placed on the ground?

3. How is the wilderness of Tennessee characterized? What words or phrases does the poet use to describe it?

The Road Not Taken (1916)
Robert Frost

Two roads diverged in a yellow wood,
And sorry I could not travel both
And be one traveler, long I stood
And looked down one as far as I could
To where it bent in the undergrowth;

Then took the other, as just as fair,
And having perhaps the better claim,
Because it was grassy and wanted wear;
Though as for that the passing there
Had worn them really about the same.

And both that morning equally lay
In leaves no step had trodden black.
Oh, I kept the first for another day!
Yet knowing how way leads on to way,
I doubted if I should ever come back.

I shall be telling this with a sigh
Somewhere ages and ages hence:
Two roads diverged in a wood, and I—
I took the one less traveled by,
And that has made all the difference.

Study Questions:

1. What symbolism do you find in this poem, if any? Back up your claim with evidence.
2. What might the two roads stand for in the speaker's mind?
3. Describe the similarities and differences of these two roads. Which one does the speaker take?

Poem (1934)
William Carlos Williams

As the cat

climbed over

the top of

the jamcloset

first the right

forefoot

carefully

then the hind

stepped down

into the pit of

the empty

flowerpot

Study Questions:

Please read the poem, and decide which description best suits it:

1. The poem has a central symbol.
2. The poem contains no symbolism, but is to be taken literally.

Bright Star! Would I Were Steadfast as Thou Art① (1819)
John Keats

Bright star! Would I were steadfast as thou art—
   Not in lone splendor hung aloft the night,
And watching, with eternal lids apart,
   Like nature's patient, sleepless eremite②
The moving waters at their priest-like task
   Of pure ablution③ round earth's human shores,

---

① While on a tour of the Lake District in 1818, Keats had said that the austere scenes "refine one's sensual vision into a sort of north star which can never cease to be open lidded and steadfast over the wonders of the great power". The thought developed into the sonnet, which Keats drafted in 1819, then copied into his volume of Shakespeare's poems at the end of September or the beginning of October 1820, while on his way to Italy, where he died.
② eremite: hermit
③ ablution: washing, as part of a religious rite

> Or gazing on the new soft-fallen mask
>
> Of snow upon the mountains and the moors—
>
> No—yet still steadfast, still unchangeable,
>
> Pillowed upon my fair love's ripening breast,
>
> To feel for ever its soft fall and swell,
>
> Awake for ever in a sweet unrest,
>
> Still, still to hear her tender-taken breath,
>
> And so live ever—or else swoon to death.

Study Questions:

1. Stars are conventional symbols for love and a loved one. (Love, Shakespeare tells us in a sonnet, "is the star to every wandering bark".) In this sonnet, why is it not possible for the star to have this meaning? How does Keats use it?

2. What seems concrete and particular in the speaker's observations?

3. Suppose Keats had said "slow" and "easy" instead of "tender-taken" in Line 13, what would have been lost?

[Reading Critically]

How to Read a Symbol

A symbol, to use poet John Drury's concise definition, is "an image that radiates meanings". Exactly what those meanings will be, however, often differs from poem to poem. In one poem *snow* may be a reassuring symbol of sleep and forgetfulness, while in another it becomes a chilling symbol of death. Both meanings easily connect to the natural image of *snow*, but in each poem, the author has nudged that image in a different direction.

The way a symbol has been used by earlier writers affects the way we grasp the image today. It would be difficult, for example, to put a great white whale in a contemporary poem without summoning up the symbolic association of Melville's *Moby Dick*. No matter how the poet chooses to handle it, the association will be there as a starting point. William Butler Yeats believed that poetic symbols acquired their special power by thousands of years of use. Poets, therefore, had to employ symbols consistent with their ancient meanings. Contemporary poets, on the other hand, often enjoy turning traditional symbols upside down.

The same image, therefore, can often convey divergent meanings in different poems—even when the poems are written by contemporaries. When reading or writing about the meaning (or meanings) of a symbol, follow the image through the poem and give it time to establish its own pattern of associations. Don't jump to quick conclusions.

If the symbol is a traditional one (the cross, a rose, a reaper and so on), is it being used in the expected way? Or is the poet playing with its associations? And finally, if the image does not seem to radiate meanings above and beyond its literal sense, don't feel you have failed as a critic. Not everything is a symbol. As Sigmund Freud once commented about symbol hunting, "Sometimes a cigar is just a cigar."

5. Figures of Speech

Speaking Figuratively

When preparing to confront his mother, Hamlet says, "I will speak daggers to her, but use none." His statement makes sense only because we realize that *daggers* are to be taken two ways: literally (denoting sharp, pointed weapons) and non-literally (referring to something that can be used like weapons—namely, words). Reading poetry, we often meet comparisons between two things whose similarity we have never noticed before. Such comparisons are called figures of speech.

In its broadest definition, a **figure of speech** may be said to occur whenever a speaker or writer, for the sake of freshness or emphasis, departs from the usual denotations of words. Certainly, when Hamlet says he will speak *daggers*, no one expects him to release pointed weapons from his lips, for *daggers* are not to be read solely for its denotation. Its connotations—sharp, stabbing, piercing, wounding—also come to mind, and we see ways in which words and daggers work alike. (Words too can hurt: by striking through pretenses, possibly, or by wounding their hearer's self-esteem.) In the statement "A razor is sharper than an ax", there is no departure from the usual denotations of *razor* and *ax*, and no figure of speech results. Both objects are of the same class; the comparison is not offensive to logic. But in "How sharper than a serpent's tooth it is to have a thankless child", the objects—snake's tooth (fang) and ungrateful offspring—are so unlike that no reasonable comparison may be made between them. To find similarity, we attend to the connotations of serpent's tooth—biting, piercing, venom, pain—rather than to its denotations. If we are aware of the connotations of red rose (beauty, softness, freshness, and so forth), then the line "My Love Is like a Red, Red Rose" need not call to mind a woman with a scarlet face and a thorny neck.

Figures of speech are not devices to state what is demonstrably untrue. Indeed they often state truths that more literal language cannot communicate; they call attention to such truths; they lend them emphasis. Let's read the following poem and gain a bit of knowledge of what figures of speech are in a poem.

The Eagle (1851)
Alfred, Lord Tennyson

He clasps the crag with crooked hands;
Close to the sun in lonely lands,
Ringed with the azure world, he stands.

The wrinkled sea beneath him crawls;
He watches from his mountain walls,
And like a thunderbolt he falls.

This brief poem is rich in figurative language. In the first line, the phrase *crooked hands* may surprise us. An eagle does not have hands, we might protest; but the objection would be a quibble, for evidently Tennyson is indicating exactly how an eagle clasps a crag, in the way that human fingers clasp a thing. By implication, too, the eagle is a person. *Close to the sun*, if taken literally, is an absurd exaggeration, the sun being a mean distance of 93,000,000 miles from the earth. For the eagle to be closer to it by the altitude of a mountain is an approach so small as to be insignificant. But figuratively, Tennyson conveys that the eagle stands above the clouds, perhaps silhouetted against the sun, and for the moment belongs to the heavens rather than to the land and sea. The word *ringed* makes a circle of the whole world's horizons and suggests that we see the world from the eagle's height; *the wrinkled sea* becomes an aged, sluggish animal; *mountain walls*, possibly literal, also suggests a fort or castle; and finally the eagle itself is likened to a thunderbolt in speed and in power, perhaps also in that its beak is—like our abstract conception of a lightning bolt—pointed. How much of the poem can be taken literally? Only *he clasps the crag*, *he stands*, *he watches*, *he falls*. The rest is made of figures of speech. The result is that, reading Tennyson's poem, we gain a bird's-eye view of sun, sea, and land—and even of bird. Like imagery, figurative language refers us to the physical world.

Read the following poem and try to understand how figurative language in it works.

The Flea[①](1633)

John Donne

Mark[②] but this flea, and mark in this
How little that which thou deny'st me is;
It sucked me first, and now sucks thee,
And in this flea our two bloods mingled be;
Thou know'st that this cannot be said
A sin, nor shame, nor loss of maidenhead[③],
Yet this enjoys before it woo,
And pampered[④] swells with one blood made of two,
And this, alas, is more than we would do.

Oh stay, three lives in one flea spare,
Where we almost, yea more than married are.
This flea is you and I, and this
Our marriage bed, and marriage temple is;
Though parents grudge, and you, we're met
And cloistered[⑤] in these living walls of jet[⑥].
Though use[⑦] make you apt to kill me[⑧],
Let not to that, self-murder added be,
And sacrilege, three sins in killing three.

Cruel and sudden, hast thou since
Purpled thy nail in blood of innocence?
Wherein could this flea guilty be,
Except in that drop it sucked from thee?
Yet thou triumph'st, and say'st that thou
Find'st not thyself, nor me, the weaker now;
'tis true; then learn how false, fears be;

[①] This insect afforded a popular erotic theme for poets all over Europe, deriving from a pseudo-Ovidian medieval poem in which a lover envies the flea for the liberties it takes with his mistress's body.
[②] mark: have a look at it
[③] maidenhead: virginity
[④] pampered: overfed
[⑤] cloistered: as in a convent or monastery
[⑥] jet: black
[⑦] use: custom
[⑧] make you apt to kill me: deny me sexual gratification

Just so much honor, when thou yield'st to me,
Will waste, as this flea's death took life from thee.

Study Questions:

1. Why does the poet say that "this cannot be said a sin, nor shame, nor loss of maidenhead"?
2. What do you think is the addressee's parents' attitude toward the poet's wooing?
3. What is the real purpose of the poet to say that in killing the flea "thou" are actually killing three lives?

Metaphor and Simile

In your reading, you may meet these lines, "Life, like a dome of many-colored glass,/Stains the white radiance of Eternity." The first of these lines (from Shelley's "Adonais") is a **simile**: a comparison of two things, indicated by some connective, usually *like*, *as*, *than*, or a verb such as *resemble*. A simile expresses a similarity. Still, for a simile to exist, the things compared have to be dissimilar in kind. It is no simile to say, "Your fingers are like mine"; it is a literal observation. But to say, "Your fingers are like sausages" is to use a simile. Omit the connective—say, "Your fingers are sausages"—and the result is a **metaphor**, a statement that one thing is something else, which, in a literal sense, it is not. In the second of Shelley's lines, it is assumed that eternity is light or radiance, and we have an implied metaphor, one that uses neither a connective nor the verb to be. Here are examples:

Oh, my love is like a red, red rose.	Simile
Oh, my love resembles a red, red rose.	Simile
Oh, my love is redder than a rose.	Simile
Oh, my love is a red, red rose.	Metaphor
Oh, my love has red petals and sharp thorns.	Implied metaphor
Oh, I placed my love into a long-stem vase And I bandaged my bleeding thumb.	Implied metaphor

Often you can tell a metaphor from a simile by much more than just the presence or absence of a connective. In general, a simile refers to only one characteristic that two things have in common, while a metaphor is not plainly limited in the number of resemblances it may indicate. To use the simile "He eats like a pig" is to compare man and animal in one respect: eating habits. But to say "He's a pig" is to use a metaphor that might involve comparisons of appearance and morality as well.

In everyday speech, simile and metaphor occur frequently. We use metaphors ("She's a doll") and similes ("The tickets are selling like hotcakes") without being fully conscious of them. If, however, we are aware that words possess literal meanings as well as figurative ones, we do not write *died in the wool* for *dyed in the wool*, or *tow the line* for *toe the line*, nor do we use mixed metaphors as did the writer who advised, "Water the spark of knowledge and it will bear fruit", or the speaker who urged, "To get ahead, keep your nose to the grindstone, your shoulder to the wheel, your ear to the ground, and your eye on the ball." Perhaps the unintended humor of these statements comes from our seeing that the writer, busy stringing together stale metaphors, was not aware that they had any physical reference.

Unlike a writer who thoughtlessly mixes metaphors, a good poet can join together incongruous things and still keep the readers' respect. A poem may make a series of comparisons, or the whole poem may be one extended comparison.

Here are two poems. Please detect how much life metaphors bring to poetry by comparing them.

Flower in the Crannied Wall (1869)
Alfred, Lord Tennyson

Flower in the crannied wall,
I pluck you out of the crannies,
I hold you here, root and all, in my hand,
Little flower—but if I could understand
What you are, root and all, and all in all,
I should know what God and man is.

To See a World in a Grain of Sand[①] (about 1803)
William Blake

To see a world in a grain of sand
And a heaven in a wild flower,
Hold infinity in the palm of your hand
And eternity in an hour.

How many metaphors does Tennyson's poem contain? None. We may compare it with a briefer poem on a similar theme: the quatrain that begins Blake's "Auguries of

---

① We follow here the opinion of W. B. Yeats, who, in editing Blake's poems, thought the lines ought to be printed separately.

Innocence". Set beside Blake's poem, Tennyson's, short though it is, seems lengthy. What contributes to the richness of "To see a world in a grain of sand" is Blake's use of a metaphor in every line. And every metaphor is loaded with suggestion. Our world does indeed resemble a grain of sand: in being round, in being stony, in being one of a myriad (the suggestions go on and on). Like Blake's grain of sand, a metaphor holds much, within a small circumference.

Read the following poem, and understand its richness the metaphor brings to you.

It Dropped So Low—in My Regard (about 1863)
Emily Dickinson

It dropped so low—in my Regard—
I heard it hit the Ground—
And go to pieces on the Stones
At bottom of my Mind—

Yet blamed the Fate that flung it—less
Than I denounced Myself,
For entertaining Plated Wares
Upon My Silver Shelf—

Study Questions:
1. What is "it" in the poem? What two things are compared?
2. How much of the poem develops and amplifies this comparison?

Other Figures of Speech

When Shakespeare asks, in a sonnet, "O! how shall summer's honey breath hold out/Against the wrackful siege of batt'ring days", it might seem at first that he mixes metaphors. How can a *breath* confront the *battering* ram of an invading army? But it is *summer's breath* and, by giving it to summer, Shakespeare makes the season a man or woman. It is as if the fragrance of summer were the breath within a person's body, and winter were the onslaught of old age.

Such is one instance of **personification**: a figure of speech in which a thing, an animal, or an abstract term (truth, nature) is made human. Hand in hand with personification often goes **apostrophe**: a way of addressing someone or something invisible or not ordinarily spoken to. In an apostrophe, a poet (in these examples Wordsworth) may address an inanimate object ("Spade! with which Wilkinson hath tilled his lands"), some dead or absent person ("Milton! thou shouldst be living at this hour"), an abstract thing ("Return, Delights!"), or a spirit ("Thou Soul that art the eternity of thought"). More often than not, the poet uses apostrophe to announce a lofty and serious tone. An "O" may even be put in front of it ("O moon!"). Apostrophe is a way of giving body to the intangible, a way of speaking to it person to person, as in the words of a moving American spiritual: "Death, ain't you got no shame?"

Most of us, from time to time, emphasize a point with a statement containing exaggeration: "Faster than greased lightning," "I've told him a thousand times." We speak, then, not literal truth but use a figure of speech called **overstatement** (or **hyperbole**). Poets too, being fond of emphasis, often exaggerate for effect. Instances are Marvell's profession of a love that should grow "Vaster than empires, and more slow". Overstatement can be used also for humorous purposes. The opposite is **understatement**, implying more than is said. Mark Twain in *Life on the Mississippi* recalls how, as an apprentice steamboat-pilot asleep when supposed to be on watch, he was roused by the pilot and sent clambering to the pilot house: "Mr. Bixby was close behind, commenting." Another example is Robert Frost's line "One could do worse than be a swinger of birches"—the conclusion of a poem that has suggested that to swing on a birch tree is one of the most deeply satisfying activities in the world.

In **metonymy**, the name of a thing is substituted for that of another closely associated with it. For instance, we say "The White House decided", and mean the President did. A kind of metonymy, **synecdoche**, is the use of a part of a thing to stand for the whole of it or vice versa. We say, "She lent a hand", and mean that she lent her entire presence. Another kind of metonymy is the **transferred epithet**: a device of emphasis in which the poet attributes some characteristic of a thing to another thing closely associated with it. When Hart Crane, describing the earth as seen from an airplane, speaks of "nimble blue plateaus", he attributes the airplane's motion to the earth.

Paradox occurs in a statement that at first strikes us as self-contradictory but that on reflection makes some sense. "The peasant," said G. K. Chesterton, "lives in a larger world than the globe-trotter". Here, two different meanings of *larger* are contrasted: "greater in spiritual values" versus "greater in miles". Some paradoxical statements, however, are much more than plays on words. In a moving sonnet, the blind John Milton tells how one night he dreamed he could see his dead wife. The poem ends in a paradox: "But oh, as to embrace me she inclined, /I waked, she fled, and day brought back my night."

To sum up: Even though figures of speech are not to be taken only literally, they refer us to a tangible world. By **personifying** an eagle, Tennyson reminds us that the bird and humankind have certain characteristics in common. Through **metonymy**, a poet can focus our attention on a particular detail in a larger object; through **hyperbole** and **understatement**, make us see the physical actuality in back of words. **Pun** and **paradox** cause us to realize this actuality, too, and probably surprise us enjoyably at the same time. Through **apostrophe**, the poet animates the inanimate and asks it to listen—speaks directly to an immediate god or to the revivified dead. Put to such uses, figures of speech have power. They are more than just ways of playing with words.

The Silken Tent (1942)
Robert Frost

She is as in a field a silken tent
At midday when a sunny summer breeze
Has dried the dew and all its ropes relent,
So that in guys① it gently sways at ease,
And its supporting central cedar pole,
That is its pinnacle to heavenward
And signifies the sureness of the soul,
Seems to owe naught to any single cord,
But strictly held by none, is loosely bound
By countless silken ties of love and thought
To everything on earth the compass round,
And only by one's going slightly taut
In the capriciousness of summer air
Is of the slightest bondage made aware.

Study Questions:

1. Is Frost's comparison of a woman and tent a simile or a metaphor?
2. What are the ropes or cords?
3. Does the poet convey any sense of this woman's character? What sort of person do you believe her to be?
4. Paraphrase the poem, and try to state its implied meaning.

The Tyger (1794)
William Blake

Tyger! Tyger! burning bright
In the forests of the night,

---

① guys: attachments that steady it

What immortal hand or eye
Could frame thy fearful symmetry①?

In what distant deeps② or skies
Burnt the fire of thine eyes?
On what wings dare he aspire③?
What the hand dare seize the fire?

And what shoulder④, and what art⑤,
Could twist the sinews⑥ of thy heart?
And when thy heart began to beat,
What dread⑦ hand? and what dread feet?

What the hammer? what the chain?
In what furnace was thy brain?
What the anvil⑧? what dread grasp
Dare its deadly terrors clasp?

When the stars threw down their spears,
And watered heaven with their tears⑨,
Did he smile his work to see?
Did he who made the Lamb make thee?

Tyger! Tyger! burning bright
In the forests of the night,
What immortal hand or eye
Dare frame thy fearful symmetry?

---

① symmetry: referring to the well-proportioned body of the tyger
② deeps: seas
③ aspire: have ambition for something
④ shoulder: referring to the strength of the maker
⑤ art: skill
⑥ sinews: muscles
⑦ dread: dreadful, terrible. It means that what powerful hands or feet can control the tyger when it is made.
⑧ anvil: iron block on which a smith shapes heated metal by hammering it
⑨ When ... tears: This line is subject to different interpretations. It may refer to the fact that in the process of making the tyger, the blacksmith waved the hammer on the red-hot iron and light shot out in all directions like the angels' tears (meteors). The stars may also refer to French aristocrats who, defeated by the people, laid down their spears, and cried bitterly for their loss.

The Sick Rose (1794)
William Blake

O Rose, thou art sick!
The invisible worm
That flies in the night,
In the howling storm,

Has found out thy bed
Of crimson joy,
And his dark secret love
Does thy life destroy.

Study Questions:
1. What figure of speech does the poet mainly use in "The Tyger"?
2. What is the symbolic meaning of the tiger? What idea does the poet want to express?
3. In what sense do you think that the rose is "sick"?
4. Should there be any symbolic meanings for the "night" and the "storm"? If so, what meanings would you suggest?
5. Compare "The Sick Rose" with Robert Burns' "A Red, Red Rose".

[Reading Critically]

How Metaphors Enlarge a Poem's Meaning

Poems have the particular power of helping us see one thing by pointing out another. One of the most distinctive ways poems manage this feat is by calling a thing by a different name, in other words, by creating a metaphor. Paradoxically, by connecting an object to something else, a metaphor can reveal interesting aspects of the original thing we might either never have noticed or have considered unimportant.

Usually we can see the main point of a good metaphor immediately, but in interpreting a poem, the practical issue sometimes arises on how far to extend a comparison. All readers recognize that metaphors enlarge meaning, but they also know that there is always some limit to the comparison and that in most poems the limit remains unstated. If at the dinner table an elder brother calls his kid brother "a pig", he probably does not mean to imply that the child has a snout and a kinky tail. Most metaphors have a finite set of associations—even insults from an elder brother.

If you plan an essay on a highly metaphorical poem, it is often useful to examine the key comparison or comparisons in the poem. Jot down the major metaphors (or similes). Under each comparison make a two-column list—one marked "true", the other "false". Now start exploring the connections between the object the poem presents and the thing to which it is being compared. What aspects of the comparison are true? Make this list as long as possible. In the second list write the aspects that the two objects do not truly share; this list soon sets the limits of the metaphorical connections. In poems in which the metaphor is rich and resonant, the "true" list will be much longer than the "false" list. In other poems, ones in which the metaphor is narrowly focused on only limited connections between the two objects, the "false" list will quickly outpace the "true" list. Finally, once you have listed the key comparisons in the poem, see if there is any obvious connection between all the metaphors or similes themselves. Do they share something in common? Are all of them threatening? Inviting? Nocturnal? Exaggerated? Their similarities, if any, will almost certainly be significant.

Don't spend more than a few minutes on each list. The object is not to list every possible connection but only to determine the general scope of the metaphor and its implications. If the poem has a central metaphor, its scope and function should now be clear.

6. Sound

Poetry, like music, appeals to the ear. However limited it may be in comparison with the sound of orchestra, the sound of words in itself gives pleasure. Listening to a symphony in which themes are repeated throughout each movement, we enjoy both their recurrence and their variation. We take similar pleasure in the repetition of a phrase or a single chord. Something like this pleasure is afforded us frequently in poetry.

Alliteration

Analogies between poetry and wordless music, it is true, tend to break down when carried far, since poetry, to mention a single difference, has denotation. But like musical compositions, poems have patterns of sounds. Among such patterns long popular in English poetry is **alliteration**, which has been defined as a succession of similar sounds.

Alliteration occurs in the repetition of the same consonant sound at the beginning of successive words, "round and round the rugged rocks the ragged rascal ran", or inside the words, as in a line by e. e. cummings, "colossal hoax of clocks and calendars", the sound of x within *hoax* alliterates with the *cks* in *clocks*.

Poetry formerly contained more alliteration than it usually contains today. In old English verse, each line was held together by alliteration, a basic pattern still evident in the 14th century, as in the following description of the world as a "fair field" in *Piers Plowman*: "A feir feld ful of folk fond I ther bi-twene,/Of alle maner of men, the mene and the riche."

Most poets nowadays save alliteration for special occasions. They may use it to give emphasis, or just point out the relationship between two things placed side by side with its aid, as in Pope's line on things of little worth: "The courtier's promises, and sick man's prayers." Alliteration, too, can be a powerful aid to memory. It is hard to forget such tongue twisters as "Peter Piper picked a peck of pickled peppers", or common expressions like "green as grass", "tried and true", and "from stem to stern". In fact, because alliteration directs our attention to something, it had best be used neither thoughtlessly nor merely for decoration, lest it call attention to emptiness.

Assonance

As we have seen, to repeat the sound of a consonant is to produce alliteration, but to repeat the sound of a vowel is to produce assonance. Like alliteration, assonance may occur either initially, "all the *a*wful *au*guries", or internally like Edmund Spenser's "Her goodly *eyes* l*i*ke sapph*i*res sh*i*ning br*i*ght,/Her forehead *i*vory wh*i*te ... " and it can help make common phrases unforgettable: "eager beaver", "holy smoke". Like alliteration, it slows the reader down and focuses attention.

Try reading aloud as rapidly as possible the following poem by Tennyson. From the difficulties you encounter, you may be able to sense the slowing effect of assonance. Then read the poem aloud a second time, with consideration.

The Splendor Falls on Castle Walls (1850)
Alfred, Lord Tennyson

The splendor falls on castle walls
   And snowy summits old in story;
The long light shakes across the lakes,
   And the wild cataract leaps in glory.
Blow, bugle, blow, set the wild echoes flying,
Blow, bugle; answer, echoes, dying, dying, dying.

  O hark, O hear! how thin and clear,
     And thinner, clearer, farther going!
  O sweet and far from cliff and scar
     The horns of Elfland faintly blowing!
Blow, let us hear the purple glens replying:
Blow, bugle; answer, echoes, dying, dying, dying.

O love, they die in yon rich sky,
   They faint on hill or field or river;
Our echoes roll from soul to soul,
   And grow for ever and for ever.
Blow, bugle, blow, set the wild echoes flying,
   And answer, echoes, answer, dying, dying, dying.

Rime

A **rime** (or rhyme), defined most narrowly, occurs when two or more words or phrases contain an identical or similar vowel-sound, usually accented, and the consonant-sounds (if any) that follow the vowel-sound are identical: h*ay* and sl*eigh*, prairie schoo*ner* and piano tu*ner*.

Some definitions of **rime** would apply the term to the repetition of any identical or similar sound, not only a vowel-sound. In this sense, assonance is a kind of rime; so is alliteration (called initial rime). From these examples it will be seen that rime depends not on spelling but on sound.

Excellent rimes surprise. It is all very well that readers may anticipate which vowel-sound is coming next, for patterns of rime give pleasure by satisfying expectations; but riming becomes dull clunking if, at the end of each line, the readers can predict the word that will end the next.

To have an exact rime, sounds following the vowel sound have to be the same: *red* and *bread*, *wealthily* and *stealthily*, *walk to her* and *talk to her*. If final consonant sounds are the same but the vowel sounds are different, the result is **slant rime**, also called **near rime**, **off rime**, or **imperfect rime**: *sun* riming with *bone*, *moon*, *rain*, *green*, *gone*, *thin*. By not satisfying the readers' expectation of an exact chime, but instead giving a clunk, a slant rime can help a poet say some things in a particular way. It works especially well for disappointed letdowns, negations, and denials, as in Blake's couplet: "He who the ox to wrath has moved/Shall never be by woman loved."

Consonance, a kind of slant rime, occurs when the rimed words or phrases have the same beginning and ending consonant sounds but a different vowel, as in *chitter* and *chatter*. **End rime**, as its name indicates, comes at the ends of lines, **internal rime** within them. Most rime tends to be end rime. Few recent poets have used internal rime so heavily as Wallace Stevens. **Masculine rime** is a rime of one-syllable words (*jail*, *bail*) or (in words of more than one syllable) stressed final syllables: *di-VORCE*, *re-MORSE*, or *h-ORSE*, *re-MORSE*. **Feminine rime** is a rime of two or more syllables, with stress on a syllable other than the last: *TUR-tle*, *FER-tile*, or (to take an example from Byron) *in-tel-LECT-u-al*, *hen-PECKED you all*. Often it lends itself to comic verse, but can occasionally be valuable to serious poems, as in Wordsworth's "Resolution and Independence": "We poets in our youth begin in gladness,/But thereof come in the end despondency and madness."

Artfully used, feminine rhyme can give a poem a heightened musical effect for the simple reason that it offers the listener twice as many rhyming syllables in each line. In the wrong hands, however, that sonic abundance has the unfortunate ability of making a bad poem twice as painful to endure.

In **eye rime**, spellings look alike but pronunciations differ: *rough* and *dough*, *idea* and *flea*, *Venus* and *menus*. Strictly speaking, eye rime is not rime at all.

Rime in American poetry suffered a significant fall from favor in the early 1960s. A new generation of poets took for models the open forms of Whitman, Pound, and William Carlos Williams. Recently, however, young poets have begun skillfully using rime again in their work. Often called the New Formalists, these poets include Julia Alvarez, Annie Finch, R. S. Gwynn, Rachel Hadas, Mark Jarman, Paul Lake, Charles Martin, Molly Peacock, Gjertrud Schnackenberg, and Timothy Steele. Their poems often use rime and meter to present unusual contemporary subjects, but they also sometimes write poems that recollect, converse, and argue with the poetry of the past.

Still, most American poets don't write in rime; some even consider it exhausted. Such a view may be a reaction against the wearing-thin of rimes by overuse or the mechanical and meaningless application of a rime scheme. Yet anyone who listens to children skipping rope in the street, making up rimes to delight themselves as they go along, may doubt that the pleasures of rime are ended; and certainly the practice of Yeats and Emily Dickinson, to name only two, suggests that the possibilities of slant rime may be nearly infinite. If successfully employed, as it.has been at times by a majority of English-speaking poets whose work we care to save, rime runs through its poem like a spine: The creature moves by means of it.

Read Frost's poem, and sense its delight the poem brings to you through the sound.

Desert Places (1936)
Robert Frost

> Snow falling and night falling fast, oh, fast
> In a field I looked into going past,
> And the ground almost covered smooth in snow,
> But a few weeds and stubble showing last.
>
> The woods around it have it—it is theirs.
> All animals are smothered in their lairs,
> I am too absent-spirited to count;

> The loneliness includes me unawares.
>
> And lonely as it is, that loneliness
> Will be more lonely ere it will be less—
> A blanker whiteness of benighted snow
> With no expression, nothing to express.
>
> They cannot scare me with their empty spaces
> Between stars—on stars where no human race is.
> I have it in me so much nearer home
> To scare myself with my own desert places.

Study Questions:

1. What are these desert places that the speaker finds in himself? (More than one theory is possible. What is yours?)

2. Notice how many times, within the short space of Lines 8–10, Frost says *lonely* (or *loneliness*). What other words in the poem contain similar sounds that reinforce these words?

3. In the closing stanza, the feminine rimes *spaces*, *race is*, and *places* might well occur in light or comic verse. Does this poem leave you laughing? If not, what does it make you feel?

Rhythm

Rhythms affect us powerfully. We are lulled by a hammock's sway, awakened by an alarm clock's repeated yammer, moved by the folk songs of railroad workers and chain gangs whose words were chanted in time to the lifting and dropping of a sledgehammer. A rhythm is produced by a series of recurrences: the returns and departures of the seasons, the repetitions of an engine's stroke, and the beats of the heart. A rhythm may be produced by the recurrence of a sound (the throb of a drum, a telephone's busy signal), but rhythm and sound are not identical. A totally deaf person at a parade can sense rhythm from the motions of the marchers' arms and feet, from the shaking of the pavement as they tramp. Rhythms inhere in the motions of the moon and stars, even though when they move we hear no sound.

In poetry, several kinds of recurrent sound are possible, including rime, alliteration, and assonance. But most often when we speak of the rhythm of a poem we mean the recurrence of stresses and pauses in it. When we hear a poem read aloud, stresses and pauses are, of course, part of its sound. It is possible to be aware of rhythms in poems read silently, too.

A stress (or accent) is a greater amount of force given to one syllable in speaking than is given to another. We favor a stressed syllable with a little more breath and emphasis, with the result that it comes out slightly louder, higher in pitch, or longer in duration than other syllables. In this manner we place a stress on the first syllable of words such as *eagle, impact, open,* and *statue,* and on the second syllable in *cigar, mystique, precise,* and *until.* Each word in English carries at least one stress, except (usually) for the articles *a, an,* and *the,* and one-syllable prepositions: *at, by, for, from, of, to, with.* One word by itself is seldom long enough for us to notice a rhythm in it. Usually a sequence of at least a few words is needed for stresses to establish their pattern: a line, a passage, a whole poem.

When stresses recur at fixed intervals, the result is called a **meter**. The line "A trot a trot a trot a trot" is in **iambic meter**, a succession of alternate unstressed and stressed syllables. Of all rhythms in the English language, this one is most familiar; most of our traditional poetry is written in it and ordinary speech tends to resemble it.

Rhythms in poetry are due not only to stresses but also to pauses. Pauses tend to recur at more prominent places after each line. End-stopped lines and run-on lines have different effects for the poem's rhythms.

To sum up: Rhythm is recurrence. In poems, it is made of stresses and pauses. The poet can produce it by doing any of several things: making the intervals between stresses fixed or varied, long or short; indicating pauses within lines; end-stopping lines or running them over; writing in short or long lines. Rhythm in itself cannot convey meaning. And yet if a poet's words have meaning, their rhythm must be one with it.

Meter

To enjoy the rhythms of a poem, no special knowledge of meter is necessary. There are four common accentual-syllable **meters** (a fixed arrangement of accented and unaccented syllables) in English: **iambic, anapestic, trochaic,** and **dactylic**. Each is named for its basic foot (usually a unit of two or three syllables that contains one strong stress) or building block. Here are some examples of each meter.

1. **Iambic**: a line made up primarily of iambs, an unstressed syllable followed by a stressed syllable (˘ ˊ). The iambic measure is the most common meter in English poetry. Many writers, such as Robert Frost, feel iambs most easily capture the natural rhythms of our speech.

But soft, | what light | through yon | der win | dow breaks?

—William Shakespeare

When I | have fears | that I | may cease | to be

—John Keats

If we | had world | e-nough | and time

This coy | ness, la | dy, were | no crime

—Andrew Marvell

My life | had stood- | a load | ed Gun

—Emily Dickinson

2. **Anapestic**: a line made up primarily of anapests, two unstressed syllables followed by a stressed syllable (˘ ˘ ˋ). Anapestic meter resembles iambic but contains an extra-unstressed syllable. Totally anapestic lines often start to gallop, so poets sometimes slow them down by substituting an iambic foot.

Now this | is the Law | of the Jun | gle—as old | and as true |

as the sky

And the Wolf | that shall keep | it may pros | per, | but the

wolf | that shall break | it must die.

—Rudyard Kipling

It was ma | ny and ma | ny a year | a ' go

In a king | dom by | the sea

That a maid | en there lived | whom you | may know

By the name | of An | na bel Lee.

—Edgar Allan Poe

3. **Trochaic**: a line made up primarily of trochees, a stressed syllable followed by an unstressed syllable (ˋ ˘). The trochaic meter is often associated with songs, chants, and magic spells in English. Trochees make a strong, emphatic meter that is often very mnemonic. Shakespeare and Blake used trochaic meter to exploit its magical associations.

Dou·ble, | dou·ble, | toil and | trou·ble

Fi·re | burn and | cau·dron | bub·ble.

—William Shakespeare

Ty·ger, | ty·ger, | burn·ing | bright

In the | forest | of the | night

—William Blake

Go and | catch a | fall·ing | star

—John Donne

4. **Dactylic**: a line made up primarily of dactyls, one stressed syllable followed by two unstressed syllables (` ˘ ˘). The dactylic meter is less common in English than in classical languages like Greek or Latin. Used carefully, dactylic meter can sound stately, as in Longfellow's *Evangeline*, but it also easily becomes a prancing, propulsive measure and is often used in comic verse. Poets often drop the unstressed syllables at the end of a dactylic line.

This is the | for·est pri | me·val. The | mur·mur·ing | pines and the | hem·lock

—Henry Wadsworth Longfellow

Take her up | ten·derly

Lift her with | care

Fash·ioned so | slen·der·ly

young and so | fair.

—Thomas Hood

Iambic and anapestic meters are called **rising meters** because their movement rises from an unstressed syllable to stress; trochaic and dactylic meters are called **falling**. A frequent heard metrical description is **iambic pentameter**: a line of five iambs, a meter especially familiar because it occurs in all blank verse (such as Shakespeare's plays and Milton's *Paradise Lost*), heroic couplets and sonnets. The commonly used names for line lengths follow:

Monometer	one foot
Dimeter	two feet
Trimeter	three feet
Tetrameter	four feet
Pentameter	five feet
Hexameter	six feet
Heptameter	seven feet
Octameter	eight feet

Lines of more than eight feet are possible but are rare. They tend to break up into shorter lengths in the listening ear.

Besides the two rising meters (iambic, anapestic) and the two falling meters (trochaic, dactylic), English poets have another valuable meter. It is **accentual meter**, in which the poet does not write in feet (as in the other meters) but instead counts accents (stresses). The idea is to have the same number of stresses in every line. The poet may place them anywhere in the line and may include practically any number of unstressed syllables, which do not count. In "Christabel", for instance, Coleridge keeps four stresses to a line, though the first line has only eight syllables and the last line has eleven:

There is not wind e·nough to twirl

The one red leaf , the last of its clan,

That dan·ces as of ·ten as dance it can,

Hang·ing so light, and hang·ing so high,

On the top-most twig that looks up at the sky.

Although less popular among poets today than formerly, meter endures. Major poets from Shakespeare to Yeats have fashioned their works by it, and if we are to read their poems with full enjoyment, we need to be aware of it.

Verse Form

Besides the rhymed verse, there is **blank verse**, which is unrhymed, and composed of lines, which normally contain 10 syllables and have the stress on every second syllable, as in the classical iambic pentameter. Blank verse is the principal English meter, used in much of the greatest English poetry, like the tragedies of Shakespeare. In America, Robert Frost is a skillful user of blank verse. For example,

> *When I see birches bend to left and right*
> *Across the line of straighter darker trees*

Don't confuse blank verse with free verse. **Free verse** is poetry that has an irregular rhythm and line length and that attempts to avoid any predetermined verse structure; instead, it uses the cadences of natural speech. While it alternates stressed and unstressed syllables as stricter verse forms do, free verse does so in a looser way. Whitman's poetry is an example of free verse at its most impressive form. Listen, for instance, to a line from "Song of Myself":

> *A child said, What is the grass? fetching it to me with full hands;*

Here, question and answer create a rising and falling effect, ending in a stop. Whitman continues:

How could I answer the child? I do not know what it is any more than he.

The same question-and-answer pattern is repeated, the same rising and falling effect. This is not prose but poetry. It is arranged rhythmically, tightened and loosened by the poet. It has a plan, although the plan seems to "grow" organically—like its subjects, nature and human beings.

Although free verse had been used before Whitman, notably in Italian opera and in the King James translation of the *Bible*, it was Whitman who pioneered the form and made it acceptable in American poetry. It has since been used by Ezra Pound, T. S. Eliot, William Carlos Williams, Wallace Stevens, and other major American poets of the 20th century.

Stanza Form

Stanza form is a division of a poem into units of the same number of lines, the same meter, and the same rhyme scheme. There are many stanza patterns in English language poetry. One of the most frequent forms in English is the **quatrain**, in which the first and third lined rhyme, and the second and fourth; thus: a-b-a-b. There are some other stanza patterns like **couplet** (a stanza of two lines), **octave** (a stanza of eight lines), **tercet** (a stanza of three lines) and etc.

In English, there are some fixed forms of poetry, for example, **ballad**, a narrative poem, usually in the stanza form of quatrains. The ballad has its fixed meter: Each of the odd-numbered-lines is written in iambic tetrameter, while each of the even-numbered lines is iambic trimeter. Several other fixed forms of poetry are direct borrowings from French and Italian sources. The most familiar fixed form in English language poetry is the **sonnet**, which began to be developed in Britain (although borrowed from the Italian poets) in the 16th century. It is a fourteen-line poem, nearly always in iambic pentameter, although the rhyme patterns and rhythm may sometimes vary. There are two basic types of sonnet in both British and American poetry, the Italian and the English.

The **Italian sonnet** (also frequently called the **Petrarchan**, after the Italian poet Petrarch) is divided into two parts. The first eight lines, rhyming a-b-b-a-a-b-b-a are the **octave**; and the second six lines are called the **sestet** usually rhyming c-d-e-c-d-e or c-d-c-e-c-e. Usually there is a division of thought between the octave and the sestet, the first presenting a problem, a situation, or a question and the second providing a solution, an example, or an answer.

The **English sonnet** (also called **Shakespearean**, because it was first developed by the English Earl of Surrey and perfected by William Shakespeare) is made up of three quatrains and a concluding couplet, rhyming a-b-a-b-c-d-c-d-e-f-e-f-g-g. As in the Italian sonnet, there is a development of thought. The three quatrains often present variations of one idea, and the concluding two lines provide a conclusion. Several American poets have used this form at times, most notably Frost and Robinson, but Shakespeare himself provides the best model of the type.

Here are four poems, read them and learn to recognize rhythms in them.

The Descent of Winter (Section 10/30) (1934)
William Carlos Williams

To freight cars in the air

all the slow

   clank, clank

   clank, clank

moving about the treetops

the

   wha, wha

of the hoarse whistle

   pah, pah, pah

   pah, pah, pah, pah, pah

   piece and piece

   piece and piece

moving still trippingly

through the morning mist

   long after the engine

has fought by

   and disappeared

in silence

   to the left

Beat! Beat! Drums! (1861)
Walt Whitman

Beat! beat! drums!—blow! bugles! blow!

Through the windows—through doors—burst like a ruthless force,

Into the solemn church, and scatter the congregation,
Into the school where the scholar is studying;
Leave not the bridegroom quiet—no happiness must he have now with his bride,
Nor the peaceful farmer any peace, ploughing his field or gathering his grain,
So fierce you whirr and pound you drums—so shrill you bugles blow.

Beat! beat! drums!—blow! bugles! blow!
Over the traffic of cities—over the rumble of wheels in the streets;
Are beds prepared for sleepers at night in the houses? no sleepers must sleep in those beds,
No bargainer's bargains by day—no brokers or speculators—would they continue?
Would the talkers be talking? would the singer attempt to sing?
Would the lawyer rise in the court to state his case before the judge?
Then rattle quicker, heavier drums—you bugles wilder blow.

Beat! beat! drums!—blow! bugles! blow!
Make no parley—stop for no expostulation,
Mind not the timid—mind not the weeper or prayer,
Mind not the old man beseeching the young man,
Let not the child's voice be heard, nor the mother's entreaties,
Make even the trestles to shake the dead where they lie awaiting the hearses.
So strong you thump O terrible drums—so loud you bugles blow.

Dream Boogle (1951)
Langston Hughes

Good morning, daddy!
Ain't you heard
The boogie-woogie rumble
Of a dream deferred?

Listen closely:
You'll hear their feet
Beating out and beating out a—

You think
It's a happy beat?

Listen to it closely:
Ain't you heard something underneath
like a—

What did I say?

Sure,
I'm happy!
Take it away!

Hey, pop!
Re-bop!
Mop!

Y-e-a-h!

She Dwelt Among the Untrodden Ways (1800)
William Wordsworth

She dwelt among the untrodden ways
Beside the springs of Dove,
A Maid whom there were none to praise
And very few to love:

A violet by a mossy stone
Half hidden from the eye!
Fair as a star, when only one
Is shining in the sky.

She lived unknown, and few could know
When Lucy cease to be;
But she is in her grave, and oh,
The difference to me

Study Questions:

Which of the poems contain predominant meters? Which poems are not whole metrical, but are metrical in certain lines? Point out any such lines.

[Reading Critically]

What Is Poetry?

What is poetry? Robert Frost made a try at its definition: "A poem is an idea caught in the act of dawning." Just in case further efforts at definition can be useful, here are a few memorable ones:

the art of uniting pleasure with truth by calling imagination to the help of reason.

—Samuel Johnson

the best words in the best order.

—Samuel Tailor Coleridge

the spontaneous overflow of powerful feelings.

—William Wordsworth

musical thought.

—Thomas Carlyle

emotion put into measure.

—Thomas Hardy

If I feel physically as if the top of my head were taken off, I know that is poetry.

—Emily Dickinson

a way of remembering what it would impoverish us to forget.

—Robert Frost

a revelation in words by means of the words.

—Wallace Stevens

Poetry is prose bewitched.

—Mina Lay

not the assertion that something is true, but the making of that truth more fully real to us.

—T. S. Eliot

the clear expression of mixed feelings.

—W. H. Auden

the body of linguistic constructions that men usually refer to as poems.

—J. V. Cunningham

hundreds of things coming together at the right moment.

—Elizabeth Bishop

Verse should have two obligations: to communicate a precise instance and to touch us physically, as the presence of the sea does.

—Jorge Luis Barges

Reduced to its simplest and most essential form, the poem is a song. Song is neither discourse nor explanation.

—Octavio Paz

anything said in such a way, or put on the page in such a way, as to invite from the hearer or the reader a certain kind of attention.

—William Stafford

Poetry is life distilled.

—Gwendolyn Brooks

A poem is something that penetrates for an instant into the unconscious.

—Robert Bly

All in all, a poem differs from most prose in several ways. For one, both writer and reader tend to regard it differently. The poet's attitude is something like this: I offer this piece of writing to be read not as prose but as a poem, that is, more perceptively, thoughtfully, and considerately, with more attention to sounds and connotations. This is a great deal to expect, but in return, the reader, too, has a right to certain expectations. Approaching the poem in the anticipation of out-of-the-ordinary knowledge and pleasure, the reader assumes that the poem may use certain enjoyable devices not available to prose: rime, alliteration, meter, and rhythms—definite, various, or emphatic. (The poet may not always decide to use these things.) The reader expects the poet to make greater use, perhaps, of resources of meaning such as figurative language, allusion, symbol, and imagery. As readers of prose we might seek no more than meaning: no more than what could be paraphrased without serious loss. Meeting any figurative language or graceful turns of word order, we think them pleasant extras. But in poetry all these "extras" matter as much as the paraphraseable content, if not more. For, when we finish reading a good poem, we cannot explain precisely to ourselves what we have experienced, without repeating, word for word, the language of the poem itself.

"Poetry is to prose as dancing is to walking," remarked Paul Valery. It is doubtful, however, that anyone can draw an immovable boundary between poetry and prose. Certain prose needs only to be arranged in lines to be seen as poetry, especially prose that conveys strong emotion in vivid, physical imagery and in terse, figurative, rhythmical language.

It may be that a poem can point beyond words to something still more essential. Language has its limits, for, of all a human being can experience and imagine, words say only part. "Human speech," said Flaubert, who strove after the best of it, "is like a cracked kettle on which we hammer out tunes to make bears dance, when what we long for is the compassion of the stars."

A poem is to be seen not as a confederation of form, rime, image, metaphor, tone, and theme, but as a whole. We study one element of a poem at a time because the intellect best comprehends what it can separate. But only our total attention, involving the participation of our blood and marrow, can see all elements in a poem fused, all dancing together. Pedagogy must have a stop; so too must the viewing of poems as if their elements fell into chapters. For the total experience of reading a poem surpasses the mind's categories. The wind in the grass, says a proverb, cannot be taken into the house.

Part Two　Fiction

For human intercourse, as soon as we look at it for its own sake and not as a social adjunct, is seen to be haunted by a specter. We cannot understand each other, except in a rough-and-ready way; we cannot reveal ourselves, even when we want to; what we call intimacy is only a makeshift; perfect knowledge is an illusion. But in the novel we can know people perfectly, and, apart from the general pleasure of reading, we can find here a compensation for their dinners in life. In this direction fiction is truer than history, because it goes beyond the evidence, and each of us knows from his own experience that there is something beyond the evidence, and even if the novelist has not got it correctly, well—he has tried.

E. M. Forster

Fiction (from the Latin *fictio*, "a shaping, a counterfeiting") is a name for stories not entirely factual, but at least partially shaped, made up, and imagined. Today, fiction almost becomes the synonym of novel. Broadly speaking, the term "novel", apparently derived from Italian *Novella* which means "tale or piece of news", is now applied to any prose work of some length, which tells a story, attempts rounded characterization, amuses, shocks and entertains the reader. In a narrow sense, a novel is a realistic fiction, complete in itself and contains the essential elements of story, character, and setting. In this way, a **novel** can be defined as a book-length prose fiction, while a **short story** is thus a brief prose fiction, usually one that can be read in a single sitting.

It is true that in some fiction, such as a historical novel, a writer draws upon factual information in presenting scenes, events, and characters. But the factual information in a historical novel, unlike that in a history book, is of secondary importance. Many first-hand accounts of the American Civil War were written by men who had fought in it, but few eyewitnesses give us so keen a sense of actual life on the battlefront as the author of *The Red Badge of Courage*, Stephen Crane, born after the war was over. In fiction, the "facts" may or may not be true, and a story is none the worse for their being entirely imaginary. We expect from fiction a sense of how people act, not an authentic chronicle of how, at some past time, a few people acted.

As children, we used to read (if we were lucky and formed the habit) to steep ourselves in romance, mystery, and adventure. As adults, we still do: at an airport, while waiting for a flight, we pass the time with some newsstand paperback full of fast action and brisk dialogue. Certain fiction, of course, calls for closer attention. To read a novel by the Russian master Dostoevsky instead of a science fiction thriller in the *Star Trek* series is somewhat like playing chess instead of a game of tic-tac-toe. Not that a great novel does not provide entertainment. In fact, it may offer more deeply satisfying entertainment than a novel of violence and soft-core pornography, in which stick figures connive, go to bed, and kill one another in accord with some market-tested formula.

Reading literary fiction (as distinguished from fiction as a commercial product—the formula kind of spy, detective, Western, romance, or science fiction story), we are not necessarily led on by the promise of thrills; we do not keep reading mainly to find out what happens next. Indeed, a literary story might even disclose in its opening lines everything that happened, then spend the rest of its length revealing what that happening meant. Reading literary fiction is no merely passive activity, but one that demands both attention and insight-lending participation. In return, it offers rewards. In some works of literary fiction, in Stephen Crane's "The Open Boat" and Flannery O'Connor's "Revelation", we see more deeply into the minds and hearts of the characters than we ever see into those of our family, our close friends, our lovers, or even ourselves.

Fables, Parables, and Tales

Modern literary fiction in English has been dominated by two forms: the novel and the short story. The two have many elements in common. Perhaps we will be able to define the short story more meaningfully—for it has traits more essential than just a particular length—if first, for comparison, we consider some related varieties of fiction: the fable and the tale. Ancient forms whose origins date back to the time of word-of-mouth storytelling, the fable and the tale are relatively simple in structure; in them we can plainly see elements also found in the short story (and in the novel). A fable is a brief story that sets forth some pointed statement of truth.

Another traditional form of storytelling is the parable. Like the fable, a parable is a brief narrative that teaches a moral, but unlike the fable, its plot is plausibly realistic, and the main characters are human rather than anthropomorphized animals or natural forces. The other key difference is that parables usually possess a more mysterious and suggestive tone. A fable customarily ends by explicitly stating its moral, but parables often present their morals implicitly, and their meanings can be open to several interpretations.

In the Western tradition, the literary conventions of the parable are largely based on the brief stories told by Jesus in his preaching. The forty-three parables recounted in the four gospels reveal how frequently he used the form to teach. Jesus designed his parables to have two levels of meaning—a literal story that could immediately be understood by the crowds he addressed, and a deeper meaning fully comprehended only by his disciples, an inner circle who understood the nature of his ministry. The parable was also widely used by Eastern philosophers. The Taoist sage, Chuang Tzu, often portrayed the principles of Tao, which he called the "Way of Nature", in witty parables.

The name tale (from the Old English *talu*, "speech") is sometimes applied to any story, whether short or long, true or fictitious. Tale, a more evocative name than story, writers sometimes call their stories "tales" as if to imply something handed down from the past. But defined in a more limited sense, a tale is a story, usually short, that sets forth strange and wonderful events in more or less bare summary, without detailed character drawing. "Tale" is pretty much synonymous with "yarn", for it implies a story in which the goal is revelation of the marvelous rather than revelation of character. In the English folk tale "Jack and the Beanstalk", we take away a more vivid impression of the miraculous beanstalk and the giant who dwells at its top than of Jack's mind or personality. Because such venerable stories were told aloud before someone set them down in writing, the storytellers had to limit themselves to brief descriptions. Probably spoken around a fire or hearth, such a tale tends to be less complicated and less closely detailed than a story written for the printed page, whose readers can linger over it. Still, such tales can be complicated. It is not merely greater length that makes a short story different from a tale or a fable: A mark of a short story is a fully delineated character.

Even modern tales favor supernatural or fantastic events: for instance, the **tall tale**, that variety of folk story, which recounts the deeds of a superhero or of the storyteller. If the storyteller is telling about his own imaginary experience, his bragging yarn is usually told with a straight face to listeners who take pleasure in scoffing at it. Although the fairy tale, set in a world of magic and enchantment, is sometimes the work of a modern author (notably Hans Christian Andersen), well-known examples are those German folktales, which probably originated in the Middle Ages, collected by the brothers Grimm. The label fairy tale is something of an English misnomer, for in the Grimm stories, though witches and goblins abound, fairies are a minority.

Short Stories

The teller of a tale relies heavily upon the method of summary: terse, general narration. But in a **short story**, a form more realistic than the tale and of modern origin, the writer usually presents the main events in greater fullness. Fine writers of short stories, although they may use summary at times (often to give some portion of a story less emphasis), are skilled in rendering a scene: a vivid or dramatic moment described in enough detail to create the illusion that the reader is practically there. Avoiding long summary, they try to *show* rather than simply to *tell*; as if following Mark Twain's advice to authors: "Don't say, 'The old lady screamed.' Bring her on and let her scream."

A short story is more than just a sequence of happenings. A finely wrought short story has the richness and conciseness of an excellent lyric poem. Spontaneous and natural as the finished story may seem, the writer has written it so artfully that there is meaning in even seemingly casual speeches and apparently trivial details. If we skim it hastily, skipping the descriptive passages, we miss significant parts. Some literary short stories, unlike commercial fiction in which the main interest is in physical action or conflict, tell of an **epiphany**: some moment of insight, discovery, or revelation by which a character's life, or view of life, is greatly altered. (For such moments in fiction, see the stories by James Joyce, John Steinbeck, and Joyce Carol Gates.) Other short stories tell of a character initiated into experience or maturity: One such story of **initiation** is William Faulkner's "Barn Burning", in which a boy finds it necessary to defy his father and suddenly to grow into manhood.

The fable and the tale are ancient forms; the short story is of more recent origin. In the 19th century, writers of fiction were encouraged by a large, literate audience of middle-class readers who wanted to see their lives reflected in faithful mirrors. Skillfully representing ordinary life, many writers perfected the art of the short story: in Russia, Anton Chekhov; in France, Honoré de Balzac, Gustave Flaubert, and Guy de Maupassant; and in America, Nathaniel Hawthorne and Edgar Allan Poe (although the Americans seem less fond of everyday life than of dream and fantasy). It would be false to claim that, in passing from the fable and the tale to the short story, fiction has made a triumphant progress; or to claim that, because short stories are modern, they are superior to fables and tales. Fable, tale, and short story are distinct forms, each achieving its own effects. (Incidentally, fable and tale are far from being extinct today: You can find many recent examples.) Lately, in the hands of Jorge Luis Borges, Joyce Carol Oates, Gabriel Garcia Marquez, and other innovative writers, the conventions of the short story have been changing; and at the moment, stories of epiphany and initiation have become scarcer.

Long Stories and Novels

Among the forms of imaginative literature in English, the novel has been the favorite of both writers and readers for more than two hundred years. Unlike other major literary forms—drama, lyric, ballad, and epic—the novel is a relative newcomer. Originally, the drama in ancient Greece came alive only when actors performed it; the epic or heroic poem (from the classic *Iliad* through the Old English *Beowulf*), only when a bard sang or chanted it. But the English **novel** came to maturity in literate times, in the 18th century, and by its nature was something different: a story to be communicated silently, at whatever moment and at whatever pace (whether quickly or slowly and meditatively) the reader desired. Akin to the French word for "news" (*nouvelles*), the word novel comes from the Italian *novella* ("something new and small"), a term applied to a newly made story taking place in recent times, and not a traditional story taking place long ago.

Many early novels were told in the form of letters. Sometimes these epistolary novels contained letters by only one character; often they contained letters by several of the characters in the book. By casting his novel, *Pamela* (1740), into the form of personal letters, Samuel Richardson helped give the story the appearance of not being invented but discovered from real documents. Alice Walker's *The Color Purple* (1982) is a more recent **epistolary novel**, though some of the letters that tell the story are addressed to God.

Another method favored by novelists is to write as though setting down a memoir or an autobiography. Daniel Defoe is a skilled writer in feigning such memoirs. His *Moll Flanders* (1722) even succeeded in writing the supposedly true confessions of a woman retired from a life of crime. It is true that some novelists place great emphasis on research and note-taking. James A. Michener, the internationally best-selling author of novels like *Chesapeake* (which describes 400 years of events on Maryland's Eastern Shore), started work on a book by studying everything available about his chosen subject. He also traveled to locations that might appear in the book, interviewed local people, and compiled immense amounts of scientific, historical, and cultural data. Research alone, however, is not enough to finish a novel. A novel grows to completion only through the slow mental process of creation, selection, and arrangement. But raw facts can sometimes provide a beginning. Many novels started when the author read some arresting episode in a newspaper or magazine. Theodore Dreiser's impressive study of a murder, *An American Tragedy* (1925), for example, was inspired by a journalist's account of a real-life case.

Since both the novel and journalism try to capture the fabric of everyday life, there has long been a close relationship between the two literary forms. Many novelists, like Ernest Hemingway, Stephen Crane, and Jack London began their writing careers as cub reporters. Journalism greatly influences how novelists depict the world around them. Stephen Crane's *The Open Boat* (1897) began as a newspaper account of his actual experiences in a small rowboat after the sinking of the Commodore in 1897. A journalist might have been content with such a gripping first-person story of surviving a shipwreck, but a great fiction writer has the gift of turning personal bad luck into art, and Crane eventually created a masterpiece of fiction based on fact.

In the 1960s there was a great deal of talk about the **nonfiction novel**, in which the author presents actual people and events in story form. The vogue of the nonfiction novel was created by Truman Capote's *In Cold Blood* (1966), which depicts an actual multiple murder and the resulting trial in Kansas. Capote traveled to the scene of the crime and interviewed all of the principal parties, including the murderers. Norman Mailer wrote a similar novel, *The Executioner's Song* (1979), chronicling the life and death of Gary Gilmore, the Utah murderer who demanded his own execution. Perhaps the name "nonfiction novel" (Capote's name for it) or "true life novel" (as Mailer calls his Gilmore story) is newer than the form. In the past, writers of autobiography have cast their memoirs into what looks like novel form such as Richard Wright in his *Black Boy* (1945). In reading such works we may nearly forget we are reading literal truth, so well do the techniques of the novel lend remembered facts an air of immediacy.

A familiar kind of fiction that claims a basis in fact is the **historical novel**, a detailed reconstruction of life in another time, perhaps in another place. In some historical novels the author attempts a faithful picture of daily life in another era. More often, history is a backdrop for an exciting story of love and heroic adventure. Nathaniel Hawthorne's *The Scarlet Letter* (set in Puritan Boston), Herman Melville's *Moby Dick* (set in the heyday of Yankee whalers); and Stephen Crane's *The Red Badge of Courage* (set in the battlefields of the Civil War) are historical novels in that their authors lived considerably later than the scenes and events that they depicted and strove for truthfulness, by imaginative means.

Other varieties of novel will be familiar to anyone such as the mystery or detective novel, the Western novel, the science fiction novel, and other enduring types. Classified according to less well-known species, novels are sometimes said to belong to a category if they contain some recognizable kind of structure or theme. Such a category is the ***Bildungsroman*** (German for "a novel of growth or development"), which is the kind of novel in which a youth struggles toward maturity, seeking, perhaps, some consistent worldview or philosophy of life. Sometimes the **apprenticeship novel** is evidently the author's recollection of his own early life: James Joyce's *Portrait of the Artist as a Young Man* and Mark Twain's *Tom Sawyer*.

In a **picaresque novel** (another famous category), a likable scoundrel wanders through adventures, living by his wits, duping the straight citizenry. The name comes from Spanish: *picaro*, "rascal" or "rogue". The classic picaresque novel is the anonymous Spanish *Life of Lazarillo de Tonmes* (1554), imitated by many English writers, among them Henry Fielding in his story of a London thief and racketeer, *Jonathan Wild* (1743). Mark Twain's *Huckleberry Finn* owes something to the tradition; like early picaresque novels, it is told in episodes rather than in one all-unifying plot and is narrated in the first person by a hero at odds with respectable society. Modern novels worthy of the name include J. P. Donleavy's *The Ginger Man* (1965), Saul Bellow's *The Adventures of Augie March* (1953), Erica Jong's *Fanny* (1981), and Seth Morgan's *Homeboy* (1990).

The death of the novel has been frequently announced. Competition from television, VCRs, video games, and the Internet, critics claim, will overwhelm the habit of reading; the public is lazy and will follow the easiest route available for entertainment. But in England and America television and films have been sending people back in vast numbers to the books they dramatize. Jane Austen has never lacked readers, but films like *Emma*, *Persuasion*, and *Sense and Sensibility* made her one of the world's best-selling novelists. Even experimental novels like Virginia Woolf's *Orlando* and William Burroughs's *Naked Lunch* have become successful films that have in turn sent a new generation of readers back to the novels. Sometimes Hollywood even helps bring a good book into print. No one would publish Thomas Disch's sophisticated children's novella, *The Brave Little Toaster*, until Walt Disney turned it into a cartoon movie.

Meanwhile, each year new novels by the hundreds continue to appear, their authors wistfully looking for a public. A chosen few reach tens of thousands of readers through book clubs, and, through paperback reprint editions, occasionally millions more. To forecast the end of the novel seems risky. For the novel exercises the imagination of the beholder. At any hour, at a touch of the hand, it opens and (with no warm-up) begins to speak. Once printed, it consumes no further energy. Often so small it may be carried in a pocket, it may yet survive by its ability to contain multitudes: a thing both a work of art and an amazingly compact system for the storage and retrieval of imagined life.

Trying to perceive a novel as a whole, we may find it helpful to look for the same elements that we do in reading short stories. By asking ourselves leading questions, we may be drawn more deeply into the novel's world, and may come to recognize and appreciate the techniques of the novelist. Does the novel have themes, or an overall theme? Who is its main character? What is the author's kind of narrative voice? What do we know about the tone, style, and use of irony? Why is this novel written from one point of view rather than from another? In the following part, we will talk about those basic elements of fiction: plot, point of view, character, setting, tone and style, theme, and symbol.

1. Plot

A fiction, especially a short story generally contains seven or eight major elements of fiction: plot, character, setting, point of view, theme, symbol, allegory, style and tone. When we refer to the **plot** of a novel or short story, we are referring to the series of events that take us from a beginning to an end. Each event in the plot is related to the **conflict**, the struggle that the main character must wage against an opposing force. Usually the events of the story are all related to the conflict. The conflict may either external, when the protagonist (who is often referred to as the hero or the focal character) is pitted against some outside object or force, or internal, in which case the issue to be resolved is one within the protagonist's own self. **External conflict** may take the form of a basic opposition between a person and nature or between a person and society. It may also take the form of an opposition between two people (between the protagonist and a human adversary, the antagonist). **Internal conflict**, on the other hand, focuses on two or more elements contesting within the protagonist's own character.

It is worth noting that some story plots contain more than one conflict and the conflicts of a story may exist prior to the formal initiation of the plot itself, rather than be explicitly dramatized. Some conflicts, in fact, are never made explicit and must be inferred by the reader from what the characters do or say as the plot unfolds. Conflict, then, is the basic opposition, or tension, that sets the plot of a short story in motion; it engages the reader, builds the suspense or the mystery of the work, and arouses expectation for the events that are to follow.

The plot of the traditional short story is often conceived of as moving through five distinct sections or stages. The first stage is the **exposition** in which the author provides the necessary background information, sets the scene, establishes the situation, and dates the action. It usually introduces the characters and the conflict, or at least the potential for conflict. The second stage is the rising action, which is sometimes referred to as the **complication**. It develops and intensifies the conflict. The third stage is the **crisis** (also referred to as the **climax**) that is the point of highest dramatic tension or excitement; it is the turning point of the plot, directly precipitating its resolution. The falling action is the fourth stage in which the tension subsides and the plot moves toward its conclusion. The final stage of the plot is the **resolution**; it records the outcome of the conflict and establishes some new equilibrium. The resolution is also referred to as the **conclusion** or the **denouement**, the latter a French word meaning "unknotting" or "untying". In some novels this five-stage structure is repeated in many of the individual chapters, while a novel as a whole builds on a series of increasing conflicts.

Although the five stages are helpful in understanding the relationship among the parts of many kinds of narrative, but all plots, unfortunately, do not lend themselves to such neat and exact formulations. Even when they do, it is not unusual for critics and readers to disagree among themselves about the precise nature of the conflict, for example, the protagonist is more in conflict with society than with himself or herself, or about where the crisis, or turning point, of the story actually occurs. Nor is there any special reason that the crisis should occur at or near the middle of the plot. It can, in fact, occur at any moment. In a number of the companion stories in James Joyce's *Dubliners*, the crisis—in the form of a sudden illumination that Joyce called an epiphany—occurs at the very end of a story, and the falling action and the resolution are dispensed with almost entirely. Exposition and rising action can also be omitted in favor of a plot that begins in the midst of things. In many modern and contemporary stories the plot consists of a "slice of life" into which we enter on the eve of crisis, and the reader is left to infer beginnings and antecedents—including the precise nature of the conflict—from what he or she is subsequently able to learn.

This is the case in such stories as Ernest Hemingway's "Hills Like White Elephants" and Doris Lessing's "Wine", in which the authors choose to eliminate not only the traditional beginning, but also the ending in order to focus our attention on a more limited moment of time, the middle, which takes the form of a single, self-contained episode. Both stories offer little in the way of a traditional plot; there is very little description and almost no action. Rather, in both instances the reader overhears a continuous dialogue between two characters—a man and woman. Conflict and complication in each case are neither shown nor prepared for, but only revealed; the situation and the "story" are to be understood and completed through the active participation of the reader. Such stories are sometimes referred to as "plotless" in order to suggest that the author's emphasis and interest have been shifted elsewhere, most frequently to character or idea.

Plot plays a desultory or irregular part in the traditional picaresque novel, which depends for movement on a succession of chance incidents. Plot plays a very important part in the Gothic novel and detective novel, and in the 19th century realistic novel. Plot plays almost no part in some works of modernist novelists, in which the consciousness of the characters provides all the fictional material.

Understanding the plot on a schematic level becomes even more difficult when dealing with works, usually novels, which have more than one plot. Many novels contain one or more subplots that reinforce by contrast or parallel the main plot. For example, Jane Austin's *Pride and Prejudice* (1813) might have been conceived as "a young couple destined to be married have first to overcome the barriers of pride on the part of the hero and prejudice on the part of the heroine". The detailed working out of the nuclear idea, however, requires much ingenuity, since the plot of one novel is expected to be somewhat different from that of another.

Pride and Prejudice (1813) (Chapters 1 and 58)
Jane Austin

Chapter 1

It is a truth universally acknowledged, that a single man in possession of a good fortune must be in want of a wife.

However little known the feelings or views of such a man may be on his first entering a neighbourhood, this truth is so well fixed in the minds of the surrounding families, that he is considered as the rightful property of some one or other of their daughters.

"My dear Mr. Bennet," said his lady to him one day, "have you heard that Netherfield Park① is let at last?"

Mr. Bennet replied that he had not.

"But it is," returned she, "for Mrs. Long② has just been here, and she told me all about it." Mr. Bennet made no answer.

"Do not you want to know who has taken it?" cried his wife impatiently.

"You want to tell me, and I have no objection to hearing it."

This was invitation enough.

"Why, my dear, you must know, Mrs. Long says that Netherfield is taken by a young man of large fortune from the north of England; that he came down on Monday in a chaise and four to see the place, and was so much delighted with it that he agreed with Mr. Morris③ immediately; that he is to take possession before Michaelmas④, and some of his servants are to be in the house by the end of next week."

"What is his name?"

"Bingley."

"Is he married or single?"

"Oh! Single, my dear, to be sure! A single man of large fortune; four or five thousand a year. What a fine thing for our girls!"

"How so? How can it affect them?"

---

① Netherfield Park: the name of a land estate near the home of the Bennets
② Mrs. Long: a neighbour and friend of the Bennets
③ Mr. Morris: the landlord of the Netherfield Park
④ Michaelmas: a festival celebrated on Sept. 29 in honor of the archangel Michael, one of the seven archangels in Jewish and Christian legend

"My dear Mr. Bennet," replied his wife, "how can you be so tiresome! You must know that I am thinking of his marrying one of them."

"Is that his design in settling here?"

"Design! Nonsense, how can you talk so! But it is very likely that he may fall in love with one of them, and therefore you must visit him as soon as he comes."

"I see no occasion for that. You and the girls may go, or you may send them by themselves, which perhaps will be still better, for as you are as handsome as any of them, Mr. Bingley might like you the best of the party."

"My dear, you flatter me. I certainly have had my share of beauty, but I do not pretend to be any thing extraordinary now. When a woman has five-grown-up daughters, she ought to give over thinking of her own beauty."

"In such cases, a woman has not often much beauty to think of."

"But, my dear, you must indeed go and see Mr. Bingley when he comes into the neighbourhood."

"It is more than I engage for, I assure you."

"But consider your daughters. Only think what an establishment① it would be for one of them. Sir William and Lady Lucas are determined to go, merely on that account, for in general you know they visit no new comers. Indeed you must go, for it will be impossible for us to visit him, if you do not."

"You are over scrupulous surely. I dare say Mr. Bingley will be very glad to see you; and I will send a few lines by you to assure him of my hearty consent to his marrying whichever he chooses of the girls; though I must throw in a good word for my little Lizzy."

"I desire you will do no such thing. Lizzy② is not a bit better than the others; and I am sure she is not half so handsome as Jane, nor half so good humoured as Lydia. But you are always giving her the preference."

"They have none of them much to recommend them," replied he, "they are all silly and ignorant like other girls; but Lizzy has something more of quickness than her sisters."

"Mr. Bennet, how can you abuse your own children in such a way? You take delight in vexing me. You have no compassion for my poor nerves."

"You mistake me, my dear. I have a high respect for your nerves. They are my old friends. I have heard you mention them with consideration these twenty years at least."

"Ah! You do not know what I suffer."

"But I hope you will get over it, and live to see many young men of four thousand a year come into the neighbourhood."

"It will be no use to us, if twenty such should come, since you will not visit them."

---

① establishment: marriage
② Lizzy: (shortened form for Elizabeth) Mr. Bennet's second daughter

"Depend upon it, my dear, that when there are twenty, I will visit them all." Mr. Bennet was so odd a mixture of quick parts①, sarcastic humour, reserve, and caprice, that the experience of three-and-twenty years had been insufficient to make his wife understand his character. Her mind was less difficult to develop. She was a woman of mean understanding, little information, and uncertain temper. When she was discontented, she fancied herself nervous. The business of her life was to get her daughters married; its solace was visiting and news. ②

Chapter 58

Instead of receiving any such letter of excuse from his friend, as Elizabeth half expected Mr. Bingley to do, he was able to bring Darcy with him to Longbourn before many days had passed after Lady Catherine's visit. The gentlemen arrived early; and, before Mrs. Bennet had time to tell him of their having seen his aunt, of which her daughter sat in momentary dread, Bingley, who wanted to be alone with Jane, proposed their all walking out. It was agreed to. Mrs. Bennet was not in the habit of walking; Mary could never spare time; but the remaining five set off together. Bingley and Jane, however, soon allowed the others to outstrip③ them. They lagged behind, while Elizabeth, Kitty, and Darcy were to entertain each other. Very little was said by either; Kitty was too much afraid of him to talk; Elizabeth was secretly forming a desperate resolution; and perhaps he might be doing the same.

They walked towards the Lucases, because Kitty wished to call upon Maria; and as Elizabeth saw no occasion for making it a general concern, when Kitty left them she went boldly on with him alone. Now was the moment for her resolution to be executed, and, while her courage was high, she immediately said, "Mr. Darcy, I am a very selfish creature; and, for the sake of giving relief to my own feelings, care not how much I may be wounding yours. I can no longer help thanking you for your unexampled kindness to my poor sister. Ever since I have known it, I have been most anxious to acknowledge to you how gratefully I feel it. Were it known to the rest of my family, I should not have merely my own gratitude to express."

"I am sorry, exceedingly sorry," replied Darcy, in a tone of surprise and emotion, "that you have ever been informed of what may, in a mistaken light, have given you uneasiness. I did not think Mrs. Gardiner was so little to be trusted."

"You must not blame my aunt. Lydia's thoughtlessness first betrayed to me that you had been concerned in the matter④; and, of course, I could not rest till I knew the particulars. Let

---

① parts: Here "parts" in the plural from is used in the archaic sense of "abilities", "intelligence".

② The comfort of her life consisted in paying visits to her neighbors and receiving visits from them and in listening to and talking about things that happened recently in the neighborhood.

③ outstrip: go faster than

④ matter: referring to Darcy's making Lydia's marriage with Wynn me thank again and again, in the name of all my family, for that generous compassion which induced you to take so much trouble, and bear so many mortifications, for the sake of discovering them."

"If you will thank me," he replied, "let it be for yourself alone. That the wish of giving happiness to you might add force to the other inducements which led me on, I shall not attempt to deny. But your family owes me nothing. Much as I respect them, I believe I thought only of you."

Elizabeth was too much embarrassed to say a word. After a short pause, her companion added, "You are too generous to trifle with me. If your feelings are still what they were last April, tell me so at once. My affections and wishes are unchanged, but one word from you will silence me on this subject for ever."

Elizabeth, feeling all the more than common awkwardness and anxiety of his situation, now forced herself to speak; and immediately, though not very fluently, gave him to understand that her sentiments had undergone so material a change, since the period to which he alluded, as to make her receive with gratitude and pleasure his present assurances. The happiness which this reply produced, was such as he had probably never felt before; and he expressed himself on the occasion as sensibly and as warmly as a man violently in love can be supposed to do. Had Elizabeth been able to encounter his eye, she might have seen how well the expression of heartfelt delight, diffused over his face, became him; but, though she could not look, she could listen, and he told her of feelings, which, in proving of what importance she was to him, made his affection every moment more valuable.

They walked on, without knowing in what direction. There was too much to be thought, and felt, and said, for attention to any other objects. She soon learnt that they were indebted for their present good understanding to the efforts of his aunt, who did call on him in her return through London, and there relate her journey to Longbourn①, its motive, and the substance of her conversation with Elizabeth; dwelling emphatically on every expression of the latter which, in her ladyship's apprehension, peculiarly denoted her perverseness and assurance; in the belief that such a relation must assist her endeavours to obtain that promise from her nephew which she had refused to give. But, unluckily for her ladyship, its effect had been exactly contrariwise.

"It taught me to hope," said he, "as I had scarcely ever allowed myself to hope before. I knew enough of your disposition to be certain that, had you been absolutely, irrevocably decided against me, you would have acknowledged it to Lady Catherine, frankly and openly."

Elizabeth coloured and laughed as she replied, "Yes, you know enough of my frankness to

---

① her journey to Longbourn: referring to the journey, which the aunt of Darcy went to Longbourn for the purpose of persuading Elizabeth to give up the idea of marrying Darcy. Out of her expectations, her visit hastens the process of love between Elizabeth and Darcy.

believe me capable of that. After abusing you so abominably to your face, I could have no scruple in abusing you to all your relations."

"What did you say of me, that I did not deserve? For, though your accusations were ill-founded, formed on mistaken premises, my behaviour to you at the time had merited the severest reproof. It was unpardonable. I cannot think of it without abhorrence."

"We will not quarrel for the greater share of blame annexed to that evening," said Elizabeth. "The conduct of neither, if strictly examined, will be irreproachable; but since then, we have both, I hope, improved in civility."

"I cannot be so easily reconciled to myself. The recollection of what I then said—of my conduct, my manners, my expressions during the whole of it—is now, and has been many months, inexpressibly painful to me. Your reproof, so well applied, I shall never forget: 'had you behaved in a more gentleman-like manner.' Those were your words. You know not, you can scarcely conceive, how they have tortured me;—though it was some time, I confess, before I was reasonable enough to allow their justice."

"I was certainly very far from expecting them to make so strong an impression. I had not the smallest idea of their being ever felt in such a way."

"I can easily believe it. You thought me then devoid of every proper feeling, I am sure you did. The turn of your countenance I shall never forget, as you said that I could not have addressed you in any possible way that would induce you to accept me."

"Oh! Do not repeat what I then said. These recollections will not do at all. I assure you that I have long been most heartily ashamed of it."

Darcy mentioned his letter. "Did it," said he, "did it soon make you think better of me? Did you, on reading it, give any credit to its contents?"

She explained what its effect on her had been, and how gradually all her former prejudices had been removed.

"I knew," said he, "that what I wrote must give you pain, but it was necessary. I hope you have destroyed the letter. There was one part especially, the opening of it, which I should dread your having the power of reading again. I can remember some expressions which might justly make you hate me."

"The letter shall certainly be burnt, if you believe it essential to the preservation of my regard; but, though we have both reason to think my opinions not entirely unalterable, they are not, I hope, quite so easily changed as that implies."

"When I wrote that letter," replied Darcy, "I believed myself perfectly calm and cool, but I am since convinced that it was written in a dreadful bitterness of spirit."

"The letter, perhaps, began in bitterness, but it did not end so. The adieu is charity itself. But think no more of the letter. The feelings of the person who wrote, and the person who received it, are now so widely different from what they were then, that every unpleasant circumstance attending it ought to be forgotten. You must learn some of my philosophy. Think only of the past as its remembrance gives you pleasure. "

"I cannot give you credit for any philosophy of the kind. Your retrospections must be so totally void of reproach, that the contentment arising from them is not of philosophy, but, what is much better, of innocence. But with me, it is not so. Painful recollections will intrude which cannot, which ought not, to be repelled. I have been a selfish being all my life, in practice, though not in principle. As a child I was taught what was right, but I was not taught to correct my temper. I was given good principles, but left to follow them in pride and conceit. Unfortunately an only son (for many years an only child), I was spoilt by my parents, who, though good themselves (my father, particularly, all that was benevolent and amiable), allowed, encouraged, almost taught me to be selfish and overbearing; to care for none beyond my own family circle; to think meanly of all the rest of the world; to wish at least to think meanly of their sense and worth compared with my own. Such I was, from eight to eight and twenty; and such I might still have been but for you, dearest, loveliest Elizabeth! What do I not owe you! You taught me a lesson, hard indeed at first, but most advantageous. By you, I was properly humbled. I came to you without a doubt of my reception. You showed me how insufficient were all my pretensions to please a woman worthy of being pleased. "

"Had you then persuaded yourself that I should?"

"Indeed I had. What will you think of my vanity? I believed you to be wishing, expecting my addresses. "

"My manners must have been in fault, but not intentionally, I assure you. I never meant to deceive you, but my spirits might often lead me wrong. How you must have hated me after that evening?"

"Hate you! I was angry perhaps at first, but my anger soon began to take a proper direction. "

"I am almost afraid of asking what you thought of me, when we met at Pemberley①. You blamed me for coming?"

"No indeed; I felt nothing but surprise. "

"Your surprise could not be greater than mine in being noticed by you. My conscience told me that I deserved no extraordinary politeness, and I confess that I did not expect to receive more than my due. "

"My object then," replied Darcy, "was to show you, by every civility in my power, that I was not so mean as to resent the past; and I hoped to obtain your forgiveness, to lessen your ill opinion, by letting you see that your reproofs had been attended to. How soon any other wishes introduced themselves I can hardly tell, but I believe in about half an hour after I had

---

① Pemberley: Darcy's house

seen you."

He then told her of Georgiana's delight in her acquaintance, and of her disappointment at its sudden interruption; which naturally leading to the cause of that interruption, she soon learnt that his resolution of following her from Derbyshire in quest of her sister had been formed before he quitted the inn, and that his gravity and thoughtfulness there had arisen from no other struggles than what such a purpose must comprehend.

She expressed her gratitude again, but it was too painful a subject to each, to be dwelt on farther.

After walking several miles in a leisurely manner, and too busy to know any thing about it, they found at last, on examining their watches, that it was time to be at home.

"What could become of Mr. Bingley and Jane!" was a wonder which introduced the discussion of their affairs. Darcy was delighted with their engagement; his friend had given him the earliest information of it.

"I must ask whether you were surprised?" said Elizabeth.

"Not at all. When I went away, I felt that it would soon happen."

"That is to say, you had given your permission. I guessed as much."

And though he exclaimed at the term, she found that it had been pretty much the case.

"On the evening before my going to London," said he, "I made a confession to him, which I believe I ought to have made long ago. I told him of all that had occurred to make my former interference in his affairs absurd and impertinent. His surprise was great. He had never had the slightest suspicion. I told him, moreover, that I believed myself mistaken in supposing, as I had done, that your sister was indifferent to him; and as I could easily perceive that his attachment to her was unabated, I felt no doubt of their happiness together."

Elizabeth could not help smiling at his easy manner of directing his friend.

"Did you speak from your own observation," said she, "when you told him that my sister loved him, or merely from my information last spring?"

"From the former. I had narrowly observed her during the two visits which I had lately made here; and I was convinced of her affection."

"And your assurance of it, I suppose, carried immediate conviction to him."

"It did. Bingley is most unaffectedly modest. His diffidence had prevented his depending on his own judgment in so anxious a case, but his reliance on mine made every thing easy. I was obliged to confess one thing, which for a time, and not unjustly, offended him. I could not allow myself to conceal that your sister had been in town three months last winter—that I had known it, and purposely kept it from him. He was angry. But his anger, I am persuaded, lasted no longer than he remained in any doubt of your sister's sentiments. He has heartily forgiven me now."

Elizabeth longed to observe that Mr. Bingley had been a most delightful friend—so easily guided that his worth was invaluable; but she checked herself. She remembered that he had yet to learn to be laughed at, and it was rather too early to begin. In anticipating the happiness of Bingley, which of course was to be inferior only to his own, he continued the conversation till they reached the house. In the hall they parted.

Study Questions:

1. Do you agree with the statement "It is a truth universally acknowledged, that a single man in possession of a good fortune must be in want of a wife"? What is the relationship between money and marriage?
2. What do you think of Mrs. Bennet? How can you characterize her?
3. What makes Elizabeth feel so grateful to Darcy? How does Darcy respond to her?

Tess of the d'Urbervilles (1891)
Thomas Hardy

XXXIV

They drove by the level road along the valley to a distance of a few miles, and, reaching Wellbridge, turned away from the village to the left, and over the great Elizabethan bridge which gives the places half its name. Immediately behind it stood the house wherein they had engaged lodgings, whose exterior features are so well known travelers through the Froom Valley; once portion of a fine manorial residence, and the property and seat of a d'Urberville, but since its partial demolition a farm-house.

"Welcome to one of your ancestral mansions!" said Clare handed her down. But he regretted the pleasantry; it was too near a satire.

On entering they found that, though they had only engaged a couple of rooms, the farmer had taken advantage of their proposed presence during the coming days to pay a New Year's visit to some friends, leaving a woman from a neighbouring cottage to minister to their few wants. The absoluteness of possession pleased them, and they realized it as the first moment of their experience under their own exclusive roof-tree①.

But he found that the mouldy old habitation somewhat depressed his bride. When the carriage was gone they ascended the stairs to wash their hands, the charwoman showing the way. On the landing Tess stopped and started.

"What's the matter?" said he.

"Those horrid women!" she answered, with a smile. "He frightened me."

He looked up, and perceived two life-size portraits on pane into the masonry. As all visitors to the mansion are aware, these paintings represent women of middle age, of a date

---

① their own exclusive roof-tree: rooms owned by themselves, here roof referring to the whole building

some two hundred years ago, whose lineaments① once seen can never be forgotten. The long pointed features, narrow eye, and smirk of the one, so suggestive of merciless treachery; the bill-hook nose, large teeth, and bold eye of the other, suggesting arrogance to the point of ferocity, haunt the beholder afterwards in his dreams.

"Whose portraits are those?" asked Clare of the charwoman.

"I have been told by old folk that they were ladies of the d'Urberville family, the ancient lords of this manor," she said. "Owing to their being builded into the wall they can't be moved away."

The unpleasantness of the matter was that, in addition to their effect upon Tess, her fine features were unquestionably traceable in these exaggerated forms. He said nothing of this, however, and, regretting that he had gone out of his way to choose the house for their bridal time, went on into the adjoining room. The place having been rather hastily prepared for them they washed their hands in one basin. Clare touched hers under the water.

"Which are my fingers and which are yours?" he said, looking up. "They are very much mixed."

"They are all yours," said she, very prettily, and endeavoured to be gayer than she was. He had not been displeased with her thoughtfulness on such an occasion; it was what every sensible woman would show; but Tess knew that she had been thoughtful to excess, and struggled against it.

The sun was so low on that short last afternoon of the year that it shone in through a small opening and formed a golden staff which stretched across to her skirt, where it made a spot like a paint-mark set upon her. They went into the ancient parlour to tea, and here they shared their first common meal alone. Such was their childishness, or rather his, that he found it interesting to use the same bread-and-butter plate as herself, and to brush crumbs from her lips with his own. He wondered a little that she did not enter into these frivolities with his own zest.

Looking at her silently for a long time; "She is a dear dear Tess," he thought to himself, as one deciding on the true construction of a difficult passage. "Do I realize solemnly enough how utterly and irretrievably this little womanly thing is the creature of my good or bad faith and fortune? I think not. I think I could not, unless I were a woman myself. What I am in worldly estate, she is. ② What I become, she must become. What I cannot be, she cannot be. And shall I ever neglect her, or hurt her, or even forget to consider her? God forbid such a crime!"

They sat on over the tea-table waiting for their luggage, which the dairyman had promised to send before it grew dark. But evening began to close in, and the luggage did not arrive, and

---

① lineaments: features
② What I am in worldly estate, she is: They share weal and woe.

they had brought nothing more than they stood in①. With the departure of the sun the calm mood of the winter day changed. Out of doors there began noises as of silk smartly rubbed; the restful dead leaves of the preceding autumn were stirred to irritated resurrection, and whirled about unwillingly, and tapped against the shutters. It soon began to rain.

"That cock knew the weather was going to change," said Clare.

The woman who had attended upon them had gone home for night, but she had placed candles upon the table, and now they lit them. Each candle-flame drew towards the fireplace.

"These old houses are so draughty," continued Angel, looking at the flames, and at the grease guttering down the sides. "I wonder where that luggage is. We haven't even a brush and comb." "I don't know," she answered, absent-minded. "Tess, you are not a bit cheerful this evening—not at all as you used to be. Those harridans on the panels upstairs have unsettled you. I am sorry I brought you here. I wonder if you really love me, after all?"

He knew that she did, and the words had no serious intent; but she was surcharged with emotion, and winced like a wounded animal. Though she tried not to shed tears she could not help showing one or two.

"I did not mean it!" said he, sorry. "You are worried at not having your things, I know. I cannot think why old Jonathan has not come with them. Why, it is seven o'clock? Ah, there he is!"

A knock had come to the door, and, there being nobody else to answer it Clare went out. He returned to the room with a small package in his hand.

"It is not Jonathan, after all," he said.

"How vexing!" said Tess.

The packet had been brought by a special messenger, who had arrived at Talbothays from Emminster Vicarage immediately after the departure of the married couple, and had followed them hither, being under injunction to deliver it into nobody's hands but theirs. Clare brought it to the light. It was less than a foot long, sewed up in canvas, sealed in red wax with his father's seal, and directed in his father's hand to "Mrs. Angel Clare".

"It is a little wedding-present for you, Tess," said he, handing it to her. "How thoughtful they are!"

Tess looked a little flustered as she took it.

"I think I would rather have you open it, dearest," said she, turning over the parcel. "I don't like to break those great seals; they look so serious. Please open it for me!"

He undid the parcel. Inside was a case of morocco leather, on the top of which lay a note and a key.

The note was for Clare, in the following words:

---

① stood in: had in

MY DEAR SON,—*Possibly you have forgotten that on the death of your godmother, Mrs. Pitney, when you were a lad, she—vain kind woman that she was—left to me a portion of the contents of her jewel-case in trust for your wife, if you should ever have one, as a mark of her affection for you and whomsoever you should choose. This trust I have fulfilled, and the diamonds have been locked up at my banker's ever since. Though I feel it to be a somewhat incongruous act in the circumstances, I am, as you will see, bound to hand over the artic to the woman to whom the use of them for her lifetime will now rightly belong, and they are therefore promptly sent. They become, I believe, heirlooms, strictly speaking, according to the terms of godmother's will. The precise words of the clause that refers to this matter are enclosed.*

"I do remember," said Clare; "but I had quite forgotten."

Unlocking the case, they found it to contain a necklace, with pendant, bracelets, and earrings; and also some other small ornaments.

Tess seemed afraid to touch them at first, but her eyes spark for a moment as much as the stones when Clare spread out the set.

"Are they mine?" she asked incredulously.

"They are, certainly," said he.

He looked into the fire. He remembered how, when he was a lad of fifteen, his godmother, the Squire's wife—the only rich person with whom he had ever come in contact—had pinned her faith to his success; had prophesied a wondrous career for him. There had seemed nothing at all out of keeping with such a conjectured career in the storing up of these showy ornaments for his wife and the wives of the descendants. They gleamed somewhat ironically now. "Yet why?" he asked himself. It was but a question of vanity throughout; and if that were admitted into one side of the equation it should be admitted into the other. His wife was a d'Urberville: whom could they become—the better than her?

Suddenly he said with enthusiasm—

"Tess, put them on; put them on!" And he turned from the fire to help her.

But as if by magic she had already donned them—necklace, earrings, bracelets, and all.

"But the gown isn't right, Tess," said Glare. "It ought to be a low one for a set of brilliants like that." "Ought it?" said Tess. "Yes," said he.

He suggested to her how to tuck in the upper edge of her bodice, so as to make it roughly approximate to the cut for evening wear; and when she had done this, and the pendant to the necklace hung isolated amid the whiteness of her throat, as it was designed to do, he stepped back to survey her.

"My heavens," said Clare, "how beautiful you are!"

As everybody knows, fine feathers make fine birds; a peasant girl but very moderately prepossessing to the casual observer in her simple condition and attire, will bloom as an amazing beauty if clothed as a woman of fashion with the aids that Art can render; while the beauty of the midnight crush① would often cut but a sorry figure if placed inside the field-woman's wrapper upon a monotonous acreage of turnips on a dull day. He had never till now estimated the artistic of excellence of Tess' limbs and features.

"If you were only to appear in a ball-room!" he said. "But no no, dearest; I think I love you best in the wing-bonnet and cotton-frock—yes, better than in this, well as you support these dignities."

Tess' sense of her striking appearance had given her a flush of excitement, which was yet not happiness.

"I'll take them off," she said, "in case Jonathan should see me. They are not fit for me, are they? They must be sold, I Suppose?"

"Let them stay a few minutes longer. Sell them? It would be a breach of faith."

Influenced by a second thought she readily obeyed. She had something to tell, and there might be help in these. She sat down with the jewels upon her; and they again indulged in conjectures as to where Jonathan could possibly be with their baggage. The ale they had poured out for his consumption when he came had gone flat with long standing②.

Shortly after this they began supper, which was already laid on a side-table. Ere they had finished there was a jerk in the fire-smoke, the rising skein of which bulged out into the room, as if some giant had laid his hand on the chimney-top for a moment. It had been caused by the opening of the outer door. A heavy step was now heard in the passage, and Angel went out.

"I couldn't make nobody hear at all by knocking," apologized Jonathan Kail, for it was he at last; "and as't was raining out I opened the door. I've brought the things, sir."

"I am very glad to see them. But you are very late."

"Well, yes, sir."

There was something subdued in Jonathan Kail's tone which had not been there in the day, and lines of concern were ploughed upon his forehead in addition to the lines of years. He continued—

"We've all been gallied at the dairy at what-might ha' been a most terrible affliction since you and your Mis'ess③—so to name her now—left us this afternoon. Perhaps you ha'nt forgot the cock's afternoon crow?"

"Dear me;—what—"

"Well, some says it do mane one thing, and some another; but what's happened is that poor little Retty Priddle hev④ tried to drown herself."

---

① crush: crowding social occasions
② gone flat with long standing: bubbles in the ale have disappeared after it was poured out for a long time
③ Mis'ess: Misses
④ hev: has or had

"No! Really! Why, she bade us good-bye with the rest—"

"Yes. Well, sir, when you and your Mis'ess—so to name what she lawful is—when you two drove away, as I say, Retty and Marian put on their bonnets and went out; and as there is not much doing now, being New Year's Eve, and folks mops and brooms① from what's inside'em, nobody took much notice. They went on to Lew Everard, where they had summut② to drink, and then on they vamped③ to Dree-armed Cross, and there they seemed to have parted, Retty striking across the water-meads as if for home, and Marian going on to the next village, where there's another public-house. Nothing more was zeed④ or heard o' Retty till the waterman, on his way home, noticed something by the Great Pool; 't was her bonnet and shawl packed up. In the water he found her. He and another man brought her home, thinking 'a⑤ was dead; but she fetched roundby degrees."

Angel, suddenly recollecting that Tess was overhearing this gloomy tale, went to shut the door between the passage and the anteroom to the inner parlour where she was; but his wife, flinging a shawl round her, had come to the outer room and was listening to the man's narrative, her eyes resting absently on the luggage and the drops of rain glistening upon it.

"And, more than this, there's Marian; she's been found dead drunk by the withy-bed—a girl who has never been known to touch anything before except shilling ale⑥; though, to be sure, 'a was always a good trencher-woman⑦, as her face showed. It seems as if the maids had all gone out o' their minds!"

"And Izz?" asked Tess.

"Izz is about house as usual; but 'a do say 'a⑧ can guess how it happened; and she seems to be very low in mind about it, poor maid, as well she mid be⑨. And so you see, sir, as all this happened just when we was packing your few traps and your Mis'ess's night-rail⑩ and dressing things into the cart, why, it belated me."

"Yes. Well, Jonathan, will you get the trunks upstairs, and drink a cup of ale, and hasten back as soon as you can, in case you lid be wanted?"

Tess had gone back to the inner parlour, and sat down by the fire, looking wistfully into it. She heard Jonathan Kail's heavy footsteps up and down the stairs till he had done placing the

---

① mops and brooms: half-drunk
② summut: something
③ vamped: tramped
④ was zeed: was seen
⑤ 'a: she
⑥ shinning ale: ale seld by a shilling per gallon, low alcohol
⑦ trencher-woman: a woman with appetite
⑧ but 'a do say 'a: but she does say she
⑨ as well she mid be: as well as she might be
⑩ night-rail: night grown

luggage, and heard him express his thanks for the ale her husband took out to him, and for the gratuity he received. Jonathan's footsteps then died from the door, and his cart creaked away.

Angel slid forward the massive oak bar which secured the door, and coming in to where she sat over the hearth, pressed her cheeks between his hands from behind. He expected her to jump up gaily and unpack the toilet-gear that she had been so anxious about, but as she did not rise he sat down with her in the firelight, the candles on the supper-table being too thin and glimmering to interfere with its glow.

"I am so sorry you should have heard this sad story about the girls," he said. "Still, don't let it depress you. Retty was naturally morbid, you know."

"Without the least cause," said Tess. "While they who have cause to be, hide it, and pretend they are not."

This incident had turned the scale① for her. They were simple and innocent girls on whom the unhappiness of unrequited love had fallen; they had deserved better at the hands of Fate. She had deserved worse—yet she was the chosen one. It was wicked of her to take all without paying. She would pay to the uttermost farthing; she would tell, there and then. This final determination she came to when she looked into the fire, he holding her hand.

A steady glare from the now flameless embers painted the sides and back of the fireplace with its colour, and the well-polished andirons, and the old brass tongs that would not meet. The underside of the mantel-shelf was flushed with the high-coloured light, and the legs of the table nearest the fire. Tess's face and neck reflected the same warmth, which each gem turned into an Aldebaran or a Sirius②—a constellation of white, red, and green flashes, that interchanged their hues with her every pulsation.

"Do you remember what we said to each other this morning about telling our faults?" he asked abruptly, finding that she still remained immovable. "We spoke lightly perhaps, and you may well have done so. But for me it was no light promise. I want to make a confession to you, Love."

This, from him, so unexpectedly apposite, had the effect upon her of a Providential interposition③.

"You have to confess something?" she said quickly, and even with gladness and relief.

"You did not expect it? Ah—you thought too highly of me. Now listen. Put your head there, because I want you to forgive me, and not to be indignant with me for not telling you before, as perhaps I ought to have done."

---

① turn the scale: weigh

② Aldebaran or a Sirius: Aldebaran is the brightest star in Venus; Sirius is the brightest star in stellar system. Fixed stars are said to be in different colors with age, usu. in blue, white, red and yellow. The first two colors signify prosperity, while the latter two ones mean declining.

③ Providential interposition: God's arrangement on purpose

How strange it was. He seemed to be her double. She did not speak, and Clare went on—

"I did not mention it because I was afraid of endangering my chance of you, darling, the great prize of my life—my Fellowship I call you. My brother's Fellowship was won at his college, mine at Talbothay's Dairy. Well, I would not risk it. I was going to tell you a month ago—at the time you agreed to be mine, but I could not; I thought it might frighten you away from me. I put it off; then I thought I would tell you yesterday, to give you a chance at least of escaping me. But I did not. And I did not this morning, when you proposed our confessing our faults on the landing—the sinner that I was! But I must, now I see you sitting there so solemnly. I wonder if you will forgive me?"

"O yes! I am sure that—"

"Well, I hope so. But wait a minute. You don't know. To begin at the beginning. Though I imagine my poor father fears that I am one of the eternally lost for my doctrines, I am of course, a believer in good morals, Tess, as much as you. I used to wish to be a teacher of men, and it was a great disappointment to me when I found I could not enter the church. I admired spotlessness, even though I could lay no claim to it, and hated impurity, as I hope I do now. Whatever one may think of plenary inspiration①, one must heartily subscribe to these of Paul: "Be thou an example—in word, in conversation, in spirit, in faith, in purity." It is the only safeguard for us or human beings. "Integer vitae②", says a Roman poet③, who is strange company for St Paul—

The man of upright life, from frailties free,
Stands not in need of Moorish spear or bow.

"Well, a certain place is paved with good intentions④, and having felt all that so strongly, you will see what a terrible remorse it bred in me when, in the midst of my fine aims for other people, I myself fell."

He then told her of that time of his life to which allusion has been made when, tossed about by doubts and difficulties in London, like a cork on the waves, he plunged into eight-and-forty hours' dissipation with a stranger.

---

① plenary inspiration: theory of complete inspiration. The Bible is based on the inspiration of God, so is absolutely right.
② Integer vitae: Blameless in life
③ a Roman poet: Horace, one poet in Rome
④ a certain place is paved with good intentions: In English there is a saying, "Hell is paved with good intentions", which means that one shall go to the hell even if he has good intentions without practice. Here "a certain place" takes the place of the hell, because in the wedding day it is unlucky to mention it.

"Happily I awoke almost immediately to a sense of my folly," he continued. "I would have no more to say to her, and I came home. I have never repeated the offence. But I felt I should like to treat you with perfect frankness and honour, and I could not do so without telling this. Do you forgive me?"

She pressed his hand tightly for an answer.

"Then we will dismiss it at once and for ever!—too painful as it is for the occasion—and talk of something lighter."

"O, Angel—I am almost glad—because now you can forgive me! I have not made my confession. I have a confession, too—remember, I said so."

"Ah, to be sure! Now then for it, wicked little one."

"Perhaps, although you smile, it is as serious as yours, or more so."

"It can hardly be more serious, dearest."

"It cannot—O no, it cannot!" She jumped up joyfully at the hope. "No, it cannot be more serious, certainly," she cried, "because 'tis just the same! I will tell you now."

She sat down again.

Their hands were still joined. The ashes under the grate were lit by the fire vertically, like a torrid waste. Imagination might have beheld a Last Day luridness in this red-coaled glow, which fell on face and hand, and on hers, peering into the loose hair about brow, and firing the delicate skin underneath. A large shadow of shape rose upon the wall and ceiling. She bent forward, at which each diamond on her neck gave a sinister wink like a toad's; and pressing her forehead against his temple she entered on her story of acquaintance with Alec d'Urberville and its results, murmuring words without flinching, and with her eyelids drooping down.

Study Questions:
1. Why was Tess horrified while she was walking on the landing? In Clare's eyes, what else could be shown from the two portraits?
2. For what reason was Tess "not a bit" cheerful on her wedding night?
3. What happened to the three girls after the young couple had driven away from the dairy? What was the sign before this incident?
4. What helped Tess come to her final determination of telling Clare about her truth completely?
5. What was Tess' reaction after she was told about Clare's fault?
6. In what sense is Tess's story tragic?

[Reading Critically]

What's the Plot?

If a friend asks you, "What was the story you just read about?" you will probably reply by summarizing the **plot**. The plot of a short story is the element most readers notice first and remember longest. Plotting is such an obvious aspect of fiction that in analyzing a short story, it is easy to overlook its importance. It seems much more profound to dig into imagery, style, or symbolism to discover hidden meanings. Although discussing those other elements can often be illuminating, don't forget the central importance of the plot in expressing the meaning of a story.

Remember that a plot is usually not just a linear sequence of events ("and then … and then … and then …"). Plotting is a pattern of actions, events, and situations. Some patterns are simple, but others are complex. The plot is also an expressive device. In a well-written work of fiction, this narrative pattern has been carefully organized by the author to create a certain effect or set of effects on the readers—suspense, humor, sadness, excitement, terror. The organization of a plot also suggests or emphasizes the relationship between characters, events, and situations. The true nature of characters is almost always revealed not by what they say in a story but by what they do.

In reading about a short story, never ignore the surface narrative. It is possible to uncover important and even profound things by focusing on the plot.

2. Character

From popular fiction and drama, both classic and contemporary, we are acquainted with many stereotyped characters. Called **stock characters**, they are often known by some outstanding trait or traits: the bragging soldier of Greek and Roman comedy, the Prince Charming of fairy tales, the mad scientist of horror movies, the fearlessly reckless police detective of urban action films, the greedy explorer of Tarzan films, the brilliant but alcoholic brain surgeon of medical thrillers on television. Stock characters are especially convenient for writers of commercial fiction: They require little detailed portaiture, for we already know them well. Most writers of the literary story, however, attempt to create characters who strike us not as stereotypes but as unique individuals. Although stock characters tend to have single dominant virtues and vices, characters in the finest contemporary short stories tend to have many facets, like people we meet.

A **character**, then, is presumably an imagined person who inhabits a story—although that simple definition may admit to a few exceptions. In George Stewart's novel *Storm*, the protagonist is the wind; in Richard Adams's *Watership Down*, the main characters are rabbits. But usually we recognize, in the main characters of a story, human personalities that become familiar to us. If the story seems "true to life", we generally find that its characters act in a reasonably consistent manner and that the author has provided them with motivation: sufficient reason to behave as they do. Should a character behave in a sudden and unexpected way, seeming to deny what we have been told about his nature or personality, we trust that he had a reason and that sooner or later we will discover it. This is not to claim that all authors insist that their characters behave with absolute consistency, for some contemporary stories feature characters who sometimes act without apparent reason. Nor can we say that, in good fiction, characters never change or develop. In *A Christmas Carol*, Charles Dickens tells how Ebenezer Scrooge, a tightfisted miser, reforms overnight, suddenly gives to the poor, and endeavors to assist his clerk's struggling family. But Dickens amply demonstrates why Scrooge had such a change of heart: four ghostly visitors, stirring kind memories the old miser had forgotten and also warning him of the probable consequences of his habits, provide the character (and hence the story) with adequate motivation.

To borrow the useful terms of the English novelist E. M. Forster, characters may seem flat or round, depending on whether a writer sketches or sculptures them. A **flat character** has only one outstanding trait or feature, or at most a few distinguishing marks: for example, the familiar stock character of the mad scientist, with his lust for absolute power and his crazily gleaming eyes. Flat characters, however, need not be stock characters: in all of literature there is probably only one Tiny Tim, though his functions in *A Christmas Carol* are mainly to invoke blessings and to remind others of their Christian duties. Some writers, notably Balzac, who peopled his many novels with hosts of characters, try to distinguish the flat ones by giving each a single odd physical feature or mannerism—a nervous twitch, a piercing gaze, an obsessive fondness for oysters. **Round characters**, however, present us with more facets—that is, their authors portray them in greater depth and in more generous detail. Such a round character may appear to us only as he appears to the other characters in the story. If their views of him differ, we will see him from more than one side. In other stories, we enter a character's mind and come to know him through his own thoughts, feelings, and perceptions.

Flat characters tend to stay the same throughout a story, but round characters often change—learn or become enlightened, grow or deteriorate. In William Faulkner's "Barn Burning", the boy Sarty Snopes, driven to defy his proud and violent father, becomes at the story's end more knowing and more mature. (Some critics call a fixed character **static**; a changing one, **dynamic**.) This is not to damn a flat character as an inferior work of art. In most fiction—even the greatest—minor characters tend to be flat instead of round. Why? Rounding them would cost time and space; and so enlarged, they might only distract us from the main characters.

"A character, first of all, is the noise of his name," according to novelist William

Gass.① Names, chosen artfully, can indicate natures. A simple illustration is the completely virtuous Squire Allworthy, the foster father in *Tom Jones* by Henry Fielding. Subtler, perhaps, is the custom of giving a character a name that makes an allusion: a reference to some famous person, place, or thing in history, in other fiction, or in actuality. For his central characters in *Moby Dick*, Herman Melville chose names from *The Old Testament*, calling his tragic and domineering Ahab after a biblical tyrant who came to a bad end, and his wandering narrator Ishmael after a biblical outcast. Whether or not it includes an allusion, a good name often reveals the character of the character. Henry James, who so loved names that he kept lists of them for characters he might someday conceive, chose for a sensitive, cultured gentleman the name of Lambert Strether; for a down-to-earth, benevolent individual, the name of Mrs. Bread. (But James may have wished to indicate that names cannot be identified with people absolutely, in giving the fragile, considerate heroine of *The Spoils of Poynton* the harsh sounding name of Fleda Vetch.)

Instead of a hero, many a recent novel has featured an **antihero**: a protagonist conspicuously lacking in one or more of the usual attributes of a traditional hero (bravery, skill, idealism, sense of purpose). If epic poets once drew their heroes as decisive leaders of their people, embodying their people's highest ideals, antiheroes tend to be loners, without perfections, just barely able to survive. A gulf separates Leopold Bloom, antihero of James Joyce's novel *Ulysses*, from the hero of the Greek *Odyssey*. In Homer's epic, Ulysses wanders the Mediterranean, battling monsters and overcoming enchantments. In Joyce's novel, Bloom wanders the littered streets of Dublin, peddling advertising space. Mersault, the title character of Albert Camus's novel *The Stranger*, is so alienated from his own life that he is unmoved at the news of his mother's death. In contemporary fiction, by the way, female antiheroes abound: Ellen, for instance, is the aimlessly drifting central character of Edna O'Brien's novel *August Is a Wicked Month*.

Evidently, not only fashions in heroes but also attitudes toward human nature have undergone change. In the 18th century, Scottish philosopher David Hume argued that the nature of an individual is relatively fixed and unalterable. Hume mentioned, however, a few exceptions: "A person of an obliging disposition gives a peevish answer; but he has the toothache or has not dined. A stupid fellow discovers an obvious alacrity in his carriage; but he has met with a sudden piece of good fortune." For a long time after Hume, novelists and short-story writers seem to have assumed that characters behave nearly always in a predictable fashion and that their actions ought to be consistent with their personalities. Now and again, a writer differed: Jane Austen in

---

① "The Concept of Character in Fiction". *Fiction and the Figures of Life*. New York: Knopf, 1970.

Pride and Prejudice has her protagonist Elizabeth Bennet remark to the citified Mr. Darcy, who fears that life in the country cannot be amusing, "But people themselves alter so much, that there is something to be observed in them forever."

Many contemporary writers of fiction would deny even that people have definite selves to alter. Following Sigmund Freud and other modern psychologists, they assume that a large part of human behavior is shaped in the unconscious—that, for instance, a person might fear horses, not because of a basically timid nature, but because of unconscious memories of having been nearly trampled by a horse in childhood. To some writers it now appears that what Hume called a "disposition" (now called a "personality") is more vulnerable to change from such causes as age, disease, neurosis, psychic shock, or brainwashing than was once believed. Hence, some characters in the 20th-century fiction appear to be shifting bundles of impulses. "You mustn't look in my novel for the old stable ego of character," wrote D. H. Lawrence to a friend about *The Rainbow*; and in that novel and other novels Lawrence demonstrated his view of individuals as bits of one vast life force, spurred to act by incomprehensible passions and urges—the "dark gods" in them. The usual limits of character are playfully violated by Virginia Woolf in *Orlando*, a novel whose protagonist, defying time, lives right on from Elizabethan days into the present, changing in mid-story from a man into a woman. Characterization, as practiced by 19th-century novelists, almost entirely disappears in Franz Kafka's *The Castle*, whose protagonist has no home, no family, no definite appearance—not even a name, just the initial K. Characters are things of the past, insists the contemporary French novelist Alain Robbe-Grillet. Still, many writers of fiction go on portraying them.

The Jilting of Granny Weatherall (1930)
Katherine Anne Porter

She flicked her wrist neatly out of Doctor Harry's pudgy careful fingers and pulled the sheet up to her chin. The brat ought to be in knee breeches. Doctoring around the country with spectacles on his nose! "Get along now, take your schoolbooks and go. There's nothing wrong with me."

Doctor Harry spread a warm paw like a cushion on her forehead where the forked green vein danced and made her eyelids twitch. "Now, now, be a good girl, and we'll have you up in no time."

"That's no way to speak to a woman nearly eighty years old just because she's down. I'd have you respect your elders, young man."

"Well, Missy, excuse me." Doctor Harry patted her cheek. "But I've got to warn you, haven't I? You're a marvel, but you must be careful or you're going to be good and sorry①."

"Don't tell me what I'm going to be. I'm on my feet now, morally speaking. It's Cornelia. I had to go to bed to get rid of her."

Her bones felt loose, and floated around in her skin, and Doctor Harry floated like a balloon around the foot of the bed. He floated and pulled down his waistcoat and swung his glasses on a cord. "Well, stay where you are, it certainly can't hurt you."

"Get along and doctor your sick," said Granny Weatherall. "Leave a well woman alone. I'll call for you when I want you ... Where were you forty years ago when I pulled through milk-leg② and double pneumonia? You weren't even born. Don't let Cornelia lead you on," she shouted, because Doctor Harry appeared to float up to the ceiling and out. "I pay my own bills, and I don't throw my money away on nonsense!"

She meant to wave good-by, but it was too much trouble. Her eyes closed of themselves, it was like a dark curtain drawn around the bed. The pillow rose and floated under her, pleasant as a hammock in a light wind. She listened to the leaves rustling outside the window. No, somebody was swishing newspapers: no, Cornelia and Doctor Harry were whispering together. She leaped broad awake, thinking they whispered in her ear.

"She was never like this, never like this!" "Well, what can we expect?" "Yes, eighty years old ..."

Well, and what if she was? She still had ears. It was like Cornelia to whisper around doors. She always kept things secret in such a public way. She was always being tactful and kind. Cornelia was dutiful; that was the trouble with her. Dutiful and good: "So good and dutiful," said Granny, "that I'd like to spank her." She saw herself spanking Cornelia and making a fine job of it.

"What'd you say, Mother?"

Granny felt her face tying up in hard knots.

"Can't a body think, I'd like to know?"

"I thought you might want something."

"I do. I want a lot of things. First off, go away and don't whisper."

She lay and drowsed, hoping in her sleep that the children would keep out and let her rest a minute. It had been a long day. Not that she was tired. It was always pleasant to snatch a minute now and then. There was always so much to be done, let me see: tomorrow.

Tomorrow was far away and there was nothing to trouble about. Things were finished somehow when the time came; thank God there was always a little margin over for peace: then a person could spread out the plan of life and tuck in the edges orderly③. It was good to have

---

① good and sorry: very sorry (informal English)
② milk-leg: painful swelling of the leg, usually as a result of infection during childbirth
③ tuck in the edges orderly: tidy up the loose ends of life

everything clean and folded away, with the hair brushes and tonic bottles sitting straight on the white embroidered linen: the day started without fuss and the pantry shelves laid out with rows of jelly glasses and brown jugs and white stone-china jars with blue whirligigs and words painted on them: coffee, tea, sugar, ginger, cinnamon, allspice: and the bronze clock with the lion on top nicely dusted off. The dust that lion could collect in twenty-four hours! The box in the attic with all those letters tied up, well, she'd have to go through that tomorrow. All those letters—George's letters and John's letters and her letters to them both—lying around for the children to find afterwards made her uneasy. Yes, that would be tomorrow's business. No use to let them know how silly she had been once.

While she was rummaging around she found death in her mind and it felt clammy and unfamiliar. She had spent so much time preparing for death there was no need for bringing it up again. Let it take care of itself now. When she was sixty she had felt very old, finished, and went around making farewell trips to see her children and grandchildren, with a secret in her mind: This is the very last of your mother, children! Then she made her will and came down with a long fever. That was all just a notion like a lot of other things, but it was lucky too, for she had once for all got over the idea of dying for a long time. Now she couldn't be worried. She hoped she had better sense now. Her father had lived to be one hundred and two years old and had drunk a noggin of strong hot toddy① on his last birthday. He told the reporters it was his daily habit, and he owed his long life to it. He had made quite a scandal and was very pleased about it. She believed she'd just plague Cornelia a little.

"Cornelia! Cornelia!" No footsteps, but a sudden hand on her cheek. "Bless you, where have you been?"

"Here, Mother."

"Well, Cornelia, I want a noggin of hot toddy."

"Are you cold, darling?"

"I'm chilly, Cornelia. Lying in bed stops the circulation. I must have told you that a thousand times."

Well, she could just hear Cornelia telling her husband that Mother was getting a little childish and they'd have to humor her. The thing that most annoyed her was that Cornelia thought she was deaf, dumb, and blind. Little hasty glances and tiny gestures tossed around her and over her head saying, "Don't cross her, let her have her way, she's eighty years old," and she sitting there as if she lived in a thin glass cage. Sometimes Granny almost made up her mind to pack up and move back to her own house where nobody could remind her every minute that she was old. Wait, wait, Cornelia, till your own children whisper behind you back!

---

① a noggin of strong hot toddy: "noggin" means "a small amount of"; "hot toddy" means "a sweetened mixture of whiskey and hot water," usually considered good for a cold

In her day she had kept a better house and had got more work done. She wasn't too old yet for Lydia to be driving eighty miles for advice when one of the children jumped the track①, and Jimmy still dropped in and talked things over: "Now, Mammy, you've a good business head, I want to know what you think of this? ..." Old. Cornelia couldn't change the furniture around without asking. Little things, little things! They had been so sweet when they were little.

Granny wished the old days were back again with the children young and everything to be done over. It had been a hard pull, but not too much for her. When she thought of all the food she had cooked, and all the clothes she had cut and sewed, and all the gardens she had made—well, the children showed it. There they were, made out of her, and they couldn't get away from that. Sometimes she wanted to see John② again and point to them and say, "Well, I didn't do so badly, did I?" But that would have to wait. That was for tomorrow. She used to think of him as a man, but now all the children were older than their father, and he would be a child beside her if she saw him now. It seemed strange and there was something wrong in the idea. Why, he couldn't possibly recognize her. She had fenced in a hundred acres once, digging the post holes herself and clamping the wires with just a negro boy to help. That changed a woman. John would be looking for a young woman with the peaked Spanish comb in her hair and the painted fan. Digging post holes changed a woman. Riding country roads in the winter when women had their babies was another thing: sitting up nights with sick horses and sick negroes and sick children and hardly ever losing one. John, I hardly ever lost one of them! John would see that in a minute, that would be something he could understand, she wouldn't have to explain anything!

It made her feel like rolling up her sleeves and putting the whole place to rights again. No matter if Cornelia was determined to be everywhere at once, there were a great many things left undone on this place. She would start tomorrow and do them. It was good to be strong enough for everything, even if all you made melted and changed and slipped under your hands, so that by the time you finished you almost forgot what you were working for. What was it I set out to do? she asked herself intently, but she could not remember. A fog rose over the valley, she saw it marching across the creek swallowing the trees and moving up the hill like an army of ghosts. Soon it would be at the near edge of the orchard, and then it was time to go in and light the lamps. Come in, children, don't stay out in the night air.

Lighting the lamps had been beautiful. The children huddled up to her and breathed like little calves waiting at the bars in the twilight. Their eyes followed the match and watched the flame rise and settle in a blue curve, then they moved away from her. The lamp was lit, they

---

① jumped the track: deviated from the right course of life, misbehaved
② John: Granny's dead husband

didn't have to be scared and hang on to mother any more. Never, never, never more. God, for all my life I thank Thee. Without Thee, my God, I could never have done it. Hail, Mary, full of grace. ①

I want you to pick all the fruit this year and see that nothing is wasted. There's always someone who can use it. Don't let good things rot for want of using. You waste life when you waste good food. Don't let things get lost. It's bitter to lose things. Now, don't let me get to thinking, not when I am tired and taking a little nap before supper …

The pillow rose about her shoulders and pressed against her heart and the memory was being squeezed out of it: oh, push down the pillow, somebody: it would smother her if she tried to hold it. Such a fresh breeze blowing and such a green day with no threats in it. But he② had not come, just the same. What does a woman do when she has put on the white veil and set out the white cake for a man and he doesn't come? She tried to remember. No, I swear he never harmed me but in that. He never harmed me but in that … and what if he did? There was the day, the day, but a whirl of dark smoke rose and covered it, crept up and over into the bright field where everything was planted so carefully in orderly rows. That was hell, she knew hell when she saw it. For sixty years she had prayed against remembering him and against losing her soul in the deep pit of hell, and now the two things were mingled in one and the thought of him was a smoky cloud from hell that moved and crept in her head when she had just got rid of Doctor Harry and was trying to rest a minute. Wounded vanity, Ellen, said a sharp voice in the top of her mind. Don't let your wounded vanity get the upper hand of you. Plenty of girls get jilted. You were jilted, weren't you? Then stand up to it. Her eyelids wavered and let in streamers of blue-gray light like tissue paper over her eyes. She must get up and pull the shades down or she'd never sleep. She was in bed again and the shades were not down. How could that happen? Better turn over, hide from the light, sleeping in the light gave you nightmares. "Mother, how do you feel now?" and a stinging wetness on her forehead. But I don't like having my face washed in cold water!

Hapsy? George? Lydia? Jimmy?③ No, Cornelia, and her features were swollen and full of little puddles. "They're coming, darling, they'll all be here soon." Go wash your face, child, you look funny.

Instead of obeying, Cornelia knelt down and put her head on the pillow. She seemed to be talking but there was no sound. "Well, are you tongue-tied? Whose birthday is it? Are you going to give a party?"

Cornelia's mouth moved urgently in strange shapes. "Don't do that, you bother me, daughter."

---

① Hail, Mary, full of grace: a prayer for a Roman Catholic
② he: referring to George, who deserted her before
③ Hapsy? George? Lydia? Jimmy?: names of Granny's children

"Oh, no, Mother. Oh, no ..."

Nonsense. It was strange about children. They disputed your every word. "No what, Cornelia?"

"Here's Doctor Harry."

"I won't see that boy again. He just left three minutes ago."

"That was this morning, Mother. It's night now. Here's the nurse."

"This is Doctor Harry, Mrs. Weatherall. I never saw you look so young and happy!"

"Ah, I'll never be young again—but I'd be happy if they'd let me lie in peace and get rested."

She thought she spoke up loudly, but no one answered. A warm weight on her forehead, a warm bracelet on her wrist, and a breeze went on whispering, trying to tell her something. A shuffle of leaves in the everlasting hand of God. He blew on them and they danced and rattled. "Mother, don't mind, we're going to give you a little hypodermic." "Look here, daughter, how do ants get in this bed? I saw sugar ants yesterday. Did you send for Hapsy too?"

It was Hapsy she really wanted. She had to go a long way back through a great many rooms to find Hapsy standing with a baby on her arm. She seemed to herself to be Hapsy also, and the baby on Hapsy's arm was Hapsy and himself and herself, all at once, and there was no surprise in the meeting. Then Hapsy melted from within and turned flimsy as gray gauze and the baby was a gauzy shadow, and Hapsy came up close and said, "I thought you'd never come," and looked at her very searchingly and said, "You haven't changed a bit!" They leaned forward to kiss, when Cornelia began whispering from a long way off, "Oh, is there anything you want to tell me? Is there anything I can do for you?"

Yes, she had changed her mind after sixty years and she would like to see George. I want you to find George. Find him and be sure to tell him I forgot him. I want him to know I had my husband just the same and my children and my house like any other woman. A good house too and a good husband that I loved and fine children out of him. Better than I hoped for even. Tell him I was given back everything he took away and more. Oh, no, oh, God, no, there was something else besides the house and the man and the children. Oh, surely they were not all? What was it? Something not given back ... Her breath crowded down under her ribs and grew into a monstrous frightening shape with cutting edges; it bored up into her head, and the agony was unbelievable: Yes, John, get the Doctor now, no more talk, my time has come①.

When this one was born it should be the last. The last. It should have been born first, for it was the one she had truly wanted. Everything came in good time. Nothing left out, left over. She was strong, in three days she would be as well as ever. Better. A woman needed milk in her to have her full health.

---

① my time has come: the due day, when she is to produce a baby

"Mother, do you hear me?"

"I've been telling you—"

"Mother, Father Connolly's here."

"I went to Holy Communion only last week. Tell him I'm not so sinful as all that."

"Father just wants to speak to you."

He could speak as much as he pleased. It was like him to drop in and inquire about her soul as if it were a teething baby, and then stay on for a cup of tea and a round of cards and gossip. He always had a funny story of some sort, usually about an Irishman who made his little mistakes and confessed them, and the point lay in some absurd thing he would blurt out in the confessional showing his struggles between native piety and original sin. Granny felt easy about her soul. Cornelia, where are your manners? Give Father Connolly a chair. She had her secret comfortable understanding with a few favorite saints who cleared a straight road to God for her. All as surely signed and sealed as the papers for the new Forty Acres. Forever ... heirs and assigns forever. Since the day the wedding cake was not cut, but thrown out and wasted. The whole bottom dropped out of the world①, and there she was blind and sweating with nothing under her feet and the walls falling away. His hand had caught her under the breast, she had not fallen, there was the freshly polished floor with the green rug on it, just as before. He had cursed like a sailor's parrot and said, "I'll kill him for you." Don't lay a hand on him, for my sake leave something to God. "Now, Ellen, you must believe what I tell you ..."

So there was nothing, nothing to worry about any more, except sometimes in the night one of the children screamed in a nightmare, and they both hustled out shaking and hunting for the matches and calling, "There, wait a minute, here we are!" John, get the doctor now, Hapsy's time has come. But there was Hapsy standing by the bed in a white cap. "Cornelia, tell Hapsy to take off her cap. I can't see her plain."

Her eyes opened very wide and the room stood out like a picture she had seen somewhere. Dark colors with the shadows rising towards the ceiling in long angles. The tall black dresser gleamed with nothing on it but John's picture, enlarged from a little one, with John's eyes very black when they should have been blue. You never saw him, so how do you know how he looked? But the man insisted the copy was perfect, it was very rich and handsome. For a picture, yes, but it's not my husband. The table by the bed had a linen cover and a candle and a crucifix. The light was blue from Cornelia's silk lampshades. No sort of light at all, just frippery. You had to live forty years with kerosene lamps to appreciate honest electricity. She felt very strong and she saw Doctor Harry with a rosy nimbus around him.

"You look like a saint, Doctor Harry, and I vow that's as near as you'll ever come to it."

"She's saying something."

---

① The whole bottom dropped out of the world: Something very bad suddenly happened.

"I heard you, Cornelia. What's all this carrying-on?"

"Father Connolly's saying—"

Cornelia's voice staggered and bumped like a cart in a bad road. It rounded corners and turned back again and arrived nowhere. Granny stepped up in the cart very lightly① and reached for the reins, but a man sat beside her and she knew him by his hands, driving the cart. She did not look in his face, for she knew without seeing, but looked instead down the road where the trees leaned over and bowed to each other and a thousand birds were singing a Mass. She felt like singing too, but she put her hand in the bosom of her dress and pulled out a rosary; and Father Connolly murmured Latin in a very solemn voice and tickled her feet. My God, will you stop that nonsense? I'm a married woman. What if he did run away and leave me to face the priest by myself? I found another a whole world better. I wouldn't have exchanged my husband for anybody except St. Michael himself, and you may tell him that for me with a thank you in the bargain.

Light flashed on her closed eyelids, and a deep roaring shook her. Cornelia, is that lightning? I hear thunder. There's going to be a storm. Close all the windows. Call the children in … "Mother, here we are, all of us." "Is that you, Hapsy?" "Oh, no, I'm Lydia. We drove as fast as we could." Their faces drifted above her, drifted away. The rosary fell out of her hands and Lydia put it back. Jimmy tried to help, their hands fumbled together, and Granny closed two fingers around Jimmy's thumb. Beads wouldn't do, it must be something alive. She was so amazed her thoughts ran round and round. So, my dear Lord, this is my death and I wasn't even thinking about it. My children have come to see me die. But I can't, it's not time. Oh, I always hated surprises. I wanted to give Cornelia the amethyst② set— Cornelia, you're to have the amethyst set, but Hapsy's to wear it when she wants, and, Doctor Harry, do shut up. Nobody sent for you. Oh, my dear Lord, do wait a minute. I meant to do something about the Forty Acres, Jimmy doesn't need it and Lydia will later on, with that worthless husband of hers. I meant to finish the altar cloth and send six bottles of wine to Sister Borgia for her dyspepsia③. I want to send six bottles of wine to Sister Borgia, Father Connolly, now don't let me forget.

Cornelia's voice made short turns and tilted over and crashed, "Oh, Mother, oh, Mother, oh, Mother …"

"I'm not going, Cornelia. I'm taken by surprise. I can't go."

You'll see Hapsy again. What about her? "I thought you'd never come." Granny made a

---

① Granny stepped up in the cart very lightly: Here it is an allusion. Emily Dickinson's poem "Because I Could Not Stop for Death" describes Death coming to pick her up in a carriage, and then they experience all the life journey, and finally went to the tomb and eternity.

② amethyst: purple or violet quartz, used in jewelry

③ dyspepsia: indigestion

long journey outward, looking for Hapsy. What if I don't find her? What then? Her heart sank down and down, there was no bottom to death, she couldn't come to the end of it. The blue light① from Cornelia's lampshade drew into a tiny point in the center of her brain, it flickered and winked like an eye, quietly it fluttered and dwindled. Granny lay curled down within herself, amazed and watchful, staring at the point of light that was herself; her body was now only a deeper mass of shadow in an endless darkness and this darkness would curl around the light and swallow it up. God, give a sign!

For the second time there was no sign. Again no bridegroom and the priest in the house. She could not remember any other sorrow because this grief wiped them all away. Oh, no, there's nothing more cruel than this—I'll never forgive it. She stretched herself with a deep breath and blew out the light.

Study Questions:

1. In the very first paragraph, what does the writer tell us about Ellen (Granny) Weatherall?

2. What does the name of Weatherall have to do with Granny's nature (or her life story)? What other traits or qualities do you find in her?

3. "Her bones felt loose, and floated around in her skin, and Doctor Harry floated like a balloon." (Para. 6) What do you understand from this statement? By what other remarks does the writer indicate Granny's condition? In Para. 56, why does Father Connolly tickle Granny's feet? At what other moments in the story does she fail to understand what is happening, or confuse the present with the past?

4. What happened to Ellen Weatherall sixty years earlier? What effects did this event have on her?

5. In Para. 49, who do you guess to be the man who "cursed like a sailor's parrot"? In Para. 56, who do you assume to be the man driving the cart? Is the fact that these persons are not clearly labeled and identified a failure on the author's part?

6. What is stream of consciousness? Would you call "The Jilting of Granny Weatherall" a stream of consciousness story? Refer to the story in your reply.

7. Sum up the character of the daughter Cornelia.

8. Why doesn't Granny's last child Hapsy come to her mother's deathbed?

9. Would you call the character of Doctor Harry "flat" or "round"? Why is his flatness (or roundness) appropriate to the story?

10. How is this the story of another "jilting"? What is similar between that fateful day of sixty years ago (described in Paras. 29, 49 and 61) and the moment when Granny is dying? This time, who is the "bridegroom" not in the house?

11. "This is the story of an eighty-year-old woman lying in bed, getting groggy, and dying. I

---

① the blue light: Here Dickinson's another poem, "I Heard a Fly Buzz—when I died—", is taken as an allusion.

can't see why it should interest anybody." How would you answer this critic?

Everyday Use (1973)

Alice Walker

I will wait for her in the yard that Maggie and I made so clean and wavy yesterday afternoon. A yard like this is more comfortable than most people know. It is not just a yard. It is like an extended living room. When the hard clay is swept clean as a floor and the fine sand around the edges lined with tiny, irregular grooves anyone can come and sit and look up into the elm tree and wait for the breezes that never come inside the house.

Maggie will be nervous until after her sister goes: she will stand hopelessly in corners, homely and ashamed of the burn scars down her arms and legs, eyeing her sister with a mixture of envy and awe. She thinks her sister has held life always in the palm of one hand, that "no" is a word the world never learned to say to her.

You've no doubt seen those TV shows where the child who has "made it"① is confronted, as a surprise, by her own mother and father, tottering in weakly from backstage. (A pleasant surprise, of course: What would they do if parent and child came on the show only to curse out and insult each other?) On TV mother and child embrace and smile into each other's faces. Sometimes the mother and father weep, the child wraps them in her arms and leans across the table to tell how she would not have made it without their help. I have seen these programs②.

Sometimes I dream a dream in which Dee and I are suddenly brought together on a TV program of this sort. Out of a dark and soft-seated limousine I am ushered into a bright room filled with many people. There I meet a smiling, gray, sporty man like Johnny Carson③ who shakes my hand and tells me what a fine girl I have. Then we are on the stage and Dee is embracing me with tears in her eyes. She pins on my dress a large orchid, even though she has told me once that she thinks orchids are tacky flowers.

In real life I am a large, big-boned woman with rough, man-working hands. In the winter I wear flannel nightgowns to bed and overalls during the day. I can kill and clean a hog as mercilessly as a man. My fat keeps me hot in zero weather. I can work outside all day, breaking ice to get water for washing. I can eat pork liver cooked over the open fire minutes after it comes steaming from the hog. One winter I knocked a bull calf straight in the brain between the eyes with a sledge hammer and had the meat hung up to chill before nightfall. But of course all this does not show on television. I am the way my daughter would want me to be: a

---

① "made it": to become a success, to succeed, either in specific endeavor or in general

② these programs: On the NEC television show *This Is Your Life*, people were publicly and often tearfully reunited with friends, relatives, and teachers they had not seen in years

③ Johnny Carson: a man who runs a late night talk show

hundred pounds lighter, my skin like an uncooked barley pancake. My hair glistens in the hot bright lights. Johnny Carson has much to do to keep up with my quick and witty tongue.

But that is a mistake. I know even before I wake up. Who ever knew a Johnson with a quick tongue? Who can even imagine me looking a strange white man in the eye? It seems to me I have talked to them always with one foot raised in flight, with my head turned in whichever way is farthest from them. Dee, though. She would always look anyone in the eye. Hesitation was no part of her nature.

"How do I look, Mama?" Maggie says, showing just enough of her thin body enveloped in pink skirt and red blouse for me to know she's there, almost hidden by the door.

"Come out into the yard," I say.

Have you ever seen a lame animal, perhaps a dog run over by some careless person rich enough to own a car, sidle up to someone who is ignorant enough to be kind to him? That is the way my Maggie walks. She has been like this, chin on chest, eyes on ground, feet in shuffle, ever since the fire that burned the other house to the ground.

Dee is lighter than Maggie, with nicer hair and a fuller figure. She's a woman now, though sometimes I forget. How long ago was it that the other house burned? Ten, twelve years? Sometimes I can still hear the flames and feel these programs: On the NEC television show *This Is Your Life*, people were publicly and often tearfully reunited with friends, relatives, and teachers they had not seen in years.

Maggie's arms sticking to me, her hair smoking and her dress falling off her in little black papery flakes. Her eyes seemed stretched open, blazed open by the flames reflected in them. And Dee. I see her standing off under the sweet gum tree she used to dig gum out of; a look of concentration on her face as she watched the last dingy gray board of the house fall in toward the red-hot brick chimney. Why don't you do a dance around the ashes? I'd wanted to ask her. She had hated the house that much.

I used to think she hated Maggie, too. But that was before we raised the money, the church and me, to send her to Augusta to school. She used to read to us without pity; forcing words, lies, other folks' habits, whole lives upon us two, sitting trapped and ignorant underneath her voice. She washed us in a river of make-believe, burned us with a lot of knowledge we didn't necessarily need to know. Pressed us to her with the serious way she read, to shove us away at just the moment, like dimwits, we seemed about to understand.

Dee wanted nice things. A yellow organdy dress to wear to her graduation from high school; black pumps to match a green suit she'd made from an old suit somebody gave me. She was determined to stare down any disaster in her efforts. Her eyelids would not flicker for minutes at a time. Often I fought off the temptation to shake her. At sixteen she had a style of her own and knew what style was.

I never had an education myself. After second grade the school was closed down. Don't ask me why: in 1927 colored asked fewer questions than they do now. Sometimes Maggie reads to me. She stumbles along good-naturedly but can't see well. She knows she is not bright. Like good looks and money, quickness passed her by. She will marry John Thomas (who has mossy teeth in an earnest face) and then I'll be free to sit here and I guess just sing church songs to myself. Although I never was a good singer. Never could carry a tune. I was always better at a man's job. I used to love to milk till I was hoofed① in the side in '49. Cows are soothing and slow and don't bother you, unless you try to milk them the wrong way.

I have deliberately turned my back on the house. It is three rooms, just like the one that burned, except the roof is tin; they don't make shingle roofs any more. There are no real windows, just some holes cut in the sides, like the portholes in a ship, but not round and not square, with rawhide holding the shutters up on the outside. This house is in a pasture, too, like the other one. No doubt when Dee sees it she will want to tear it down. She wrote me once that no matter where we "choose" to live, she will manage to come see us. But she will never bring her friends. Maggie and I thought about this and Maggie asked me, "Mama, when did Dee ever have any friends?"

She had a few. Furtive boys in pink shirts hanging about on washday after school. Nervous girls who never laughed. Impressed with her they worshiped the well-turned phrase, the cute shape, the scalding humor that erupted like bubbles in lye. She read to them.

When she was courting Jimmy T② she didn't have much time to pay to us, but turned all her faultfinding power on him. He flew to marry a cheap city girl from a family of ignorant flashy people. She hardly had time to recompose herself.

When she comes I will meet—but there they are!

Maggie attempts to make a dash for the house, in her shuffling way, but I stay her with my hand. "Come back here," I say. And she stops and tries to dig a well in the sand with her toe.

It is hard to see them clearly through the strong sun. But even the first glimpse of leg out of the car tells me it is Dee. Her feet were always neat-looking, as if God himself had shaped them with a certain style. From the other side of the car comes a short, stocky man. Hair is all over his head a foot long and hanging from his chin like a kinky mule tail. I hear Maggie suck in her breath. "Uhnnnh," is what it sounds like. Like when you see the wriggling end of a snake just in front of your foot on the road. "Uhnnnh."

Dee next. A dress down to the ground, in this hot weather. A dress so loud it hurts my eyes. There are yellows and oranges enough to throw back the light of the sun. I feel my whole face warming from the heat waves it throws out. Earrings, too, gold and hanging down to her shoulders. Bracelets dangling and making noises when she moves her arm up to shake the folds

---

① hoofed: injured by the horn of the cow being milked
② Jimmy T: "T" is the initial of the surname of the boy Dee courts

of the dress out of her armpits. The dress is loose and flows, and as she walks closer, I like it. I hear Maggie go "Uhnnnh" again. It is her sister's hair. It stands straight up like the wool on a sheep. It is black as night and around the edges are two long pigtails that rope about like small lizards disappearing behind her ears.

"Wa-su-zo-Tean-o①!" she says, coming on in that gliding way the dress makes her move. The short stocky fellow with the hair to his navel is all grinning and he follows up with "Asalamalakim②, my mother and sister!" He moves to hug Maggie but she falls back, right up against the back of my chair. I feel her trembling there and when I look up I see the perspiration falling off her chin.

"Don't get up," says Dee. Since I am stout it takes something of a push. You can see me trying to move a second or two before I make it. She turns, showing white heels through her sandals, and goes back to the car. Out she peeks next with a Polaroid③. She stoops down quickly and lines up picture after picture of me sitting there in front of the house with Maggie cowering behind me. She never takes a shot without making sure the house is included. When a cow comes nibbling around the edge of the yard she snaps it and me and Maggie and the house. Then she puts the Polaroid in the back seat of the car, and comes up and kisses me on the forehead.

Meanwhile Asalamalakim is going through the motions with Maggie's hand. Maggie's hand is as limp as a fish, and probably as cold, despite the sweat, and she keeps trying to pull it back. It looks like Asalamalakim wants to shake hands but wants to do it fancy. Or maybe he doesn't know how people shake hands. Anyhow, he soon gives up on Maggie.

"Well," I say. "Dee."

"No, Mama," she says. "Not 'Dee', Wangero Leewanika Kemanjo!"

"What happened to 'Dee'?" I wanted to know.

"She's dead," Wangero said. "I couldn't bear it any longer, being named after the people who oppress me."

"You know as well as me you was named after your aunt Dicie," I said. Dicie is my sister. She named Dee. We called her "Big Dee" after Dee was born.

"But who was she named after?" asked Wangero.

"I guess after Grandma Dee," I said.

"And who was she named after?" asked Wangero.

"Her mother," I said, and saw Wangero was getting tired. "That's about as far back as I can trace it," I said. Though, in fact, I probably could have carried it back beyond the Civil

---

① Wa-su-zo-Tean-o: salutation in Swahili, an African language. Notice that Dee has to sound it out, syllable by syllable.

② Asalamalakim: salutation in Arabic: "Peace be upon you."

③ Polaroid: a camera that produces instant pictures

War through the branches.

"Well," said Asalamalakim, "there you are."

"Uhnnnh," I heard Maggie say.

"There I was not," I said, "before 'Dicie' cropped up in our family, so why should I try to trace it that far back?"

He just stood there grinning, looking down on me like somebody inspecting a Model A car①. Every once in a while he and Wangero sent eye signals over my head.

"How do you pronounce this name?" I asked.

"You don't have to call me by it if you don't want to," said Wangero.

"Why shouldn't I?" I asked. "If that's what you want us to call you, we'll call you."

"I know it might sound awkward at first," said Wangero.

"I'll get used to it," I said. "Read it out again."

Well, soon we got the name out of the way. Asalamalakim had a name twice as long and three times as hard. After I tripped over it two or three times he told me to just call him Hakim-a-barber. I wanted to ask him was he a barber, but I didn't really think he was, so I didn't ask.

"You must belong to those beef-cattle peoples down the road," I said. They said "Asalamalakim" when they met you, too, but they didn't shake hands. Always too busy: feeding the cattle, fixing the fences, putting up salt-lick shelters, throwing down hay. When the white folks poisoned some of the herd the men stayed up all night with rifles in their hands. I walked a mile and a half just to see the sight.

Hakim-a-barber said, "I accept some of their doctrines, but farming and raising cattle is not my style." (They didn't tell me, and I didn't ask, whether Wangero (Dee) had really gone and married him.)

We sat down to eat and right away he said he didn't eat collards and pork was unclean②. Wangero, though, went on through the chitlins③ and corn bread, the greens and everything else. She talked a blue streak over the sweet potatoes. Everything delighted her. Even the fact that we still used the benches her daddy made for the table when we couldn't afford to buy chairs.

"Oh, Mama!" she cried. Then turned to Hakim-a-barber. "I never knew how lovely these benches are. You can feel the rump prints," she said, running her hands underneath her and along the bench. Then she gave a sigh and her hand closed over Grandma Dee's butter dish. "That's it!" she said. "I knew there was something I wanted to ask you if I could have."

---

① Model A car: popular low-priced automobile introduced by the Ford Motor Company in 1927

② pork was unclean: Muslims are forbidden by their religion to eat pork because it is considered to be unclean.

③ chitlins: also chitlings or chitterlings, the small intestines of pigs, used for food, a common dish in Afro-American household

She jumped up from the table and went over in the corner where the churn stood, the milk in it clabber① by now. She looked at the churn and looked at it.

"This churn top is what I need," she said. "Didn't Uncle Buddy whittle it out of a tree you all used to have?"

"Yes," I said.

"Uh huh," she said happily. "And I want the dasher, too."

"Uncle Buddy whittle that, too?" asked the barber.

Dee (Wangero) looked up at me.

"Aunt Dee's first husband whittled the dash," said Maggie so low you almost couldn't hear her. "His name was Henry, but they called him Stash."

"Maggie's brain is like an elephant's," Wangero said, laughing. "I can use the churn top as a centerpiece for the alcove table," she said, sliding a plate over the churn, "and I'll think of something artistic to do with the dasher."

When she finished wrapping the dasher the handle stuck out. I took it for a moment in my hands. You didn't even have to look close to see where hands pushing the dasher up and down to make butter had left a kind of sink in the wood. In fact, there were a lot of small sinks; you could see where thumbs and fingers had sunk into the wood. It was beautiful light yellow wood, from a tree that grew in the yard where Big Dee and Stash had lived.

After dinner Dee (Wangero) went to the trunk at the foot of my bed and started rifling through it. Maggie hung back in the kitchen over the dishpan. Out came Wangero with two quilts. They had been pieced by Grandma Dee and then Big Dee and me had hung them on the quilt frames on the front porch and quilted them. One was in the Lone Star pattern②. The other was Walk Around the Mountain③. In both of them were scraps of dresses Grandma Dee had worn fifty and more years ago. Bits and pieces of Grandpa Jarrell's paisley shirts④. And one teeny faded blue piece, about the piece of a penny matchbox, that was from Great Grandpa Ezra's uniform that he wore in the Civil War.

"Mama," Wangero said sweet as a bird. "Can I have these old quilts?"

I heard something fall in the kitchen, and a minute later the kitchen door slammed.

"Why don't you take one or two of the others?" I asked. "These old things was just done by me and Big Dee from some tops your grandma pieced before she died."

"No," said Wangero. "I don't want those. They are stitched around the borders by machine."

---

① clabber: sour milk or buttermilk

② Lone Star pattern: the design on the quilt had, perhaps, a single star

③ Walk Around the Mountain: perhaps a quilt design showing a mountain

④ paisley shirts: shirts having an elaborate, colorful pattern of intricate figures. It is called after Paisley, a city in Scotland where shawls of such design were originally made.

"That'll make them last better," I said.

"That's not the point," said Wangero. "These are all pieces of dresses Grandma used to wear. She did all this stitching by hand. Imagine!" She held the quilts securely in her arms, stroking them.

"Some of the pieces, like those lavender ones, come from old clothes her mother handed down to her," I said, moving up to touch the quilts. Dee (Wangero) moved back just enough so that I couldn't reach the quilts. They already belonged to her.

"Imagine!" she breathed again, clutching them closely to her bosom.

"The truth is," I said, "I promised to give them quilts to Maggie, for when she marries John Thomas."

She gasped like a bee had stung her.

"Maggie can't appreciate these quilts!" she said. "She'd probably be backward enough to put them to everyday use."

"I reckon she would," I said. "God knows I been saving'em for long enough with nobody using'em. I hope she will!" I didn't want to bring up how I had offered Dee (Wangero) a quilt when she went away to college. Then she had told me they were old-fashioned, out of style.

"But they're priceless!" she was saying now, furiously; for she has a temper. "Maggie would put them on the bed and in five years they'd be in rags. Less than that!"

"She can always make some more," I said. "Maggie knows how to quilt."

Dee (Wangero) looked at me with hatred. "You just will not understand. The point is these quilts, these quilts!"

"Well," I said, stumped. "What would you do with them?"

"Hang them," she said. As if that was the only thing you could do with quilts.

Maggie by now was standing in the door. I could almost hear the sound her feet made as they scraped over each other.

"She can have them, Mama," she said, like somebody used to never winning anything, or having anything reserved for her. "I can'member Grandma Dee without the quilts."

I looked at her hard. She had filled her bottom lip with checkerberry snuff and it gave her face a kind of dopey, hangdog look. It was Grandma Dee and Big Dee who taught her how to quilt herself. She stood there with her scarred hands hidden in the folds of her skirt. She looked at her sister with something like fear but she wasn't mad at her. This was Maggie's portion. This was the way she knew God to work.

When I looked at her like that something hit me in the top of my head and ran down to the soles of my feet. Just like when I'm in church and the spirit of God touches me and I get happy and shout. I did something I never had done before: hugged Maggie to me, then dragged her on into the room, snatched the quilts out of Miss Wangero's hands and dumped them into Maggie's lap. Maggie just sat there on my bed with her mouth open.

"Take one or two of the others," I said to Dee.

But she turned without a word and went out to Hakim-a-barber.

"You just don't understand," she said, as Maggie and I came out to the car.

"What don't I understand?" I wanted to know.

"Your heritage," she said. And then she turned to Maggie, kissed her, and said, "You ought to try to make something of yourself, too, Maggie. It's really a new day for us. But from the way you and Mama still live you'd never know it."

She put on some sunglasses that hid everything above the tip of her nose and her chin. Maggie smiled; maybe at the sunglasses. But a real smile, not scared. After we watched the car dust settle I asked Maggie to bring me a dip of snuff. And then the two of us sat there just enjoying, until it was time to go in the house and go to bed.

Study Questions:

1. What is the basic conflict in "Everyday Use"?
2. What is the tone of Walker's story? By what means does the author communicate it?
3. From whose point of view is "Everyday Use" told? What does the story gain from this point of view, instead of, say, from the point of view of Dee (Wangero)?
4. What does the narrator of the story feel toward Dee? What seems to be Dee's present attitude toward her mother and sister?
5. What do you take to be the author's attitude toward each of her characters? How does she convey it?
6. What levels of meaning do you find in the story's title?
7. Contrast Dee's attitude toward her heritage with the attitudes of her mother and sister. How much truth is there in Dee's accusation that her mother and sister don't understand their heritage?
8. Does the knowledge that "Everyday Use" was written by a black writer in any way influence your reactions to it? Explain.

[Reading Critically]

How Does Character Create Action?

Although the average readers may consider plot the basic element of fiction, writers often remark that stories begin with characters. They imagine a certain person and then wait to see what that character will do. "By the time I write a story," remarked Katherine Anne Porter, "my people are up and alive and walking around and taking things into their own hands." The action of a story usually grows out of the personality of its protagonist and the situation he or she faces. As critic Phyllis Bottome observed, "If a writer is true to his characters they will give him his plot."

In reading about the protagonist (or any other figure) in a short story, novel, or other literary works, begin by studying his or her personality. What makes this individual different from the other characters in the story? Jot down a quick list of individual physical, mental, moral, or behavioral traits the character displays. Does one trait seem especially significant? Do any of these qualities foreshadow the action of the story? Now jot down what the character's primary motivation appears to be. Does this motivation seem as reasonable to the reader as it does to the protagonist? If not, what does the gap between the protagonist's motivation and the reader's reaction suggest? (The odd motivation of the narrator in Edgar Allan Poe's "The Tell-Tale Heart", for instance, suggests that the speaker is insane.) Does the protagonist fully understand his or her own motivation?

3. Setting

By the **setting** of a story, we mean its time and place. But often, in an effective short story, setting may figure as more than mere background or underpinning. It can make things happen. It can prompt characters to act, bring them to realizations, or cause them to reveal their inmost natures.

To be sure, the idea of setting includes the physical environment of a story: a house, a street, a city, a landscape, a region. Physical places mattered so greatly to some novelists, such as French novelist Honoré de Balzac, which helps to provide what we call verisimilitude; while they serve as little to some stories more than incidental and decorative backdrops, which have little or no necessary relationship to either the plot or the characters.

But besides place, setting may crucially involve the time of the story—hour, year, or century. It might matter greatly that a story takes place at dawn, or on the day of the first moon landing. When we begin to read a historical novel, we are soon made aware that we are not reading about life in the 21st century. In *The Scarlet Letter*, the 19th-century author Nathaniel Hawthorne, by a long introduction and a vivid opening scene at a prison door, prepares us to witness events in the Puritan community of Boston in the earlier 17th century. This setting, together with scenes of Puritan times, helps us understand what happens in the novel. We can appreciate the shocked agitation in town when a woman is accused of adultery: she has given illegitimate birth. Such an event might seem common today, but in the stern, God-fearing New England Puritan community, it was a flagrant defiance of church and state, which were all-powerful (and were all one). That readers will make no sense of *The Scarlet Letter* who ignores its setting—if to ignore the setting is possible, so much attention does Hawthorne pay to it.

Besides time and place, setting may also include the weather, which in some stories may be crucial. Climate seems as substantial as any character in William Faulkner's "Dry September". After sixty-two rainless days, a long-unbroken spell of late-summer heat has frayed every nerve in a small town and caused the main character, a hotheaded white supremacist, to feel more and more irritation. The weather, someone remarks, is "enough to make a man do anything". When a false report circulates that a woman has been raped by a black man, the rumor, like a match flung into a dry field, ignites rage and provokes a lynching. Evidently, to understand the story we have to recognize its locale (where a story takes place is sometimes called its locale), a small town in Mississippi in the 1930s during an infernal heat wave. Fully to take in the meaning of Faulkner's story, we have to take in the setting in its entirety.

Physical place, by the way, is especially vital to a regional writer, who usually sets stories (or other works) in one geographic area. Such a writer, often a native of the place, tries to bring it alive to readers who live elsewhere. William Faulkner, a distinguished regional writer, almost always sets his novels and stories in his native Mississippi. Though born in St. Louis, Kate Chopin became known as a regional writer for writing about Louisiana in many of her short stories and in her novel *The Awakening*. Willa Cather, for her novels of frontier Nebraska, often is regarded as another outstanding regionalist (though she also set fiction in Quebec, the Southwest, and in "Paul's Case", in Pittsburgh and New York). There is often something arbitrary, however, about calling an author a regional writer. The label often has a political tinge; it means the author describes an area outside the political and economic centers of a society. In a sense, we might think of James Joyce as a regional writer, in that all his fiction takes place in the city of Dublin, but instead we usually call him an Irish one.

As such writers show, a place can profoundly affect the character who grew up in it. Willa Cather is fond of portraying strong-minded, independent women, such as the heroine of her novel *My Ántonia*, strengthened in part by years of coping with the hardships of life on the wind-lashed prairie. Not that every writer of stories in which a place matters greatly will draw the characters as helpless puppets of their environment. Few writers do so, although that may be what you find in novels of naturalism—fiction of grim realism, in which the writer observes human characters like a scientist observing ants, seeing them as the products and victims of environment and heredity.

Setting may operate subtly. Often, setting and character will reveal each other. Recall how Faulkner, at the start of "A Rose for Emily", depicts Emily Grierson's house, once handsome but now "an eyesore among eyesores" surrounded by gas stations. Still standing, refusing to yield its old-time horse-and-buggy splendor to the age of the automobile, the house in "its stubborn and coquettish decay" embodies the character of its owner. In some fiction, setting is closely bound with theme (what the story is saying)—as you will find in John Steinbeck's "The Chrysanthemums", a story beginning with a fog that has sealed off a valley from the rest of the world—a fog like the lid on a pot.

In some stories, a writer will seem to draw a setting mainly to evoke atmosphere. In such a story, setting starts us feeling whatever the storyteller would have us feel. In "The Tell-Tale Heart", Poe's setting the action in an old, dark, lantern-lit house greatly contributes to our sense of unease—and so helps the story's effectiveness.

In conclusion, setting, in its broadest sense, encompasses both the physical locale that frames the action and the time of day or year, the climatic conditions, and the historical period during which the action takes place. At its most basic, setting helps the readers visualize the action of the work and thus adds credibility and authenticity to the story.

There are many different kinds of setting in fiction and they function in a variety of ways. To be specific, among them are the following:

1. Setting as a background for action.
2. Setting as antagonist.
3. Setting as a means of creating appropriate atmosphere.
4. Setting as a means of revealing character.
5. Setting as a means of reinforcing theme.

In this chapter, you will meet two fine stories in which setting, for one reason or another, counts greatly. Without it, nothing will happen.

The Storm (1898)
Kate Chopin

I

The leaves were so still that even Bibi thought it was going to rain. Bobinôt, who was accustomed to converse on terms of perfect equality with his little son, called the child's attention to certain somber clouds that were rolling with sinister intention from the west, accompanied by a sullen, threatening roar. They were at Friedheimer's store and decided to remain there till the storm had passed. They sat within the door on two empty kegs. Bibi was four years old and looked very wise.

"Mama'll be 'fraid, yes," he suggested with blinking eyes.

"She'll shut the house. Maybe she got Sylvie helpin' her this evenin'," Bobinôt responded reassuringly.

"No; she didn' get Sylvie. Sylvie was helpin' her yistiday," piped Bibi.

Bobinôt arose and going across to the counter purchased a can of shrimps, of which Calixta was very fond. Then he returned to his perch on the keg and sat stolidly holding the can of shrimps while the storm burst. It shook the wooden store and seemed to be ripping great furrows in the distant field. Bibi laid his little hand on his father's knee and was not afraid.

II

Calixta, at home, felt no uneasiness for their safety. She sat at a side window sewing furiously on a sewing machine. She was greatly occupied and did not notice the approaching storm. But she felt very warm and often stopped to mop her face on which the perspiration gathered in beads. She unfastened her white sacque at the throat. It began to grow dark, and suddenly realizing the situation she got up hurriedly and went about closing windows and doors.

Out on the small front gallery she had hung Bobinôt's Sunday clothes to air and she hastened out to gather them before the rain fell. As she stepped outside, Alcée Laballière rode in at the gate. She had not seen him very often since her marriage, and never alone. She stood there with Bobinôt's coat in her hands, and the big rain drops began to fall. Alcée rode his horse under the shelter of a side projection where the chickens had huddled and there were plows and a harrow piled up in the corner.

"May I come and wait on your gallery till the storm is over, Calixta?" he asked.

"Come'long in, M'sieur Alcée."

His voice and her own startled her as if from a trance, and she seized Bobinôt's vest. Alcée, mounting to the porch, grabbed the trousers and snatched Bibi's braided jacket that was about to be carried away by a sudden gust of wind. He expressed an intention to remain outside, but it was soon apparent that he might as well have been out in the open: the water beat in upon the boards in driving sheets, and he went inside, closing the door after him. It was even necessary to put something beneath the door to keep the water out.

"My! what a rain! It's good two years since it rain like that," exclaimed Calixta as she rolled up a piece of bagging and Alcée helped her to thrust it beneath the crack.

She was a little fuller of figure than five years before when she married; but she had lost nothing of her vivacity. Her blue eyes still retained their melting quality; and her yellow hair, dishevelled by the wind and rain, kinked more stubbornly than ever about her ears and temples.

The rain beat upon the low, shingled roof with a force and clatter that threatened to break an entrance and deluge them there. They were in the dining room—the sitting room—the general utility room. Adjoining was her bed room, with Bibi's couch along side her own. The door stood open, and the room with its white, monumental bed, its closed shutters, looked dim and mysterious.

Alcée flung himself into a rocker and Calixta nervously began to gather up from the floor the lengths of a cotton sheet which she had been sewing.

"If this keeps up, *Dieu sait* ① if the levees goin' to stan' it!" she exclaimed.

---

① *Dieu sait*: God only knows

"What have you got to do with the levees?"

"I got enough to do! An' there's Bobinôt with Bibi out in that storm—if he only didn' left Friedheimer's!"

"Let us hope, Calixta, that Bobinôt's got sense enough to come in out of a cyclone."

She went and stood at the window with a greatly disturbed look on her face. She wiped the frame that was clouded with moisture. It was stiflingly hot. Alcée got up and joined her at the window, looking over her shoulder. The rain was coming down in sheets obscuring the view of far-off cabins and enveloping the distant wood in a gray mist. The playing of the lightning was incessant. A bolt struck a tall chinaberry tree at the edge of the field. It filled all visible space with a blinding glare and the crash seemed to invade the very boards they stood upon.

Calixta put her hands to her eyes, and with a cry, staggered backward. Alcée's arm encircled her, and for an instant he drew her close and spasmodically to him.

"Bonté①!" she cried, releasing herself from his encircling arm and retreating from the window, "the house'll go next! If I only knew w'ere Bibi was!" She would not compose herself; she would not be seated. Alcée clasped her shoulders and looked into her face. The contact of her warm, palpitating body when he had unthinkingly drawn her into his arms, had aroused all the old-time infatuation and desire for her flesh.

"Calixta," he said, "don't be frightened. Nothing can happen. The house is too low to be struck, with so many tall trees standing about. There! aren't you going to be quiet? say, aren't you?" He pushed her hair back from her face that was warm and steaming. Her lips were as red and moist as pomegranate seed. Her white neck and a glimpse of her full, firm bosom disturbed him powerfully. As she glanced up at him the fear in her liquid blue eyes had given place to a drowsy gleam that unconsciously betrayed a sensuous desire. He looked down into her eyes and there was nothing for him to do but gather her lips in a kiss. It reminded him of Assumption②.

"Do you remember—in Assumption, Calixta?" he asked in a low voice broken by passion. Oh! she remembered; for in Assumption he had kissed her and kissed and kissed her; until his senses would well nigh fail, and to save her he would resort to a desperate flight. If she was not an immaculate dove in those days, she was still inviolate; a passionate creature whose very defenselessness had made her defense, against which his honor forbade him to prevail. Now—well, now—her lips seemed in a manner free to be tasted, as well as her round, white throat and her whiter breasts.

They did not heed the crashing torrents, and the roar of the elements made her laugh as

---

① Bonté: Heavens
② Assumption: a parish west of New Orleans

she lay in his arms. She was a revelation in that dim, mysterious chamber; as white as the couch she lay upon. Her firm, elastic flesh that was knowing for the first time its birthright, was like a creamy lily that the sun invites to contribute its breath and perfume to the undying life of the world.

The generous abundance of her passion, without guile or trickery, was like a white flame which penetrated and found response in depths of his own sensuous nature that had never yet been reached.

When he touched her breasts they gave themselves up in quivering ecstasy, inviting his lips. Her mouth was a fountain of delight. And when he possessed her, they seemed to swoon together at the very borderland of life's mystery.

He stayed cushioned upon her, breathless, dazed, enervated, with his heart beating like a hammer upon her. With one hand she clasped his head, her lips lightly touching his forehead. The other hand stroked with a soothing rhythm his muscular shoulders.

The growl of the thunder was distant and passing away. The rain beat softly upon the shingles, inviting them to drowsiness and sleep. But they dared not yield.

The rain was over; and the sun was turning the glistening green world into a palace of gems. Calixta, on the gallery, watched Alcée ride away. He turned and smiled at her with a beaming face; and she lifted her pretty chin in the air and laughed aloud.

III

Bobinôt and Bibi, trudging home, stopped without at the cistern to make themselves presentable.

"My! Bibi, w'at will yo' mama say! You ought to be ashame'. You oughtn' put on those good pants. Look at 'em! An' that mud on yo' collar! How you got that mud on yo' collar, Bibi? I never saw such a boy!" Bibi was the picture of pathetic resignation. Bobinôt was the embodiment of serious solicitude as he strove to remove from his own person and his son's the signs of their tramp over heavy roads and through wet fields. He scraped the mud off Bibi's bare legs and feet with a stick and carefully removed all traces from his heavy brogans. Then, prepared for the worst—the meeting with an overscrupulous housewife, they entered cautiously at the back door.

Calixta was preparing supper. She had set the table and was dripping coffee at the hearth. She sprang up as they came in.

"Oh, Bobinôt! You back! My! but I was uneasy. Were you been during the rain? An' Bibi? he ain't wet? he ain't hurt?" She had clasped Bibi and was kissing him effusively. Bobinôt's explanations and apologies which he had been composing all along the way, died on his lips as Calixta felt him to see if he were dry, and seemed to express nothing but satisfaction at their safe return.

"I brought you some shrimps, Calixta," offered Bobinôt, hauling the can from his ample side pocket and laying it on the table.

"Shrimps! Oh, Bobinôt! you too good fo' anything!" and she gave him a smacking kiss on the cheek that resounded. "*J'vous réponds*①, we'll have feas' tonight! umph-umph!"

Bobinôt and Bibi began to relax and enjoy themselves, and when the three seated themselves at table they laughed much and so loud that anyone might have heard them as far away as Laballière's.

IV

Alcée Laballière wrote to his wife, Clarisse, that night. It was a loving letter, full of tender solicitude. He told her not to hurry back, but if she and the babies liked it at Biloxi, to stay a month longer. He was getting on nicely; and though he missed them, he was willing to bear the separation a while longer—realizing that their health and pleasure were the first things to be considered.

V

As for Clarisse, she was charmed upon receiving her husband's letter. She and the babies were doing well. The society was agreeable; many of her old friends and acquaintances were at the bay. And the first free breath since her marriage seemed to restore the pleasant liberty of her maiden days. Devoted as she was to her husband, their intimate conjugal life was something which she was more than willing to forego for a while.

So the storm passed and everyone was happy.

Study Questions:

1. Where does Chopin's story take place exactly? How can you tell?

2. What circumstances introduced in Part I turn out to have a profound effect on events in the story?

3. What details in "The Storm" emphasize the fact that Bobinôt loves his wife? What details reveal how imperfectly he comprehends her nature?

4. What general attitudes toward sex, love, and marriage does Chopin imply? Cite evidence to support your answer.

5. What meanings do you find in the title "The Storm"?

6. In the story as a whole, how do setting and plot reinforce each other?

To Build a Fire (1910)

Jack London

Day had broken cold and gray, exceedingly cold and gray, when the man turned aside

---

① *J'vous réponds:* Let me tell you.

from the main Yukon trail① and climbed the high earth-bank, where a dim and little-traveled trail led eastward through the fat spruce timberland. It was a steep bank, and he paused for breath at the top, excusing the act to himself by looking at his watch. It was nine o'clock. There was no sun nor hint of sun, though there was not a cloud in the sky. It was a clear day, and yet there seemed an intangible pall over the face of things, a subtle gloom that made the day dark, and that was due to the absence of sun. This fact did not worry the man. He was used to the lack of sun. It had been days since he had seen the sun, and he knew that a few more days must pass before that cheerful orb, due south, would just peep above the sky line and dip immediately from view.

  The man flung a look back along the way he had come. The Yukon lay a mile wide and hidden under three feet of ice. On top of this ice were as many feet of snow. It was all pure white, rolling in gentle undulations where the ice jams of the freeze-up had formed. North and south, as far as the eye could see, it was unbroken white, save for a dark hairline that curved and twisted from around the spruce-covered island to the south, and that curved and twisted away into the north, where it disappeared behind another spruce-covered island. This dark hairline was the trail—the main trail—that led south five hundred miles to the Chilcoot Pass, Dyea②, and salt water; and that led north seventy miles to Dawson, and still on to the north a thousand miles to Nulato③, and finally to St. Michael, on Bering Sea, a thousand miles and half a thousand more.

  But all this—the mysterious, far-reaching hairline trail, the absence of sun from the sky, the tremendous cold, and the strangeness and weirdness of it all—made no impression on the man. It was not because he was long used to it. He was a newcomer in the land, a *chechaquo*④, and this was his first winter. The trouble with him was that he was without imagination. He was quick and alert in the things of life, but only in the things, and not in the significances. Fifty degrees below zero meant eighty-odd degrees of frost. Such fact impressed him as being cold and uncomfortable, and that was all. It did not lead him to meditate upon his frailty as a creature of temperature, and upon man's frailty in general, able only to live within certain narrow limits of heat and cold; and from there on it did not lead him to the conjectural field of immortality and man's place in the universe. Fifty degrees below zero stood for a bite of frost that hurt and that must be guarded against by the use of mittens, ear flaps, warm moccasins, and thick socks. Fifty degrees below zero was to him just precisely fifty degrees below zero. That there should be anything more to it than that was a thought that never entered his head.

---

  ① Yukon trail: trail extending from southeastern Alaska through the Yukon territory of northwestern Canada and along the Yukon River through central Alaska to the Bering Sea
  ② Dyea: the former town at the start of the trail
  ③ Dawson, Nulato: the former gold-mining centers in the Yukon
  ④ *chechaquo*: slang for "a newcomer" in the Pacific Northwest

As he turned to go on, he spat speculatively. There was a sharp, explosive crackle that startled him. He spat again. And again, in the air, before it could fall to the snow, the spittle crackled. He knew that at fifty below spittle crackled on the snow, but this spittle had crackled in the air. Undoubtedly it was colder than fifty below—how much colder he did not know. But the temperature did not matter. He was bound for the old claim on the left fork of Henderson Creek, where the boys were already. They had come over across the divide from the Indian Creek country, while he had come the roundabout way to take a look at the possibilities of getting out logs in the spring from the islands in the Yukon. He would be in to camp by six o'clock; a bit after dark, it was true, but the boys would be there, a fire would be going, and a hot supper would be ready. As for lunch, he pressed his hand against the protruding bundle under his jacket. It was also under his shirt, wrapped up in a handkerchief and lying against the naked skin. It was the only way to keep the biscuits from freezing. He smiled agreeably to himself as he thought of those biscuits, each cut open and sopped in bacon grease, and each enclosing a generous slice of fried bacon.

He plunged in among the big spruce trees. The trail was faint. A foot of snow had fallen since the last sled had passed over, and he was glad he was without a sled, traveling light. In fact, he carried nothing but the lunch wrapped in the handkerchief. He was surprised, however, at the cold. It certainly was cold, he concluded, as he rubbed his numb nose and cheekbones with his mittened hand. He was a warm-whiskered man, but the hair on his face did not protect the high cheekbones and the eager nose that thrust itself aggressively into the frosty air.

At the man's heels trotted a dog, a big native husky, the proper wolf dog, gray-coated and without any visible or temperamental difference from its brother, the wild wolf. The animal was depressed by the tremendous cold. It knew that it was no time for traveling. Its instinct told it a truer tale than was told to the man by the man's judgment. In reality, it was not merely colder than fifty below zero; it was colder than sixty below, than seventy below. It was seventy-five below zero. Since the freezing point is thirty-two above zero, it meant that one hundred and seven degrees of frost obtained. The dog did not know anything about thermometers. Possibly in its brain there was no sharp consciousness of a condition of very cold such as was in the man's brain. But the brute had its instinct. It experienced a vague but menacing apprehension that subdued it and made it slink along at the man's heels, and that made it question eagerly every unwonted① movement of the man as if expecting him to go into camp or to seek shelter somewhere and build a fire. The dog had learned fire, and it wanted fire, or else to burrow under the snow and cuddle its warmth away from the air.

The frozen moisture of its breathing had settled on its fur in a fine powder of frost, and

---

① unwonted: unusual

especially were its jowls, muzzle, and eyelashes whitened by its crystalled breath. The man's red beard and mustache were likewise frosted, but more solidly, the deposit taking the form of ice and increasing with every warm, moist breath he exhaled. Also, the man was chewing tobacco, and the muzzle of ice held his lips so rigidly that he was unable to clear his chin when he expelled the juice. The result was that a crystal beard of the color and solidity of amber was increasing its length on his chin. If he fell down it would shatter itself, like glass, into brittle fragments. But he did not mind the appendage. It was the penalty all tobacco chewers paid in that country, and he had been out before in two cold snaps. They had not been so cold as this, he knew, but by the spirit thermometer① at Sixty Mile he knew they had been registered at fifty below and at fifty-five.

He held on through the level stretch of woods for several miles, crossed a wide flat, and dropped down a bank to the frozen bed of a small stream. This was Henderson Creek, and he knew he was ten miles from the forks. He looked at his watch. It was ten o'clock. He was making four miles an hour, and he calculated that he would arrive at the forks at half past twelve. He decided to celebrate that event by eating his lunch there.

The dog dropped in again at his heels, with a tail drooping discouragement, as the man swung along the creek bed. The furrow of the old sled trail was plainly visible, but a dozen inches of snow covered the marks of the last runners. In a month no man had come up or down that silent creek. The man held steadily on. He was not much given to thinking, and just then particularly he had nothing to think about save that he would eat lunch at the forks and that at six o'clock he would be in camp with the boys. There was nobody to talk to; and, had there been, speech would have been impossible because of the ice muzzle on his mouth. So he continued monotonously to chew tobacco and to increase the length of his amber beard.

Once in a while the thought reiterated itself that it was very cold and that he had never experienced such cold. As he walked along he rubbed his cheekbones and nose with the back of his mittened hand. He did this automatically, now and again changing hands. But, rub as he would, the instant he stopped his cheekbones were numb, and the following instant the end of his nose went numb. He was sure to frost his cheeks; he knew that, and experienced a pang of regret that he had not devised a nose strap of the sort Bud wore in cold snaps. Such a strap passed across the cheeks, as well, and saved them. But it didn't matter much, after all. What were frosted cheeks? A bit painful, that was all; they were never serious.

Empty as the man's mind was of thoughts, he was keenly observant, and he noticed the changes in the creek, the curves and bends and timber jams, and always he sharply noted where he placed his feet. Once, coming around a bend, he shied abruptly, like a startled horse, curved away from the place where he had been walking, and retreated several paces back along

---

① spirit thermometer: thermometer that contains alcohol instead of mercury and is used in extreme cold

the trail. The creek he knew was frozen clear to the bottom—no creek could contain water in that arctic winter—but he knew also that there were springs that bubbled out from the hillsides and ran along under the snow and on top the ice of the creek. He knew that the coldest snaps never froze these springs, and he knew likewise their danger. They were traps. They hid pools of water under the snow that might be three inches deep, or three feet. Sometimes a skin of ice half an inch thick covered them, and in turn was covered by the snow. Sometimes there were alternate layers of water and ice skin, so that when one broke through he kept on breaking through for a while, sometimes wetting himself to the waist.

That was why he had shied in such panic. He had felt the give under his feet and heard the crackle of a snow-hidden ice skin. And to get his feet wet in such a temperature meant trouble and danger. At the very least it meant delay, for he would be forced to stop and build a fire, and under its protection to bare his feet while he dried his socks and moccasins. He stood and studied the creek bed and its banks, and decided that the flow of water came from the right. He reflected awhile, rubbing his nose and cheeks, then skirted to the left, stepping gingerly and testing the footing for each step. Once clear of the danger, he took a fresh chew of tobacco and swung along at his four-mile gait.

In the course of the next two hours he came upon several similar traps. Usually the snow above the hidden pools had a sunken, candied appearance that advertised the danger. Once again, however, he had a close call; and once, suspecting danger, he compelled the dog to go on in front. The dog did not want to go. It hung back until the man shoved it forward, and then it went quickly across the white, unbroken surface. Suddenly it broke through, floundered to one side, and got away to firmer footing. It had wet its forefeet and legs, and almost immediately the water that clung to it turned to ice. It made quick efforts to lick the ice off its legs, then dropped down in the snow and began to bite out the ice that had formed between the toes. This was a matter of instinct. To permit the ice to remain would mean sore feet. It did not know this. It merely obeyed the mysterious prompting that arose from the deep crypts of its being. But the man knew, having achieved a judgment on the subject, and he removed the mitten from his right hand and helped tear out the ice particles. He did not expose his fingers more than a minute, and was astonished at the swift numbness that smote them. It certainly was cold. He pulled on the mitten hastily, and beat the hand savagely across his chest.

At twelve o'clock the day was at its brightest. Yet the sun was too far south on its winter journey to clear the horizon. The bulge of the earth intervened between it and Henderson Creek, where the men walked under a clear sky at noon and cast no shadow. At half past twelve, to the minute, he arrived at the forks of the creek. He was pleased at the speed he had made. If he kept it up, he would certainly be with the boys by six. He unbuttoned his jacket and shirt and drew forth his lunch. The action consumed no more than a quarter of a minute, yet in that brief moment the numbness laid hold of the exposed fingers. He did not put the mitten on, but, instead, struck the fingers a dozen sharp smashes against his leg. Then he sat down on a snow-covered log to eat. The sting that followed upon the striking of his fingers against his leg ceased so quickly that he was startled. He had no chance to take a bite of biscuit. He struck the fingers repeatedly and returned them to the mitten, baring the other hand for the purpose of eating. He tried to take a mouthful, but the ice muzzle prevented. He had forgotten to build a fire and thaw out. He chuckled at his foolishness, and as he chuckled he noted the numbness creeping into the exposed fingers. Also, he noted that the stinging which had first come to his toes when he sat down was already passing away. He wondered whether the toes were warm or numb. He moved them inside the moccasins and decided that they were numb.

He pulled the mitten on hurriedly and stood up. He was a bit frightened. He stamped up and down until the stinging returned into the feet. It certainly was cold, was his thought. That man from Sulphur Creek had spoken the truth when telling how cold it sometimes got in the country. And he had laughed at him at the time! That showed one must not be too sure of things. There was no mistake about it, it was cold. He strode up and down, stamping his feet and threshing his arms, until reassured by the returning warmth. Then he got out matches and proceeded to make a fire. From the undergrowth, where high water of the previous spring had lodged a supply of seasoned twigs, he got his firewood. Working carefully from a small beginning, he soon had a roaring fire, over which he thawed the ice from his face and in the protection of which he ate his biscuits. For the moment the cold of space was outwitted. The dog took satisfaction in the fire, stretching out close enough for warmth and far enough away to escape being singed.

When the man had finished, he filled his pipe and took his comfortable time over a smoke. Then he pulled on his mittens, settled the ear flaps of his cap firmly about his ears, and took the creek trail up the left fork. The dog was disappointed and yearned back toward the fire. This man did not know cold. Possibly all the generations of his ancestry had been ignorant of cold, of real cold, of cold one hundred and seven degrees below freezing point. But the dog knew; all its ancestry knew, and it had inherited the knowledge. And it knew that it was not good to walk abroad in such fearful cold. It was the time to lie snug in a hole in the snow and wait for a curtain of cloud to be drawn across the face of outer space whence this cold came. On the other hand, there was no keen intimacy between the dog and the man. The one was the toil slave of the other, and the only caresses it had ever received were the caresses of the whip lash and of harsh and menacing throat sounds that threatened the whip lash. So the dog made no effort to communicate its apprehension to the man. It was not concerned in the welfare of the man; it was for its own sake that it yearned back toward the fire. But the man whistled, and spoke to it with the sound of whip lashes, and the dog swung in at the man's heels and followed after.

The man took a chew of tobacco and proceeded to start a new amber beard. Also, his moist breath quickly powdered with white his mustache, eyebrows, and lashes. There did not seem to be so many springs on the left fork of the Henderson, and for half an hour the man saw no signs of any. And then it happened. At a place where there were no signs, where the soft, unbroken snow seemed to advertise solidity beneath, the man broke through. It was not deep. He wet himself halfway to the knees before he floundered out to the firm crust.

He was angry, and cursed his luck aloud. He had hoped to get into camp with the boys at six o'clock, and this would delay him an hour, for he would have to build a fire and dry out his footgear. This was imperative at that low temperature—he knew that much; and he turned aside to the bank, which he climbed. On top, tangled in the underbrush about the trunks of several small spruce trees, was a high-water deposit of dry firewood—sticks and twigs, principally, but also larger portions of seasoned branches and fine, dry, last year's grasses. He threw down several large pieces on top of the snow. This served for a foundation and prevented the young flame from drowning itself in the snow it otherwise would melt. The flame he got by touching a match to a small shred of birch bark that he took from his pocket. This burned even more readily than paper. Placing it on the foundation, he fed the young flame with wisps of dry grass and with the tiniest dry twigs.

He worked slowly and carefully, keenly aware of his danger. Gradually, as the flame grew stronger, he increased the size of the twigs with which he fed it. He squatted in the snow, pulling the twigs out from their entanglement in the brush and feeding directly to the flame. He knew there must be no failure. When it is seventy-five below zero, a man must not fail in his first attempt to build a fire—that is, if his feet are wet. If his feet are dry, and he fails, he can run along the trail for half a mile and restore his circulation. But the circulation of wet and freezing feet cannot be restored by running when it is seventy-five below. No matter how fast he runs, the wet feet will freeze the harder.

All this the man knew. The old-timer on Sulphur Creek had told him about it the previous fall, and now he was appreciating the advice. Already all sensation had gone out of his feet. To build the fire he had been forced to remove his mittens, and the fingers had quickly gone numb. His pace of four miles an hour had kept his heart pumping blood to the surface of his body and to all the extremities. But the instant he stopped, the action of the pump eased down. The cold of space smote the unprotected tip of the planet, and he, being on that unprotected tip, received the full force of the blow. The blood of his body recoiled before it. The blood was alive, like the dog, and like the dog it wanted to hide away and cover itself up from the fearful cold. So long as he walked four miles an hour, he pumped that blood, willy-nilly①, to the surface; but now it ebbed away and sank down into the recesses of his body. The extremities were the first to feel its absence. His wet feet froze the faster, and his exposed fingers numbed the faster, though they had not yet begun to freeze. Nose and cheeks were already

---

① willy-nilly: inevitably

freezing, while the skin of all his body chilled as it lost its blood.

But he was safe. Toes and nose and cheeks would be only touched by the frost, for the fire was beginning to burn with strength. He was feeding it with twigs the size of his finger. In another minute he would be able to feed it with branches the size of his wrist, and then he could remove his wet footgear, and, while it dried, he could keep his naked feet warm by the fire, rubbing them at first, of course, with snow. The fire was a success. He was safe. He remembered the advice of the old-timer on Sulphur Creek, and smiled. The old-timer had been very serious in laying down the law that no man must travel alone in the Klondike① after fifty below. Well, here he was; he had had the accident; he was alone; and he had saved himself. Those old-timers were rather womanish, some of them, he thought. All a man had to do was to keep his head, and he was all right. Any man who was a man could travel alone. But it was surprising, the rapidity with which his cheeks and nose were freezing. And he had not thought his fingers could go lifeless in so short a time. Lifeless they were, for he could scarcely make them move together to grip a twig, and they seemed remote from his body and from him. When he touched a twig, he had to look and see whether or not he had held of it. The wires were pretty well down between him and his finger ends.

All of which counted for little. There was the fire, snapping and crackling and promising life with every dancing flame. He started to untie his moccasins. They were coated with ice; the thick German socks were like sheaths of iron halfway to the knees; and the moccasin strings were like rods of steel all twisted and knotted as by some conflagration②. For a moment he tugged with his numb fingers, then, realizing the folly of it, he drew his sheath knife.

But before he could cut the strings, it happened. It was his own fault or, rather, his mistake. He should not have built the fire under the spruce tree. He should have built it in the open. But it had been easier to pull the twigs from the brush and drop them directly on the fire. Now the tree under which he had done this carried a weight of snow on its boughs. No wind had blown for weeks, and each bough was fully freighted. Each time he had pulled a twig he had communicated a slight agitation to the tree—an imperceptible agitation, so far as he was concerned, but an agitation sufficient to bring about the disaster. High up in the tree one bough capsized its load of snow. This fell on the boughs beneath, capsizing them. This process continued, spreading out and involving the whole tree. It grew like an avalanche, and it descended without warning upon the man and the fire, and the fire was blotted out! Where it had burned was a mantle of fresh and disordered snow.

The man was shocked. It was as though he had just heard his own sentence of death. For a moment he sat and stared at the spot where the fire had been. Then he grew very calm.

---

① Klondike: Yukon gold-mining region
② conflagration: destructive fire

Perhaps the old-timer on Sulphur Creek was right. If he had only had a trail mate he would have been in no danger now. The trail mate could have built the fire. Well, it was up to him to build the fire over again, and this second time there must be no failure. Even if he succeeded, he would most likely lose some toes. His feet must be badly frozen by now, and there would be some time before the second fire was ready.

Such were his thoughts, but he did not sit and think them. He was busy all the time they were passing through his mind. He made a new foundation for a fire, this time in the open, where no treacherous tree could blot it out. Next he gathered dry grasses and tiny twigs from the high-water flotsam. He could not bring his fingers together to pull them out, but he was able to gather them by the handful. In this way he got many rotten twigs and bits of green moss that were undesirable, but it was the best he could do. He worked methodically, even collecting an armful of the larger branches to be used later when the fire gathered strength. And all the while the dog sat and watched him, a certain yearning wistfulness in its eye, for it looked upon him as the fire provider, and the fire was slow in coming.

When all was ready, the man reached in his pocket for a second piece of birch bark. He knew the bark was there, and, though he could not feel it with his fingers, he could hear its crisp rustling as he fumbled for it. Try as he would, he could not clutch hold of it. And all the time, in his consciousness, was the knowledge that each instant his feet were freezing. This thought tended to put him in a panic, but he fought against it and kept calm. He pulled on his mittens with his teeth, and threshed his arms back and forth, beating his hands with all his might against his sides. He did this sitting down, and he stood up to do it; and all the while the dog sat in the snow, its wolf brush of a tail curled around warmly over its forefeet, its sharp wolf ears pricked forward intently as it watched the man. And the man, as he beat and threshed with his arms and hands, felt a great surge of envy as he regarded the creature that was warm and secure in its natural covering.

After a time he was aware of the first faraway signals of sensation in his beaten fingers. The faint tingling grew stronger till it evolved into a stinging ache that was excruciating, but which the man hailed with satisfaction. He stripped the mitten from his right hand and fetched forth the birch bark. The exposed fingers were quickly going numb again. Next he brought out his bunch of sulphur matches. But the tremendous cold had already driven the life out of his fingers. In his effort to separate one match from the others, the whole bunch fell in the snow. He tried to pick it out of the snow, but failed. The dead fingers could neither touch nor clutch. He was very careful. He drove the thought of his freezing feet, and nose, and cheeks, out of his mind, devoting his whole soul to the matches. He watched, using the sense of vision in place of that of touch, and when he saw his fingers on each side the bunch, he closed them—that is, he willed to close them, for the wires were down, and the fingers did not obey. He pulled the mitten on the right hand, and beat it fiercely against his knee. Then, with both mittened hands, he scooped the bunch of matches, along with much snow, into his lap. Yet he was no better off.

After some manipulation he managed to get the bunch between the heels of his mittened hands. In this fashion he carried it to his mouth. The ice crackled and snapped when by a violent effort he opened his mouth. He drew the lower jaw in, curled the upper lip out of the way, and scraped the bunch with his upper teeth in order to separate a match. He succeeded in getting one, which he dropped on his lap. He was no better off. He could not pick it up. Then he devised a way. He picked it up in his teeth and scratched it on his leg. Twenty times he scratched before he succeeded in lighting it. As it flamed he held it with his teeth to the birch bark. But the burning brimstone went up his nostrils and into his lungs, causing him to cough spasmodically. The match fell into the snow and went out.

The old-timer on Sulphur Creek was right, he thought in the moment of controlled despair that ensued: after fifty below, a man should travel with a partner. He beat his hands, but failed in exciting any sensation. Suddenly he bared both hands, removing the mittens with his teeth. He caught the whole bunch between the heels of his hands. His arm muscles not being frozen enabled him to press the hand heels tightly against the matches. Then he scratched the bunch along his leg. It flared into flame, seventy sulphur matches at once! There was no wind to blow them out. He kept his head to one side to escape the strangling fumes, and held the blazing bunch to the birch bark. As he so held it, he became aware of sensation in his hand. His flesh was burning. He could smell it. Deep down below the surface he could feel it. The sensation developed into pain that grew acute. And still he endured it, holding the flame of the matches clumsily to the bark that would not light readily because his own burning hands were in the way, absorbing most of the flame.

At last, when he could endure no more, he jerked his hands apart. The blazing matches fell sizzling into the snow, but the birch bark was alight. He began laying dry grasses and the tiniest twigs on the flame. He could not pick and choose, for he had to lift the fuel between the heels of his hands. Small pieces of rotten wood and green moss clung to the twigs, and he bit them off as well as he could with his teeth. He cherished the flame carefully and awkwardly. It meant life, and it must not perish. The withdrawal of blood from the surface of his body now made him begin to shiver, and he grew more awkward. A large piece of green moss fell squarely on the little fire. He tried to poke it out with his fingers, but his shivering frame made him poke too far, and he disrupted the nucleus of the little fire, the burning grasses and tiny twigs separating and scattering. He tried to poke them together again, but in spite of the tenseness of the effort, his shivering got away from him, and the twigs were hopelessly scattered. Each twig gushed a puff of smoke and went out. The fire provider had failed. As he looked apathetically about him, his eyes chanced on the dog, sitting across the ruins of the fire from him, in the snow, making restless, hunching movements, slightly lifting one forefoot and then the other, shifting its weight back and forth on them with wistful eagerness.

The sight of the dog put a wild idea into his head. He remembered the tale of the man, caught in the blizzard, who killed a steer and crawled inside the carcass, and so was saved. He would kill the dog and bury his hands in the warm body until the numbness went out of them. Then he could build another fire. He spoke to the dog, calling it to him; but in his voice was a strange note of fear that frightened the animal, who had never known the man to speak in such a way before. Something was the matter, and its suspicious nature sensed danger—it knew not what danger, but somewhere, somehow, in its brain arose an apprehension of the man. It flattened its ears down at the sound of the man's voice, and its restless, hunching movements and the liftings and shiftings of its forefeet became more pronounced; but it would not come to the man. He got on his hands and knees and crawled toward the dog. This unusual posture again excited suspicion, and the animal sidled mincingly away.

The man sat up in the snow for a moment and struggled for calmness. Then he pulled on his mittens, by means of his teeth, and got upon his feet. He glanced down at first in order to assure himself that he was really standing up, for the absence of sensation in his feet left him unrelated to the earth. His erect position in itself started to drive the webs of suspicion from the dog's mind; and when he spoke peremptorily①, with the sound of whip lashes in his voice, the dog rendered its customary allegiance and came to him. As it came within reaching distance, the man lost his control. His arms flashed out to the dog, and he experienced genuine surprise when he discovered that his hands could not clutch, that there was neither bend nor feeling in the fingers. He had forgotten for the moment that they were frozen and that they were freezing more and more. All this happened quickly, and before the animal could get away, he encircled its body with his arms. He sat down in the snow, and in this fashion held the dog, while it snarled and whined and struggled.

But it was all he could do, hold its body encircled in his arms and sit there. He realized that he could not kill the dog. There was no way to do it. With his helpless hands he could neither draw nor hold his sheath knife nor throttle the animal. He released it, and it plunged wildly away, with tail between its legs, and still snarling. It halted forty feet away and surveyed him curiously, with ears sharply pricked forward.

The man looked down at his hands in order to locate them, and found them hanging on the ends of his arms. It struck him as curious that one should have to use his eyes in order to find out where his hands were. He began threshing his arms back and forth, beating the mittened hands against his sides. He did this for five minutes, violently, and his heart pumped enough blood up to the surface to put a stop to his shivering. But no sensation was aroused in the hands. He had an impression that they hung like weights on the ends of his arms, but when he tried to run the impression down, he could not find it.

---

① peremptorily: dictatorially

A certain fear of death, dull and oppressive, came to him. This fear quickly became poignant as he realized that it was no longer a mere matter of freezing his fingers and toes, or of losing his hands and feet, but that it was a matter of life and death with the chances against him. This threw him into a panic, and he turned and ran up the creek bed along the old, dim trail. The dog joined in behind and kept up with him. He ran blindly, without intention, in fear such as he had never known in his life. Slowly, as he plowed and floundered through the snow, he began to see things again—the banks of the creek, the old timber jams, the leafless aspens, and the sky. The running made him feel better. He did not shiver. Maybe, if he ran on, his feet would thaw out; and anyway, if he ran far enough, he would reach camp and the boys. Without doubt he would lose some fingers and toes and some of his face; but the boys would take care of him, and save the rest of him when he got there. And at the same time there was another thought in his mind that said he would never get to the camp and the boys; that it was too many miles away, that the freezing had too great a start on him, and that he would soon be stiff and dead. This thought he kept in the background and refused to consider. Sometimes it pushed itself forward and demanded to be heard, but he thrust it back and strove to think of other things.

It struck him as curious that he could run at all on feet so frozen that he could not feel them when they struck the earth and took the weight of his body. He seemed to himself to skim along above the surface, and to have no connection with the earth. Somewhere he had once seen a winged Mercury①, and he wondered if Mercury felt as he felt when skimming over the earth.

His theory of running until he reached the camp and the boys had one flaw in it; he lacked the endurance. Several times he stumbled, and finally he tottered, crumpled up, and fell. When he tried to rise, he failed. He must sit and rest, he decided, and next time he would merely walk and keep on going. As he sat and regained his breath, he noted that he was feeling quite warm and comfortable. He was not shivering, and it even seemed that a warm glow had come to his chest and trunk. And yet, when he touched his nose and cheeks, there was no sensation. Running would not thaw them out. Nor would it thaw out his hands and feet. Then the thought came to him that the frozen portions of his body must be extending. He tried to keep this thought down, to forget it, to think of something else; he was aware of the panicky feeling that it caused, and he was afraid of the panic. But the thought asserted itself, and persisted, until it produced a vision of his body totally frozen. This was too much, and he made another wild run along the trail. Once he slowed down to a walk, but the thought of the freezing extending itself made him run again.

And all the time the dog ran with him, at his heels. When he fell down a second time, it

---

① Mercury: in Roman mythology, messenger of the gods, considered to have winged feet

curled its tail over its forefeet and sat in front of him, facing him, curiously eager and intent. The warmth and security of the animal angered him, and he cursed it till it flattened down its ears appeasingly. This time the shivering came more quickly upon the man. He was losing in his battle with the frost. It was creeping into his body from all sides. The thought of it drove him on, but he ran no more than a hundred feet, when he staggered and pitched headlong. It was his last panic. When he had recovered his breath and control, he sat up and entertained in his mind the conception of meeting death with dignity. However, the conception did not come to him in such terms. His idea of it was that he had been making a fool of himself, running around like a chicken with its head cut off—such was the simile that occurred to him. Well, he was bound to freeze anyway, and he might as well take it decently. With this new-found peace of mind came the first glimmerings of drowsiness. A good idea, he thought, to sleep off to death. It was like taking an anesthetic①. Freezing was not so bad as people thought. There were lots worse ways to die.

He pictured the boys finding his body next day. Suddenly he found himself with them, coining along the trail and looking for himself. And, still with them, he came around a turn in the trail and found himself lying in the snow. He did not belong with himself any more, for even then he was out of himself, standing with the boys and looking at himself in the snow. It certainly was cold, was his thought. When he got back to the States he could tell the folks what real cold was. He drifted on from this to a vision of the old-timer on Sulphur Creek. He could see him quite clearly, warm and comfortable, and smoking a pipe.

"You were right, old hoss; you were right," the man mumbled to the old-timer of Sulphur Creek.

Then the man drowsed off into what seemed to him the most comfortable and satisfying sleep he had ever known. The dog sat facing him and waiting. The brief day drew to a close in a long, slow twilight. There were no signs of a fire to be made, and, besides, never in the dog's experience had it known a man to sit like that in the snow and make no fire. As the twilight drew on, its eager yearning for the fire mastered it, and with a great lifting and shifting of forefeet, it whined softly, then flattened its ears down in anticipation of being chidden② by the man. But the man remained silent. Later the dog whined loudly. And still later it crept close to the man and caught the scent of death. This made the animal bristle and back away. A little longer it delayed, howling under the stars that leaped and danced and shone brightly in the cold sky. Then it turned and trotted up the trail in the direction of the camp it knew, where were the other food providers and fire providers.

---

① anesthetic: something that produces a loss of sensation
② chidden: scolded

Study Questions:

1. Roughly how much of London's story is devoted to describing the setting? What particular details make it memorable?

2. To what extent does the setting determine what happens in this story?

3. From what point of view is London's story told?

4. In "To Build a Fire", the man is never given a name. What is the effect of his being called simply "the man" throughout the story?

5. From the evidence London gives us, what stages are involved in the process of freezing to death? What does the story gain from London's detailed account of the man's experience with each successive stage?

6. What are the most serious mistakes the man makes? To what factors do you attribute these errors?

[Reading Critically]

How Do Time and Place Set a Story?

When you read a short story, do not consider only the plot and character—the **what** and **who** of the tale. What happens and who is involved are essential, but those two elements are not the whole story. You should also examine **where** and **when** the story unfolds.

A story's setting constitutes the external reality that surrounds the internal reality of the character's personalities. The external pressure of the setting is often the key factor that compels or invites the protagonist into action. To study a story's setting, therefore, invites you to study not only the setting itself but also its relation to the protagonist.

Before studying the setting, it may help to ask yourself the following questions:

1. When does the story take place? Is the time of year or time of day of any significance?

2. Does the weather play a meaningful role in the story's action?

3. Where does the story take place? Does its location suggest anything about the character's lives?

4. Do different characters become associated with different locations?

5. Do any external elements of time or place suggest something about the protagonists?

4. Point of View

In the opening lines of *Adventures of Huckleberry Finn*, Mark Twain takes care to separate himself from the leading character, who is to tell his own story:

> You don't know about me, without you have read a book by the name of The Adventures of Tom Sawyer, but that ain't no matter. That book was made by Mr. Mark Twain, and he told the truth, mainly.

Twain wrote the novel, but the narrator or speaker is Huck Finn, the one from whose perspective the story is told. Obviously, in *Adventures of Huckleberry Finn*, the narrator of a story is not the same person as the "real-life" author, the one given the byline. In employing Huck as his narrator, Twain selects a special angle of vision: not his own, exactly, but that of a resourceful boy moving through the thick of events, with a mind at times shrewd, at other times innocent. Through Huck's eyes, Twain takes in certain scenes, actions, and characters and—as only Huck's angle of vision could have enabled Twain to do so well—records them memorably.

Not every narrator in fiction is, like Huck Finn, a main character, one in the thick of events. Some narrators play only minor parts in the stories they tell; others take no active part at all. A story may even be told by a narrator who seems so impartial and aloof that he limits himself to reporting only overheard conversation and to describing, without comment or opinion, the appearances of things. Evidently, narrators greatly differ in kind; however, because stories usually are told by someone, almost every story has some kind of narrator. It is rare in modern fiction for the "real-life" author to try to step out from behind the typewriter and tell the story. Real persons can tell stories, but when such a story is written, the result is usually nonfiction: a memoir, an account of travels, and an autobiography.

To identify the narrator of a story, describing any part he or she plays in the events and any limits placed upon his knowledge, is to identify the story's point of view. In a short story, it is usual for the writer to maintain one point of view from the beginning to the end, but there is nothing to stop him from introducing other points of view as well.

Theoretically, a great many points of view are possible. A narrator who says "I" might conceivably be involved in events to a much greater or a much lesser degree: as the protagonist, as some other major character, as some minor character, as a mere passive spectator, or even as a character who arrives late upon the scene and then tries to piece together what happened. Evidently, too, a narrator's knowledge might vary in gradations from total omniscience to almost total ignorance. But in reading fiction, again and again we encounter familiar and recognizable points of view. Here is a list of them—admittedly just a rough abstraction—that may provide a few terms with which to discuss the stories that you read and to describe their points of view:

Narrator: a Participant (Writing in the First Person):

1. a major character;
2. a minor character.

Narrator: a Non-participant (Writing in the Third Person):

3. all-knowing (seeing into any of the characters);
4. seeing into one major character;
5. seeing into one minor character;
6. objective (not seeing into any characters).

When the narrator is cast as a participant in the events of the story, he or she is a dramatized character who says "I". Such a narrator may be the protagonist (Huck Finn) or may be an observer, a minor character standing a little to one side, watching a story unfold that mainly involves someone else.

A narrator who remains a non-participant does not appear in the story as a character. Viewing the characters, perhaps seeing into the minds of one or more of them, such a narrator refers to them as "he", "she", or "they". When **all-knowing** (or **omniscient**), the narrator sees into the minds of all (or some) characters, moving when necessary from one to another. This narrator is said to show **editorial omniscience**. A narrator who shows **impartial omniscience** presents the thoughts and actions of the characters, but does not judge them or comment on them.

When a nonparticipating narrator sees events through the eyes of a single character, whether a major character or a minor one, the resulting point of view is sometimes called **limited omniscience** or **selective omniscience**. The author, of course, selects which character to see through; the omniscience is his and not the narrator's. In William Faulkner's "Barn Burning", the narrator is almost entirely confined to knowing the thoughts and perceptions of a boy, the central character.

In the objective point of view, the narrator does not enter the mind of any character but describes events from the outside. Telling us what people say and how their faces look, he leaves us to infer their thoughts and feelings. So inconspicuous is the narrator that this point of view has been called "the fly on the wall". This metaphor assumes the existence of a fly with a highly discriminating gaze, who knows which details to look for to communicate the deepest meaning. Some critics would say that in the objective point of view, the narrator disappears altogether.

Also possible, but unusual, is a story written in the second person, you. This point of view results in an attention-getting directness, such an arresting way to tell a story is effective, too.

The attitudes and opinions of a narrator are not necessarily those of the author; in fact, we may notice a lively conflict between what we are told and what, apparently, we are meant to believe. A story may be told by an innocent narrator or a naive narrator, a character who fails to understand all the implications of the story. One such innocent narrator (despite his sometimes shrewd perceptions) is Huckleberry Finn. Because Huck accepts without question the morality and lawfulness of slavery, he feels guilty about helping Jim, a runaway slave. But, far from condemning Huck for his defiance of the law—"All right, then, I'll go to hell," Huck tells himself, deciding against returning Jim to captivity—the author, and the readers along with him, silently applaud. Naive in the extreme is the narrator of one part of William Faulkner's novel *The Sound and the Fury*, the idiot Benjy, a grown man with the intellect of a child. In a story told by an **unreliable narrator**, the point of view is that of a person who, we perceive, is deceptive, self-deceptive, deluded, or deranged. As though seeking ways to be faithful to uncertainty, contemporary writers have been particularly fond of unreliable narrators.

Modern writers of fiction have employed many strategies such as stream of consciousness and interior monologue to present complicated reality of life. In fiction, the **stream of consciousness** is a kind of **selective omniscience**: the presentation of thoughts and sense impressions in a lifelike fashion—not in a sequence arranged by logic, but mingled randomly. Stream-of-consciousness writing usually occurs in relatively short passages, but in *Ulysses*, Joyce employs it extensively. Similar in method, an **interior monologue** is an extended presentation of a character's thoughts, not in the seemingly order of a stream of consciousness, but in an arrangement as if the character were speaking out loud to himself, for us to overhear. A famous interior monologue comes at the end of *Ulysses* when Joyce gives us the rambling memories and reflections of earth-mother Molly Bloom.

Every point of view has limitations. Even total omniscience, a knowledge of the minds of all the characters, has its disadvantages. Such a point of view requires high skill to manage, without the storyteller's losing his way in a multitude of perspectives. In fact, there are evident advantages in having a narrator not know everything. We are accustomed to seeing the world through one pair of eyes, to having truths gradually occur to us.

By using a particular point of view, an author may artfully withhold information, if need be, rather than immediately present it to us. If, for instance, the suspense in a story depends on our not knowing until the end that the protagonist is a spy, the author would be ill advised to tell the story from the protagonist's point of view. If a character acts as the narrator, the author must make sure that the character possesses (or can obtain) enough information to tell the story adequately. Clearly, the author makes a fundamental decision in selecting, from many possibilities, a story's point of view. What we readers admire, if the story is effective, is not only skill in execution, but also judicious choice.

A Rose For Emily (1931)
William Faulkner

I

When Miss Emily Grierson died, our whole town went to her funeral: the men through a sort of respectful affection for a fallen monument①, the women mostly out of curiosity to see the inside of her house, which no one save an old manservant—a combined gardener and cook—had seen in at least ten years.

It was a big, squarish frame house that had once been white, decorated with cupolas and spires and scrolled balconies in the heavily lightsome style of the seventies②, set on what had once been our most select street. But garages and cotton gins had encroached and obliterated even the august names of that neighborhood; only Miss Emily's house was left, lifting its stubborn and coquettish decay above the cotton wagons and the gasoline pumps—an eyesore among eyesores③. And now Miss Emily had gone to join the representatives of those august names where they lay in the cedar-bemused cemetery among the ranked and anonymous graves of Union and Confederate soldiers④ who fell at the battle of Jefferson.

Alive, Miss Emily had been a tradition, a duty, and a care; a sort of hereditary obligation upon the town, dating from that day in 1894 when Colonel Sartoris, the mayor—he who fathered the edict that no Negro woman should appear on the streets without an apron—remitted her taxes, the dispensation dating from the death of her father on into perpetuity. Not that Miss Emily would have accepted charity. Colonel Sartoris invented an involved tale to the effect that Miss Emily's father had loaned money to the town, which the town, as a matter of business, preferred this way of repaying. Only a man of Colonel Sartoris' generation and thought could have invented it, and only a woman could have believed it.

When the next generation, with its more modern ideas, became mayors and aldermen⑤, this arrangement created some little dissatisfaction. On the first of the year they mailed her a tax notice. February came, and there was no reply. They wrote her a formal letter, asking her to call at the sheriff's office at her convenience. A week later the mayor wrote her himself, offering to call or to send his car for her, and received in reply a note on paper of an archaic shape, in

---

① a fallen monument: Emily is the symbol of tradition and the old way of life. Therefore, her death is like the falling of a monument.
② the seventies: the 1870s
③ an eyesore among eyesores: the most unpleasant thing to look at
④ Union and Confederate soldiers: soldiers of the warring parties in the American Civil War (1861–1865)
⑤ aldermen: members of the municipal legislative body

a thin, flowing calligraphy in faded ink, to the effect that she no longer went out at all. The tax notice was also enclosed, without comment.

They called a special meeting of the Board of Aldermen. A deputation waited upon her, knocked at the door through which no visitor had passed since she ceased giving china-painting lessons eight or ten years earlier. They were admitted by the old Negro into a dim hall from which a stairway mounted into still more shadow. It smelled of dust and disuse—a close, dank smell. The Negro led them into the parlor. It was furnished in heavy, leather-covered furniture. When the Negro opened the blinds of one window, they could see that the leather was cracked; and when they sat down, a faint dust rose sluggishly about their thighs, spinning with slow motes in the single sun-ray. On a tarnished gilt easel before the fireplace stood a crayon portrait of Miss Emily's father.

They rose when she entered—a small, fat woman in black, with a thin gold chain descending to her waist and vanishing into her belt, leaning on an ebony cane with a tarnished gold head. Her skeleton was small and spare; perhaps that was why what would have been merely plumpness in another was obesity in her①. She looked bloated, like a body long submerged in motionless water, and of that pallid hue. Her eyes, lost in the fatty ridges of her face, looked like two small pieces of coal pressed into a lump of dough as they moved from one face to another while the visitors stated their errand.

She did not ask them to sit. She just stood in the door and listened quietly until the spokesman came to a stumbling halt②. Then they could hear the invisible watch ticking at the end of the gold chain.

Her voice was dry and cold. "I have no taxes in Jefferson. Colonel Sartoris explained it to me. Perhaps one of you can gain access to the city records and satisfy yourselves."

"But we have. We are the city authorities, Miss Emily. Didn't you get a notice from the sheriff, signed by him?"

"I received a paper, yes," Miss Emily said. "Perhaps he considers himself the sheriff … I have no taxes in Jefferson."

"But there is nothing on the books to show that, you see. We must go by the—"

"See Colonel Sartoris. I have no taxes in Jefferson."

"But, Miss Emily—"

"See Colonel Sartoris." (Colonel Sartoris had been dead almost ten years.) "I have no taxes in Jefferson. To be!" The Negro appeared. "Show these gentlemen out."

---

① what would have been … obesity in her: because Emily was short, a little extra weight, which made women of large frame look fat, made her look excessively fat

② a stumbling halt: a pause caused by hesitation in the speaking

II

So she vanquished them, horse and foot①, just as she had vanquished their fathers thirty years before about the smell. That was two years after her father's death and a short time after her sweetheart—the one we believed would marry her—had deserted her. After her father's death she went out very little; after her sweetheart went away, people hardly saw her at all. A few of the ladies had the temerity to call, but were not received, and the only sign of life about the place was the Negro man—a young man then—going in and out with a market basket.

"Just as if a man—any man—could keep a kitchen properly," the ladies said; so they were not surprised when the smell developed. It was another link between the gross, teeming world and the high and mighty Griersons.

A neighbor, a woman, complained to the mayor, Judge Stevens, eighty years old.

"But what will you have me do about it, madam?" he said.

"Why, send her word to stop it," the woman said. "Isn't there a law?"

"I'm sure that won't be necessary," Judge Stevens said. "It's probably just a snake or a rat that nigger of hers killed in the yard. I'll speak to him about it."

The next day he received two more complaints, one from a man who came in diffident deprecation. "We really must do something about it, Judge. I'd be the last one in the world to bother Miss Emily, but we've got to do something." That night the Board of Aldermen met—three graybeards and one younger man, a member of the rising generation.

"It's simple enough," he said. "Send her word to have her place cleaned up. Give her a certain time to do it in, and if she doesn't ..."

"Dammit, sir," Judge Stevens said, "will you accuse a lady to her face of smelling bad?"

So the next night, after midnight, four men crossed Miss Emily's lawn and slunk about the house like burglars, sniffing along the base of the brickwork and at the cellar openings while one of them performed a regular sowing motion with his hand out of a sack slung from his shoulder. They broke open the cellar door and sprinkled lime there, and in all the outbuildings②. As they recrossed the lawn, a window that had been dark was lighted and Miss Emily sat in it, the light behind her, and her upright torso motionless as that of an idol. They crept quietly across the lawn and into the shadow of the locusts that lined the street. After a week or two the smell went away.

That was when people had begun to feel really sorry for her. People in our town, remembering how old lady Wyatt, her great-aunt, had gone completely crazy at last, believed that the Griersons held themselves a little too high for what they really were. None of the young men were quite good enough for Miss Emily and such. We had long thought of them as

---

① horse and foot: (idiom) completely

② outbuildings: buildings, e.g. a shed or stable, separate from the main building

a tableau①, Miss Emily a slender figure in white in the background, her father a spraddled silhouette② in the foreground, his back to her and clutching a horsewhip, the two of them framed by the back-flung front door. So when she got to be thirty and was still single, we were not pleased exactly, but vindicated; even with insanity in the family she wouldn't have turned down all of her chances if they had really materialized.

When her father died, it got about that the house was all that was left to her; and in a way, people were glad. At last they could pity Miss Emily. Being left alone, and a pauper, she had become humanized. Now she too would know the old thrill and the old despair of a penny more or less③.

The day after his death all the ladies prepared to call at the house and offer condolence and aid, as is our custom. Miss Emily met them at the door, dressed as usual and with no trace of grief on her face. She told them that her father was not dead. She did that for three days, with the ministers calling on her, and the doctors, trying to persuade her to let them dispose of the body. Just as they were about to resort to law and force, she broke down, and they buried her father quickly.

We did not say she was crazy then. We believed she had to do that. We remembered all the young men her father had driven away, and we knew that with nothing left, she would have to cling to that which had robbed her, as people will.

III

She was sick for a long time. When we saw her again, her hair was cut short, making her look like a girl, with a vague resemblance to those angels in colored church windows—sort of tragic and serene.

The town had just let the contracts for paving the sidewalks, and in the summer after her father's death they began the work. The construction company came with niggers and mules and machinery, and a foreman named Homer Barron, a Yankee—a big, dark, ready man, with a big voice and eyes lighter than his face. The little boys would follow in groups to hear him cuss the niggers, and the niggers singing in time to the rise and fall of picks. Pretty soon he knew everybody in town. Whenever you heard a lot of laughing anywhere about the square, Homer Barron would be in the center of the group. Presently we began to see him and Miss Emily on Sunday afternoons driving in the yellow-wheeled buggy and the matched team of bays④ from the livery stable.

---

① tableau: striking and lifelike representation, esp. scene in which living models pose silent and without moving

② a spraddled silhouette: a dark image, whose legs are wide open

③ the old thrill and the old despair of a penny more or less: the great excitement and despair caused by the gain or loss of a small amount of money

④ the matched team of bays: a pair of reddish-brown horses that are similar in size and appearance

At first we were glad that Miss Emily would have an interest, because the ladies all said, "Of course a Grierson would not think seriously of a Northerner, a day laborer." But there were still others, older people, who said that even grief could not cause a real lady to forget *noblesse oblige*①—without calling it *noblesse oblige*. They just said, "Poor Emily. Her kinsfolk should come to her." She had some kin in Alabama; but years ago her father had fallen out with② them over the estate of old lady Wyatt, the crazy woman, and there was no communication between the two families. They had not even been represented at the funeral.

And as soon as the old people said, "Poor Emily," the whispering began. "Do you suppose it's really so?" they said to one another. "Of course it is. What else could ..." This behind their hands③; rustling of craned silk and satin④ behind jalousies closed upon the sun of Sunday afternoon as the thin, swift clop-clop-clop of the matched team passed: "Poor Emily."

She carried her head high enough—even when we believed that she was fallen⑤. It was as if she demanded more than ever the recognition of her dignity as the last Grierson; as if it had wanted that touch of earthiness to reaffirm her imperviousness⑥. Like when she bought the rat poison, the arsenic. That was over a year after they had begun to say "Poor Emily," and while the two female cousins were visiting her.

"I want some poison," she said to the druggist. She was over thirty then, still a slight woman, though thinner than usual, with cold, haughty black eyes in a face the flesh of which was strained across the temples and about the eye-sockets as you imagine a lighthouse-keeper's face⑦ ought to look. "I want some poison," she said.

"Yes, Miss Emily. What kind? For rats and such? I'd recom—"

"I want the best you have. I don't care what kind."

The druggist named several. "They'll kill anything up to an elephant. But what you want is—"

"Arsenic," Miss Emily said. "Is that a good one?"

"Is ... arsenic? Yes, ma'am. But what you want—"

"I want arsenic."

The druggist looked down at her. She looked back at him, erect, her face like a strained

---

① *noblesse oblige:* the obligation of a member of the nobility to behave with honor and dignity
② fallen out with: quarreled with
③ This behind their hands: They gossiped with their hands covering the mouths.
④ rustling of craned silk and satin: the rustling sound of their silk and satin dresses caused by the movement
⑤ fallen: morally degraded
⑥ that touch of earthiness to reaffirm her imperviousness: the eagerness in showing that she was unaffected by the outside world
⑦ a lighthouse-keeper's face: a face with the stained and intense expression as that of a lighthouse-keeper's

flag. "Why, of course," the druggist said. "If that's what you want. But the law requires you to tell what you are going to use it for."

Miss Emily just stared at him, her head tilted back in order to look him eye for eye, until he looked away and went and got the arsenic and wrapped it up. The Negro delivery boy brought her the package; the druggist didn't come back. When she opened the package at home there was written on the box, under the skull and bones: "For rats."

IV

So the next day we all said, "She will kill herself"; and we said it would be the best thing. When she had first begun to be seen with Homer Barron, we had said, "She will marry him." Then we said, "She will persuade him yet," because Homer himself had remarked—he liked men, and it was known that he drank with the younger men in the Elks' Club—that he was not a marrying man. Later we said, "Poor Emily," behind the jalousies as they passed on Sunday afternoon in the glittering buggy, Miss Emily with her head high and Homer Barron with his hat cocked and a cigar in his teeth, reins and whip in a yellow glove.

Then some of the ladies began to say that it was a disgrace to the town and a bad example to the young people. The men did not want to interfere, but at last the ladies forced the Baptist minister—Miss Emily's people were Episcopal①—to call upon her. He would never divulge what happened during that interview, but he refused to go back again. The next Sunday they again drove about the streets, and the following day the minister's wife wrote to Miss Emily's relations in Alabama.

So she had blood-kin under her roof again and we sat back to watch developments. At first nothing happened. Then we were sure that they were to be married. We learned that Miss Emily had been to the jeweler's and ordered a man's toilet set in silver, with the letters H. B. on each piece. Two days later we learned that she had bought a complete outfit of men's clothing, including a nightshirt, and we said, "They are married." We were really glad. We were glad because the two female cousins were even more Grierson than Miss Emily had ever been.

So we were not surprised when Homer Barren—the streets had been finished some time since—was gone. We were a little disappointed that there was not a public blowing-off②, but we believed that he had gone on to prepare for Miss Emily's coming, or to give her a chance to get rid of the cousins. (By that time it was a cabal③, and we were all Miss Emily's allies to help circumvent the cousins.) Sure enough, after another week they departed. And, as we had expected all along, within three days Homer Barren was back in town. A neighbor saw the Negro man admit him at the kitchen door at dusk one evening.

---

① Episopal: of the Anglican Church, a Protestant sect of the Christian Church
② a public blowing-off: a big sensation
③ cabal: a group of people who carry on secret intrigue

And that was the last we saw of Homer Barren. And of Miss Emily for some time. The Negro man went in and out with the market basket, but the front door remained closed. Now and then we would see her at a window for a moment, as the men did that night when they sprinkled the lime, but for almost six months she did not appear on the streets. Then we knew that this was to be expected too; as if that quality of her father which had thwarted her woman's life so many times had been too virulent and too furious to die.

When we next saw Miss Emily, she had grown fat and her hair was turning gray. During the next few years it grew grayer and grayer until it attained an even pepper-and-salt iron-gray, when it ceased turning. Up to the day of her death at seventy-four it was still that vigorous iron-gray, like the hair of an active man.

From that time on her front door remained closed, save for a period of six or seven years, when she was about forty, during which she gave lessons in china-painting. She fitted up a studio in one of the downstairs rooms, where the daughters and granddaughters of Colonel Sartoris' contemporaries were sent to her with the same regularity and in the same spirit that they were sent to church on Sundays with a twenty-five-cent piece for the collection plate①. Meanwhile her taxes had been remitted.

Then the newer generation became the backbone and the spirit of the town, and the painting pupils grew up and fell away and did not send their children to her with boxes of color and tedious brushes and pictures cut from the ladies' magazines. The front door closed upon the last one and remained closed for good. When the town got free postal delivery, Miss Emily alone refused to let them fasten the metal numbers above her door and attach a mailbox to it. She would not listen to them.

Daily, monthly, yearly we watched the Negro grow grayer and more stooped, going in and out with the market basket. Each December we sent her a tax notice, which would be returned by the post office a week later, unclaimed. Now and then we would see her in one of the downstairs windows—she had evidently shut up the top floor of the house—like the carven torso of an idol in a niche, looking or not looking at us, we could never tell which. Thus she passed from generation to generation—dear, inescapable, impervious, tranquil, and perverse.

And so she died. Fell ill in the house filled with dust and shadows, with only a doddering Negro man to wait on her. We did not even know she was sick; we had long since given up trying to get any information from the Negro. He talked to no one, probably not even to her, for his voice had grown harsh and rusty, as if from disuse.

She died in one of the downstairs rooms, in a heavy walnut bed with a curtain, her gray head propped on a pillow yellow and moldy with age and lack of sunlight.

V

The Negro met the first of the ladies at the front door and let them in, with their hushed,

---

① the collection plate: the plate used to collect money during a church service sibilant voices and their quick, curious glances, and then he disappeared. He walked right through the house and out the back and was not seen again.

The two female cousins came at once. They held the funeral on the second day, with the town coming to look at Miss Emily beneath a mass of bought flowers, with the crayon face of her father musing profoundly above the bier and the ladies sibilant and macabre①; and the very old men—some in their brushed Confederate uniforms—on the porch and the lawn, talking of Miss Emily as if she had been a contemporary of theirs, believing that they had danced with her and courted her perhaps, confusing time with its mathematical progression, as the old do, to whom all the past is not a diminishing road but, instead, a huge meadow which no winter ever quite touches, divided from them now by the narrow bottleneck② of the most recent decade of years.

Already we knew that there was one room in that region above stairs which no one had seen in forty years, and which would have to be forced. They waited until Miss Emily was decently in the ground before they opened it.

The violence of breaking down the door seemed to fill this room with pervading dust. A thin, acrid pall as of the tomb seemed to lie everywhere upon this room decked and furnished as for a bridal: upon the valance curtains③ of faded rose color, upon the rose-shaded lights, upon the dressing table, upon the delicate array of crystal and the man's toilet things backed with tarnished silver, silver so tarnished that the monogram④ was obscured. Among them lay collar and tie, as if they had just been removed, which, lifted, left upon the surface a pale crescent in the dust. Upon a chair hung the suit, carefully folded; beneath it the two mute shoes and the discarded socks.

The man himself lay in the bed.

For a long while we just stood there, looking down at the profound and fleshless grin. The body had apparently once lain in the attitude of an embrace, but now the long sleep that outlasts love, that conquers even the grimace of love⑤, had cuckolded him⑥. What was left of him, rotted beneath what was left of the nightshirt, had become inextricable from the bed in which he lay; and upon him and upon the pillow beside him lay that even coating of the patient and biding dust.

Then we noticed that in the second pillow was the indentation of a head. One of us lifted something from it, and leaning forward, that faint and invisible dust dry and acrid in the

---

① the ladies sibilant and macabre: the ladies whispering about the death
② bottleneck: a short, narrow passage; here it refers to something that connects the past and the future
③ valance curtains: short curtains around the frame of a bed
④ monogram: a person's initials combined in one design
⑤ grimace of love: pretended and false love
⑥ cuckolded him: made him the man whose wife has continued adultery

nostrils, we saw a long strand of iron-gray hair.

Study Questions:

1. What is meaningful in the final detail that the strand of hair on the second pillow is *iron-gray*?

2. Who is the unnamed narrator? For whom does he profess to be speaking?

3. Why does "A Rose for Emily" seem better told from his point of view than if it were told from the point of view of the main character?

4. What foreshadowings of the discovery of the body of Homer Barren are given earlier in the story? Share your experience in reading "A Rose for Emily" : Did the foreshadowings give away the ending for you? Did they heighten your interest?

5. What contrasts does the narrator draw between changing reality and Emily's refusal or inability to recognize change?

6. How do the character and background of Emily Grierson differ from those of Homer Barron? What general observations about the society that Faulkner depicts can be made from his portraits of these two characters and from his account of life in this one Mississippi town?

7. Does the story seem to you totally grim, or do you find any humor in it?

8. What do you infer to be the author's attitude toward Emily Grierson? Is she simply a murderous madwoman? Why do you suppose Faulkner calls his story "A Rose ..."?

The Tell-Tale Heart (1843, 1850)

Edgar Allan Poe

True!—nervous—very, very dreadfully nervous I had been and am; but why will you say that I am mad? The disease had sharpened my senses—not destroyed—not dulled them. Above all was the sense of hearing acute. I heard all things in the heaven and in the earth. I heard many things in hell. How, then, am I mad? Hearken! and observe how healthily—how calmly I can tell you the whole story.

It is impossible to say how first the idea entered my brain; but once conceived, it haunted me day and night. Object there was none. Passion there was none. I loved the old man. He had never wronged me. He had never given me insult. For his gold I had no desire. I think it was his eye! yes, it was this! One of his eyes resembled that of a vulture—a pale blue eye, with a film over it. Whenever it fell upon me, my blood ran cold; and so by degrees—very gradually—I made up my mind to take the life of the old man, and thus rid myself of the eye for ever.

Now this is the point. You fancy me mad. Madmen know nothing. But you should have seen me. You should have seen how wisely I proceeded—with what caution—with what foresight—with what dissimulation I went to work! I was never kinder to the old man than during the whole week before I killed him. And every night, about midnight, I turned the latch of his door and opened it—oh, so gently! And then, when I had made an opening sufficient for my head, I put in a dark lantern, all closed, closed, so that no light shone out, and then I thrust in my head. Oh, you would have laughed to see how cunningly I thrust it in! I moved it slowly—very, very slowly, so that I might not disturb the old man's sleep. It took me an hour to place my whole head within the opening so far that I could see him as he lay upon his bed. Ha!—would a madman have been so wise as this? And then, when my head was well in the room, I undid the lantern cautiously—oh, so cautiously—cautiously (for the hinges creaked)—I undid it just so much that a single thin ray fell upon the vulture eye. And this I did for seven long nights—every night just at midnight—but I found the eye always closed; and so it was impossible to do the work; for it was not the old man who vexed me, but his Evil Eye. And every morning, when the day broke, I went boldly into the chamber, and spoke courageously to him, calling him by name in a hearty tone, and inquiring how he had passed the night. So you see he would have been a very profound old man, indeed, to suspect that every night, just at twelve, I looked in upon him while he slept.

Upon the eighth night I was more than usually cautious in opening the door. A watch's minute hand moves more quickly than did mine. Never before that night had I felt the extent of my own powers—of my sagacity. I could scarcely contain my feelings of triumph. To think that there I was, opening the door, little by little, and he not even to dream of my secret deeds or thoughts. I fairly chuckled at the idea; and perhaps he heard me; for he moved on the bed suddenly, as if startled. Now you may think that I drew back—but no. His room was as black as pitch with the thick darkness (for the shutters were close fastened, through fear of robbers), and so I knew that he could not see the opening of the door, and I kept pushing it on steadily, steadily.

I had my head in, and was about to open the lantern, when my thumb slipped upon the tin fastening, and the old man sprang up in the bed, crying out—"Who's there?"

I kept quite still and said nothing. For a whole hour I did not move a muscle, and in the meantime I did not hear him lie down. He was still sitting up in the bed, listening;—just as I have done, night after night, hearkening to the death watches① in the wall.

Presently I heard a slight groan, and I knew it was the groan of mortal terror. It was not a groan of pain or of grief—oh, no!—it was the low stifled sound that arises from the bottom of the soul when overcharged with awe. I knew the sound very well. Many a night, just at midnight, when all the world slept, it has welled up from my own bosom, deepening, with its dreadful echo, the terrors that distracted me. I say I knew it well. I knew what the old man felt, and pitied him, although I chuckled at heart. I knew that he had been lying awake ever

---

① death watches: beetles that infest timbers, whose clicking sound was thought to be an omen of death

since the first slight noise, when he had turned in the bed. His fears had been ever since growing upon him. He had been trying to fancy them causeless, but could not. He had been saying to himself—"It is nothing but the wind in the chimney—it is only a mouse crossing the floor," or "it is merely a cricket which has made a single chirp." Yes, he had been trying to comfort himself with these suppositions; but he had found all in vain. All in vain; because Death, in approaching him, had stalked with his black shadow before him, and enveloped the victim. And it was the mournful influence of the unperceived shadow that caused him to feel—although he neither saw nor heard—to feel the presence of my head within the room.

When I had waited a long time, very patiently, without hearing him lie down, I resolved to open a little—a very, very little crevice in the lantern. So I opened it—you cannot imagine how stealthily, stealthily—until, at length, a single dim ray, like the thread of the spider, shot from out the crevice and fell upon the vulture eye.

It was open—wide, wide open—and I grew furious as I gazed upon it. I saw it with perfect distinctness—all a dull blue, with a hideous veil over it that chilled the very marrow in my bones; but I could see nothing else of the old man's face or person: for I had directed the ray as if by instinct, precisely upon the damned spot.

And now have I not told you that what you mistake for madness is but over-acuteness of the senses?—now, I say, there came to my ears a low, dull, quick sound, such as a watch makes when enveloped in cotton. I knew that sound well, too. It was the beating of the old man's heart. It increased my fury, as the beating of a drum stimulates the soldier into courage.

But even yet I refrained and kept still. I scarcely breathed. I held the lantern motionless. I tried how steadily I could maintain the ray upon the eye. Meantime the hellish tattoo of the heart increased. It grew quicker and quicker, and louder and louder every instant. The old man's terror must have been extreme! It grew louder, I say, louder every moment!—do you mark me well? I have told you that I am nervous: so I am. And now at the dead hour of the night, amid the dreadful silence of that old house, so strange a noise as this excited me to uncontrollable terror. Yet, for some minutes longer I refrained and stood still. But the beating grew louder, louder! I thought the heart must burst. And now a new anxiety seized me—the sound would be heard by a neighbor! The old man's hour had come! With a loud yell, I threw open the lantern and leaped into the room. He shrieked once—once only. In an instant I dragged him to the floor, and pulled the heavy bed over him. I then smiled gaily, to find the deed so far done. But, for many minutes, the heart beat on with a muffled sound. This, however, did not vex me; it would not be heard through the wall. At length it ceased. The old man was dead. I removed the bed and examined the corpse. Yes, he was stone, stone dead. I placed my hand upon the heart and held it there many minutes. There was no pulsation. He was stone dead. His eye would trouble me no more.

If still you think me mad, you will think so no longer when I describe the wise precautions

I took for the concealment of the body. The night waned, and I worked hastily, but in silence. First of all I dismembered the corpse. I cut off the head and the arms and the legs.

I then took up three planks from the flooring of the chamber, and deposited all between the scantlings. I then replaced the boards so cleverly, so cunningly, that no human eye—not even his—could have detected anything wrong. There was nothing to wash out—no stain of any kind—no blood-spot whatever. I had been too wary for that. A tub had caught all—ha! ha!

When I had made an end of these labors, it was four o'clock—still dark as midnight. As the bell sounded the hour, there came a knocking at the street door. I went down to open it with a light heart,—for what had I now to fear? There entered three men, who introduced themselves, with perfect suavity, as officers of the police. A shriek had been heard by a neighbor during the night; suspicion of foul play had been aroused; information had been lodged at the police office, and they (the officers) had been deputed to search the premises.

I smiled,—for what had I to fear? I bade the gentlemen welcome. The shriek, I said, was my own in a dream. The old man, I mentioned, was absent in the country. I took my visitors all over the house. I bade them search—search well. I led them, at length, to his chamber. I showed them his treasures, secure, undisturbed. In the enthusiasm of my confidence, I brought chairs into the room, and desired them *here* to rest from their fatigues, while I myself, in the wild audacity of my perfect triumph, placed my own seat upon the very spot beneath which reposed the corpse of the victim.

The officers were satisfied. My manner had convinced them. I was singularly at ease. They sat, and while I answered cheerily, they chatted of familiar things. But, ere long, I felt myself getting pale and wished them gone. My head ached, and I fancied a ringing in my ears: but still they sat and still chatted. The ringing became more distinct:—it continued and became more distinct: I talked more freely to get rid of the feeling: but it continued and gained definitiveness—until, at length, I found that the noise was *not* within my ears.

No doubt I now grew very pale:—but I talked more fluently, and with a heightened voice. Yet the sound increased—and what could I do? It was a low, dull, quick sound—much such a sound as a watch makes when enveloped in cotton. I gasped for breath—and yet the officers heard it not. I talked more quickly—more vehemently; but the noise steadily increased. I arose and argued about trifles, in a high key and with violent gesticulations; but the noise steadily increased. *Why would* they not be gone? I paced the floor to and fro with heavy strides, as if excited to fury by the observations of the men—but the noise steadily increased. Oh God! what *could* I do? I foamed—I raved—I swore! I swung the chair upon which I had been sitting, and grated it upon the boards, but the noise arose over all and continually increased. It grew louder—louder—*louder*! And still the men chatted pleasantly, and smiled. Was it possible they heard not? Almighty God!—no, no! They heard!—they suspected!—they *knew*!—they were making a mockery of my horror!—this I thought, and this I think. But anything was better than this agony! Anything was more tolerable than this derision! I could bear those hypocritical smiles no longer! I felt that I must scream or die!—and now—again!—hark! louder! louder! louder! Louder!—

"Villains!" I shrieked, "dissemble no more! I admit the deed!—tear up the planks!—here, here!—it is the beating of his hideous heart!"

Study Questions:

1. From what point of view is Poe's story told? Why is this point of view particularly effective for "The Tell-Tale Heart"?

2. Point out details in the story that identify its speaker as an unreliable narrator.

3. What do we know about the old man in the story? What motivates the narrator to kill him?

4. In spite of all his precautions, the narrator does not commit the perfect crime. What trips him up?

5. How do you account for the police officers' chatting calmly with the murderer instead of reacting to the sound that stirs the murderer into a frenzy?

[Reading Critically]

How Does Point of View Shape a Story?

The point of view from which a narrative work is told does not merely affect the story; it is an important part of the story. From the first sentence till the final word, the point of view shapes what the reader experiences in a work of fiction.

Often the point of view also demonstrates how well readers will understand a story's theme. A third-person omniscient point of view, for example, may give the readers a sense of authority and stability that makes the narrative seem reliable. A first-person narrator, however, often suggests a certain bias, especially when the narrator describes events in which he or she played a part. In such cases the narrator sometimes has an obvious interest in the audience's accepting his or her particular version of the story as truth.

In analyzing, a story always determines the point of view from which it is narrated. If the tale is told by a participant in the action, question the speaker's motivation. What is the speaker's main reason for telling the story? Does he or she have something to gain by the version of the facts presented? Sometimes the narrator's special point of view greatly enriches a story that might not seem as memorable from another narrative angle. Do we gain something from the speaker's perspective we might not discover elsewhere? Understanding the limits and rewards of a narrator's point of view is a key to interpreting everything a story says.

5. Tone and Style

In many Victorian novels it was customary for some commentator, presumably the author, to interrupt the story from time to time, remarking upon the action, offering philosophical asides, or explaining the procedures to be followed in telling the story. For example,

> Two hours later, Dorothea was seated in an inner room or boudoir of a handsome apartment in the Via Sistina. I am sorry to add that she was sobbing bitterly ...
>
> —George Eliot, *Middlemarch*

> But let the gentle-hearted reader be under no apprehension whatsoever. It is not destined that Eleanor shall marry Mr. Slope or Bertie Stanhope.
>
> —Anthony Trollope, *Barchester Towers*

> And, as we bring our characters forward, I will ask leave, as a man and a brother, not only to introduce, but occasionally step down from the platform, and talk about them: if they are good and kindly, to love them and shake them by the hand; if they are silly, to laugh at them confidentially in the reader's sleeve; if they are wicked and heartless, to abuse them in the strongest terms which politeness admits of.
>
> —William Makepeace Thackeray, *Vanity Fair*

Of course, the voice of this commentator was not identical with that of the "real life" author—the one toiling over an ink pot, worrying about publication deadlines and whether the rent would be paid. At times the living author might have been far different in personality from that usually wise and cheerful intruder who kept addressing the readers of the book. Much of the time, to be sure, the author probably agreed with whatever attitudes his alter ego expressed. But, in effect, the author created the character of a commentator to speak for him and throughout the novel artfully sustained that character's voice.

Such intrusions, although sometimes useful to the "real" author and enjoyable to the readers, are today rare. Modern storytellers, carefully keeping out of sight, seldom comment on their plots and characters. Apparently they agree with Anton Chekhov that a writer should not judge the characters but should serve as their "impartial witness". And yet, no less definitely than Victorian novelists who introduced commentators, writers of effective stories no doubt have feelings toward their characters and events. The authors presumably care about these imaginary people and, in order for the story to grasp and sustain our interest, have to make us see these people in such a way that we, too, will care about them. When at the beginning of the short story, "In Exile", Chekhov introduces us to a character, he does so with a description that arouses sympathy:

> The Tartar was worn out and ill, and wrapping himself in his rags, he talked about how good it was in the province of Simbirsk, and what a beautiful and clever wife he had left at home. He was not more than twenty-five, and in the firelight his pale, sickly face and woebegone expression made him seem like a boy.

Other than the comparison of the Tartar to a child, the details in this passage seem mostly factual: the young man's illness, ragged clothes, facial expression, and topics of conversation. But these details form a portrait that stirs pity. By his selection of these imaginary details out of countless others that he might have included, Chekhov firmly directs our feelings about the Tartar, so miserable and pathetic in his sickness and his homesickness. We cannot know, of course, exactly what the living Chekhov felt; but at least we can be sure that we are supposed to share the compassion and tenderness of the narrator—Chekhov's impartial (but human) witness.

Not only the author's choice of details may lead us to infer his or her attitude, but also choice of characters, events, and situations, and choice of words. When the narrator of Joseph Conrad's *Heart of Darkness* comes upon an African outpost littered with abandoned machines and notices "a boiler wallowing in the grass", the exact word *wallowing* conveys an attitude: That there is something swinish about this scene of careless waste. Whatever leads us to infer the author's attitude is commonly called tone. Like a tone of voice, the tone of a story may communicate amusement, anger, affection, sorrow, contempt. It implies the feelings of the author, so far as we can sense them. Those feelings may be similar to feelings expressed by the narrator of the story (or by any character), but sometimes they may be dissimilar, even sharply opposed. The characters in a story may regard an event as sad, but we sense that the author regards it as funny. To understand the tone of a story, then, is to understand some attitude more fundamental to the story than whatever attitude the characters explicitly declare.

The tone of a story, like a tone of voice, may convey not simply one attitude, but a medley. Often the tone of a literary story will be too rich and complicated to sum up in one or two words. But to try to describe the tone of such a story may be a useful way to penetrate to its center and to grasp the whole of it.

One of the clearest indications of the tone of a story is the style in which it is written. In general, style refers to the individual traits or characteristics of a piece of writing: to a writer's particular ways of managing words that we come to recognize as habitual or customary. A distinctive style marks the work of a fine writer: We can tell his or her work from that of anyone else. From one story to another, however, the writer may fittingly change style; and in some stories, style may be altered meaningful as the story goes along. In his novel *As I Lay Dying*, William Faulkner changes narrators with every chapter, and he distinguishes the narrators one from another by giving each an individual style or manner of speaking. Though each narrator has his or her own style, the book as a whole demonstrates Faulkner's style as well. For instance, one chapter is written from the point of view of a small boy, Vardaman Bundren, member of a family of poor Mississippi tenant farmers, whose view of a horse in a barn reads like this:

> *It is as though the dark were resolving him out of his integrity, into an unrelated scattering of components—snuffings and stampings; smells of cooling flesh and ammoniac hair; an illusion of a coordinated whole of splotched hide and strong bones within which, detached and secret and familiar, an is different from my is.*

How can a small boy unaccustomed to libraries use words like *integrity*, *components*, *illusion*, and *coordinated*? Elsewhere in the story, Vardaman says aloud, with no trace of literacy, "Hit was a-laying right there on the ground." Apparently, in the passage it is not the voice of the boy that we are hearing, but something resembling the voice of William Faulkner, elevated and passionate, expressing the boy's thoughts in a style that admits Faulknerian words.

Usually, style indicates a mode of expression: the language a writer uses. In this sense, the notion of **style** includes such traits as the length and complexity of sentences, and diction, or choice of words: abstract or concrete, bookish ("unrelated scattering of components") or close to speech ("Hit was a-laying right there on the ground"). Involved in the idea of style, too, is any habitual use of imagery, patterns of sound, figures of speech, or other devices.

More recently, several writers of realistic fiction, called minimalists—Ann Beattie, Raymond Carver, Bobbie Ann Mason—have written with a flat, laid-back, unemotional tone, in an appropriately bare, unadorned style. Minimalists seem to give nothing but facts drawn from ordinary life, sometimes in picayune detail. Here is a sample passage, from Raymond Carver's story "A Small, Good Thing":

> She pulled into the driveway and cut the engine. She closed her eyes and leaned her head against the wheel for a minute. She listened to the ticking sounds the engine made as it began to cool. Then she got out of the car. She could hear the dog barking inside the house. She went to the front door, which was unlocked. She went inside and turned on lights and put on a kettle of water for tea. She opened some dog food and fed Slug on the back porch. The dog ate in hungry little smacks. It kept running into the kitchen to see that she was going to stay.

Explicit feeling and showy language are kept at a minimum here. Taken out of context, this description may strike you as banal, as if the writer himself was bored; but it works effectively as a part of Carver's entire story. As in all good writing, the style here seems a faithful mirror of what is said in it.

To see what style means, compare the stories in this chapter by William Faulkner ("Barn Burning") and by Ernest Hemingway ("A Clean, Well-Lighted Place"). Faulkner frequently falls into a style in which a statement, as soon as uttered, is followed by another statement expressing the idea in a more emphatic way. Sentences are interrupted with parenthetical elements (asides, like this) thrust into them unexpectedly. At times, Faulkner writes of seemingly ordinary matters as if giving a speech in a towering passion. Here, from "Barn Burning", is a description of how a boy's father delivers a rug:

> "Don't you want me to help?" he whispered. His father did not answer and now he heard again that stiff foot striking the hollow portico with that wooden and clocklike deliberation, that outrageous overstatement of the weight it carried. The rug, hunched, not flung (the boy could tell that even in the darkness) from his father's shoulder struck the angle of wall and floor with a sound unbelievably loud, thunderous, then the foot again, unhurried and enormous; a light came on in the house and the boy sat, tense, breathing steadily and quietly and just a little fast, though the foot itself did not increase its beat at all, descending the steps now; now the boy could see him.

Faulkner is not merely indulging in language for its own sake. As you will find when you read the whole story, this rug delivery is vital to the story, and so too is the father's profound defiance—indicated by his walk. By devices of style—by metaphor and simile ("wooden and clocklike"), by exact qualification ("not flung"), by emphatic adjectives ("loud, thunderous")—Faulkner is carefully placing his emphases. By the words he selects to describe the father's stride, Faulkner directs how we feel toward the man and perhaps also indicates his own wondering but skeptical attitude toward a character whose very footfall is "outrageous" and "enormous". (Fond of long sentences like the last one in the quoted passage, Faulkner remarked that there are sentences that need to be written in the way a circus acrobat pedals a bicycle on a high wire: rapidly, so as not to fall off.)

Hemingway's famous style includes both short sentences and long, but when the sentences are long they tend to be relatively simple in construction. Hemingway likes long compound sentences (clause plus clause plus clause), sometimes joined with "ands". He interrupts such a sentence with a dependent clause or a parenthetical element much less frequently than Faulkner does. The effect is like listening to speech:

> In the day time the street was dusty, but at night the dew settled the dust and the old man liked to sit late because he was deaf and now at night it was quiet and he felt the difference.

Hemingway is a master of swift, terse dialogue, and often casts whole scenes in the form of conversation. As if he were a closemouthed speaker unwilling to let his feelings loose, the narrator of a Hemingway story often addresses us in understatement, implying greater depths of feeling than he puts into words. Read the following story and you will see that its style and tone cannot be separated.

A Clean, Well-Lighted Place (1933)

Ernest Hemingway

It was late and every one had left the café except an old man who sat in the shadow the leaves of the tree made against the electric light. In the day time the street was dusty, but at night the dew settled the dust and the old man liked to sit late because he was deaf and now at night it was quiet and he felt the difference. The two waiters inside the café knew that the old man was a little drunk, and while he was a good client they knew that if he became too drunk he would leave without paying, so they kept watch on him.

"Last week he tried to commit suicide," one waiter said.

"Why?"

"He was in despair."

"What about?"

"Nothing."

"How do you know it was nothing?"

"He has plenty of money."

They sat together at a table that was close against the wall near the door of the café and looked at the terrace where the tables were all empty except where the old man sat in the shadow of the leaves of the tree that moved slightly in the wind. A girl and a soldier went by in the street. The street light shone on the brass number on his collar. The girl wore no head covering and hurried beside him.

"The guard will pick him up," one waiter said.

"What does it matter if he gets what he's after?"

"He had better get off the street now. The guard will get him. They went by five minutes ago."

The old man sitting in the shadow rapped on his saucer with his glass. The younger waiter went over to him.

"What do you want?"

The old man looked at him. "Another brandy," he said.

"You'll be drunk," the waiter said. The old man looked at him. The waiter went away.

"He'll stay all night," he said to his colleague. "I'm sleepy now. I never get into bed before three o'clock. He should have killed himself last week."

The waiter took the brandy bottle and another saucer from the counter inside the café and marched out to the old man's table. He put down the saucer and poured the glass full of brandy.

"You should have killed yourself last week," he said to the deaf man. The old man motioned with his finger. "A little more," he said. The waiter poured on into the glass so that the brandy slopped over and ran down the stem into the top saucer of the pile. "Thank you," the old man said. The waiter took the bottle back inside the café. He sat down at the table with his colleague again.

"He's drunk now," he said.

"He's drunk every night."①

"What did he want to kill himself for?"

"How should I know?"

"How did he do it?"

"He hung himself with a rope."

"Who cut him down?"

"His niece."

"Why did they do it?"

---

① "He's drunk now," he said. "He's drunk every night.": The younger waiter perhaps says both these lines. A device of Hemingway's style is sometimes to have a character pause, then speak again—as often happens in actual speech. "*He must be eighty years old.*" "*Anyway I should say he was eighty*": Is this another instance of the same character's speaking twice? Clearly, it is the younger waiter who says the next line, "I wish he would go home."

"Fear for his soul."

"How much money has he got?"

"He's got plenty."

"He must be eighty years old."

"Anyway I should say he was eighty."

"I wish he would go home. I never get to bed before three o'clock. What kind of hour is that to go to bed?"

"He stays up because he likes it."

"He's lonely. I'm not lonely. I have a wife waiting in bed for me."

"He had a wife once too."

"A wife would be no good to him now."

"You can't tell. He might be better with a wife."

"His niece looks after him."

"I know. You said she cut him down."

"I wouldn't want to be that old. An old man is a nasty thing."

"Not always. This old man is clean. He drinks without spilling. Even now, drunk. Look at him."

"I don't want to look at him. I wish he would go home. He has no regard for those who must work."

The old man looked from his glass across the square, then over at the waiters.

"Another brandy," he said, pointing to his glass. The waiter who was in a hurry came over.

"Finished," he said, speaking with that omission of syntax stupid people employ when talking to drunken people or foreigners. "No more tonight. Close now."

"Another," said the old man.

"No. Finished." The waiter wiped the edge of the table with a towel and shook his head.

The old man stood up, slowly counted the saucers, took a leather coin purse from his pocket and paid for the drinks, leaving half a peseta tip.

The waiter watched him go down the street, a very old man walking unsteadily but with dignity.

"Why didn't you let him stay and drink?" the unhurried waiter asked. They were putting up the shutters. "It is not half past two."

"I want to go home to bed."

"What is an hour?"

"More to me than to him."

"An hour is the same."

"You talk like an old man yourself. He can buy a bottle and drink at home."

"It's not the same."

"No, it is not," agreed the waiter with a wife. He did not wish to be unjust. He was only in a hurry.

"And you? You have no fear of going home before the usual hour?"

"Are you trying to insult me?"

"No, hombre, only to make a joke."

"No," the waiter who was in a hurry said, rising from pulling down the metal shutters. "I have confidence. I am all confidence."

"You have youth, confidence, and a job," the older waiter said. "You have everything."

"And what do you lack?"

"Everything but work."

"You have everything I have."

"No. I have never had confidence and I am not young."

"Come on. Stop talking nonsense and lock up."

"I am of those who like to stay late at the café," the older waiter said. "With all those who do not want to go to bed. With all those who need a light for the night."

"I want to go home and into bed."

"We are of two different kinds," the older waiter said. He was not dressed to go home. "It is not only a question of youth and confidence although those things are very beautiful. Each night I am reluctant to close up because there may be someone who needs the café."

"Hombre, there are bodegas① open all night long."

"You do not understand. This is a clean and pleasant café. It is well lighted. The light is very good and also, now, there are shadows of the leaves."

"Good night," said the younger waiter.

"Good night," the other said. Turning off the electric light he continued the conversation with himself. It is the light of course but it is necessary that the place be clean and pleasant. You do not want music. Certainly you do not want music. Nor can you stand before a bar with dignity although that is all that is provided for these hours. What did he fear? It was not fear or dread. It was a nothing that he knew too well. It was all a nothing and a man was nothing too. It was only that and light was all it needed and a certain cleanness and order. Some lived in it and never felt it but he knew it all was nada y pues nada y nada y pues nada② Our nada who art in nada, nada be thy name thy kingdom nada thy will be nada in nada as it is in nada. Give us this nada our daily nada and nada us our nada as we nada our nadas and nada us not into nada but deliver us from nada; pues nada. Hail nothing full of nothing, nothing is with thee. He

---

① bodegas: wine shops

② nada y pues .... nada: nothing and then nothing and nothing and then nothing

smiled and stood before a bar with a shining steam pressure coffee machine.

"What's yours?" asked the barman.

"Nada."

"Otro loco más①," said the barman and turned away.

"A little cup," said the waiter.

The barman poured it for him.

"The light is very bright and pleasant but the bar is unpolished," the waiter said.

The barman looked at him but did not answer. It was too late at night for conversation.

"You want another copita②?" the barman asked.

"No, thank you," said the waiter and went out. He disliked bars and bodegas. A clean, well-lighted café was a very different thing. Now, without thinking further, he would go home to his room. He would lie in the bed and finally, with daylight, he would go to sleep. After all, he said to himself, it is probably only insomnia. Many must have it.

Study Questions:

1. What besides insomnia makes the older waiter reluctant to go to bed? Comment especially on his meditation with its nada refrain. Why does he so well understand the old man's need for a café? What does the café represent for the two of them?

2. Compare the younger waiter and the older waiter in their attitudes toward the old man. Whose attitude do you take to be closer to that of the author? Even though Hemingway does not editorially state his own feelings, how does he make them clear to us?

3. Point out sentences that establish the style of the story. What is distinctive in them? What repetitions of words or phrases seem particularly effective? Does Hemingway seem to favor a simple or an erudite vocabulary?

4. What is the story's point of view? Discuss its appropriateness.

Barn Burning③ (1939)

William Faulkner

The store in which the Justice of the Peace's court was sitting smelled of cheese. The boy, crouched on his nail keg at the back of the crowded room, knew he smelled cheese, and more: from where he sat he could see the ranked shelves close-packed with the solid, squat, dynamic shapes of tin cans whose labels his stomach read, not from the lettering which meant nothing to

---

① Otro loco más: another lunatic

② copita: little cup

③ Faulkner's "Barn Burning" is among his many contributions to the history of Yoknapatawpha, an imaginary Mississippi county in which the Sartorises and the de Spains are landed aristocrats living by a code of honor and the Snopeses—most of them—shiftless ne'er-do-wells.

his mind but from the scarlet devils and the silver curve of fish—this, the cheese which he knew he smelled and the hermetic meat① which his intestines believed he smelled coming in intermittent gusts momentary and brief between the other constant one, the smell and sense just a little of fear because mostly of despair and grief, the old fierce pull of blood. He could not see the table where the Justice sat and before which his father and his father's enemy (our *enemy* he thought in that despair; *ourn! mine and hisn both! He's my father!*) stood, but he could hear them, the two of them that is, because his father had said no word yet:

"But what proof have you, Mr. Harris?"

"I told you. The hog got into my corn. I caught it up and sent it back to him. He had no fence that would hold it. I told him so, warned him. The next time I put the hog in my pen. When he came to get it I gave him enough wire to patch up his pen. The next time I put the hog up and kept it. I rode down to his house and saw the wire I gave him still rolled on to the spool in his yard. I told him he could have the hog when he paid me a dollar pound fee. That evening a nigger came with the dollar and got the hog. He was a strange nigger. He said, 'He say to tell you wood and hay kin burn.' I said, 'What?' 'That whut he say to tell you,' the nigger said. 'Wood and hay kin burn.' That night my barn burned. I got the stock out but I lost the barn."

"Where's the nigger? Have you got him?"

"He was a strange nigger, I tell you. I don't know what became of him."

"But that's not proof. Don't you see that's not proof?"

"Get that boy up here. He knows." For a moment the boy thought too that the man meant his older brother until Harris said, "Not him. The little one. The boy," and, crouching, small for his age, small and wiry like his father, in patched and faded jeans even too small for him, with straight, uncombed, brown hair and eyes gray and wild as storm scud, he saw the men between himself and the table part and become a lane of grim faces, at the end of which he saw the Justice, a shabby, collarless, graying man in spectacles, beckoning him. He felt no floor under his bare feet; he seemed to walk beneath the palpable weight of the grim turning faces. His father, still in his black Sunday coat donned not for the trial but for the moving, did not even look at him. *He aims far me to lie*, he thought, again with that frantic grief and despair. *And I will have to do hit.*

"What's your name, boy?" the Justice said.

"Colonel Sartoris② Snopes," the boy whispered.

"Hey?" the Justice said. "Talk louder. Colonel Sartoris? I reckon anybody named for Colonel Sartoris in this country can't help but tell the truth, can they?" The boy said nothing.

---

① hermetic meat: canned meat

② Colonel Sartoris: a famous man in Faulkner's imaginary Jefferson town, who is an officer from the South in the Civil War

Enemy! Enemy! he thought; for a moment he could not even see, could not see that the Justice's face was kindly nor discern that his voice was troubled when he spoke to the man named Harris: "Do you want me to question this boy?" But he could hear, and during those subsequent long seconds while there was absolutely no sound in the crowded little room save that of quiet and intent breathing it was as if he had swung outward at the end of a grape vine, over a ravine, and at the top of the swing had been caught in a prolonged instant of mesmerized gravity, weightless in time.

"No!" Harris said violently, explosively. "Damnation! Send him out of here!" Now time, the fluid world, rushed beneath him again, the voices coming to him again through the smell of cheese and sealed meat, the fear and despair and the old grief of blood:

"This case is closed. I can't find against you, Snopes, but I can give you advice. Leave this country and don't come back to it."

His father spoke for the first time, his voice cold and harsh, level, without emphasis: "I aim to. I don't figure to stay in a country among people who ..." he said something unprintable and vile, addressed to no one.

"That'll do," the Justice said. "Take your wagon and get out of this country before dark. Case dismissed."

His father turned, and he followed the stiff black coat, the wiry figure walking a little stiffly from where a Confederate provost's man's musket ball had taken him in the heel on a stolen horse thirty years ago, followed the two backs now, since his older brother had appeared from somewhere in the crowd, no taller than the father but thicker, chewing tobacco steadily, between the two lines of grim-faced men and out of the store and across the worn gallery and down the sagging steps and among the dogs and half-grown boys in the mild May dust, where as he passed a voice hissed:

"Barn burner!"

Again he could not see, whirling; there was a face in a red haze, moonlike, bigger than the full moon, the owner of it half again his size, he leaping in the red haze toward the face, feeling no blow, feeling no shock when his head struck the earth, scrabbling up and leaping again, feeling no blow this time either and tasting no blood, scrabbling up to see the other boy in full flight and himself already leaping into pursuit as his father's hand jerked him back, the harsh, cold voice speaking above him: "Go get in the wagon."

It stood in a grove of locusts and mulberries across the road. His two hulking sisters in their Sunday dresses and his mother and her sister in calico and sun-bonnets were already in it, sitting on and among the sorry residue of the dozen and more movings which even the boy could remember—the battered stove, the broken beds and chairs, the clock inlaid with mother-of-pearl, which would not run, stopped at some fourteen minutes past two o'clock of a dead and forgotten day and time, which had been his mother's dowry. She was crying, though when she saw him she drew her sleeve across her face and began to descend from the wagon. " Get back," the father said.

"He's hurt. I got to get some water and wash his ..."

"Get back in the wagon," his father said. He got in too, over the tail-gate. His father mounted to the seat where the older brother already sat and struck the gaunt mules two savage blows with the peeled willow, but without heat. It was not even sadistic; it was exactly that same quality which in later years would cause his descendants to over-run the engine before putting a motor car into motion, striking and reining back in the same movement. The wagon went on, the store with its quiet crowd of grimly watching men dropped behind; a curve in the road hid it. *Forever* he thought. *Maybe he's done satisfied-now, now that he has ...* stopping himself, not to say it aloud even to himself. His mother's hand touched his shoulder.

"Does hit hurt?" she said.

"Naw," he said. "Hit don't hurt. Lemme be."

"Can't you wipe some of the blood off before hit dries?"

"I'll wash to-night," he said. "Lemme be, I tell you."

The wagon went on. He did not know where they were going. None of them ever did or ever asked, because it was always somewhere, always a house of sorts waiting for them a day or two days or even three days away. Likely his father had already arranged to make a crop on another farm before he ... Again he had to stop himself. He (the father) always did. There was something about his wolflike independence and even courage when the advantage was at least neutral which impressed strangers, as if they got from his latent ravening ferocity not so much a sense of dependability as a feeling that his ferocious conviction in the rightness of his own actions would be of advantage to all whose interest lay with his.

That night they camped, in a grove of oaks and beeches where a spring ran. The nights were still cool and they had a fire against it, of a rail lifted from a nearby fence and cut into lengths—a small fire, neat, niggard almost, a shrewd fire; such fires were his father's habit and custom always, even in freezing weather. Older, the boy might have remarked this and wondered why not a big one; why should not a man who had not only seen the waste and extravagance of war, but who had in his blood an inherent voracious prodigality with material not his own, have burned everything in sight? Then he might have gone a step farther and thought that that was the reason: that niggard blaze was the living fruit of nights passed during those four years in the woods hiding from all men, blue and gray[①], with his strings of horses (captured horses, he called them). And older still, he might have divined the true reason: that the element of fire spoke to some deep mainspring of his father's being, as the element of steel

---

① blue or gray: "blue" and "gray" refer to the color of uniforms dressed by the Union Army and the Confederate Army in the Civil War. Here it refers to the Union Army and the Confederate one.

or of powder spoke to other men, as the one weapon for the preservation of integrity, else breath were not worth the breathing, and hence to be regarded with respect and used with discretion.

But he did not think this now and he had seen those same niggard blazes all his life. He merely ate his supper beside it and was already half asleep over his iron plate when his father called him, and once more he followed the stiff back, the stiff and ruthless limp, up the slope and on to the starlit road where, turning, he could see his father against the stars but without face or depth—a shape black, flat, and bloodless as though cut from tin in the iron folds of the frockcoat which had not been made for him, the voice harsh like tin and without heat like tin:

"You were fixing to tell them. You would have told him."

He didn't answer. His father struck him with the flat of his hand on the side of the head, hard but without heat, exactly as he had struck the two mules at the store, exactly as he would strike either of them with any stick in order to kill a horse fly, his voice without heat or anger: "You're getting to be a man. You got to learn. You got to learn to stick to your own blood or you ain't going to have any blood to stick to you. Do you think either of them, any man there this morning, would? Don't you know all they wanted was a chance to get at me because they knew I had them beat? Eh?" Later, twenty years later, he was to tell himself, "If I had said they wanted only truth, justice, he would have hit me again." But now he said nothing. He was not crying. He just stood there. "Answer me," his father said.

"Yes," he whispered. His father turned.

"Get on to bed. We'll be there tomorrow."

Tomorrow they were there. In the early afternoon the wagon stopped before a paintless two-room house identical almost with the dozen others it had stopped before even in the boy's ten years, and again, as on the other dozen occasions, his mother and aunt got down and began to unload the wagon, although his two sisters and his father and brother had not moved.

"Likely hit ain't fitten for hawgs," one of the sisters said.

"Nevertheless, fit it will and you'll hog it and like it," his father said. "Get out of them chairs and help your Ma unload."

The two sisters got down, big, bovine, in a flutter of cheap ribbons; one of them drew from the jumbled wagon bed a battered lantern, the other a worn broom. His father handed the reins to the older son and began to climb stiffly over the wheel. "When they get unloaded, take the team to the barn and feed them." Then he said, and at first the boy thought he was still speaking to his brother: "Come with me."

"Me?" he said.

"Yes," his father said. "You."

"Abner," his mother said. His father paused and looked back—the harsh level stare beneath the shaggy, graying, irascible brows.

"I reckon I'll have a word with the man that aims to begin tomorrow owning me body and soul for the next eight months."

They went back up the road. A week ago—or before last night, that is—he would have asked where they were going, but not now. His father had struck him before last night but never before had he paused afterward to explain why; it was as if the blow and the following calm, outrageous voice still rang, repercussed, divulging nothing to him save the terrible handicap of being young, the light weight of his few years, just heavy enough to prevent his soaring free of the world as it seemed to be ordered but not heavy enough to keep him footed solid in it, to resist it and try to change the course of its events.

Presently he could see the grove of oaks and cedars and the other flowering trees and shrubs where the house would be, though not the house yet. They walked beside a fence massed with honeysuckle and Cherokee roses and came to a gate swinging open between two brick pillars, and now, beyond a sweep of drive, he saw the house for the first time and at that instant he forgot his father and the terror and despair both, and even when he remembered his father again (who had not stopped) the terror and despair did not return. Because, for all the twelve movings, they had sojourned until now in a poor country, a land of small farms and fields and houses, and he had never seen a house like this before. *Hit's big as a courthouse*, he thought quietly, with a surge of peace and joy whose reason he could not have thought into words, being too young for that: *They are safe from him. People whose lives are a part of this peace and dignity are beyond his touch, he no more to them than a buzzing wasp: capable of stinging for a little moment but that's all; the spell of this peace and dignity rendering even the barns and stable and cribs which belong to it impervious to the puny flames he might contrive* ... this, the peace and joy, ebbing for an instant as he looked again at the stiff black back, the stiff and implacable limp of the figure which was not dwarfed by the house, for the reason that it had never looked big anywhere and which now, against the serene columned backdrop, had more than ever that impervious quality of something cut ruthlessly from tin, depthless, as though, sidewise to the sun, it would cast no shadow. Watching him, the boy remarked the absolutely undeviating course which his father held and saw the stiff foot come squarely down in a pile of fresh droppings where a horse had stood in the drive and which his father could have avoided by a simple change of stride. But it ebbed only a moment, though he could not have thought this into words either, walking on in the spell of the house, which he could even want but without envy, without sorrow, certainly never with that ravening and jealous rage which unknown to him walked in the ironlike black coat before him: *Maybe he will feel it too. Maybe it will even change him now from what maybe he couldn't help but be.*

They crossed the portico. Now he could hear his father's stiff foot as it came down on the boards with clocklike finality, a sound out of all proportion to the displacement of the body it bore and which was not dwarfed either by the white door before it, as though it had attained to a sort of vicious and ravening minimum not to be dwarfed by anything—the flat, wide, black hat, the formal coat of broadcloth which had once been black but which had now that friction-glazed greenish cast of the bodies of old house flies, the lifted sleeve which was too large, the lifted hand like a curled claw. The door opened so promptly that the boy knew the Negro must have been watching them all the time, an old man with neat grizzled hair, in a linen jacket, who stood barring the door with his body, saying, "Wipe yo foots, white man, fo you come in here. Major ain't home nohow."

"Get out of my way, nigger," his father said, without heat too, flinging the door back and the Negro also and entering, his hat still on his head. And now the boy saw the prints of the stiff foot on the doorjamb and saw them appear on the pale rug behind the machinelike deliberation of the foot which seemed to bear (or transmit) twice the weight which the body compassed. The Negro was shouting "Miss Lula! Miss Lula!" somewhere behind them, then the boy, deluged as though by a warm wave by a suave turn of the carpeted stair and a pendant glitter of chandeliers and a mute gleam of gold frames, heard the swift feet and saw her too, a lady—perhaps he had never seen her like before either—in a gray, smooth gown with lace at the throat and an apron tied at the waist and the sleeves turned back, wiping cake or biscuit dough from her hands with a towel as she came up the hall, looking not at his father at all but at the tracks on the blond rug with an expression of incredulous amazement.

"I tried," the Negro cried. "I tole him to …"

"Will you please go away?" she said in a shaking voice. "Major de Spain is not at home. Will you please go away?"

His father had not spoken again. He did not speak again. He did not even look at her. He just stood stiff in the center of the rug, in his hat, the shaggy iron-gray brows twitching slightly above the pebble-colored eyes as he appeared to examine the house with brief deliberation. Then with the same deliberation he turned; the boy watched him pivot on the good leg and saw the stiff foot drag around the arc of the turning, leaving a final long and fading smear. His father never looked at it, he never once looked down at the rug. The Negro held the door. It closed behind them, upon the hysteric and indistinguishable woman-wail. His father stopped at the top of the steps and scraped his boot clean on the edge of it. At the gate he stopped again. He stood for a moment, planted stiffly on the stiff foot, looking back at the house. "Pretty and white, ain't it?" he said. "That's sweat. Nigger sweat. Maybe it ain't white enough yet to suit him. Maybe he wants to mix some white sweat with it."

Two hours later the boy was chopping wood behind the house within which his mother and aunt and the two sisters (the mother and aunt, not the two girls, he knew that; even at this distance and muffled by walls the flat loud voices of the two girls emanated an incorrigible idle inertia) were setting up the stove to prepare a meal, when he heard the hooves and saw the linen-clad man on a fine sorrel mare, whom he recognized even before he saw the rolled rug in front of the Negro youth following on a fat bay carriage horse—a suffused, angry face vanishing, still at full gallop, beyond the corner of the house where his father and brother were sitting in the two tilted chairs; and a moment later, almost before he could have put the axe down, he heard the hooves again and watched the sorrel mare go back out of the yard, already galloping again. Then his father began to shout one of the sisters' names, who presently emerged backward from the kitchen door dragging the rolled rug along the ground by one end while the other sister walked behind it.

"If you ain't going to tote, go on and set up the wash pot," the first said.

"You, Sarty!" the second shouted. "Set up the wash pot!" His father appeared at the door, framed against that shabbiness, as he had been against that other bland perfection, impervious to either, the mother's anxious face at his shoulder.

"Go on," the father said. "Pick it up." The two sisters stooped, broad, lethargic; stooping, they presented an incredible expanse of pale cloth and a flutter of tawdry ribbons.

"If I thought enough of a rug to have to git hit all the way from France I wouldn't keep hit where folks coming in would have to tromp on hit," the first said. They raised the rug.

"Abner," the mother said. "Let me do it."

"You go back and git dinner," his father said. "I'll tend to this."

From the woodpile through the rest of the afternoon the boy watched them, the rug spread flat in the dust beside the bubbling wash pot, the two sisters stooping over it with that profound and lethargic reluctance, while the father stood over them in turn, implacable and grim, driving them though never raising his voice again. He could smell the harsh homemade lye they were using; he saw his mother come to the door once and look toward them with an expression not anxious now but very like despair; he saw his father turn, and he fell to with the axe and saw from the corner of his eye his father raise from the ground a flattish fragment of field stone and examine it and return to the pot, and this time his mother actually spoke: "Abner. Abner. Please don't. Please, Abner."

Then he was done too. It was dusk; the whippoorwills had already begun. He could smell coffee from the room where they would presently eat the cold food remaining from the midafternoon meal, though when he entered the house he realized they were having coffee again probably because there was a fire on the hearth, before which the rug now lay spread over the backs of the two chairs. The tracks of his father's foot were gone. Where they had been were now long, water-cloudy scoriations resembling the sporadic course of a lilliputian mowing machine.

It still hung there while they ate the cold food and then went to bed, scattered without order or claim up and down the two rooms, his mother in one bed, where his father would later lie, the older brother in the other, himself, the aunt, and the two sisters on pallets on the floor. But his father was not in bed yet. The last thing the boy remembered was the depthless, harsh silhouette of the hat and coat bending over the rug and it seemed to him that he had not even closed his eyes when the silhouette was standing over him, the fire almost dead behind it, the stiff foot prodding him awake. "Catch up the mule," his father said.

When he returned with the mule his father was standing in the back door, the rolled rug over his shoulder. "Ain't you going to ride?" he said.

"No. Give me your foot."

He bent his knee into his father's hand, the wiry, surprising power flowed smoothly, rising, he rising with it, on to the mule's bare back (they had owned a saddle once; the boy could remember it though not when or where) and with the same effortlessness his father swung the rug up in front of him. Now in the starlight they retraced the afternoon's path, up the dusty road rife with honeysuckle, through the gate and up the black tunnel of the drive to the lightless house, where he sat on the mule and felt the rough warp of the rug drag across his thighs and vanish.

"Don't you want me to help?" he whispered. His father did not answer and now he heard again that stiff foot striking the hollow portico with that wooden and clocklike deliberation, that outrageous overstatement of the weight it carried. The rug, hunched, not flung (the boy could tell that even in the darkness) from his father's shoulder struck the angle of wall and floor with a sound unbelievably loud, thunderous, then the foot again, unhurried and enormous; a light came on in the house and the boy sat, tense, breathing steadily and quietly and just a little fast, though the foot itself did not increase its beat at all, descending the steps now; now the boy could see him.

"Don't you want to ride now?" he whispered. "We kin both ride now," the light within the house altering now, flaring up and sinking. *He's coming down the stairs now*, he thought. He had already ridden the mule up beside the horse block; presently his father was up behind him and he doubled the reins over and slashed the mule across the neck, but before the animal could begin to trot the hard, thin arm came around him, the hard, knotted hand jerking the mule back to a walk.

In the first red rays of the sun they were in the lot, putting plow gear on the mules. This time the sorrel mare was in the lot before he heard it at all, the rider collarless and even bareheaded, trembling, speaking in a shaking voice as the woman in the house had done, his father merely looking up once before stooping again to the hame he was buckling, so that the man on the mare spoke to his stooping back:

"You must realize you have ruined that rug. Wasn't there anybody here, any of your women ..." he ceased, shaking, the boy watching him, the older brother leaning now in the stable door, chewing, blinking slowly and steadily at nothing apparently. "It cost a hundred dollars. But you never had a hundred dollars. You never will. So I'm going to charge you twenty bushels of corn against your crop. I'll add it in your contract and when you come to the commissary you can sign it. That won't keep Mrs. de Spain quiet but maybe it will teach you to wipe your feet off before you enter her house again."

Then he was gone. The boy looked at his father, who still had not spoken or even looked up again, who was now adjusting the logger-head in the hame.

"Pap," he said. His father looked at him—the inscrutable face, the shaggy brows beneath where the gray eyes glinted coldly. Suddenly the boy went toward him, fast, stopping as suddenly. "You done the best you could!" he cried. "If he wanted hit done different why didn't he wait and tell you how? He won't git no twenty bushels! He won't git none! We'll gather hit and hide hit! I kin watch ..."

"Did you put the cutter back in that straight stock like I told you?"

"No, sir," he said.

"Then go do it."

That was Wednesday. During the rest of that week he worked steadily, at what was within his scope and some which was beyond it, with an industry that did not need to be driven nor even commanded twice; he had this from his mother, with the difference that some at least of what he did he liked to do, such as splitting wood with the half-size axe which his mother and aunt had earned, or saved money somehow, to present him with at Christmas. In company with the two older women (and on one afternoon, even one of the sisters), he built pens for the shoat and the cow which were a part of his father's contract with the landlord, and one afternoon, his father being absent, gone somewhere on one of the mules, he went to the field.

They were running a middle buster now, his brother holding the plow straight while he handled the reins, and walking beside the straining mule, the rich black soil shearing cool and damp against his bare ankles, he thought *Maybe this is the end of it. Maybe even that twenty bushels that seems hard to have to pay for just a rug will be a cheap price for him to stop forever and always from being what he used to be*; thinking, dreaming now, so that his brother had to speak sharply to him to mind the mule: *Maybe he even won't collect the twenty bushels. Maybe it will all add up and balance and vanish—corn, rug, fire; the terror and grief; the being pulled two ways like between two teams of horses—gone, done with for ever and ever.*

Then it was Saturday; he looked up from beneath the mule he was harnessing and saw his father in the black coat and hat. "Not that," his father said. "The wagon gear." And then, two hours later, sitting in the wagon bed behind his father and brother on the seat, the wagon accomplished a final curve, and he saw the weathered paintless store with its tattered tobacco- and patent-medicine posters and the tethered wagons and saddle animals below the gallery. He mounted the gnawed steps behind his father and brother, and there again was the lane of quiet, watching faces for the three of them to walk through. He saw the man in spectacles sitting at the plank table and he did not need to be told this was a Justice of the Peace; he sent one glare of fierce, exultant, partisan defiance at the man in collar and cravat now, whom he had seen but twice before in his life, and that on a galloping horse, who now wore on his face an expression not of rage but of amazed unbelief which the boy could not have known was at the incredible circumstance of being sued by one of his own tenants, and came and stood against his father and cried at the Justice: "He ain't done it! He ain't burnt …"

"Go back to the wagon," his father said.

"Burnt?" the Justice said. "Do I understand this rug was burned too?"

"Does anybody here claim it was?" his father said. "Go back to the wagon." But he did not, he merely retreated to the rear of the room, crowded as that other had been, but not to sit down this time, instead, to stand pressing among the motionless bodies, listening to the voices:

"And you claim twenty bushels of corn is too high for the damage you did to the rug?"

"He brought the rug to me and said he wanted the tracks washed out of it. I washed the tracks out and took the rug back to him."

"But you didn't carry the rug back to him in the same condition it was in before you made the tracks on it."

His father did not answer, and now for perhaps half a minute there was no sound at all save that of breathing, the faint, steady suspiration of complete and intent listening.

"You decline to answer that, Mr. Snopes?" Again his father did not answer. "I'm going to find against you, Mr. Snopes. I'm going to find that you were responsible for the injury to Major de Spain's rug and hold you liable for it. But twenty bushels of corn seems a little high for a man in your circumstances to have to pay. Major de Spain claims it cost a hundred dollars. October corn will be worth about fifty cents. I figure that if Major de Spain can stand a ninety-five dollar loss on something he paid cash for, you can stand a five-dollar loss you haven't earned yet. I hold you in damages to Major de Spain to the amount of ten bushels of corn over and above your contract with him, to be paid to him out of your crop at gathering time. Court adjourned."

It had taken no time hardly, the morning was but half begun. He thought they would return home and perhaps back to the field, since they were late, far behind all other farmers. But instead his father passed on behind the wagon, merely indicating with his hand for the older brother to follow with it, and crossed the road toward the blacksmith shop opposite, pressing on after his father, overtaking him, speaking, whispering up at the harsh, calm face beneath the weathered hat: "He won't git no ten bushels either. He won't git one. We'll …" until his father glanced for an instant down at him, the face absolutely calm, the grizzled eyebrows tangled above the cold eyes, the voice almost pleasant, almost gentle:

"You think so? Well, we'll wait till October anyway."

The matter of the wagon—the setting of a spoke or two and the tightening of the tires—did not take long either, the business of the tires accomplished by driving the wagon into the spring branch behind the shop and letting it stand there, the mules nuzzling into the water from time to time, and the boy on the seat with the idle reins, looking up the slope and through the sooty tunnel of the shed where the slow hammer rang and where his father sat on an upended cypress bolt, easily, either talking or listening, still sitting there when the boy brought the dripping wagon up out of the branch and halted it before the door.

"Take them on to the shade and hitch," his father said. He did so and returned. His father and the smith and a third man squatting on his heels inside the door were talking, about crops and animals; the boy, squatting too in the ammoniac dust and hoof-parings and scales of rust, heard his father tell a long and unhurried story out of the time before the birth of the older brother even when he had been a professional horsetrader. And then his father came up beside him where he stood before a tattered last year's circus poster on the other side of the store, gazing rapt and quiet at the scarlet horses, the incredible poisings and convulsions of tulle and tights and the painted leers of comedians, and said, "It's time to eat."

But not at home. Squatting beside his brother against the front wall, he watched his father emerge from the store and produce from a paper sack a segment of cheese and divide it carefully and deliberately into three with his pocket knife and produce crackers from the same sack. They all three squatted on the gallery and ate, slowly, without talking; then in the store again, they drank from a tin dipper tepid water smelling of the cedar bucket and of living beech trees. And still they did not go home. It was a horse lot this time, a tall rail fence upon and along which men stood and sat and out of which one by one horses were led, to be walked and trotted and then cantered back and forth along the road while the slow swapping and buying went on and the sun began to slant westward, they—the three of them—watching and listening, the older brother with his muddy eyes and his steady, inevitable tobacco, the father commenting now and then on certain of the animals, to no one in particular.

It was after sundown when they reached home. They ate supper by lamplight, then, sitting on the doorstep, the boy watched the night fully accomplish, listening to the whippoorwills and the frogs, when he heard his mother's voice: "Abner! No! No! Oh, God. Oh, God. Abner!" and he rose, whirled, and saw the altered light through the door where a candle stub now burned in a bottle neck on the table and his father, still in the hat and coat, at once formal and burlesque as though dressed carefully for some shabby and ceremonial violence, emptying the reservoir of the lamp back into the five-gallon kerosene can from which it had been filled, while the mother tugged at his arm until he shifted the lamp to the other hand and flung her back, not savagely or viciously, just hard, into the wall, her hands flung out against the wall for balance, her mouth open and in her face the same quality of hopeless despair as had been in her voice. Then his father saw him standing in the door.

"Go to the barn and get that can of oil we were oiling the wagon with," he said. The boy did not move. Then he could speak.

"What ..." he cried. "What are you ..."

"Go get that oil," his father said. "Go."

Then he was moving, running, outside the house, toward the stable: this the old habit, the old blood which he had not been permitted to choose for himself, which had been bequeathed him willy nilly and which had run for so long (and who knew where, battening on what of outrage and savagery and lust) before it came to him. *I could keep on*, he thought. *I could run on and on and never look back, never need to see his face again. Only I can't. I can't*, the rusted can in his hand now, the liquid sploshing in it as he ran back to the house and into it, into the sound of his mother's weeping in the next room, and handed the can to his father.

"Ain't you going to even send a nigger?" he cried. "At least you sent a nigger before!"

This time his father didn't strike him. The hand came even faster than the blow had, the same hand which had set the can on the table with almost excruciating care flashing from the can toward him too quick for him to follow it, gripping him by the back of his shirt and on to tiptoe before he had seen it quit the can, the face stooping at him in breathless and frozen ferocity, the cold, dead voice speaking over him to the older brother who leaned against the table, chewing with that steady, curious, sidewise motion of cows:

"Empty the can into the big one and go on. I'll catch up with you."

"Better tie him up to the bedpost," the brother said.

"Do like I told you," the father said. Then the boy was moving, his bunched shirt and the hard, bony hand between his shoulder-blades, his toes just touching the floor, across the room and into the other one, past the sisters sitting with spread heavy thighs in the two chairs over the cold hearth, and to where his mother and aunt sat side by side on the bed, the aunt's arm about his mother's shoulders.

"Hold him," the father said. The aunt made a startled movement. "Not you," the father said. "Lennie. Take hold of him. I want to see you do it." His mother took him by the wrist. "You'll hold him better than that. If he gets loose don't you know what he is going to do? He will go up yonder." He jerked his head toward the road. "Maybe I'd better tie him."

"I'll hold him," his mother whispered.

"See you do then." Then his father was gone, the stiff foot heavy and measured upon the boards, ceasing at last.

Then he began to struggle. His mother caught him in both arms, he jerking and wrenching at them. He would be stronger in the end, he knew that. But he had no time to wait for it. "Lemme go!" he cried. "I don't want to have to hit you!"

"Let him go!" the aunt said. "If he don't go, before God, I am going up there myself!"

"Don't you see I can't?" his mother cried. "Sarty! Sarty! No! No! Help me, Lizzie!"

Then he was free. His aunt grasped at him but it was too late. He whirled, running, his mother stumbled forward on to her knees behind him, crying to the nearer sister: "Catch him, Net! Catch him!" But that was too late too, the sister (the sisters were twins, born at the same time, yet either of them now gave the impression of being, encompassing as much living meat and volume and weight as any other two of the family) not yet having begun to rise from the chair, her head, face, alone merely turned, presenting to him in the flying instant an astonishing expanse of young female features untroubled by any surprise even, wearing only an expression of bovine interest. Then he was out of the room, out of the house, in the mild dust of the starlit road and the heavy rifeness of honeysuckle, the pale ribbon unspooling with terrific slowness under his running feet, reaching the gate at last and turning in, running, his heart and lungs drumming, on up the drive toward the lighted house, the lighted door. He did not knock, he burst in, sobbing for breath, incapable for the moment of speech; he saw the astonished face of the Negro in the linen jacket without knowing when the Negro had appeared.

"De Spain!" he cried, panted. "Where's ..." then he saw the white man too emerging from a white door down the hall. "Barn!" he cried. "Barn!"

"What?" the white man said. "Barn?"

"Yes!" the boy cried. "Barn!"

"Catch him!" the white man shouted.

But it was too late this time too. The Negro grasped his shirt, but the entire sleeve, rotten with washing, carried away, and he was out that door too and in the drive again, and had actually never ceased to run even while he was screaming into the white man's face.

Behind him the white man was shouting. "My horse! Fetch my horse!" and he thought for an instant of cutting across the park and climbing the fence into the road, but he did not know the park nor how the vine-massed fence might be and he dared not risk it. So he ran on down the drive, blood and breath roaring; presently he was in the road again though he could not see it. He could not hear either: the galloping mare was almost upon him before he heard her, and even then he held his course, as if the very urgency of his wild grief and need must in a moment more find him wings, waiting until the ultimate instant to hurl himself aside and into the weed-choked roadside ditch as the horse thundered past and on, for an instant in furious silhouette against the stars, the tranquil early summer night sky which, even before the shape of the horse and rider vanished, stained abruptly and violently upward: a long, swirling roar incredible and soundless, blotting the stars, and he springing up and into the road again, running again, knowing it was too late yet still running even after he heard the shot and an instant later, two shots, pausing now without knowing he had ceased to run, crying, "Pap! Pap!", running again before he knew he had begun to run, stumbling, tripping over something and scrabbling up again without ceasing to run, looking backward over his shoulder at the glare as he got up, running on among the invisible trees, panting, sobbing, "Father! Father!"

At midnight he was sitting on the crest of a hill. He did not know it was midnight and he did not know how far he had come. But there was no glare behind him now and he sat now, his back toward what he had called home for four days anyhow, his face toward the dark woods which he would enter when breath was strong again, small, shaking steadily in the chill darkness, hugging himself into the remainder of his thin, rotten shirt, the grief and despair now no longer terror and fear but just grief and despair. *Father. My father*, he thought. "He was brave!" he cried suddenly, aloud but not loud, no more than a whisper. "He was! He was in the war! He was in Colonel Sartoris' cav'ry!" not knowing that his father had gone to that war a private in the fine old European sense, wearing no uniform, admitting the authority of and giving fidelity to no man or army or flag, going to war as Malbrouck① himself did; for booty—it meant nothing and less than nothing to him if it were enemy booty or his own.

The slow constellations wheeled on. It would be dawn and then sun-up after a while and he would be hungry. But that would be tomorrow and now he was only cold, and walking would cure that. His breathing was easier now and he decided to get up and go on, and then he found that he had been asleep because he knew it was almost dawn, the night almost over. He could tell that from the whippoorwills. They were everywhere now among the dark trees below him, constant and inflectioned and ceaseless, so that, as the instant for giving over to the day birds drew nearer and nearer, there was no interval at all between them. He got up. He was a little stiff, but walking would cure that too as it would the cold, and soon there would be the sun. He went on down the hill, toward the dark woods within which the liquid silver voices of the birds called unceasing—the rapid and urgent beating of the urgent and quiring heart of the late spring night. He did not look back.

Study Questions:

1. After delivering his warning to Major de Spain, the boy Snopes does not actually witness what happens to his father and brother, nor what happens to the Major's barn. But what do you assume happens? What evidence is given in the story?

2. What do you understand is Faulkner's opinion of Abner Snopes? Make a guess, indicating details in the story that convey attitudes.

3. Which adjectives best describe the general tone of the story: calm, amused, disinterested, scornful, marveling, excited, impassioned? Point out passages that may be so described. What do you notice about the style in which these passages are written?

4. In tone and style, how does "Barn Burning" compare with Faulkner's story "A Rose for Emily"? To what do you attribute any differences?

5. Suppose that, instead of "Barn Burning", Faulkner had written another story told by Abner Snopes in the first person. Why would such a story need a style different from that of "Barn Burning"? (Suggestion: Notice Faulkner's descriptions of Abner Snopes' voice.)

6. Although "Barn Burning" takes place some thirty years after the Civil War, how does the war figure in it?

---

① Malbrouck: John Churchill, Duke of Marlborough (1650–1722), English general victorious in the Battle of Blenheim (1704), whose triumph drove the French army out of Germany. The French called him Malbrouck, a name they found easier to pronounce.

[Reading Critically]

Be Style Conscious

If you look around a crowded classroom, you will notice, consciously or not, the styles of your fellow students. The way they dress, talk, and even sit conveys information on their attitudes. A haircut, a tattoo, a piece of jewelry all silently say something. Style is not merely a literary concept. It is a phenomenon we encounter every day in society.

Use the same powers of observation when discussing a writer's style. It may help to begin with a checklist of four elements—diction, sentence structure, tone, and organization:

1. Diction: Does the writer use word choice in a distinctive way? In "A Clean, Well-Lighted Place", for example, Hemingway favors simple, unemotional, and descriptive language whereas in "The Tell-Tale Heart" Poe seemingly delights in extravagant and emotionally charged diction. Each choice reveals something important about the story.

2. Sentence Structure: Does the author characteristically use long or short sentences? Are there perhaps even sentence fragments? Hemingway is famous for his short, clipped sentences, which often repeat certain key words. Faulkner, however, favors long, elaborate syntax that immerses the readers in the emotional situation of the narrative.

3. Tone: What is the writer's evident attitude toward the material? In "The Gospel According to Mark", Borges unfolds the story over a central irony, a tragic misunderstanding that will doom his protagonist. Tan's "A Pair of Tickets", by contrast, creates a tone of hushed excitement and direct emotional involvement. The tone of each story is an important element in its total design.

4. Organization: How does a writer go about arranging the material of the story? Borges presents his story in a straightforward, chronological manner, which eventually makes it possible for us to appreciate the tale's complex undercurrents.

Focus on the specifics of the story you are discussing. Examine the obvious elements of style and note what seems characteristic. Remember that style is personality.

6. Symbol

In F. Scott Fitzgerald's novel *The Great Gatsby*, a huge pair of bespectacled eyes stares across a wilderness of ash heaps, from a billboard advertising the services of an oculist. Repeatedly entering into the story, the advertisement comes to mean more than simply the availability of eye examinations. Fitzgerald has a character liken it to the eyes of God; he hints that some sad, compassionate spirit is brooding as it watches the passing procession of humanity. Such an object is a **symbol**: in literature, a thing that suggests more than its literal meaning. Symbols generally do not "stand for" any one meaning, nor for anything absolutely definite; they point, they hint, or, as Henry James put it, they cast long shadows. To take a large example, in Herman Melville's *Moby Dick*, the great white whale of the book's title apparently means more than the literal dictionary-definition meaning of an aquatic mammal. He also suggests more than the devil, to whom some of the characters liken him. The great whale, as the story unfolds, comes to imply an amplitude of meanings; among them the forces of nature and the whole created universe.

This indefinite multiplicity of meanings is characteristic of a symbolic story and distinguishes it from an **allegory**, a story in which persons, places, and things form a system of clearly labeled equivalents. In a simple allegory, characters and other ingredients often stand for other definite meanings, which are often abstractions. In Nathaniel Hawthorne's "Young Goodman Brown", the tale's main female character, Faith, represents the religious virtue suggested by her name. Supreme allegories are found in some biblical parables ("The Kingdom of Heaven is like a man who sowed good seed in his field ... " Matthew 13: 24 –30). A classic allegory is the medieval play *Everyman*, whose hero represents us all, and who, deserted by false friends called Kindred and Goods, faces the judgment of God accompanied only by a faithful friend called Good Deeds. In John Bunyan's 17th-century *Pilgrim's Progress*, the protagonist, Christian, struggles along the difficult road toward salvation, meeting along the way persons such as Mr. Worldly Wiseman, who directs him into a more comfortable path (a wrong turn), and the residents of a town called Fair Speech, among them a hypocrite named Mr. Facing-both-ways. Not all allegories are simple: Dante's *Divine Comedy*, written in the Middle Ages, continues to reveal new meanings to careful readers. Allegory was much beloved in the Middle Ages, but in contemporary fiction it is rare. One modem instance is George Orwell's long fable *Animal Farm*, in which (among its double meanings) barnyard animals stand for human victims and totalitarian oppressors.

Symbols in fiction are not generally abstract terms like *love* or *truth*, but are likely to be perceptible objects (or worded descriptions that cause us to imagine them). In William Faulkner's "A Rose for Emily", Miss Emily's invisible watch ticking at the end of a golden chain not only indicates the passage of time, but suggests that time passes without even being noticed by the watch's owner, and the golden chain carries suggestions of wealth and authority. Often the symbols we meet in fiction are inanimate objects, but other things also may function symbolically. In James Joyce's "Araby", the very name of the bazaar, Araby—the poetic name for Arabia—suggests magic, romance, and *The Arabian Nights*; its syllables (the narrator tells us) "cast an Eastern enchantment over me". Even a locale, or a feature of physical topography, can provide rich suggestions. Recall Ernest Hemingway's "A Clean, Well-Lighted Place", in which the café is not merely a café, but an island of refuge from night, chaos, loneliness, old age, and impending death.

In some novels and stories, symbolic characters make brief cameo appearances. Such characters often are not well-rounded and fully known, but are seen fleetingly and remain slightly mysterious. In *Heart of Darkness*, a short novel by Joseph Conrad, a steamship company that hires men to work in the Congo maintains in its waiting room two women who knit black wool—like the classical Fates. Usually such a symbolic character is more a portrait than a person—or somewhat portrait-like, as Faulkner's Miss Emily, who twice appears at a window of her house "like the carven torso of an idol in a niche". Though Faulkner invests Miss Emily with life and vigor, he also clothes her in symbolic hints: She seems almost to personify the vanishing aristocracy of the antebellum South, still maintaining a black servant and being ruthlessly betrayed by a moneymaking Yankee. Sometimes a part of a character's body or an attribute may convey symbolic meaning: a baleful eye, as in Edgar Allan Poe's "The Tell-Tale Heart".

Much as a symbolic whale holds more meaning than an ordinary whale, a symbolic act is a gesture with larger significance than usual. For the boy's father in Faulkner's "Barn Burning", the act of destroying a barn is no mere act of spite, but an expression of his profound hatred for anything not belonging to him. Faulkner adds that burning a barn reflects the father's memories of the "waste and extravagance of war"; and further adds that "the element of fire spoke to some deep mainspring" in his being. A symbolic act, however, does not have to be a gesture as large as starting a conflagration. Before setting out in pursuit of the great white whale, Melville's Captain Ahab in *Moby Dick* deliberately snaps his tobacco pipe and throws it away, as if to suggest (among other things) that he will let no pleasure or pastime distract him from his vengeance.

Why do writers have to symbolize—why don't they tell us outright? One advantage of a symbol is that it is so compact, and yet so fully laden. Both starkly concrete and slightly mysterious, like Miss Emily's invisible ticking watch, it may impress us with all the force of something beheld in a dream or in a nightmare. The watch suggests, among other things, the slow and invisible passage of time. What this symbol says, it says more fully and more memorably than could be said, perhaps, in a long essay on the subject.

To some extent (it may be claimed), all stories are symbolic. Merely by holding up for our inspection these characters and their actions, the writer lends them some special significance. But this is to think of symbol in an extremely broad and inclusive way. For the usual purposes of reading a story and understanding it, there is probably little point in looking for symbolism in every word, in every stick or stone, in every striking of a match, in every minor character. Still, to be on the alert for symbols when reading fiction is perhaps wiser than to ignore them. Not to admit that symbolic meanings may be present, or to refuse to think about them, would be another way to misread a story— or to read no further than its outer edges.

How, then, do you recognize a symbol in fiction when you meet it? Fortunately, the storyteller often gives the symbol particular emphasis. It may be mentioned repeatedly throughout the story; it may even supply the story with a title ("Barn Burning", "A Clean, Well-Lighted Place", "Araby"). At times, a crucial symbol will open a story or end it. Unless an object, act, or character is given some such special emphasis and importance, we may generally feel safe in taking it at face value. Probably, it is not a symbol if it points clearly and unmistakably toward some one meaning, like a whistle in a factory, whose blast at noon means lunch. But an object, an act, or a character is surely symbolic (and almost as surely displays high literary art) if, when we finish the story, we realize that it was that item—those gigantic eyes; that clean, well-lighted café; that burning of a barn—which led us to the author's theme, the essential meaning.

Read the following novels, recognize symbols and try to compare them.

The Chrysanthemums (1938)
John Steinbeck

The high grey-flannel fog of winter closed off the Salinas Valley① from the sky and from all the rest of the world. On every side it sat like a lid on the mountains and made of the great valley a closed pot. On the broad, level land floor the gang plows bit deep and left the black earth shining like metal where the shares had cut. On the foothill ranches across the Salinas River, the yellow stubble fields seemed to be bathed in pale cold sunshine, but there was no sunshine in the valley now in December. The thick willow scrub along the river flamed with sharp and positive yellow leaves.

It was a time of quiet and of waiting. The air was cold and tender. A light wind blew up from the southwest so that the farmers were mildly hopeful of a good rain before long; but fog and rain do not go together.

Across the river, on Henry Allen's foothill ranch there was little work to be done, for the hay was cut and stored and the orchards were plowed up to receive the rain deeply when it should come. The cattle on the higher slopes were becoming shaggy and rough-coated.

---

① Salinas Valley: south of San Francisco in the Coast Ranges region of California

Elisa Allen, working in her flower garden, looked down across the yard and saw Henry, her husband, talking to two men in business suits. The three of them stood by the tractor shed, each man with one foot on the side of the little Fordson. They smoked cigarettes and studied the machine as they talked.

Elisa watched them for a moment and then went back to her work. She was thirty-five. Her face was lean and strong and her eyes were as clear as water. Her figure looked blocked and heavy in her gardening costume, a man's black hat pulled low down over her eyes, clod-hopper shoes, a figured print dress almost completely covered by a big corduroy apron with four big pockets to hold the snips, the trowel and scratcher, the seeds and the knife she worked with. She wore heavy leather gloves to protect her hands while she worked.

She was cutting down the old year's chrysanthemum stalks with a pair of short and powerful scissors. She looked down toward the men by the tractor shed now and then. Her face was eager and mature and handsome; even her work with the scissors was over-eager, over-powerful. The chrysanthemum stems seemed too small and easy for her energy.

She brushed a cloud of hair out of her eyes with the back of her glove, and left a smudge of earth on her cheek in doing it. Behind her stood the neat white farm house with red geraniums close-banked around it as high as the windows. It was a hard-swept looking little house with hard-polished windows, and a clean mud-mat on the front steps.

Elisa cast another glance toward the tractor shed. The strangers were getting into their Ford coupe. She took off a glove and put her strong fingers down into the forest of new green chrysanthemum sprouts that were growing around the old roots. She spread the leaves and looked down among the close-growing stems. No aphids were there, no sow bugs or snails or cutworms. Her terrier fingers destroyed such pests before they could get started.

Elisa started at the sound of her husband's voice. He had come near quietly, and he leaned over the wire fence that protected her flower garden from cattle and dogs and chickens.

"At it again," he said. "You've got a strong new crop coming."

Elisa straightened her back and pulled on the gardening glove again. "Yes. They'll be strong this coming year." In her tone and on her face there was a little smugness.

"You've got a gift with things," Henry observed. "Some of those yellow chrysanthemums you had this year were ten inches across. I wish you'd work out in the orchard and raise some apples that big."

Her eyes sharpened. "Maybe I could do it, too. I've a gift with things, all right. My mother had it. She could stick anything in the ground and make it grow. She said it was having planters' hands that knew how to do it."

"Well, it sure works with flowers," he said.

"Henry, who were those men you were talking to?"

"Why, sure, that's what I came to tell you. They were from the Western Meat Company. I sold those thirty head of three-year-old steers. Got nearly my own price, too."

"Good," she said. "Good for you."

"And I thought," he continued, "I thought how it's Saturday afternoon, and we might go into Salinas for dinner at a restaurant, and then to a picture show—to celebrate, you see."

"Good," she repeated. "Oh, yes. That will be good."

Henry put on his joking tone. "There's fights tonight. How'd you like to go to the fights?"

"Oh, no," she said breathlessly. "No, I wouldn't like fights."

"Just fooling, Elisa. We'll go to a movie. Let's see. It's two now. I'm going to take Scotty and bring down those steers from the hill. It'll take us maybe two hours. We'll go in town about five and have dinner at the Cominos Hotel. Like that?"

"Of course I'll like it. It's good to eat away from home."

"All right, then. I'll go get up a couple of horses."

She said, "I'll have plenty of time to transplant some of these sets, I guess."

She heard her husband calling Scotty down by the barn. And a little later she saw the two men ride up the pale yellow hillside in search of the steers.

There was a little square sandy bed kept for rooting the chrysanthemums. With her trowel she turned the soil over and over, and smoothed it and patted it firm. Then she dug ten parallel trenches to receive the sets. Back at the chrysanthemum bed she pulled out the little crisp shoots, trimmed off the leaves of each one with her scissors and laid it on a small orderly pile.

A squeak of wheels and plod of hoofs came from the road. Elisa looked up. The country road ran along the dense bank of willows and cottonwoods that bordered the river, and up this road came a curious vehicle, curiously drawn. It was an old spring-wagon, with a round canvas top on it like the cover of a prairie schooner. It was drawn by an old bay horse and a little grey-and-white burro. A big stubble-bearded man sat between the cover flaps and drove the crawling team. Underneath the wagon, between the hind wheels, a lean and rangy mongrel dog walked sedately. Words were painted on the canvas, in clumsy, crooked letters. "Pots, pans, knives, scissors, lawn mores, Fixed." Two rows of articles, and the triumphantly definitive "Fixed" below. The black paint had run down in little sharp points beneath each letter.

Elisa, squatting on the ground, watched to see the crazy, loose-jointed wagon pass by. But it didn't pass. It turned into the farm road in front of her house, crooked old wheels skirling and squeaking. The rangy dog darted from between the wheels and ran ahead. Instantly the two ranch shepherds flew out at him. Then all three stopped, and with stiff and quivering tails, with taut straight legs, with ambassadorial dignity, they slowly circled, sniffing daintily. The caravan pulled up to Elisa's wire fence and stopped. Now the newcomer dog, feeling outnumbered, lowered his tail and retired under the wagon with raised hackles and bared teeth.

The man on the wagon seat called out, "That's a bad dog in a fight when he gets started."

Elisa laughed. "I see he is. How soon does he generally get started?"

The man caught up her laughter and echoed it heartily. "Sometimes not for weeks and weeks," he said. He climbed stiffly down, over the wheel. The horse and the donkey drooped like unwatered flowers.

Elisa saw that he was a very big man. Although his hair and beard were greying, he did not look old. His worn black suit was wrinkled and spotted with grease. The laughter had disappeared from his face and eyes the moment his laughing voice ceased. His eyes were dark, and they were full of the brooding that gets in the eyes of teamsters and of sailors. The calloused hands he rested on the wire fence were cracked, and every crack was a black line. He took off his battered hat.

"I'm off my general road, ma'am," he said. "Does this dirt road cut over across the river to the Los Angeles highway?"

Elisa stood up and shoved the thick scissors in her apron pocket. "Well, yes, it does, but it winds around and then fords the river. I don't think your team could pull through the sand."

He replied with some asperity. "It might surprise you what them beasts can pull through."

"When they get started?" she asked.

He smiled for a second. "Yes. When they get started."

"Well," said Elisa, "I think you'll save time if you go back to the Salinas road and pick up the highway there."

He drew a big finger down the chicken wire and made it sing. "I ain't in any hurry, ma'am. I go from Seattle to San Diego and back every year. Takes all my time. About six months each way. I aim to follow nice weather."

Elisa took off her gloves and stuffed them in the apron pocket with the scissors. She touched the under edge of her man's hat, searching for fugitive hairs. "That sounds like a nice kind of a way to live," she said.

He leaned confidentially over the fence. "Maybe you noticed the writing on my wagon. I mend pots and sharpen knives and scissors. You got any of them things to do?"

"Oh, no," she said quickly. "Nothing like that." Her eyes hardened with resistance.

"Scissors is the worst thing," he explained. "Most people just ruin scissors trying to sharpen 'em, but I know how. I got a special tool. It's a little bobbit kind of thing, and patented. But it sure does the trick."

"No. My scissors are all sharp."

"All right, then. Take a pot," he continued earnestly, "a bent pot, or a pot with a hole. I can make it like new so you don't have to buy no new ones. That's a saving for you."

"No," she said shortly. "I tell you I have nothing like that for you to do."

His face fell to an exaggerated sadness. His voice took on a whining undertone. "I ain't had a thing to do today. Maybe I won't have no supper tonight. You see I'm off my regular road. I know folks on the highway clear from Seattle to San Diego. They save their things for me to sharpen up because they know I do it so good and save them money."

"I'm sorry," Elisa said irritably. "I haven't anything for you to do."

His eyes left her face and fell to searching the ground. They roamed about until they came to the chrysanthemum bed where she had been working. "What's them plants, ma'am?"

The irritation and resistance melted from Elisa's face. "Oh, those are chrysanthemums, giant whites and yellows. I raise them every year, bigger than anybody around here."

"Kind of a long-stemmed flower? Looks like a quick puff of colored smoke?" he asked.

"That's it. What a nice way to describe them."

"They smell kind of nasty till you get used to them," he said.

"It's a good bitter smell," she retorted, "not nasty at all."

He changed his tone quickly. "I like the smell myself."

"I had ten-inch blooms this year," she said.

The man leaned farther over the fence. "Look. I know a lady down the road a piece, has got the nicest garden you ever seen. Got nearly every kind of flower but no chrysanthemums. Last time I was mending a copper-bottom washtub for her (that's a hard job but I do it good), she said to me, 'If you ever run across some nice chrysanthemums I wish you'd try to get me a few seeds.' That's what she told me."

Elisa's eyes grew alert and eager. "She couldn't have known much about chrysanthemums. You can raise them from seed, but it's much easier to root the little sprouts you see there."

"Oh," he said. "I s'pose I can't take none to her, then."

"Why yes you can," Elisa cried. "I can put some in damp sand, and you can carry them right along with you. They'll take root in the pot if you keep them damp. And then she can transplant them."

"She'd sure like to have some, ma'am. You say they're nice ones?"

"Beautiful," she said. "Oh, beautiful." Her eyes shone. She tore off the battered hat and shook out her dark pretty hair. "I'll put them in a flower pot, and you can take them right with you. Come into the yard."

While the man came through the picket gate Elisa ran excitedly along the geranium-bordered path to the back of the house. And she returned carrying a big red flower pot. The gloves were forgotten now. She kneeled the ground by the starting bed and dug up the sandy soil with her fingers and scooped it into the bright new flower pot. Then she picked up the little pile of shoots she had prepared. With her strong fingers she pressed them in the sand and tamped around them with her knuckles. The man stood over her. "I'll tell you what to do," she said. "You remember so you can tell the lady."

"Yes, I'll try to remember."

"Well, look. These will take root in about a month. Then she must set them out, about a foot apart in good rich earth like this, see?" She lifted a handful of dark soil for him to look at. "They'll grow fast and tall. Now remember this: In July tell her to cut them down, about eight inches from the ground."

"Before they bloom?" he asked.

"Yes, before they bloom." Her face was tight with eagerness. "They'll grow right up again. About the last of September the buds will start."

She stopped and seemed perplexed. "It's the budding that takes the most care," she said hesitantly. "I don't know how to tell you." She looked deep into his eyes, searchingly. Her mouth opened a little, and she seemed to be listening. "I'll try to tell you," she said. "Did you ever hear of planting hands?"

"Can't say I have, ma'am."

"Well, I can only tell you what it feels like. It's when you're picking off the buds you don't want. Everything goes right down into your fingertips. You watch your fingers work. They do it themselves. You can feel how it is. They pick and pick the buds. They never make a mistake. They're with the plant. Do you see? Your fingers and the plant. You can feel that, right up your arm. They know. They never make a mistake. You can feel it. When you're like that you can't do anything wrong. Do you see that? Can you understand that?"

She was kneeling on the ground looking up at him. Her breast swelled passionately.

The man's eyes narrowed. He looked away self-consciously. "Maybe I know," he said. "Sometimes in the night in the wagon there—"

Elisa's voice grew husky. She broke in on him, "I've never lived as you do, but I know what you mean. When the night is dark—why, the stars are sharp-pointed, and there's quiet. Why, you rise up and up! Every pointed star gets driven into your body. It's like that. Hot and sharp and—lovely."

Kneeling there, her hand went out toward his legs in the greasy black trousers. Her hesitant ringers almost touched the cloth. Then her hand dropped to the ground. She crouched low like a fawning dog.

He said, "It's nice, just like you say. Only when you don't have no dinner, it ain't."

She stood up then, very straight, and her face was ashamed. She held the flower pot out to him and placed it gently in his arms. "Here. Put it in your wagon, on the seat, where you can watch it. Maybe I can find something for you to do."

At the back of the house she dug in the can pile and found two old and battered aluminum saucepans. She carried them back and gave them to him. "Here, maybe you can fix these."

His manner changed. He became professional. "Good as new I can fix them." At the back of his wagon he set a little anvil, and out of an oily tool box dug a small machine hammer. Elisa came through the gate to watch him while he pounded out the dents in the kettles. His mouth grew sure and knowing. At a difficult part of the work he sucked his under-lip.

"You sleep right in the wagon?" Elisa asked.

"Right in the wagon, ma'am. Rain or shine I'm dry as a cow in there."

"It must be nice," she said. "It must be very nice. I wish women could do such things."

"It ain't the right kind of a life for a woman."

Her upper lip raised a little, showing her teeth. "How do you know? How can you tell?" she said.

"I don't know, ma'am," he protested. "Of course I don't know. Now here's your kettles, done. You don't have to buy no new ones."

"How much?"

"Oh, fifty cents'll do. I keep my prices down and my work good. That's why I have all them satisfied customers up and down the highway."

Elisa brought him a fifty-cent piece from the house and dropped it in his hand. "You might be surprised to have a rival some time. I can sharpen scissors, too. And I can beat the dents out of little pots. I could show you what a woman might do."

He put his hammer back in the oily box and shoved the little anvil out of sight. "It would be a lonely life for a woman, ma'am, and a scary life, too, with animals creeping under the wagon all night." He climbed over the singletree, steadying himself with a hand on the burro's white rump. He settled himself in the seat, picked up the lines. "Thank you kindly, ma'am," he said. "I'll do like you told me; I'll go back and catch the Salinas road."

"Mind," she called, "if you're long in getting there, keep the sand damp."

"Sand, ma'am? ... Sand? Oh, sure. You mean around the chrysanthemums. Sure I will." He clucked his tongue. The beasts leaned luxuriously into their collars. The mongrel dog took his place between the back wheels. The wagon turned and crawled out the entrance road and back the way it had come, along the river.

Elisa stood in front of her wire fence watching the slow progress of the caravan. Her shoulders were straight, her head thrown back, her eyes half-closed, so that the scene came vaguely into them. Her lips moved silently, forming the words "Good-bye—good-bye." Then she whispered, "That's a bright direction. There's a glowing there." The sound of her whisper startled her. She shook herself free and looked about to see whether anyone had been listening. Only the dogs had heard. They lifted their heads toward her from their sleeping in the dust, and then stretched out their chins and settled asleep again. Elisa turned and ran hurriedly into the house.

In the kitchen she reached behind the stove and felt the water tank. It was full of hot water from the noonday cooking. In the bathroom she tore off her soiled clothes and flung them into the corner. And then she scrubbed herself with a little block of pumice, legs and thighs, loins and chest and arms, until her skin was scratched and red. When she had dried herself she stood in front of a mirror in her bedroom and looked at her body. She tightened her stomach and threw out her chest. She turned and looked over her shoulder at her back.

After a while she began to dress, slowly. She put on her newest under-clothing and her nicest stockings and the dress which was the symbol of her prettiness. She worked carefully on her hair, penciled her eyebrows and rouged her lips.

Before she was finished she heard the little thunder of hoofs and the shouts of Henry and his helper as they drove the red steers into the corral. She heard the gate bang shut and set herself for Henry's arrival.

His step sounded on the porch. He entered the house calling, "Elisa, where are you?"

"In my room, dressing. I'm not ready. There's hot water for your bath. Hurry up. It's getting late."

When she heard him splashing in the tub, Elisa laid his dark suit on the bed, and shirt and socks and tie beside it. She stood his polished shoes on the floor beside the bed. Then she went to the porch and sat primly and stiffly down. She looked toward the river road where the willow-line was still yellow with frosted leaves so that under the high grey fog they seemed a thin band of sunshine. This was the only color in the grey afternoon. She sat unmoving for a long time. Her eyes blinked rarely.

Henry came banging out of the door, shoving his tie inside his vest as he came. Elisa stiffened and her face grew tight. Henry stopped short and looked at her. "Why—why, Elisa. You look so nice!"

"Nice? You think I look nice? What do you mean by 'nice'?"

Henry blundered on. "I don't know. I mean you look different, strong and happy."

"I am strong? Yes, strong. What do you mean 'strong'?"

He looked bewildered. "You're playing some kind of a game," he said helplessly. "It's a kind of a play. You look strong enough to break a calf over your knee, happy enough to eat it like a watermelon."

For a second she lost her rigidity. "Henry! Don't talk like that. You didn't know what you said." She grew complete again. "I'm strong," she boasted. "I never knew before how strong."

Henry looked down toward the tractor shed, and when he brought his eyes back to her, they were his own again. "I'll get out the car. You can put on your coat while I'm starting."

Elisa went into the house. She heard him drive to the gate and idle down his motor, and then she took a long time to put on her hat. She pulled it here and pressed it there. When Henry turned the motor off she slipped into her coat and went out.

The little roadster bounced along on the dirt road by the river, raising the birds and driving the rabbits into the brush. Two cranes flapped heavily over the willow-line and dropped into the river-bed.

Far ahead on the road Elisa saw a dark speck. She knew.

She tried not to look as they passed it, but her eyes would not obey. She whispered to herself sadly, "He might have thrown them off the road. That wouldn't have been much trouble, not very much. But he kept the pot," she explained. "He had to keep the pot. That's why he couldn't get them off the road."

The roadster turned a bend and she saw the caravan ahead. She swung full around toward her husband so she could not see the little covered wagon and the mismatched team as the car passed them.

In a moment it was over. The thing was done. She did not look back.

She said loudly, to be heard above the motor, "It will be good, tonight, a good dinner."

"Now you're changed again," Henry complained. He took one hand from the wheel and patted her knee. "I ought to take you in to dinner oftener. It would be good for both of us. We get so heavy out on the ranch."

"Henry," she asked, "could we have wine at dinner?"

"Sure we could. Say! That will be fine."

She was silent for a while; then she said, "Henry, at those prize fights, do the men hurt each other very much?"

"Sometimes a little, not often. Why?"

"Well, I've read how they break noses, and blood runs down their chests. I've read how the fighting gloves get heavy and soggy with blood."

He looked around at her. "What's the matter, Elisa? I didn't know you read things like that." He brought the car to a stop, then turned to the right over the Salinas River bridge.

"Do any women ever go to the fights?" she asked.

"Oh, sure, some. What's the matter, Elisa? Do you want to go? I don't think you'd like it, but I'll take you if you really want to go."

She relaxed limply in the seat. "Oh, no. No. I don't want to go. I'm sure I don't." Her face was turned away from him. "It will be enough if we can have wine. It will be plenty." She turned up her coat collar so he could not see that she was crying weakly—like an old woman.

Study Questions:

1. When we first meet Elisa in her garden, with what details does Steinbeck delineate her character for us?

2. Elisa works inside a "wire fence that protected her flower garden from cattle and dogs and chickens" (Para. 9). What does this wire fence suggest?

3. How would you describe Henry and Elisa's marriage? Cite details from the story.

4. For what motive does the traveling salesman take an interest in Elisa's chrysanthemums? What immediate effect does his interest have on Elisa?

5. For what possible purpose does Steinbeck give us such a detailed account of Elisa's preparations for her evening out? Notice her tearing off her soiled clothes, her scrubbing her body

with pumice (Paras. 93-94).

6. Of what significance to Elisa is the sight of the contents of the flower pot discarded in the road? Notice that, as her husband's car overtakes the covered wagon, Elisa averts her eyes; and then Steinbeck adds, "In a moment it was over. The thing was done. She did not look back" (Para. 111). Explain this passage.

7. How do you interpret Elisa's asking for wine with dinner? How do you account for her new interest in prize fights?

8. Try to state this short story's theme in a sentence.

9. Why are Elisa Allen's chrysanthemums so important to this story? Sum up your understanding.

Odour of Chrysanthemums (1911, 1914)
D. H. Lawrence

I

The small locomotive engine, Number 4, came clanking, stumbling down from Selston with seven full wagons. It appeared round the corner with loud threats of speed, but the colt that it startled from among the gorse①, which still flickered indistinctly in the raw afternoon, out-distanced it at a canter. A woman, walking up the railway line to Underwood, drew back into the hedge, held her basket aside, and watched the footplate of the engine advancing. The trucks② thumped heavily past, one by one, with slow inevitable movement, as she stood insignificantly trapped between the jolting black wagons and the hedge; then they curved away towards the coppice③ where the withered oat leaves dropped noiselessly, while the birds, pulling at the scarlet hips beside the track, made off into the dusk that had already crept into the spinney④. In the open, the smoke from the engine sank and cleaved to the rough grass. The fields were dreary and forsaken, and in the marshy strip that led to the whimsey⑤, a reedy pit-pond, the fowls had already abandoned their run among the alders, to roost in the tarred fowl-house. The pit-bank loomed up beyond the pond, flames like red sores licking its ashy sides, in the afternoon's stagnant light. Just beyond rose the tapering chimneys and the clumsy black headstocks of Brinsley Colliery⑥.

The two wheels were spinning fast up against the sky, and the winding engine rapped out its little spasms. The miners were being turned up.

The engine whistled as it came into the wide bay of railway lines beside the colliery, where

---

① gorse: common prickly bush with yellow flowers
② trucks: open freight cars
③ coppice: a wood of small trees or shrubs
④ spinney: thicket
⑤ whimsey: a machine for raising ore or water from a mine
⑥ Brinsley Colliery: coal mine. "Headstocks" support revolving parts of a machine.

rows of trucks stood in harbour.

　　Miners, single, trailing and in groups, passed like shadows diverging home. At the edge of the ribbed level of sidings squat a low cottage, three steps down from the cinder track. A large bony vine clutched at the house, as if to claw down the tiled roof. Round the bricked yard grew a few wintry primroses. Beyond, the long garden sloped down to a bush-covered brook course. There were some twiggy apple trees, winter-crack trees, and ragged cabbages. Beside the path hung disheveled pink chrysanthemums, like pink cloths hung on bushes. A woman came stooping out of the felt-covered fowl-house, half-way down the garden. She closed and padlocked the door, then drew herself erect, having brushed some bits from her white apron.

　　She was a tall woman of imperious mien, handsome, with definite black eyebrows. Her smooth black hair was parted exactly. For a few moments she stood steadily watching the miners as they passed along the railway: then she turned towards the brook course. Her face was calm and set, her mouth was closed with disillusionment. After a moment she called:

　　"John!" There was no answer. She waited, and then said distinctly:

　　"Where are you?"

　　"Here!" replied a child's sulky voice from among the bushes. The woman looked piercingly through the dusk.

　　"Are you at that brook?" she asked sternly.

　　For answer the child showed himself before the raspberry-canes that rose like whips. He was a small, sturdy boy of five. He stood quite still, defiantly.

　　"Oh!" said the mother, conciliated. "I thought you were down at that wet brook—and you remember what I told you—"

　　The boy did not move or answer.

　　"Come, come on in," she said more gently, " it's getting dark. There's your grandfather's engine coming down the line!"

　　The lad advanced slowly, with resentful, taciturn movement. He was dressed in trousers and waistcoat of cloth that was too thick and hard for the size of the garments. They were evidently cut down from a man's clothes.

　　As they went slowly towards the house he tore at the ragged wisps of chrysanthemums and dropped the petals in handfuls along the path.

　　"Don't do that—it does look nasty," said his mother. He refrained, and she, suddenly pitiful, broke off a twig with three or four wan flowers and held them against her face. When mother and son reached the yard her hand hesitated, and instead of laying the flower aside, she pushed it in her apron-band. The mother and son stood at the foot of the three steps looking across the bay of lines at the passing home of the miners. The trundle of the small train was imminent. Suddenly the engine loomed past the house and came to a stop opposite the gate.

　　The engine-driver, a short man with round grey beard, leaned out of the cab high above the woman.

"Have you got a cup of tea?" he said in a cheery, hearty fashion.

It was her father. She went in, saying she would mash①. Directly, she returned.

"I didn't come to see you on Sunday," began the little grey-bearded man.

"I didn't expect you," said his daughter.

The engine-driver winced; then, reassuming his cheery, airy manner, he said:

"Oh, have you heard then? Well, and what do you think—?"

"I think it is soon enough," she replied.

At her brief censure the little man made an impatient gesture, and said coaxingly, yet with dangerous coldness:

"Well, what's a man to do? It's no sort of life for a man of my years, to sit at my own hearth like a stranger. And if I'm going to marry again it may as well be soon as late—what does it matter to anybody?"

The woman did not reply, but turned and went into the house. The man in the engine-cab stood assertive, till she returned with a cup of tea and a piece of bread and butter on a plate. She went up the steps and stood near the footplate of the hissing engine.

"You needn't a' brought me bread an' butter," said her father. "But a cup of tea"—he sipped appreciatively—"it's very nice." He sipped for a moment or two, then: "I hear as Walter's got another bout② on," he said.

"When hasn't he?" said the woman bitterly.

"I heerd tell of him in the 'Lord Nelson' braggin' as he was going to spend that before he went: half a sovereign③ that was."

"When?" asked the woman.

"A Sat'day night—I know that's true."

"Very likely," she laughed bitterly. "He gives me twenty-three shillings."

"Aye, it's a nice thing, when a man can do nothing with his money but make a beast of himself!" said the grey-whiskered man. The woman turned her head away. Her father swallowed the last of his tea and handed her the cup.

"Aye," he sighed, wiping his mouth. "It's a settler④, it is—"

He put his hand on the lever. The little engine strained and groaned, and the train rumbled towards the crossing. The woman again looked across the metals. Darkness was settling over the spaces of the railway and trucks: the miners, in grey somber groups, were still passing

---

① mash: steep the tea
② bout: session; i.e., bout of drinking
③ sovereign: gold coin worth twenty shillings. Half a sovereign is worth ten. Lord Nelson is the name of a public house (pub).
④ settler: crushing (or final) blow

home. The winding engine pulsed hurriedly, with brief pauses. Elizabeth Bates looked at the dreary flow of men, then she went indoors. Her husband did not come.

The kitchen was small and full of firelight; red coals piled glowing up the chimney mouth. All the life of the room seemed in the white, warm hearth and the steel fender reflecting the red fire. The cloth was laid for tea; cups glinted in the shadows. At the back, where the lowest stairs protruded into the room, the boy sat struggling with a knife and a piece of white wood. He was almost hidden in the shadow. It was half-past four. They had but to await the father's coming to begin tea. As the mother watched her son's sullen little struggle with the wood, she saw herself in his silence and pertinacity; she saw the father in her child's indifference to all but himself. She seemed to be occupied by her husband. He had probably gone past his home, slunk past his own door, to drink before he came in, while his dinner spoiled and wasted in waiting. She glanced at the clock, then took the potatoes to strain them in the yard. The garden and fields beyond the brook were closed in uncertain darkness. When she rose with the saucepan, leaving the drain steaming into the night behind her, she saw the yellow lamps were lit along the high road that went up the hill away beyond the space of the railway lines and the field.

Then again she watched the men trooping home, fewer now and fewer.

Indoors the fire was sinking and the room was dark red. The woman put her saucepan on the hob①, and set a batter-pudding near the mouth of the oven. Then she stood unmoving. Directly, gratefully, came quick young steps to the door. Someone hung on the latch a moment, then a little girl entered and began pulling off her outdoor things, dragging a mass of curls, just ripening from gold to brown, over her eyes with her hat.

Her mother chid her for coming late from school, and said she would have to keep her at home the dark winter days.

"Why, mother, it's hardly a bit dark yet. The lamp's not lighted, and my father's not home."

"No, he isn't. But it's a quarter to five! Did you see anything of him?" The child became serious. She looked at her mother with large, wistful blue eyes.

"No, mother, I've never seen him. Why? Has he come up an' gone past, to Old Brinsley? He hasn't, mother,'cos I never saw him."

"He'd watch that," said the mother bitterly, "he'd take care as you didn't see him. But you may depend upon it, he's seated in the 'Prince o' Wales'②. He wouldn't be this late." The girl looked at her mother piteously. "Let's have our teas, mother, should we?" said she.

The mother called John to table. She opened the door once more and looked out across the darkness of the lines. All was deserted; she could not hear the winding-engines.

---

① hob: part of the fireplace
② Prince o' Wales': name of a pub

"Perhaps," she said to herself, "he's stopped to get some ripping① done." They sat down to tea. John, at the end of the table near the door, was almost lost in the darkness. Their faces were hidden from each other. The girl crouched against the fender② slowly moving a thick piece of bread before the fire. The lad, his face a dusky mark on the shadow, sat watching her who was transfigured in the red glow.

"I do think it's beautiful to look in the fire," said the child.

"Do you?" said her mother. "Why?"

"It's so red, and full of little caves—and it feels so nice, and you can fair smell it."

"It'll want mending directly," replied her mother, "and then if your father comes he'll carry on and say there never is a fire when a man comes home sweating from the pit. A public-house is always warm enough."

There was silence till the boy said complainingly: "Make haste, our Annie."

"Well, I am doing! I can't make the fire do it no faster, can I?"

"She keeps wafflin' it about so's to make 'er slow," grumbled the boy.

"Don't have such an evil imagination, child," replied the mother.

Soon the room was busy in the darkness with the crisp sound of crunching. The mother ate very little. She drank her tea determinedly, and sat thinking. When she rose her anger was evident in the stern unbending of her head. She looked at the pudding in the fender, and broke out:

"It is a scandalous thing as a man can't even come home to his dinner! If it's crozzled③ up to a cinder I don't see why I should care. Past his very door he goes to get to a public-house, and here I sit with his dinner waiting for him—"

She went out. As she dropped piece after piece of coal on the red fire, the shadows fell on the walls, till the room was almost in total darkness.

"I canna see," grumbled the invisible John. In spite of herself, the mother laughed.

"You know the way to your mouth," she said. She set the dust pan outside the door. When she came again like a shadow on the hearth, the lad repeated, complaining sulkily:

"I canna see."

"Good gracious!" cried the mother irritably, "you're as bad as your father if it's a bit dusk!"

Nevertheless, she took a paper spill from a sheaf on the mantelpiece and proceeded to light the lamp that hung from the ceiling in the middle of the room. As she reached up, her figure displayed itself just rounding with maternity.

"Oh, mother—!" exclaimed the girl.

---

① ripping: taking out or cutting away coal or stone (a mining and quarrying term)
② fender: frame that keeps coals in the fireplace
③ crozzled: curled

"What?" said the woman, suspended in the act of putting the lamp-glass over the flame. The copper reflector shone handsomely on her, as she stood with uplifted arm, turning to face her daughter.

"You've got a flower in your apron!" said the child, in a little rapture at this unusual event.

"Goodness me!" exclaimed the woman, relieved. "One would think the house was afire." She replaced the glass and waited a moment before turning up the wick. A pale shadow was seen floating vaguely on the floor.

"Let me smell!" said the child, still rapturously, coming forward and putting her face to her mother's waist.

"Go along, silly!" said the mother, turning up the lamp. The light revealed their suspense so that the woman felt it almost unbearable. Annie was still bending at her waist. Irritably, the mother took the flowers out from her apron-band.

"Oh, mother—don't take them out!" Annie cried, catching her hand and trying to replace the sprig.

"Such nonsense!" said the mother, turning away. The child put the pale chrysanthemums to her lips, murmuring:

"Don't they smell beautiful!"

Her mother gave a short laugh.

"No," she said, "not to me. It was chrysanthemums when I married him, and chrysanthemums when you were born, and the first time they ever brought him home drunk, he'd got brown chrysanthemums in his buttonhole."

She looked at the children. Their eyes and their parted lips were wondering. The mother sat rocking in silence for some time. Then she looked at the clock.

"Twenty minutes to six!" In a tone of fine bitter carelessness she continued: "Eh, he'll not come now till they bring him. There he'll stick! But he needn't come rolling in here in his pit-dirt, for I won't wash him. He can lie on the floor—eh, what a fool I've been, what a fool! And this is what I came here for, to this dirty hole, rats and all, for him to slink past his very door. Twice last week—he's begun now—"

She silenced herself and rose to clear the table.

While for an hour or more the children played, subduedly intent, fertile of imagination, united in fear of the mother's wrath, and in dread of their father's home-coming, Mrs. Bates sat in her rocking chair making a "singlet" of thick cream-coloured flannel, which gave a dull wounded sound as she tore off the grey edge. She worked at her sewing with energy, listening to the children, and her anger wearied itself, lay down to rest, opening its eyes from time to time and steadily watching, its ears raised to listen. Sometimes even her anger quailed and shrank, and the mother suspended her sewing, tracing the footsteps that thudded along the sleepers① outside; she would lift her head sharply to bid the children "hush," but she recovered herself in time, and the footsteps went past the gate, and the children were not flung out of their play-world.

But at last Annie sighed, and gave in. She glanced at her wagon of slippers, and loathed the game. She turned plaintively to her mother.

"Mother!"—but she was inarticulate.

John crept out like a frog from under the sofa. His mother glanced up.

"Yes," she said, "just look at those shirt-sleeves!"

The boy held them out to survey them, saying nothing. Then somebody called in a hoarse voice away down the line, and suspense bristled in the room, till two people had gone by outside, talking.

"It is time for bed," said the mother.

"My father hasn't come," wailed Annie plaintively. But her mother was primed with courage.

"Never mind. They'll bring him when he does come—like a log." She meant there would be no scene. "And he may sleep on the floor till he wakes himself. I know he'll not go to work tomorrow after this!"

The children had their hands and faces wiped with a flannel. They were very quiet. When they had put on their night-dresses, they said their prayers, the boy mumbling. The mother looked down at them, at the brown silken bush of intertwining curls in the nape of the girl's neck, at the little black head of the lad, and her heart burst with anger at their father, who caused all three such distress. The children hid their faces in her skirts for comfort.

When Mrs. Bates came down, the room was strangely empty, with a tension of expectancy. She took up her sewing and stitched for some time without raising her head. Meantime her anger was tinged with fear.

II

The clock struck eight and she rose suddenly, dropping her sewing on her chair. She went to the stair-foot door, opened it, listening. Then she went out, looking the door behind her.

Something scuffled in the yard, and she started, though she knew it was only the rats with which the place was over-run. The night was very dark. In the great bay of railway lines, bulked with trucks, there was no trace of light, only away back she could see a few yellow lamps at the pit-top, and the red smear of the burning pit-bank on the night. She hurried along the edge of the track, then, crossing the converging lines, came to the stile by the white gates, whence she emerged on the road. Then the fear which had led her shrank. People were

---

① sleepers: railroad ties

walking up to New Brinsley; she saw the lights in the houses; twenty yards farther on were the broad windows of the "Prince of Wales," very warm and bright, and the loud voices of men could be heard distinctly. What a fool she had been to imagine that anything had happened to him! He was merely drinking over there at the "Prince of Wales." She faltered. She had never yet been to fetch him, and she never would go. So she continued her walk towards the long straggling line of houses, standing back on the highway, She entered a passage between the dwellings.

"Mr. Rigley?—Yes! Did you want him? No, he's not in at this minute."

The raw-boned woman leaned forward from her dark scullery① and peered at the other, upon whom fell a dim light through the blind of the kitchen window.

"Is it Mrs. Bates?" she asked in a tone tinged with respect.

"Yes. I wondered if your Master was at home. Mine hasn't come yet."

"'Asn't 'e! Oh, Jack's been 'ome an' 'ad 'is dinner an' gone out. 'E's just gone for 'alf an hour afore bed-time. Did you call at the 'Prince of Wales'?"

"No—"

"No, you didn't like—! It's not very nice." The other woman was indulgent. There was an awkward pause. "Jack never said nothing about—about your Master," she said.

"No!—I expect he's stuck in there!"

Elizabeth Bates said this bitterly, and with recklessness. She knew that the woman across the yard was standing at her door listening, but she did not care. As she turned:

"Stop a minute! I'll just go an' ask Jack if 'e knows anything," said Mrs. Rigley.

"Oh no—I wouldn't like to put—!"

"Yes, I will, if you'll just step inside an' see as th' childer doesn't come downstairs and set theirselves afire."

Elizabeth Bates, murmuring a remonstrance, stepped inside. The other woman apologized for the state of the room.

The kitchen needed apology. There were little frocks and trousers and childish undergarments on the squab② and on the floor, and a litter of playthings everywhere. On the black American cloth③ of the table were pieces of bread and cake, crusts, slops, and a teapot with cold tea.

"Eh, ours is just as bad," said Elizabeth Bates, looking at the woman, not at the house. Mrs. Rigley put a shawl over her head and hurried out, saying:

"I shanna be a minute."

The other sat, noting with faint disapproval the general untidiness of the room. Then she

---

① scullery: back kitchen
② squab: couch
③ cloth: oilcloth

fell to counting the shoes of various sizes scattered over the floor. There were twelve. She sighed and said to herself: "No wonder!"—glancing at the litter. There came the scratching of two pairs of feet on the yard, and the Rigleys entered. Elizabeth Bates rose. Rigley was a big man, with very large bones. His head looked particularly bony. Across his temple was a blue scar, caused by a wound got in the pit, a wound in which the coal dust remained blue like tattooing.

"'Asna 'e come whoam yit?" asked the man, without any form of greeting, but with deference and sympathy. "I couldna say wheer he is—'e's non ower theer!"—he jerked his head to signify the "Prince of Wales."

"'E's'appen gone up to th' Yew"①, said Mrs. Rigley.

There was another pause. Rigley had evidently something to get off his mind:

"Ah left'im finishin' a stint," he began. "Loose-all②'ad bin gone about ten minutes when we com'n away, an' I shouted: 'Are ter comin', Walt?' an' 'e said: 'Go on, Ah shanna be but a'ef a minnit,' so we com'n ter th' bottom, me an' Bowers, thinkin' as 'e wor just behint, an' 'ud come up i' th' next bantle③——"

He stood perplexed, as if answering a charge of deserting his mate. Elizabeth Bates, now again certain of disaster, hastened to reassure him:

"I expect 'es gone up to th' 'Yew Tree,' as you say. It's not the first time. I've fretted myself into a fever before now. He'll come home when they carry him."

"Ay, isn't it too bad!" deplored the other woman.

"I'll just step up to Dick's an' see if 'e is theer," offered the man, afraid of appearing alarmed, afraid of taking liberties.

"Oh, I wouldn't think of bothering you that far," said Elizabeth Bates, with emphasis, but he knew she was glad of his offer.

As they stumbled up the entry, Elizabeth Bates heard Rigley's wife run across the yard and open her neighbour's door. At this, suddenly all the blood in her body seemed to switch away from her heart.

"Mind!" warned Rigley. "Ah've said many a time as Ah'd fill up them ruts in this entry, sumb'dy'll be breakin' their legs yit."

She recovered herself and walked quickly along with the miner.

"I don't like leaving the children in bed, and nobody in the house," she said.

"No, you dunna!" he replied courteously. They were'dsoon at the gate of the cottage.

"Well, I shanna be many minnits. Dunna you be frettin' now, 'e'll be all right," said the

---

① th' Yew: i.e., the Yew Tree (a pub)
② Loose-all: signal for end of work
③ bantle: group

butty①.

"Thank you very much, Mr. Rigley," she replied.

"You're welcome!" he stammered, moving away. "I shanna be many minnits."

The house was quiet. Elizabeth Bates took off her hat and shawl, and rolled back the rug. When she had finished, she sat down. It was a few minutes past nine. She was startled by the rapid chuff of the winding-engine at the pit, and the sharp whirr of the brakes on the rope as it descended. Again she felt the painful sweep of her blood, and she put her hand to her side, saying aloud: "Good gracious!—it's only the nine o'clock deputy② going down," rebuking herself.

She sat still, listening. Half an hour of this, and she was wearied out.

"What am I working myself up like this for?" she said pitiably to herself, "I s'll only be doing myself some damage."

She took out her sewing again.

At a quarter to ten there were footsteps. One person! She watched for the door to open. It was an elderly woman, in a black bonnet and a black woollen shawl—his mother. She was about sixty years old, pale, with blue eyes, and her face all wrinkled and lamentable. She shut the door and turned to her daughter-in-law peevishly.

"Eh, Lizzie, whatever shall we do, whatever shall we do!" she cried.

Elizabeth drew back a little, sharply.

"What is it, mother?" she said.

The elder woman seated herself on the sofa.

"I don't know, child, I can't tell you!"—she shook her head slowly. Elizabeth sat watching her, anxious and vexed.

"I don't know," replied the grandmother, sighing very deeply. "There's no end to my troubles, there isn't. The things I've gone through, I'm sure it's enough—!" She wept without wiping her eyes, the tears running.

"But, mother," interrupted Elizabeth, "what do you mean? What is it?"

The grandmother slowly wiped her eyes. The fountains of her tears were stopped by Elizabeth's directness. She wiped her eyes slowly.

"Poor child! Eh, you poor thing!" she moaned. "I don't know what we're going to do, I don't—and you as you are—it's a thing, it is indeed!"

Elizabeth waited.

"Is he dead?" she asked, and at the words her heart swung violently, though she felt a slight flush of shame at the ultimate extravagance of the question. Her words sufficiently

---

① the butty: workmate (cf. "buddy"). Among English coal miners it means a supervisor intermediary between the employers and the men.

② deputy: minor coalmine official

frightened the old lady, almost brought her to herself.

"Don't say so, Elizabeth! We'll hope it's not as bad as that; no, may the Lord spare us that, Elizabeth. Jack Rigley came just as I was sittin' down to a glass afore going to bed, an' 'e said: ''Appen you'll go down th' line, Mrs. Bates; Walt's had an accident. 'Appen you'll go an' sit wi' 'er till we can get him home.' I hadn't time to ask him a word afore he was gone. An' I put my bonnet on an' come straight down, Lizzie. I thought to myself: 'Eh, that poor blessed child, if anybody should come an' tell her of a sudden, there's no knowin' what'll'appen to'er.' You mustn't let it upset you, Lizzie—or you know what to expect. How long is it, six months—or is it five, Lizzie? Ay!"—the old woman shook her head—"time slips on, it slips on! Ay!"

Elizabeth's thoughts were busy elsewhere. If he was killed—would she be able to manage on the little pension and what she could earn?—she counted up rapidly. If he was hurt—they wouldn't take him to the hospital—how tiresome he would be to nurse!—but perhaps she'd be able to get him away from the drink and his hateful ways. She would—while he was ill. The tears offered to come to her eyes at the picture. But what sentimental luxury was this she was beginning? She turned to consider the children. At any rate she was absolutely necessary for them. They were her business.

"Ay!" repeated the old woman, "it seems but a week or two since he brought me his first wages. Ay—he was a good lad, Elizabeth, he was, in his way. I don't know why he got to be such a trouble, I don't. He was a happy lad at home, only full of spirits. But there's no mistake he's been a handful of trouble he has! I hope the Lord'll spare him to mend his ways. I hope so, I hope so. You've had a sight o' trouble with him, Elizabeth, you have indeed. But he was a jolly enough lad wi' me, he was, I can assure you. I don't know how it is ... "

The old woman continued to muse aloud, a monotonous irritating sound while Elizabeth thought concentratedly, startled once, when she heard the winding-engine chuff quickly, and the brakes skirr with a shriek. Then she heard the engine more slowly, and the brakes made no sound. The old woman did not notice. Elizabeth waited in suspense. The mother-in-law talked, with lapses into silence.

"But he wasn't your son, Lizzie, an' it makes a difference. Whatever he was, I remember him when he was little, an' I learned to understand him and to make allowances. You've got to make allowances for them—"

It was half-past ten, and the old woman was saying: "But it's trouble from beginning to end; you're never too old for trouble, never too old for that—" when the gate banged back, and there were heavy feet on the steps.

"I'll go, Lizzie, let me go," cried the old woman, rising. But Elizabeth was at the door. It was a man in pit-clothes.

"They're bringin' 'im, Missis," he said. Elizabeth's heart halted a moment. Then it surged on again, almost suffocating her.

"Is he—is it bad?" she asked.

The man turned away, looking at the darkness:

"The doctor says 'e'd been dead hours. 'E saw 'im i' th' lamp-cabin."

The old woman, who stood just behind Elizabeth, dropped into a chair, and folded her hands, crying: "Oh, my boy, my boy!"

"Hush!" said Elizabeth, with a sharp twitch of a frown. "Be still, mother, don't waken th' children: I wouldn't have them down for anything!"

The old woman moaned softly, rocking herself. The man was drawing away. Elizabeth took a step forward.

"How was it?" she asked.

"Well, I couldn't say for sure," the man replied, very ill at ease. " 'E wor finishin' a stint an' th' butties 'ad gone, an' a lot o' stuff come down atop 'n 'im."

"And crushed him?" cried the widow, with a shudder.

"No," said the man, "it fell at th' back of im. 'E wor under th' face an' it niver touched 'im. It shut 'im in. It seems 'e wor smothered."

Elizabeth shrank back. She heard the old woman behind her cry:

"What?—what did 'e say it was?"

The man replied, more loudly: " 'E wor smothered!"

Then the old woman wailed aloud, and this relieved Elizabeth.

"Oh, mother," she said, putting her hand on the old woman, "don't waken th' children, don't waken th' children."

She wept a little, unknowing, while the old mother rocked herself and moaned. Elizabeth remembered that they were bringing him home, and she must be ready. "They'll lay him in the parlour," she said to herself, standing a moment pale and perplexed.

Then she lighted a candle and went into the tiny room. The air was cold and damp, but she could not make a fire, there was no fireplace. She set down the candle and looked round. The candlelight glittered on the lustre-glasses, on the two vases that held some of the pink chrysanthemums, and on the dark mahogany. There was a cold, deathly smell of chrysanthemums in the room. Elizabeth stood looking at the flowers. She turned away, and calculated whether there would be room to lay him on the floor, between the couch and the chiffonier. She pushed the chairs aside. There would be room to lay him down and to step round him. Then she fetched the old red tablecloth, and another old cloth, spreading them down to save her bit of carpet. She shivered on leaving the parlour; so, from the dresser drawer she took a clean shirt and put it at the fire to air. All the time her mother-in-law was rocking herself in the chair and moaning.

"You'll have to move from there, mother," said Elizabeth. "They'll be bringing him in.

Come in the rocker."

The old mother rose mechanically, and seated herself by the fire, continuing to lament. Elizabeth went into the pantry for another candle, and there, in the little pent-house under the naked tiles, she heard them coming. She stood still in the pantry doorway, listening. She heard them pass the end of the house, and come awkwardly down the three steps, a jumble of shuffling footsteps and muttering voices. The old woman was silent. The men were in the yard.

Then Elizabeth heard Matthews, the manager of the pit, say: "You go in first, Jim. Mind!"

The door came open, and the two women saw a collier backing into the room, holding one end of a stretcher, on which they could see the nailed pit-boots of the dead man. The two carriers halted, the man at the head stooping to the lintel of the door.

"Wheer will you have him?" asked the manager, a short, white-bearded man.

Elizabeth roused herself and came from the pantry carrying the unlighted candle.

"In the parlour," she said.

"In there, Jim!" pointed the manager, and the carriers backed round into the tiny room. The coat with which they had covered the body fell off as they awkwardly turned through the two doorways, and the women saw their man, naked to the waist, lying stripped for work. The old woman began to moan in a low voice of horror.

"Lay th'stretcher at th'side," snapped the manager, "an'put'im on th'cloths. Mind now, mind! Look you now—!"

One of the men had knocked off a vase of chrysanthemums. He stared awkwardly, then they set down the stretcher. Elizabeth did not look at her husband. As soon as she could get in the room, she went and picked up the broken vase and the flowers.

"Wait a minute!" she said.

The three men waited in silence while she mopped up the water with a duster.

"Eh, what a job, what a job, to be sure!" the manager was saying, rubbing his brow with trouble and perplexity. "Never knew such a thing in my life, never! He'd no business to ha' been left. I never knew such a thing in my life! Fell over him clean as a whistle, an' shut him in. Not four foot of space, there wasn't—yet it scarce bruised him."

He looked down at the dead man, lying prone, half naked, all grimed with coal-dust.

"'Sphyxiated,' the doctor said. It is the most terrible job I've ever known; Seems as if it was done o' purpose. Clean over him, an' shut 'im in, like a mouse-trap"—he made a sharp, descending gesture with his hand.

The colliers standing by jerked aside their heads in hopeless comment.

The horror of the thing bristled upon them all.

Then they heard the girl's voice upstairs calling shrilly: "Mother, mother—who is it?

Mother, who is it?"

Elizabeth hurried to the foot of the stairs and opened the door:

"Go to sleep!" she commanded sharply. "What are you shouting about? Go to sleep at once—there's nothing—"

Then she began to mount the stairs. They could hear her on the boards, and on the plaster floor of the little bedroom. They could hear her distinctly:

"What's the matter now?—what's the matter with you, silly thing?"—her voice was much agitated, with an unreal gentleness.

"I thought it was some men come," said the plaintive voice of the child. "Has he come?"

"Yes, they've brought him. There's nothing to make a fuss about. Go to sleep now, like a good child."

They could hear her voice in the bedroom, they waited whilst she covered the children under the bedclothes.

"Is he drunk?" asked the girl, timidly, faintly.

"No! No—he's not! He—he's asleep."

"Is he asleep downstairs?"

"Yes—and don't make a noise."

There was silence for a moment, then the men heard the frightened child again:

"What's that noise?"

"It's nothing, I tell you, what are you bothering for?"

The noise was the grandmother moaning. She was oblivious of everything, sitting on her chair rocking and moaning. The manager put his hand on her arm and bade her "Sh—sh!"

The old woman opened her eyes and looked at him. She was shocked by this interruption, and seemed to wonder.

"What time is it?" the plaintive thin voice of the child, sinking back unhappily into sleep, asked this last question.

"Ten o'clock," answered the mother more softly. Then she must have bent down and kissed the children.

Matthews beckoned to the men to come away. They put on their caps and took up the stretcher. Stepping over the body, they tiptoed out of the house. None of them spoke till they were far from the wakeful children.

When Elizabeth came down she found her mother alone on the parlour floor, leaning over the dead man, the tears dropping on him.

"We must lay him out," the wife said. She put on the kettle, then returning knelt at the feet, and began to unfasten the knotted leather laces. The room was clammy and dim with only one candle, so that she had to bend her face almost to the floor. At last she got off the heavy boots and put them away.

"You must help me now," she whispered to the old woman. Together they stripped the man.

When they arose, saw him lying in the naive dignity of death, the women stood arrested in fear and respect. For a few moments they remained still, looking down, the old mother whimpering. Elizabeth felt countermanded①. She saw him, how utterly inviolable he lay in himself. She had nothing to do with him. She could not accept it. Stooping, she laid her hand on him, in claim. He was still warm, for the mine was hot where he had died. His mother had his face between her hands, and was murmuring incoherently. The old tears fell in succession as drops from wet leaves; the mother was not weeping, merely her tears flowed. Elizabeth embraced the body of her husband, with cheek and lips. She seemed to be listening, inquiring, trying to get some connection. But she could not. She was driven away. He was impregnable.

She rose, went into the kitchen where she poured warm water into a bowl, brought soap and flannel and a soft towel. "I must wash him," she said.

Then the old mother rose stiffly, and watched Elizabeth as she carefully washed his face, carefully brushing his big blond moustache from his mouth with the flannel. She was afraid with a bottomless fear, so she ministered to him. The old woman, jealous, said:

"Let me wipe him!"—and she kneeled on the other side drying slowly as Elizabeth washed, her big black bonnet sometimes brushing the dark head of her daughter-in-law. They worked thus in silence for a long time. They never forgot it was death, and the touch of the man's dead body gave them strange emotions, different in each of the women; a great dread possessed them both, the mother felt the lie was given to her womb, she was denied; the wife felt the utter isolation of the human soul, the child within her was a weight apart from her.

At last it was finished. He was a man of handsome body, and his face showed no traces of drink. He was blond, full-fleshed, with fine limbs. But he was dead.

"Bless him," whispered his mother, looking always at his face, and speaking out of sheer terror. "Dear lad—bless him!" She spoke in a faint, sibilant ecstasy of fear and mother love.

Elizabeth sank down again to the floor, and put her face against his neck, and trembled and shuddered. But she had to draw away again. He was dead, and her living flesh had no place against his. A great dread and weariness held her: she was so unavailing. Her life was gone like this.

"White as milk he is, clear as a twelve-month baby, bless him, the darling!" the old mother murmured to herself. "Not a mark on him, clear and clean and white, beautiful as ever a child was made," she murmured with pride. Elizabeth kept her face hidden.

"He went peaceful, Lizzie—peaceful as sleep. Isn't he beautiful, the lamb? Ay—he must

---

① countermanded: contradicted

ha' made his peace, Lizzie. 'Appen he made it all right, Lizzie, shut in there. He'd have time. He wouldn't look like this if he hadn't made his peace. The lamb, the dear lamb. Eh, but he had a hearty laugh. I loved to hear it. He had the heartiest laugh, Lizzie, as a lad—"

Elizabeth looked up. The man's mouth was fallen back, slightly open under the cover of the moustache. The eyes, half shut, did not show glazed in the obscurity. Life with its smoky burning gone from him, had left him apart and utterly alien to her. And she knew what a stranger he was to her. In her womb was ice of fear, because of this separate stranger with whom she had been living as one flesh. Was this what it all meant—utter, intact separateness, obscured by heat of living? In dread she turned her face away. The fact was too deadly. There had been nothing between them, and yet they had come together, exchanging their nakedness repeatedly. Each time he had taken her, they had been two isolated beings, far apart as now. He was no more responsible than she. The child was like ice in her womb. For as she looked at the dead man, her mind, cold and detached, said clearly: "Who am I? What have I been doing? I have been fighting a husband who did not exist. He existed all the time. What wrong have I done? What was that I have been living with? There lies the reality, this man." And her soul died in her for fear: she knew she had never seen him, he had never seen her, they had met in the dark and had fought in the dark, not knowing whom they met or whom they fought. And now she saw, and turned silent in seeing. For she had been wrong. She had said he was something he was not; she had felt familiar with him. Whereas he was apart all the while, living as she never lived, feeling as she never felt.

In fear and shame she looked at his naked body, that she had known falsely. And he was the father of her children. Her soul was torn from her body and stood apart. She looked at his naked body and was ashamed, as if she had denied it. After all, it was itself. It seemed awful to her. She looked at his face, and she turned her own face to the wall. For his look was other than hers, his way was not her way. She had denied him what he was—she saw it now. She had refused him as himself. And this had been her life, and his life. She was grateful to death, which restored the truth. And she knew she was not dead.

And all the while her heart was bursting with grief and pity for him. What had he suffered? What stretch of horror for this helpless man! She was rigid with agony. She had not been able to help him. He had been cruelly injured, this naked man, this other being, and she could make no reparation. There were the children—but the children belonged to life. This dead man had nothing to do with them. He and she were only channels through which life had flowed to issue in the children. She was a mother—but how awful she knew it now to have been a wife. And he, dead now, how awful he must have felt it to be a husband. She felt that in the next world he would be a stranger to her. If they met there, in the beyond, they would only be ashamed of what had been before. The children had come, for some mysterious reason, out of both of them. But the children did not unite them. Now he was dead, she knew how eternally he was apart from her, how eternally he had nothing more to do with her. She saw this episode of her life closed. They had denied each other in life. Now he had withdrawn. An anguish came over her. It was finished then: it had become hopeless between them long before he died. Yet he had been her husband. But how little!

"Have you got his shirt, 'Lizabeth?"

Elizabeth turned without answering, though she strove to weep and behave as her mother-in-law expected. But she could not, she was silenced. She went into the kitchen and returned with the garment.

"It is aired," she said, grasping the cotton shirt here and there to try. She was almost ashamed to handle him; what right had she or anyone to lay hands on him; but her touch was humble on his body. It was hard work to clothe him. He was so heavy and inert. A terrible dread gripped her all the while: that he could be so heavy and utterly inert, unresponsive, apart. The horror of the distance between them was almost too much for her—it was so infinite a gap she must look across.

At last it was finished. They covered him with a sheet and left him lying, with his face bound. And she fastened the door of the little parlour, lest the children should see what was lying there. Then, with peace sunk heavy on her heart, she went about making tidy the kitchen. She knew she submitted to life, which was her immediate master. But from death, her ultimate master, she winced with fear and shame.

Study Questions:

1. Describe Elizabeth's character. What do we learn about her from her encounters with her children, her father, her neighbours, and her mother-in-law? Is she unrelentingly harsh, or is she sympathetic in any way? What circumstances have made her what she is?

2. Why did Lawrence title his story "Odour of Chrysanthemums"? What symbolic value do chrysanthemums have here? Although Elizabeth is portrayed as stern and bitter, she nonetheless breaks off a few of the flowers, holds them to her face, and puts a few in her pocket. How can we reconcile these contrasting descriptions?

3. Discuss the difference between the way that Elizabeth reacts to the presence of her husband's dead body and the way that her mother-in-law reacts. What does this scene tell you about honesty, love, or human relationships?

4. Describing Elizabeth, the narrator of "Odour of Chrysanthemums" says, "she was grateful to death, which restored the truth. And she knew she was not dead." What "truth" does Elizabeth discover?

[Reading Critically]

Recognizing Symbols

The most important thing to remember when studying symbolism is to avoid far-fetched interpretations. Not every image or event in a short story is symbolic. In literature, few symbols are hidden; most are right out in the open. Don't hunt for symbols. As you read or reread a story, any real symbol will usually find you.

An image that has acquired symbolic resonance in the course of a story will feel different to the reader. It has acquired enough associations to suggest something else. A genuine symbol has an emotional or intellectual power beyond its literal importance. You will recognize its power intuitively, even if you don't initially understand why.

If recognizing a symbol can be done by most experienced readers, understanding its meaning requires critical analysis. The temptation is usually to make the symbol mean too much or too little—to limit it to one narrow association or else to claim it summons up many different things.

7. Theme

The **theme** of a story is whatever the general idea or insight the entire story reveals. In some stories the theme is unmistakable. At the end of Aesop's fable about the council of the mice that can't decide who will bell the cat, the theme is stated in the moral: It is easier to propose a thing than to carry it out. In a work of commercial fiction, too, the theme (if any) is usually obvious. Consider a typical detective thriller in which, say, a rookie police officer trained in scientific methods of crime detection sets out to solve a mystery sooner than his or her rival, a veteran sleuth whose only laboratory is carried under his hat. Perhaps the veteran solves the case, leading to the conclusion (and the theme), "The old ways are the best ways after all." Another story by the same writer might dramatize the same rivalry but reverse the outcome, having the rookie win, thereby reversing the theme: "The times are changing! Let's shake loose from old-fashioned ways." In such commercial entertainments, a theme is like a length of rope with which the writer, patently and mechanically, trusses the story neatly (usually too neatly) into meaningful shape.

In literary fiction, a theme is seldom so obvious. That is, a theme need not be a moral or a message; it may be what the happenings add up to, what the story is about. When we come to the end of a finely wrought short story such as Ernest Hemingway's "A Clean, Well-Lighted Place", it may be easy to sum up the plot—to say what happens—but it is more difficult to sum up the story's main idea. Evidently, Hemingway relates events—how a younger waiter gets rid of an old man and how an older waiter then goes to a coffee bar—but in themselves these events seem relatively slight, though the story as a whole seems large (for its size) and full of meaning. For the meaning, we must look to other elements in the story besides what happens in it. And it is clear that Hemingway is most deeply interested in the thoughts and feelings of the older waiter, the character who has more and more to say as the story progresses, until at the end the story is entirely confined to his thoughts and perceptions. What is meaningful in these thoughts and perceptions? The older waiter understands the old man and sympathizes with his need for a clean, well-lighted place. If we say that, we are still talking about what happens in the story, though we have gone beyond merely recording its external events. But a theme is usually stated in general words. Another try: "Solitary people who cannot sleep need a cheerful, orderly place where they can drink with dignity." That's a little better. We have indicated, at least, that Hemingway's story is about more than just an old man and a couple of waiters. But what about the older waiter's meditation on *nada*, nothingness? Coming near the end of the story, it takes great emphasis; and probably no good statement of Hemingway's theme can leave it out. Still another try at a statement: "Solitary people need a place of refuge from their terrible awareness that their lives (or perhaps, human lives) are essentially meaningless." Neither this nor any other statement of the story's theme is unarguably right, but at least the sentence helps the reader to bring into focus one primary idea that Hemingway seems to be driving at. When we finish reading "A Clean, Well-Lighted Place", we feel that there is such a theme, a unifying vision, even though we cannot reduce it absolutely to a tag. Like some freshwater lake alive with creatures, Hemingway's story is a broad expanse, reflecting in many directions. No wonder that many readers will view it differently.

Moral inferences may be drawn from the story, no doubt—for Hemingway is indirectly giving us advice for properly regarding and sympathizing with the lonely, the uncertain, and the old. But the story does not set forth a lesson that we are supposed to put into practice. One could argue that "A Clean, Well-Lighted Place" contains several themes—and other statements could be made to take in Hemingway's views of love, of communication between people, of dignity. Great short stories, like great symphonies, frequently have more than one theme.

In many a fine short story, theme is the center, the moving force, the principle of unity. Clearly, such a theme is something other than the characters and events of its story. To say of James Joyce's "Araby" that it is about a boy who goes to a bazaar to buy a gift for a young woman, only to arrive too late, is to summarize plot, not theme. (The theme might be put, "The illusions of a romantic child are vulnerable", or it might be put in any of a few hundred other ways.) Although the title of Isaac Bashevis Singer's "Gimpel the Fool" indicates the main character and suggests the subject (his "foolishness"), the theme—the larger realization that the story leaves us with—has to do not with foolishness, but with how to be wise.

Sometimes you will hear it said that the theme of a story (say, Faulkner's "Barn Burning") is "loss of innocence" or "initiation into maturity"; or that the theme of some other story (Hurston's "Sweat", for instance) is "the revolt of the downtrodden". This is to use theme in a larger and more abstract sense than we use it here. Although such general descriptions of theme can be useful—as in sorting a large number of stories into rough categories—we suggest that, in the beginning, you look for whatever truth or insight you think the writer of a story reveals. Try to sum it up in a sentence. By doing so, you will find yourself looking closely at the story, trying to define its principal meaning. You may find it helpful, in making your sentence-statement of theme, to consider these points:

1. Look back once more at the title of the story. From what you have read, what does it indicate?
2. Does the main character in any way change in the story? Does this character arrive at any eventual realization or understanding? Are you left with any realization or understanding you did not have before?
3. Does the author make any general observations about life or human nature? Do the characters make any? (Caution: Characters now and again will utter opinions with which the reader is not necessarily supposed to agree.)
4. Does the story contain any especially curious objects, mysterious flat characters, significant animals, repeated names, song titles, or whatever, that hint toward meanings larger than such things ordinarily have? In literary stories, such symbols may point to central themes.
5. When you have worded your statement of theme, have you cast your statement into general language, not just given a plot summary?
6. Does your statement hold true for the story as a whole, not for just part of it?

In distilling a statement of theme from a rich and complicated story, we have, of course, no more encompassed the whole story than a paleontologist taking a plaster mold of a petrified footprint has captured a living brontosaurus. A writer (other than a fabulist) does not usually set out with theme in hand, determined to make every detail in the story work to demonstrate it. Well then, the skeptical reader may ask, if only some stories have themes, if those themes may be hard to sum up, and if readers will probably disagree in their summations, why bother to state themes? Is not it too much trouble? Surely it is, unless the effort to state a theme ends in pleasure and profit. Trying to sum up the point of a story in our own words is merely one way to make ourselves better aware of whatever we may have understood vaguely and tentatively. Attempted with loving care, such statements may bring into focus our scattered impressions of a rewarding story, may help to clarify and hold fast whatever wisdom the storyteller has offered us.

The Open Boat (1897)

Stephen Crane

A tale intended to be after the fact:
being the experience of four men from the sunk steamer commodore

I

None of them knew the color of the sky. Their eyes glanced level, and were fastened upon the waves that swept toward them. These waves were of the hue of slate, save for the tops, which were of foaming white, and all of the men knew the colors of the sea. The horizon narrowed and widened, and dipped and rose, and at all times its edge was jagged with waves that seemed thrust up in points like rocks.

Many a man ought to have a bathtub larger than the boat which here rode upon the sea. These waves were most wrongfully and barbarously abrupt and tall, and each frothtop was a problem in small-boat navigation.

The cook squatted in the bottom, and looked with both eyes at the six inches of gunwale which separated him from the ocean. His sleeves were rolled over his fat forearms, and the two flaps of his unbuttoned vest dangled as he bent to bail out the boat. Often he said, "Gawd! that was a narrow clip." As he remarked it he invariably gazed eastward over the broken sea.

The oiler[①], steering with one of the two oars in the boat, sometimes raised himself suddenly to keep clear of water that swirled in over the stern. It was a thin little oar, and it seemed often ready to snap.

The correspondent[②], pulling at the other oar, watched the waves and wondered why he was there.

The injured captain, lying in the bow, was at this time buried in that profound dejection and indifference which comes, temporarily at least, to even the bravest and most enduring when, willy-nilly, the firm fails, the army loses, the ship goes down. The mind of the master of a vessel is rooted deep in the timbers of her, though he command for a day or a decade; and this captain had on him the stern impression of a scene in the grays of dawn of seven turned faces, and later a stump of a topmast with a white ball on it, that slashed to and fro at the waves, went low and lower, and down. Thereafter there was something strange in his voice. Although steady, it was deep with mourning, and of a quality beyond oration or tears.

---

① oiler: one who oils machinery in the engine room of a ship
② correspondent: foreign correspondent, newspaper reporter

"Keep'er a little more south, Billie," said he.

"A little more south, sir," said the oiler in the stern.

A seat in this boat was not unlike a seat upon a bucking broncho, and by the same token a broncho is not much smaller. The craft pranced and reared and plunged like an animal. As each wave came, and she rose for it, she seemed like a horse making at a fence outrageously high. The manner of her scramble over these walls of water is a mystic thing, and, moreover, at the top of them were ordinarily these problems in white water, the foam racing down from the summit of each wave requiring a new leap, and a leap from the air. Then, after scornfully bumping a crest, she would slide and race and splash down a long incline, and arrive bobbing and nodding in front of the next menace.

A singular disadvantage of the sea lies in the fact that after successfully surmounting one wave you discover that there is another behind it just as important and just as nervously anxious to do something effective in the way of swamping boats. In a ten-foot dinghy one can get an idea of the resources of the sea in the line of waves that is not probable to the average experience which is never at sea in a dinghy. As each slaty wall of water approached, it shut all else from the view of the men in the boat, and it was not difficult to imagine that this particular wave was the final outburst of the ocean, the last effort of the grim water. There was a terrible grace in the move of the waves, and they came in silence, save for the snarling of the crests.

In the wan light the faces of the men must have been gray. Their eyes must have glinted in strange ways as they gazed steadily astern. Viewed from a balcony, the whole thing would doubtless have been weirdly picturesque. But the men in the boat had no time to see it, and if they had had leisure, there were other things to occupy their minds. The sun swung steadily up the sky, and they knew it was broad day because the color of the sea changed from slate to emerald green streaked with amber lights, and the foam was like tumbling snow. The process of the breaking day was unknown to them. They were aware only of this effect upon the color of the waves that rolled toward them.

In disjointed sentences the cook and the correspondent argued as to the difference between a life-saving station and a house of refuge. The cook had said: "There's a house of refuge just north of the Mosquito Inlet Light, and as soon as they see us they'll come off in their boat and pick us up."

"As soon as who see us?" said the correspondent.

"The crew," said the cook.

"Houses of refuge don't have crews," said the correspondent. "As I understand them, they are only places where clothes and grub are stored for the benefit of shipwrecked people. They don't carry crews."

"Oh, yes, they do," said the cook.

"No, they don't," said the correspondent.

"Well, we're not there yet, anyhow," said the oiler, in the stern.

"Well," said the cook, "perhaps it's not a house of refuge that I'm thinking of as being near Mosquito Inlet Light; perhaps it's a life-saving station."

"We're not there yet," said the oiler in the stern.

II

As the boat bounced from the top of each wave the wind tore through the hair of the hatless men, and as the craft plopped her stern down again the spray slashed past them. The crest of each of these waves was a hill, from the top of which the men surveyed for a moment a broad tumultuous expanse, shining and wind-riven. It was probably splendid, it was probably glorious, this play of the free sea, wild with lights of emerald and white and amber.

"Bully good thing it's an on'shore wind," said the cook. "If not, where would we be? Wouldn't have a show."

"That's right," said the correspondent.

The busy oiler nodded his assent.

Then the captain, in the bow, chuckled in a way that expressed humor, contempt, tragedy, all in one. "Do you think we've got much of a show now, boys?" said he.

Whereupon the three were silent, save for a trifle of hemming and hawing. To express any particular optimism at this time they felt to be childish and stupid, but they all doubtless possessed this sense of the situation in their minds. A young man thinks doggedly at such times. On the other hand, the ethics of their condition was decidedly against any open suggestion of hopelessness. So they were silent.

"Oh, well," said the captain, soothing his children, "we'll get ashore all right."

But there was that in his tone which made them think; so the oiler quoth, "Yes! If this wind holds."

The cook was bailing. "Yes! If we don't catch hell in the surf."

Canton-flannel① gulls flew near and far. Sometimes they sat down on the sea, near patches of brown seaweed that rolled over the waves with a movement like carpets on a line in a gale. The birds sat comfortably in groups, and they were envied by some in the dinghy, for the wrath of the sea was no more to them than it was to a covey of prairie chickens a thousand miles inland. Often they came very close and stared at the men with black bead-like eyes. At these times they were uncanny and sinister in their unblinking scrutiny, and the men hooted angrily at them, telling them to be gone. One came, and evidently decided to alight on the top of the captain's head. The bird flew parallel to the boat and did not circle, but made short sidelong jumps in the air in chicken-fashion. His black eyes were wistfully fixed upon the captain's head. "Ugly brute," said the oiler to the bird. "You look as if you were made with a jacknife." The cook and the correspondent swore darkly at the creature. The captain naturally wished to knock

---

① Canton-flannel: stout cotton fabric

it away with the end of the heavy painter, but he did not dare do it, because anything resembling an emphatic gesture would have capsized this freighted boat; and so, with his open hand, the captain gently and carefully waved the gull away. After it had been discouraged from the pursuit the captain breathed easier on account of his hair, and others breathed easier because the bird struck their minds at this time as being somehow gruesome and ominous.

In the meantime the oiler and the correspondent rowed. And also they rowed. They sat together in the same seat, and each rowed an oar. Then the oiler took both oars; then the correspondent took both oars; then the oiler; then the correspondent. They rowed and they rowed. The very ticklish part of the business was when the time came for the reclining one in the stem to take his turn at the oars. By the very last star of truth, it is easier to steal eggs from under a hen than it was to change seats in the dinghy. First the man in the stern slid his hand along the thwart and moved with care, as if he were of Sèvres①. Then the man in the rowing-seat slid his hand along the other thwart. It was all done with the most extraordinary care. As the two sidled past each other, the whole party kept watchful eyes on the coming wave, and the captain cried: "Look out, now! Steady, there!"

The brown mats of seaweed that appeared from time to time were like islands, bits of earth. They were traveling, apparently, neither one way nor the other. They were, to all intents, stationary. They informed the men in the boat that it was making progress slowly toward the land.

The captain, rearing cautiously in the bow after the dinghy soared on a great swell, said that he had seen the lighthouse at Mosquito Inlet. Presently the cook remarked that he had seen it. The correspondent was at the oars then, and for some reason he too wished to look at the lighthouse; but his back was toward the far shore, and the waves were important, and for some time he could not seize an opportunity to turn his head. But at last there came a wave more gentle than the others, and when at the crest of it he swiftly scoured the western horizon.

"See it?" said the captain.

"No," said the correspondent, slowly; "I didn't see anything."

"Look again," said the captain. He pointed. "It's exactly in that direction."

At the top of another wave the correspondent did as he was bid, and this time his eyes chanced on a small, still thing on the edge of the swaying horizon. It was precisely like the point of a pin. It took an anxious eye to find a lighthouse so tiny.

"Think we'll make it, Captain?"

"If this wind holds and the boat don't swamp, we can't do much else," said the captain.

The little boat, lifted by each towering sea and splashed viciously by the crests, made progress that in the absence of seaweed was not apparent to those in her. She seemed just a wee

---

① Sèvres: chinaware made in this French town

thing wallowing, miraculously top up, at the mercy of five oceans. Occasionally a great spread of water, like white flames, swarmed into her.

"Bail her, cook," said the captain, serenely.

"All right, Captain," said the cheerful cook.

III

It would be difficult to describe the subtle brotherhood of men that was here established on the seas. No one said that it was so. No one mentioned it. But it dwelt in the boat, and each man felt it warm him. They were a captain, an oiler, a cook, and a correspondent, and they were friends—friends in a more curiously iron-bound degree than may be common. The hurt captain, lying against the water-jar in the bow, spoke always in a low voice and calmly; but he could never command a more ready and swiftly obedient crew than the motley three of the dinghy. It was more than a mere recognition of what was best for the common safety. There was surely in it a quality that was personal and heart-felt. And after this devotion to the commander of the boat, there was this comradeship, that the correspondent, for instance, who had been taught to be cynical of men, knew even at the time was the best experience of his life. But no one said that it was so. No one mentioned it.

"I wish we had a sail," remarked the captain. "We might try my overcoat on the end of an oar, and give you two boys a chance to rest." So the cook and the correspondent held the mast and spread wide the overcoat; the oiler steered; and the little boat made good way with her new rig. Sometimes the oiler had to scull sharply to keep a sea from breaking into the boat, but otherwise sailing was a success.

Meanwhile the lighthouse had been growing slowly larger. It had now almost assumed color, and appeared like a little gray shadow on the sky. The man at the oars could not be prevented from turning his head rather often to try for a glimpse of this little gray shadow.

At last, from the top of each wave, the men in the tossing boat could see land. Even as the lighthouse was an upright shadow on the sky, this land seemed but a long black shadow on the sea. It certainly was thinner than paper. "We must be about opposite New Smyrna," said the cook, who had coasted this shore often in schooners. "Captain, by the way, I believe they abandoned that life-saving station there about a year ago."

"Did they?" said the captain.

The wind slowly died away. The cook and the correspondent were not now obliged to slave in order to hold high the oar. But the waves continued their old impetuous swooping at the dinghy, and the little craft, no longer under way, struggled woundily over them. The oiler or the correspondent took the oars again.

Shipwrecks are *apropos* of nothing. If men could only train for them and have them occurred when the men had reached pink condition, there would be less drowning at sea. Of the four in the dinghy none had slept any time worth mentioning for two days and two nights previous to embarking in the dinghy, and in the excitement of clambering about the deck of a foundering ship they had also forgotten to eat heartily.

For these reasons, and for others, neither the oiler nor the correspondent was fond of rowing at this time. The correspondent wondered ingenuously how in the name of all that was sane could there be people who thought it amusing to row a boat. It was not an amusement; it was a diabolical punishment, and even a genius of mental aberrations could never conclude that it was anything but a horror to the muscles and crime against the back. He mentioned to the boat in general how the amusement of rowing struck him, and the weary-faced oiler smiled in full sympathy. Previously to the foundering, by the way, the oiler had worked double watch in the engine-room of the ship.

"Take her easy now, boys," said the captain. "Don't spend yourselves. If we have to run a surf you'll need all your strength, because we'll sure have to swim for it. Take your time."

Slowly the land arose from the sea. From a black line it became a line of black and a line of white—trees and sand. Finally the captain said that he could make out a house on the shore. "That's the house of refuge, sure," said the cook. "They'll see us before long, and come out after us."

The distant lighthouse reared high. "The keeper ought to be able to make us out now, if he's looking through a glass," said the captain. "He'll notify the life-saving people."

"None of those other boats could have got ashore to give word of the wreck," said the oiler, in a low voice, "else the life-boat would be out hunting us."

Slowly and beautifully the land loomed out of the sea. The wind came again. It had veered from the north-east to the south-east. Finally a new sound struck the ears of the men in the boat. It was the low thunder of the surf on the shore. "We'll never be able to make the lighthouse now," said the captain. "Swing her head a little more north, Billie."

"A little more north, sir," said the oiler.

Whereupon the little boat turned her nose once more down the wind, and all but the oarsman watched the shore grow. Under the influence of this expansion doubt and direful apprehension were leaving the minds of the men. The management of the boat was still most absorbing, but it could not prevent a quiet cheerfulness. In an hour, perhaps, they would be ashore.

Their backbones had become thoroughly used to balancing in the boat, and they now rode this wild colt of a dinghy like circus men. The correspondent thought that he had been drenched to the skin, but happening to feel in the top pocket of his coat, he found therein eight cigars. Four of them were soaked with seawater; four were perfectly scatheless. After a search, somebody produced three dry matches; and thereupon the four waifs rode impudently in their little boat and, with an assurance of an impending rescue shining in their eyes, puffed at the big cigars, and judged well and ill of all men. Everybody took a drink of water.

IV

"Cook," remarked the captain, "there don't seem to be any signs of life about your house of refuge."

"No," replied the cook. "Funny they don't see us!"

A broad stretch of lowly coast lay before the eyes of the men. It was of low dunes topped with dark vegetation. The roar of the surf was plain, and sometimes they could see the white lip of a wave as it spun up the beach. A tiny house was blocked out black upon the sky. Southward, the slim lighthouse lifted its little gray length.

Tide, wind, and waves were swinging the dinghy northward. "Funny they don't see us," said the men.

The surfs roar was here dulled, but its tone was nevertheless thunderous and mighty. As the boat swam over the great rollers the men sat listening to this roar. "We'll swamp sure," said everybody.

It is fair to say here that there was not a life-saving station within twenty miles in either direction; but the men did not know this fact, and in consequence they made dark and opprobrious remarks concerning the eyesight of the nation's life-savers. Four scowling men sat in the dinghy and surpassed records in the invention of epithets.

"Funny they don't see us."

The light-heartedness of a former time had completely faded. To their sharpened minds it was easy to conjure pictures of all kinds of incompetency and blindness and, indeed, cowardice. There was the shore of the populous land, and it was bitter and bitter to them that from it came no sign.

"Well," said the captain, ultimately, "I suppose we'll have to make a try for ourselves. If we stay out here too long, we'll none of us have strength left to swim after the boat swamps."

And so the oiler, who was at the oars, turned the boat straight for the shore. There was a sudden tightening of muscles. There was some thinking.

"If we don't all get ashore," said the captain— "if we don't all get ashore, I suppose you fellows know where to send news of my finish?"

They then briefly exchanged some addresses and admonitions. As for the reflections of the men, there was a great deal of rage in them. Perchance they might be formulated thus: "If I am going to be drowned—if I am going to be drowned—if I am going to be drowned, why, in the name of the seven mad gods who rule the sea, was I allowed to come thus far and contemplate sand and trees? Was I brought here merely to have my nose dragged away as I was about to nibble the sacred cheese of life? It is preposterous. If this old ninny-woman, Fate, cannot do better than this, she should be deprived of the management of men's fortunes. She is an old hen who knows not her intention. If she has decided to drown me, why did she not do it in the beginning and save me all this trouble? The whole affair is absurd. —But no; she cannot mean to drown me. She dare not drown me. She cannot drown me. Not after all this work. " Afterward the man might have had an impulse to shake his fist at the clouds. "Just you drown me, now, and then hear what I call you!"

The billows that came at this time were more formidable. They seemed always just about to break and roll over the little boat in a turmoil of foam. There was a preparatory and long growl in the speech of them. No mind unused to the sea would have concluded that the dinghy could ascend these sheer heights in time. The shore was still afar. The oiler was a wily surfman. "Boys," he said swiftly, "she won't live three minutes more, and we're too far out to swim. Shall I take her to sea again, Captain?"

"Yes; go ahead!" said the captain.

This oiler, by a series of quick miracles and fast and steady oarsmanship, turned the boat in the middle of the surf and took her safely to sea again. There was a considerable silence as the boat bumped over the furrowed sea to deeper water. Then somebody in gloom spoke: "Well, anyhow, they must have seen us from the shore by now. "

The gulls went in slanting flight up the wind toward the gray, desolate east. A squall, marked by dinghy clouds and clouds brick-red like smoke from a burning building, appeared from the south-east.

"What do you think of those life-saving people? Ain't they peaches?"

"Funny they haven't seen us. "

"Maybe they think we're out here for sport! Maybe they think we're fishin'. Maybe they think we're damned fools. "

It was a long afternoon. A changed tide tried to force them southward, but wind and wave said northward. Far ahead, where coast-line, sea, and sky formed their mighty angle, there were little dots which seemed to indicate a city on the shore.

"St. Augustine?"

The captain shook his head. "Too near Mosquito Inlet. "

And the oiler rowed, and then the correspondent rowed; then the oiler rowed. It was a weary business. The human back can become the seat of more aches and pains than are registered in books for the composite anatomy of a regiment. It is a limited area, but it can become the theatre of innumerable muscular conflicts, tangles, wrenches, knots, and other comforts.

"Did you ever like to row, Billie?" asked the correspondent.

"No," said the oiler; "hang it!"

When one exchanged the rowing-seat for a place in the bottom of the boat, he suffered a bodily depression that caused him to be careless of everything save an obligation to wiggle one finger. There was cold sea-water swashing to and fro in the boat, and he lay in it. His head, pillowed on a thwart, was within an inch of the swirl of a wave-crest, and sometimes a particularly obstreperous sea came inboard and drenched him once more. But these matters did not annoy him. It is almost certain that if the boat had capsized he would have tumbled comfortably upon the ocean as if he felt sure that it was a great soft mattress.

"Look! There's a man on the shore!"

"Where?"

"There! See 'im?"

"Yes, sure! He's walking along."

"Now he's stopped. Look! He's facing us!"

"He's waving at us!"

"So he is! By thunder!"

"Ah, now we're all right! Now we're all right! There'll be a boat out here for us in half an hour."

"He's going on. He's running. He's going up to that house there."

The remote beach seemed lower than the sea, and it required a searching glance to discern the little black figure. The captain saw a floating stick, and they rowed to it. A bath towel was by some weird chance in the boat, and, tying this on the stick, the captain waved it. The oarsman did not dare turn his head, so he was obliged to ask questions. "What's he doing now?"

"He's standing still again. He's looking, I think. —There he goes again—toward the house. —Now he's stopped again."

"Is he waving at us?"

"No, not now; he was, though."

"Look! There comes another man!"

"He's running."

"Look at him go, would you!"

"Why, he's on a bicycle. Now he's met the other man. They're both waving at us. Look!"

"There comes something up the beach."

"What the devil is that thing?"

"Why, it looks like a boat."

"Why, certainly, it's a boat."

"No; it's on wheels."

"Yes, so it is. Well, that must be the life-boat. They drag them along shore on a wagon."

"That's the life-boat, sure."

"No, by God, it's—it's an omnibus."

"I tell you it's a life-boat."

"It is not! It's an omnibus. I can see it plain. See? One of these big hotel omnibuses."

"By thunder, you're right. It's an omnibus, sure as fate. What do you suppose they are doing with an omnibus? Maybe they are going around collecting the life-crew, hey?"

"That's it, likely. Look! There's a fellow waving a little black flag. He's standing on the steps of the omnibus. There come those other two fellows. Now they're all talking together. Look at the fellow with the flag. Maybe he ain't waving it!"

"That ain't a flag, is it? That's his coat. Why, certainly, that's his coat."

"So it is; it's his coat. He's taken it off and is waving it around his head. But would you look at him swing it!"

"Oh, say, there isn't any life-saving station there. That's just a winter-resort hotel omnibus that has brought over some of the boarders to see us drown."

"What's that idiot with the coat mean? What's he signaling anyhow?"

"It looks as if he were trying to tell us to go north. There must be a life-saving station up there."

"No; he thinks we're fishing. Just giving us a merry hand. See? Ah, there, Willie!"

"Well, I wish I could make something out of those signals. What do you suppose he means?"

"He don't mean anything; he's just playing."

"Well, if he'd just signal us to try the surf again, or to go to sea and wait, or go north, or go south, or go to hell, there would be some reason in it. But look at him! He just stands there and keeps his coat revolving like a wheel. The ass!"

"There come more people."

"Now there's quite a mob. Look! Isn't that a boat?"

"Where? Oh, I see where you mean. No, that's no boat."

"That fellow is still waving his coat."

"He must think we like to see him do that. Why don't he quit it? It don't mean anything."

"I don't know. I think he is trying to make us go north. It must be that there's a life-saving station there somewhere."

"Say, he ain't tired yet. Look at'im wave!"

"Wonder how long he can keep that up. He's been revolving his coat ever since he caught sight of us. He's an idiot. Why aren't they getting men to bring a boat out? A fishing boat—one of those big yawls—could come out here all right. Why don't he do something?"

"Oh, it's all right now."

"They'll have a boat out here for us in less than no time, now that they've seen us."

A faint yellow tone came into the sky over the low land. The shadows on the sea slowly deepened. The wind bore coldness with it, and the men began to shiver.

"Holy smoke!" said one, allowing his voice to express his impious mood, "If we keep on monkeying out here! If we've got to flounder out here all night!"

"Oh, we'll never have to stay here all night! Don't you worry. They've seen us now, and it won't be long before they'll come chasing out after us."

The shore grew dusky. The man waving a coat blended gradually into this gloom, and it swallowed in the same manner the omnibus and the group of people. The spray, when it dashed uproariously over the side, made the voyagers shrink and swear like men who were being branded.

"I'd like to catch the chump who waved the coat. I feel like socking him one, just for luck."

"Why? What did he do?"

"Oh, nothing, but then he seemed so damned cheerful."

In the meantime the oiler rowed, and then the correspondent rowed, and then the oiler rowed. Gray-faced and bowed forward, they mechanically, turn by turn, plied the leaden oars. The form of the lighthouse had vanished from the southern horizon, but finally a pale star appeared, just lifting from the sea. The streaked saffron in the west passed before the all-merging darkness, and the sea to the east was black. The land had vanished, and was expressed only by the low and drear thunder of the surf.

"If I am going to be drowned—if I am going to be drowned—if I am going to be drowned, why, in the name of the seven gods who rule the sea, was I allowed to come thus far and contemplate sand and trees? Was I brought here merely to have my nose dragged away as I was about to nibble the sacred cheese of life?"

The patient captain, drooped over the water-jar, was sometimes obliged to speak to the oarsman.

"Keep her head up! Keep her head up!"

"Keep her head, up, sir." The voices were weary and low.

This was surely a quiet evening. All save the oarsman lay heavily and listlessly in the boat's bottom. As for him, his eyes were just capable of noting the tall black waves that swept forward in a most sinister silence, save for an occasional subdued growl of a crest.

The cook's head was on a thwart, and he looked without interest at the water under this nose. He was deep in other scenes. Finally he spoke. "Billie," he murmured, dreamfully, "what kind of pie do you like best?"

V

"Pie!" said the oiler and the correspondent, agitatedly. "Don't talk about those things, blast you!"

"Well," said the cook, "I was just thinking about ham sandwiches, and—"

A night on the sea in an open boat is a long night. As darkness settled finally, the shine of the light, lifting from the sea in the south, changed to full gold. On the northern horizon a new light appeared, a small bluish gleam on the edge of the waters. These two lights were the furniture of the world. Otherwise there was nothing but waves.

Two men huddled in the stern, and distances were so magnificent in the dinghy that the rower was enabled to keep his feet partly warm by thrusting them under his companions. Their legs indeed extended far under the rowing seat until they touched the feet of the captain forward. Sometimes, despite the efforts of the tired oarsman, a wave came piling into the boat, an icy wave of the night, and the chilling water soaked them anew. They would twist their bodies for a moment and groan, and sleep the dead sleep once more, while the water in the boat gurgled about them as the craft rocked.

The plan of the oiler and the correspondent was for one to row until he lost the ability, and then arouse the other from his sea-water couch in the bottom of the boat.

The oiler plied the oars until his head drooped forward and the overpowering sleep blinded him; and he rowed yet afterward. Then he touched a man in the bottom of the boat, and called his name.

"Will you spell me for a little while?" he said meekly.

"Sure, Billie," said the correspondent, awaking and dragging himself to a sitting position. They exchanged places carefully, and the oiler, cuddling down in the sea-water at the cook's side, seemed to go to sleep instantly.

The particular violence of the sea had ceased. The waves came without snarling. The obligation of the man at the oars was to keep the boat headed so that the tilt of the roller would not capsize her, and to preserve her from filling when the crests rushed past. The black waves were silent and hard to be seen in the darkness. Often one was almost upon the boat before the oarsman was aware.

In a low voice the correspondent addressed the captain. He was not sure that the captain was awake, although this iron man seemed to be always awake. "Captain, shall I keep her making for that light north, sir?"

The same steady voice answered him. "Yes. Keep it about two points off the port bow."

The cook had tied a life-belt around himself in order to get even the warmth which this clumsy cork contrivance could donate, and he seemed almost stove-like when a rower, whose teeth invariably chattered wildly as soon as he ceased his labor, dropped down to sleep.

The correspondent, as he rowed, looked down at the two men sleeping underfoot. The cook's arm was around the oiler's shoulders, and, with their fragmentary clothing and haggard faces, they were the babes of the sea—a grotesque rendering of the old babes in the wood.

Later he must have grown stupid at his work, for suddenly there was a growling of water, and a crest came with a roar and a swash into the boat, and it was a wonder that it did not set the cook afloat in his life-belt. The cook continued to sleep, but the oiler sat up, blinking his eyes and shaking with the new cold.

"Oh, I'm awful sorry, Billie," said the correspondent, contritely.

"That's all right, old boy," said the oiler, and lay down again and was asleep.

Presently it seemed that even the captain dozed, and the correspondent thought that he was the one man afloat on all the oceans. The wind had a voice as it came over the waves, and it was sadder than the end.

There was a long, loud swishing astern of the boat, and a gleaming trail of phosphorescence, like blue flame, was furrowed on the black waters. It might have been made by a monstrous knife.

Then there came a stillness, while the correspondent breathed with open mouth and looked at the sea.

Suddenly there was another swish and another long flash of bluish light, and this time it was alongside the boat, and might almost have been reached with an oar. The correspondent saw an enormous fin speed like a shadow through the water, hurling the crystalline spray and leaving the long glowing trail.

The correspondent looked over his shoulder at the captain. His face was hidden, and he seemed to be asleep. He looked at the babes of the sea. They certainly were asleep. So, being bereft of sympathy, he leaned a little way to one side and swore softly into the sea.

But the thing did not then leave the vicinity of the boat. Ahead or astern, on one side or the other, at intervals long or short, fled the long sparkling streak, and there was to be heard the whiroo of the dark fin. The speed and power of the thing was greatly to be admired. It cut the water like a gigantic and keen projectile.

The presence of this biding thing did not affect the man with the same horror that it would if he had been a picnicker. He simply looked at the sea dully and swore in an undertone.

Nevertheless, it is true that he did not wish to be alone with the thing. He wished one of his companions to awake by chance and keep him company with it. But the captain hung motionless over the water-jar, and the oiler and the cook in the bottom of the boat were plunged in slumber.

VI

"If I am going to be drowned—if I am going to be drowned—if I am going to be drowned, why, in the name of the seven mad gods who rule the sea, was I allowed to come thus far and contemplate sand and trees?"

During this dismal night, it may be remarked that a man would conclude that it was really the intention of the seven mad gods to drown him, despite the abominable injustice of it. For it was certainly an abominable injustice to drown a man who had worked so hard, so hard. The man felt it would be a crime most unnatural. Other people had drowned at sea since galleys swarmed with painted sails, but still—

When it occurs to a man that nature does not regard him as important, and that she feels she would not maim the universe by disposing of him, he at first wishes to throw bricks at the temple, and he hates deeply the fact that there are no bricks and no temples. Any visible expression of nature would surely be pelleted with his jeers.

Then, if there be no tangible thing to hoot, he feels, perhaps, the desire to confront a personification and indulge in pleas, bowed to one knee, and with hands supplicant, saying, "Yes, but I love myself."

A high cold star on a winter's night is the word he feels that she says to him. Thereafter he knows the pathos of his situation.

The men in the dinghy had not discussed these matters, but each had, no doubt, reflected upon them in silence and according to his mind. There was seldom any expression upon their faces save the general one of complete weariness. Speech was devoted to the business of the boat.

To chime the notes of his emotion, a verse mysteriously entered the correspondent's head. He had even forgotten that he had forgotten this verse, but it suddenly was in his mind.

A soldier of the Legion lay dying in Algiers;
There was lack of woman's nursing, there was dearth of woman's tears;
But a comrade stood beside him, and he took that comrade's hand,
And he said, "I never more shall see my own, my native land." ①

In his childhood the correspondent had been made acquainted with the fact that a soldier of the Legion lay dying in Algiers, but he had never regarded the fact as important. Myriads of his school-fellows had informed him of the soldier's plight, but the dinning had naturally ended by making him perfectly indifferent. He had never considered it his affair that a soldier of the Legion lay dying in Algiers, nor had it appeared to him as a matter for sorrow. It was less to him than the breaking of a pencil's point.

Now, however, it quaintly came to him as a human, living thing. It was no longer merely a picture of a few throes in the breast of a poet, meanwhile drinking tea and warming his feet at the grate; it was an actuality—stern, mournful, and fine.

The correspondent plainly saw the soldier. He lay on the sand with his feet out straight and still. While his pale left hand was upon his chest in an attempt to thwart the going of his life, the blood came between his fingers. In the far Algerian distance, a city of low square forms was set against a sky that was faint with the last sunset hues. The correspondent, plying the oars and dreaming of the slow and slower movements of the lips of the soldier, was moved by a profound

---

① *A soldier of the Legion … native land."*: The correspondent remembers a Victorian ballad about a German dying in the French Foreign Legion, "Bingen on the Rhine" by Caroline Norton.

and perfectly impersonal comprehension. He was sorry for the soldier of the Legion who lay dying in Algiers.

The thing which had followed the boat and waited had evidently grown bored at the delay. There was no longer to be heard the slash of the cutwater, and there was no longer the flame of the long trail. The light in the north still glimmered, but it was apparently no nearer to the boat. Sometimes the boom of the surf rang in the correspondent's ears, and he turned the craft seaward then and rowed harder. Southward, some one had evidently built a watch-fire on the beach. It was too low and too far to be seen, but it made a shimmering, roseate reflection upon the bluff in back of it, and this could be discerned from the boat. The wind came stronger, and sometimes a wave suddenly raged out like a mountain cat, and there was to be seen the sheen and sparkle of a broken crest.

The captain, in the bow, moved on his water-jar and sat erect. "Pretty long night," he observed to the correspondent. He looked at the shore. "Those life-saving people take their time."

"Did you see that shark playing around?"

"Yes, I saw him. He was a big fellow, all right."

"Wish I had known you were awake."

Later the correspondent spoke into the bottom of the boat.

"Billie!" There was a slow and gradual disentanglement.

"Billie, will you spell me?"

"Sure," said the oiler.

As soon as the correspondent touched the cold, comfortable sea-water in the bottom of the boat and had huddled close to the cook's life-belt he was deep in sleep, despite the fact that his teeth played all the popular airs. This sleep was so good to him that it was but a moment before he heard a voice call his name in a tone that demonstrated the last stages of exhaustion. "Will you spell me?"

"Sure, Billie."

The light in the north had mysteriously vanished, but the correspondent took his course from the wide-awake captain.

Later in the night they took the boat farther out to sea, and the captain directed the cook to take one oar at the stern and keep the boat facing the seas. He was to call out if he should hear the thunder of the surf. This plan enabled the oiler and the correspondent to get respite together. "We'll give those boys a chance to get into shape again," said the captain. They curled down and, after a few preliminary chatterings and trembles, slept once more the dead sleep. Neither knew they had bequeathed to the cook the company of another shark, or perhaps the same shark.

As the boat caroused on the waves, spray occasionally bumped over the side and gave them a fresh soaking, but this had no power to break their repose. The ominous slash of the wind and the water affected them as it would have affected mummies.

"Boys," said the cook, with the notes of every reluctance in his voice, "she's drifted in pretty close. I guess one of you had better take her to sea again." The correspondent, aroused, heard the crash of the toppled crests.

As he was rowing, the captain gave him some whisky-and-water, and this steadied the chills out of him. "If I ever get ashore and anybody shows me even a photograph of an oar—"

At last there was a short conversation.

"Billie!—Billie, will you spell me?"

"Sure," said the oiler.

VII

When the correspondent again opened his eyes, the sea and sky were each of the gray hue of the dawning. Later, carmine and gold was painted upon the waters. The morning appeared finally, in its splendor, with a sky of pure blue, and the sunlight flamed on the tips of the waves.

On the distant dunes were set many little black cottages, and a tall white windmill reared above them. No man, nor dog, nor bicycle appeared on the beach. The cottages might have formed a deserted village.

The voyagers scanned the shore. A conference was held in the boat. "Well," said the captain, "if no help is coming, we might better try a run through the surf right away. If we stay out here much longer we will be too weak to do anything for ourselves at all." The others silently acquiesced in this reasoning. The boat was headed for the beach. The correspondent wondered if none ever ascended the tall wind-tower, and if they never looked seaward. This tower was a giant, standing with its back to the plight of the ants. It represented in a degree, to the correspondent, the serenity of nature amid the struggles of the individual—nature in the wind, and nature in the vision of men. She did not seem cruel to him then, nor beneficent, nor treacherous, nor wise. But she was indifferent, flatly indifferent. It is, perhaps, plausible that a man in this situation, impressed with the unconcern of the universe, should see the innumerable flaws of life, and have them taste wickedly in his mind, and wish for another chance. A distinction between right and wrong seems absurdly clear to him, then, in this new ignorance of the grave-edge, and he understands that if he were given another opportunity he would mend his conduct and his words, and be better and brighter during an introduction or at a tea.

"Now, boys," said the captain, "she is going to swamp sure. All we can do is to work her in as far as possible, and then when she swamps, pile out and scramble for the beach. Keep cool now, and don't jump until she swamps sure."

The oiler took the oars. Over his shoulders he scanned the surf. "Captain," he said, "I think I'd better bring her about and keep her head-on to the seas and back her in."

"All right, Billie," said the captain. "Back her in." The oiler swung the boat then, and, seated in the stern, the cook and the correspondent were obliged to look over their shoulders to contemplate the lonely and indifferent shore.

The monstrous inshore rollers heaved the boat high until the men were again enabled to see the white sheets of water scudding up the slanted beach. "We won't get in very close," said the captain. Each time a man could wrest his attention from the rollers, he turned his glance toward the shore, and in the expression of the eyes during this contemplation there was a singular quality. The correspondent, observing the others, knew that they were not afraid, but the full meaning of their glances was shrouded.

As for himself, he was too tired to grapple fundamentally with the fact. He tried to coerce his mind into thinking of it, but the mind was dominated at this time by the muscles, and the muscles said they did not care. It merely occurred to him that if he should drown it would be a shame.

There were no hurried words, no pallor, no plain agitation. The men simply looked at the shore. "Now, remember to get well clear of the boat when you jump," said the captain.

Seaward the crest of a roller suddenly fell with a thunderous crash, and the long white comber came roaring down upon the boat.

"Steady now," said the captain. The men were silent. They turned their eyes from the shore to the comber and waited. The boat slid up the incline, leaped at the furious top, bounced over it, and swung down the long back of the wave. Some water had been shipped, and the cook bailed it out.

But the next crest crashed also. The tumbling, boiling flood of white water caught the boat and whirled it almost perpendicular. Water swarmed in from all sides. The correspondent had his hands on the gunwale at this time, and when the water entered at that place he swiftly withdrew his fingers, as if he objected to wetting them.

The little boat, drunken with this weight of water, reeled and snuggled deeper into the sea.

"Bail her out, cook! Bail her out!" said the captain.

"All right, Captain," said the cook.

"Now, boys, the next one will do for us sure," said the oiler. "Mind to jump clear of the boat."

The third wave moved forward, huge, furious, implacable. It fairly swallowed the dinghy, and almost simultaneously the men tumbled into the sea. A piece of life-belt had lain in the bottom of the boat, and as the correspondent went overboard he held this to his chest with his left hand.

The January water was icy, and he reflected immediately that it was colder than he had expected to find it off the coast of Florida. This appeared to his dazed mind as a fact important enough to be noted at the time. The coldness of the water was sad; it was tragic. This fact was somehow mixed and confused with his opinion of his own situation, so that it seemed almost a proper reason for tears. The water was cold.

When he came to the surface he was conscious of little but the noisy water. Afterward he saw his companions in the sea. The oiler was ahead in the race. He was swimming strongly and rapidly. Off to the correspondent's left, the cook's great white and corked back bulged out of the water; and in the rear the captain was hanging with his one good hand to the keel of the overturned dinghy.

There is a certain immovable quality to a shore, and the correspondent wondered at it amid the confusion of the sea.

It seemed also very attractive; but the correspondent knew that it was a long journey, and he paddled leisurely. The piece of life-preserver lay under him, and sometimes he whirled down the incline of a wave as if he were on a hand-sled.

But finally he arrived at a place in the sea where travel was beset with difficulty. He did not pause swimming to inquire what manner of current had caught him, but there his progress ceased. The shore was set before him like a bit of scenery on a stage, and he looked at it and understood with his eyes each detail of it.

As the cook passed, much farther to the left, the captain was calling to him, "Turn over on your back, cook! Turn over on your back and use the oar."

"All right, sir." The cook turned on his back, and, paddling with an oar, went ahead as if he were a canoe.

Presently the boat also passed to the left of the correspondent, with the captain clinging with one hand to the keel. He would have appeared like a man raising himself to look over a board fence if it were not for the extraordinary gymnastics of the boat. The correspondent marvelled that the captain could still hold to it.

They passed on nearer to shore—the oiler, the cook, the captain—and following them went the water-jar, bouncing gaily over the seas.

The correspondent remained in the grip of this strange new enemy—a current. The shore, with its white slope of sand and its green bluff topped with little silent cottages, was spread like a picture before him. It was very near to him then, but he was impressed as one who, in a gallery, looks at a scene from Brittany or Algiers.

He thought: "I am going to drown? Can it be possible? Can it be possible? Can it be possible?" Perhaps an individual must consider his own death to be the final phenomenon of nature.

But later a wave perhaps whirled him out of this small deadly current, for he found suddenly that he could again make progress toward the shore. Later still he was aware that the captain, clinging with one hand to the keel of the dinghy, had his face turned away from the shore and toward him, and was calling his name. "Come to the boat! Come to the boat!"

In his struggle to reach the captain and the boat, he reflected that when one gets properly wearied drowning must really be a comfortable arrangement—a cessation of hostilities accompanied by a large degree of relief; and he was glad of it, for the main thing in his mind for some moments had been horror of the temporary agony. He did not wish to be hurt.

Presently he saw a man running along the shore. He was undressing with most remarkable speed. Coat, trousers, shirt, everything flew magically off him.

"Come to the boat!" called the captain.

"All right, Captain." As the correspondent paddled, he saw the captain let himself down to bottom and leave the boat. Then the correspondent performed his one little marvel of the voyage. A large wave caught him and flung him with ease and supreme speed completely over the boat and far beyond it. It struck him even then as an event in gymnastics and a true miracle of the sea. An overturned boat in the surf is not a plaything to a swimming man.

The correspondent arrived in water that reached only to his waist, but his condition did not enable him to stand for more than a moment. Each wave knocked him into a heap, and the undertow pulled at him.

Then he saw the man who had been running and undressing, and undressing and running, come bounding into the water. He dragged ashore the cook, and then waded toward the captain; but the captain waved him away and sent him to the correspondent. He was naked—naked as a tree in winter; but a halo was about his head, and he shone like a saint. He gave a strong pull, and a long drag, and a bully heave at the correspondent's hand. The correspondent, schooled in the minor formulae, said, "Thanks, old man." But suddenly the man cried, "What's that?" He pointed a swift finger. The correspondent said, "Go."

In the shallows, face downward, lay the oiler. His forehead touched sand that was periodically, between each wave, clear of the sea.

The correspondent did not know all that transpired afterward. When he achieved safe ground he fell, striking the sand with each particular part of his body. It was as if he had dropped from a roof, but the thud was grateful to him.

It seems that instantly the beach was populated with men with blankets, clothes, and flasks, and women with coffee-pots and all the remedies sacred to their minds. The welcome of the land to the men from the sea was warm and generous; but a still and dripping shape was carried slowly up the beach, and the land's welcome for it could only be the different and sinister hospitality of the grave.

When it came night, the white waves paced to and fro in the moonlight, and the wind brought the sound of the great sea's voice to the men on the shore, and they felt that they could then be interpreters.

Study Questions:

1. In actuality, Crane, the captain of the Commodore, and the two crew members spent

nearly thirty hours in the open boat. William Higgins, the oiler, was drowned as Crane describes. Does a knowledge of these facts in any way affect your response to the story? Would you admire the story less if you believed it to be pure fiction?

2. Sum up the personalities of each of the four men in the boat: captain, cook, oiler, and correspondent.

3. What is the point of view of the story?

4. In Para. 9, we are told that as each wave came, the boat "seemed like a horse making at a fence outrageously high". Point out the other vivid similes or figures of speech. What do they contribute to the story's effectiveness?

5. Notice some of the ways in which Crane, as a storyteller conscious of plot, builds suspense. What enemies or obstacles do the men in the boat confront? What is the effect of the scene of the men who wave from the beach (Paras. 86–141)? What is the climax of the story?

6. In Para. 70 (and again in Para. 143), the men wonder, "Was I brought here merely to have my nose dragged away as I was about to nibble the sacred cheese of life?" What variety of irony do you find in this quotation?

7. Why does the scrap of verse about the soldier dying in Algiers (Para. 178) suddenly come to mean so much to the correspondent?

8. What theme in "The Open Boat" seems most important to you? Where is it stated?

9. What secondary themes also enrich the story? See for instance Para. 43 (the thoughts on comradeship).

10. How do you define heroism? Who is a hero in "The Open Boat"?

The Garden Party[①] (1922)

Katherine Mansfield

And after all the weather was ideal. They could not have had a more perfect day for a garden party if they had ordered it. Windless, warm, the sky without a cloud. Only the blue was veiled with a haze of light gold, as it is sometimes in early summer. The gardener had been up since dawn, mowing the lawns and sweeping them, until the grass and the dark flat rosettes where the daisy plants had been seemed to shine. As for the roses, you could not help feeling they understood that roses are the only flowers that impress people at garden parties; the only flowers that everybody is certain of knowing. Hundreds, yes, literally hundreds, had come out in a single night; the green bushes bowed down as though they had been visited by archangels.

Breakfast was not yet over before the men came to put up the marquee.

"Where do you want the marquee put, mother?"

"My dear child, it's no use asking me. I'm determined to leave everything to you children this year. Forget I am your mother. Treat me as an honoured guest."

[①] This story draws upon an incident from Mansfield's life. In March 1907 her mother gave a garden party in their Wellington house, but a street accident befell a neighbor living in a poor quarter nearby.

But Meg could not possibly go and supervise the men. She had washed her hair before breakfast, and she sat drinking her coffee in a green turban, with a dark wet curl stamped on each cheek. Jose, the butterfly, always came down in a silk petticoat and a kimono jacket.

"You'll have to go, Laura; you're the artistic one."

Away Laura flew, still holding her piece of bread-and-butter. It's so delicious to have an excuse for eating out of doors, and besides, she loved having to arrange things; she always felt she could do it so much better than anybody else.

Four men in their shirt-sleeves stood grouped together on the garden path. They carried staves covered with rolls of canvas, and they had big tool-bags slung on their backs. They looked impressive. Laura wished now that she had not got the bread-and-butter, but there was nowhere to put it, and she couldn't possibly throw it away. She blushed and tried to look severe and even a little bit short-sighted as she came up to them.

"Good morning," she said, copying her mother's voice. But that sounded fearfully affected that she was ashamed, and stammered like a little girl, "Oh—er—have you come—is it about the marquee?"

"That's right, miss," said the tallest of the men, a lanky, freckled fellow, and he shifted his tool-bag, knocked back his straw hat and smiled down, "That's about it."

His smile was so easy, so friendly that Laura recovered. What nice eyes he had, small, but such a dark blue! And now she looked at the others, they were smiling too. "Cheer up, we won't bite," their smile seemed to say. How very nice workmen were! And what a beautiful morning! She mustn't mention morning; she must be business-like. The marquee.

"Well, what about the lily-lawn? Would that do?"

And she pointed to the lily-lawn with the hand that didn't hold the bread-and-butter. They turned, they stared in the direction. A little fat chap thrust out his under-lip, and the tall fellow frowned.

"I don't fancy it," said he. "Not conspicuous enough. You see, with a thing like a marquee," and he turned to Laura in his easy way, "you want to put it somewhere where it'll give you a bang slap in the eye, if you follow me."

Laura's upbringing made her wonder for a moment whether it was quite respectful of a workman to talk to her of bangs slap in the eye. But she did quite follow him.

"A corner of the tennis-court," she suggested. "But the band's going to be in one corner."

"H'm, going to have a band, are you?" said another of the workmen. He was pale. He had a haggard look as his dark eyes scanned the tennis-court. What was he thinking?

"Only a very small band," said Laura gently. Perhaps he wouldn't mind so much if the band was quite small. But the tall fellow interrupted.

"Look here, miss, that's the place. Against those trees. Over there. That'll do fine."

against the karakas. Then the karaka-trees would be hidden. And they were so lovely, with their broad, gleaming leaves, and their clusters of yellow fruit. They were like trees you imagined growing on a desert island, proud, solitary, lifting their leaves and fruits to the sun in a kind of silent splendour. Must they be hidden by a marquee?

They must. Already the men had shouldered their staves and were making for the place. Only the tall fellow was left. He bent down, pinched a sprig of lavender, put his thumb and forefinger to his nose and snuffed up the smell. When Laura saw that gesture she forgot all about the karakas in her wonder at him caring for things like that—caring for the smell of lavender. How many men that she knew would have done such a thing? Oh, how extraordinarily nice workmen were, she thought. Why couldn't she have workmen for friends I rather than the silly boys she danced with and who came to Sunday night supper? She would get on much better with men like these.

It's all the fault, she decided, as the tall fellow drew something on the back of an envelope, something that was to be looped up or left to hang, of these absurd class distinctions. Well, for her part, she didn't feel them. Not a bit, not an atom … And now there came the chock-chock of wooden hammers. Some one whistled, some one sang out, "Are you right there, matey?" "Matey!" The friendliness of it, the—the—Just to prove how happy she was, just to show the tall fellow how at home she felt, and how she despised stupid conventions, Laura took a big bite of her bread-and-butter as she stared at the little drawing. She felt just like a work-girl.

"Laura, Laura, where are you? Telephone, Laura!" a voice cried from the house.

"Coming!" Away she skimmed, over the lawn, up the path, up the steps, across the veranda, and into the porch. In the hall her father and Laurie were brushing their hats ready to go to the office.

"I say, Laura," said Laurie very fast, "you might just give a squiz① at my coat before this afternoon. See if it wants pressing."

"I will," said she. Suddenly she couldn't stop herself. She ran at Laurie and gave him a small, quick squeeze. "Oh, I do love parties, don't you?" gasped Laura.

"Ra-ther," said Laurie's warm, boyish voice, and he squeezed his sister too, and gave her a gentle push. "Dash off to the telephone, old girl."

The telephone. "Yes, yes; oh yes. Kitty? Good morning, dear. Come to lunch? Do, dear. Delighted of course. It will only be a very scratch meal—just the sandwich crusts and broken meringue-shells and what's left over. Yes, isn't it a perfect morning? Your white? Oh, I certainly should. One moment—hold the line. Mother's calling." And Laura sat back. "What, mother? Can't hear."

---

① squiz: glance

Mrs. Sheridan's voice floated down the stairs. "Tell her to wear that sweet hat she had on last Sunday."

"Mother says you're to wear that sweet hat you had on last Sunday. Good. One o'clock. Bye-bye."

Laura put back the receiver, flung her arms over her head, took a deep breath, stretched and let them fall. "Huh," she sighed, and the moment after the sigh she sat up quickly. She was still, listening. All the doors in the house seemed to be open. The house was alive with soft, quick steps and running voices. The green baize① door that led to the kitchen regions swung open and shut with a muffled thud. And now there came a long, chuckling absurd sound. It was the heavy piano being moved on its stiff castors. But the air! If you stopped to notice, was the air always like this? Little faint winds were playing chase in at the tops of the windows, out at the doors. And there were two tiny spots of sun, one on the inkpot, one on a silver photograph frame, playing too. Darling little spots. Especially the one on the inkpot lid. It was quite warm. A warm little silver star. She could have kissed it.

The front door bell pealed, and there sounded the rustle of Sadie's print skirt on the stairs. A man's voice murmured; Sadie answered, careless, "I'm sure I don't know. Wait. I'll ask Mrs. Sheridan."

"What is it, Sadie?" Laura came into the hall.

"It's the florist, Miss Laura."

It was, indeed. There, just inside the door, stood a wide, shallow tray full of pots of pink lilies. No other kind. Nothing but lilies—canna lilies, big pink flowers, wide open, radiant, almost frighteningly alive on bright crimson stems.

"O-oh, Sadie!" said Laura, and the sound was like a little moan. She crouched down as if to warm herself at that blaze of lilies; she felt they were in her fingers, on her lips, growing in her breast.

"It's some mistake," she said faintly. "Nobody ever ordered so many. Sadie, go and find mother."

But at that moment Mrs. Sheridan joined them.

"It's quite right," she said calmly. "Yes, I ordered them. Aren't they lovely?" She pressed Laura's arm. "I was passing the shop yesterday, and I saw them in the window. And I suddenly thought for once in my life I shall have enough canna lilies. The garden party will be a good excuse."

"But I thought you said you didn't mean to interfere," said Laura. Sadie had gone. The florist's man was still outside at his van. She put her arm round her mother's neck and gently, very gently, she bit her mother's ear.

---

① baize: coarse woolen

"My darling child, you wouldn't like a logical mother, would you? Don't do that. Here's the man."

He carried more lilies still, another whole tray.

"Bank them up, just inside the door, on both sides of the porch; please," said Mrs. Sheridan. "Don't you agree, Laura?"

"Oh, I do mother."

In the drawing-room Meg, Jose and good little Hans had at last succeeded in moving the piano.

"Now, if we put this chesterfield against the wall and move everything out of the room except the chairs, don't you think?"

"Quite."

"Hans, move these tables into the smoking-room, and bring a sweeper to take these marks off the carpet and—one moment, Hans—" Jose loved giving orders to the servants, and they loved obeying her. She always made them feel they were taking part in some drama. "Tell mother and Miss Laura to come here at once."

"Very good, Miss Jose."

She turned to Meg. "I want to hear what the piano sounds like, just in case I'm asked to sing this afternoon. Let's try over 'This life is Weary.'"

Pom! *Ta-ta-ta Tee-ta*! The piano burst out so passionately that Jose's face changed. She clasped her hands. She looked mournfully and enigmatically at her mother and Laura as they came in.

> This Life is *Wee-ary*,
> A Tear—a Sigh.
> A Love that Chan-ges,
> This Life is Wee-ary,
> A Tear—a Sigh.
> A Love that Chan-ges,
> And then ... Good-bye!

But at the word "Good-bye", and although the piano sounded more desperate than ever, her face broke into a brilliant, dreadfully unsympathetic smile.

"Aren't I in good voice, mummy?" she beamed.

> This Life is *Wee-ary*,
> Hope comes to Die.
> A Dream—a Wa-kening.

But now Sadie interrupted them. "What is it, Sadie?"

"If you please, m'm, cook says have you got the flags① for the sandwiches?"

"The flags for the sandwiches, Sadie?" echoed Mrs. Sheridan dreamily. And the children knew by her face that she hadn't got them. "Let me see." And she said to Sadie firmly, "Tell cook I'll let her have them in ten minutes."

Sadie went.

"Now, Laura," said her mother quickly. "Come with me into the smoking-room. I've got the names② somewhere on the back of an envelope. You'll have to write them out for me. Meg, go upstairs this minute and take that wet thing off your head. Jose, run and finish dressing this instant. Do you hear me, children, or shall I have to tell your father when he comes home to-night? And,—and, Jose, pacify cook if you do go into the kitchen, will you? I'm terrified of her this morning."

The envelope was found at last behind the dining-room clock, though how it had got there Mrs. Sheriden could not imagine.

"One of you children must have stolen it out of my bag, because I remember vividly—cream cheese and lemon-curd. Have you done that?"

"Yes."

"Egg and—" Mrs. Sheridan held the envelope away from her. "It looks like mice. It can't be mice, can it?"

"Olive, pet," said Laura, looking over her shoulder.

"Yes, of course, olive. What a horrible combination it sounds. Egg and olive."

They were finished at last, and Laura took them off to the kitchen. She found Jose there pacifying the cook, who did not look at all terrifying.

"I have never seen such exquisite sandwiches," said Jose's rapturous voice. "How many kinds did you say there were, cook? Fifteen?"

"Fifteen, Miss Jose."

"Well, cook, I congratulate you."

Cook swept up crusts with the long sandwich knife and smiled broadly.

"Godber's has come," announced Sadie, issuing out of the pantry. She had seen the man pass the window.

That meant the cream puffs had come. Godber's were famous for their cream puffs. Nobody ever thought of making them at home.

"Bring them in and put them on the table, my girl," ordered cook.

Sadie brought them in and went back to the door. Of course Laura and Jose were far too

---

① Little paper flags stuck in a plate of small triangular sandwiches indicating what is inside the sandwiches on each plate—an English custom adopted by the New Zealand middle class as a sign of gentility.

② the names: the names of the sandwich filling to be written on each flag

grown-up to really care about such things. All the same, they couldn't help agreeing that the puffs looked very attractive. Very. Cook began arranging them, shaking off the extra icing sugar.

"Don't they carry one back to all one's parties?" said Laura.

"I suppose they do," said practical Jose, who never liked to be carried back. "They look beautifully light and feathery, I must say."

"Have one each, my dears," said cook in her comfortable voice. "Yer ma won't know."

Oh, impossible. Fancy cream puffs so soon after breakfast. The very idea made one shudder. All the same, two minutes later Jose and Laura were licking their fingers with that absorbed inward look that only comes from whipped cream.

"Let's go into the garden, out by the back way," suggested Laura. "I want to see how the men are getting on with the marquee. They're such awfully nice men."

But the back door was blocked by cook, Sadie, Godber's man and Hans.

Something had happened.

"Tuk-tuk-tuk," clucked cook like an agitated hen. Sadie had her hand clapped to her cheek as though she had toothache. Hans's face was screwed up in the effort to understand. Only Godber's man seemed to be enjoying himself. It was his story.

"What's the matter? What's happened?"

"There's been a horrible accident," said cook. "A man killed."

"A man killed! Where? How? When?"

But Godber's man wasn't going to have his story snatched from under his very nose.

"Know those little cottages just below here, miss?" Know them? Of course, she knew them. "Well, there's a young chap living there, name of Scott, a carter. His horse shied at a traction-engine, corner of Hawke Street this morning, and he was thrown out on the back of his head. Killed."

"Dead!" Laura stared at Godber's man.

"Dead when they picked him up," said Godber's man with relish. "They were taking the body home as I come up here." And he said to the cook, "He's left a wife and five little ones."

"Jose, come here." Laura caught hold of her sister's sleeve and dragged her through the kitchen to the other side of the green baize door. There she paused and leaned against it. "Jose!" she said, horrified, "however are we going to stop everything?"

"Stop everything, Laura!" cried Jose in astonishment. "What do you mean?" "Stop the garden party, of course." Why did Jose pretend?

But Jose was still more amazed. "Stop the garden party? My dear Laura, don't be so absurd. Of course we can't do anything of the kind. Nobody expects us to. Don't be so extravagant."

"But we can't possibly have a garden party with a man dead just outside the front gate."

That really was extravagant, for the little cottages were in a lane to themselves at the very bottom of a steep rise that led up to the house. A broad road ran between. True, they were far too near. They were the greatest possible eyesore, and they had no right to be in that neighbourhood at all. They were little mean dwellings painted a chocolate brown. In the garden patches there was nothing but cabbage stalks, sick hens and tomato cans. The very smoke coming out of their chimneys was poverty-stricken. Little rags and shreds of smoke, so unlike the great silvery plumes that uncurled from the Sheridans' chimneys. Washerwomen lived in the lane and sweeps and a cobbler, and a man whose house-front was studded all over with minute bird-cages. Children swarmed. When the Sheridans were little they were forbidden to set foot there because of the revolting language and of what they might catch. But since they were grown up, Laura and Laurie on their prowls sometimes walked through. It was disgusting and sordid. They came out with a shudder. But still one must go everywhere; one must see everything. So through they went.

"And just think of what the band would sound like to that poor woman," said Laura.

"Oh, Laura!" Jose began to be seriously annoyed. "If you're going to stop a band playing every time someone has an accident, you'll lead a very strenuous life. I'm every bit as sorry about it as you. I feel just as sympathetic." Her eyes hardened. She looked at her sister just as she used to when they were little and fighting together. "You won't bring a drunken workman back to life by being sentimental," she said softly.

"Drunk! Who said he was drunk?" Laura turned furiously on Jose. She said, just as they had used to say on those occasions, "I'm going straight up to tell mother."

"Do, dear," cooed Jose.

"Mother, can I come into your room?" Laura turned the big glass door-knob.

"Of course, child. Why, what's the matter? What's given you such a colour?" And Mrs. Sheridan turned round from her dressing-table. She was trying on a new hat.

"Mother, a man's been killed," began Laura.

"Not in the garden?" interrupted her mother.

"O, no!"

"Oh, what a fright you gave me!" Mrs. Sheridan sighed with relief, and took off the big hat and held it on her knees.

"But listen, mother," said Laura. Breathless, half-choking, she told the dreadful story. "Of course, we can't have our party, can we?" she pleaded. "The band and everybody arriving. They'd hear us, mother; they're nearly neighbours!"

To Laura's astonishment her mother behaved just like Jose; it was harder to bear because she seemed amused. She refused to take Laura seriously.

"But, my dear child, use your common sense. It's only by accident we've heard of it. If some one had died there normally—and I can't understand how they keep alive in those poky little holes—we should still be having our party, shouldn't we?"

Laura had to say "yes" to that, but she felt it was all wrong. She sat down on her mother's sofa and pinched the cushion frill.

"Mother, isn't it really terribly heartless of us?" she asked.

"Darling!" Mrs. Sheridan got up and came over to her, carrying the hat. Before Laura could stop her she had popped it on. "My child!" said her mother, "the hat is yours. It's made for you. It's much too young for me. I have never seen you look such a picture. Look at yourself!" And she held up her hand-mirror.

"But, mother," Laura began again. She couldn't look at herself; she turned aside.

This time Mrs. Sheridan lost patience just as Jose had done.

"You are being very absurd, Laura," she said coldly. "People like that don't expect sacrifices from us. And it's not very sympathetic to spoil everybody's enjoyment as you're doing now."

"I don't understand," said Laura, and she walked quickly out of the room into her own bedroom. There, quite by chance, the first thing she saw was this charming girl in the mirror, in her black hat trimmed with gold daisies, and a long black velvet ribbon. Never had she imagined she could look like that. Is mother right? she thought. And now she hoped her mother was right; Am I being extravagant? Perhaps it was extravagant. Just for a moment she had another glimpse of that poor woman and those little children, and the body being carried into the house. But it all seemed blurred, unreal, like a picture in the newspaper. I'll remember it again after the party's over, she decided. And somehow that seemed quite the best plan …

Lunch was over by half past one. By half past two they were all ready for the fray. The green-coated band had arrived and was established in a cornet of the tennis-court.

"My dear!" trilled Kitty Maitland, "aren't they too like frogs for words? You ought to have arranged them round the pond with the conductor in the middle on a leaf."

Laurie arrived and hailed them on his way to dress. At the sight of him Laura remembered the accident again. She wanted to tell him. If Laurie agreed with the others, then it was bound to be all right. And she followed him into the hall.

"Laurie!"

"Hallo!" He was half-way upstairs, but when he turned round and saw Laura he suddenly puffed out his cheeks and goggled his eyes at her. "My word, Laura! You do look stunning," said Laurie. "What an absolutely topping hat!"

Laura said faintly "Is it?" and smiled up at Laurie, and didn't tell him at all.

Soon after that people began coming in streams. The band struck up; the hired waiters ran from the house to the marquee. Wherever you looked there were couples strolling, bending to the flowers, greeting, moving on over the lawn. They were like bright birds that had alighted in the Sheridans' garden for this one afternoon, on their way to—where? Ah, what happiness it is to be with people who all are happy, to press hands, press cheeks, smile into eyes.

"Darling Laura, how well you look!"

"What a becoming hat, child!"

"Laura, you look quite Spanish. I've never seen you look so striking."

And Laura, glowing, answered softly, "Have you had tea? Won't you have an ice? The passion-fruit ices really are rather special." She ran to her father and begged him. "Daddy darling, can't the band have something to drink?"

And the perfect afternoon slowly ripened, slowly faded, slowly its petals closed.

"Never a more delightful garden party ..." "The greatest success ..." "Quite the most ..."

Laura helped her mother with the goodbyes. They stood side by side in the porch till it was all over.

"All over, all over, thank heaven," said Mrs. Sheridan. "Round up the others, Laura. Let's go and have some fresh coffee. I'm exhausted. Yes, it's been very successful. But oh, these parties, these parties! Why will you children insist on giving parties!" And they all of them sat down in the deserted marquee.

"Have a sandwich, daddy dear. I wrote the flag."

"Thanks." Mr. Sheridan took a bite and the sandwich was gone. He took another. "I suppose you didn't hear of a beastly accident that happened today?" he said.

"My dear," said Mrs. Sheridan, holding up her hand, "we did. It nearly ruined the party. Laura insisted we should put it off."

"Oh, mother!" Laura didn't want to be teased about it.

"It was a horrible affair all the same," said Mr. Sheridan. "The chap was married too. Lived just below in the lane, and leaves a wife and half a dozen kiddies, so they say."

An awkward little silence fell. Mrs. Sheridan fidgeted with her cup. Really, it was very tactless of father ...

Suddenly she looked up. There on the table were all those sandwiches, cakes, puffs, all un-eaten, all going to be wasted. She had one of her brilliant ideas.

"I know," she said. "Let's make up a basket. Let's send that poor creature some of this perfectly good food. At any rate, it will be the greatest treat for the children. Don't you agree? And she's sure to have neighbours calling in and so on. What a point to have it all ready prepared. Laura!" She jumped up. "Get me the big basket out of the stairs cupboard."

"But, mother, do you really think it's a good idea?" said Laura.

Again, how curious, she seemed to be different from them all. To take scraps from their party. Would the poor woman really like that?

"Of course! What's the matter with you today? An hour or two ago you were insisting on us being sympathetic, and now—"

Oh well! Laura ran for the basket. It was filled, it was heaped by her mother.

"Take it yourself, darling," said she. "Run down just as you are. No, wait, take the arum lilies too. People of that class are so impressed by arum lilies."

"The stems will ruin her lace frock," said practical Jose.

So they would. Just in time. "Only the basket, then. And, Laura!"—her mother followed her out of the marquee—"don't on any account—"

"What mother?"

No, better not put such ideas into the child's head! "Nothing! Run along."

It was just growing dusky as Laura shut their garden gates. A big dog ran by like a shadow. The road gleamed white, and down below in the hollow the little cottages were in deep shade. How quiet it seemed after the afternoon. Here she was going down the hill to somewhere where a man lay dead, and she couldn't realize it. Why couldn't she? She stopped a minute. And it seemed to her that kisses, voices, tinkling spoons, laughter, the smell of crushed grass were somehow inside her. She had no room for anything else. How strange! She looked up at the pale sky, and all she thought was, "Yes, it was the most successful."

Now the broad road was crossed. The lane began, smoky and dark. Women in shawls and men's tweed caps hurried by. Men hung over the palings; the children played in the doorways. A low hum came from the mean little cottages. In some of them there was a flicker of light, and a shadow, crab-like, moved across the window. Laura bent her head and hurried on. She wished now she had put on a coat. How her frock shone! And the big hat with the velvet streamer—if only it was another hat! Were the people looking at her? They must be. It was a mistake to have come; she knew all along it was a mistake. Should she go back even now?

No, too late. This was the house. It must be. A dark knot of people stood outside. Beside the gate an old, old woman with a crutch sat in a chair, watching. She had her feet on a newspaper. The voices stopped as Laura drew near. The group parted. It was as though she was expected, as though they had known she was coming here.

Laura was terribly nervous. Tossing the velvet ribbon over her shoulder, she said to a woman standing by, "Is this Mrs. Scott's house?" and the woman, smiling queerly, said, "It is, my lass."

Oh, to be away from this! She actually said, "Help me, God," as she walked up the tiny path and knocked. To be away from those staring eyes, or to be covered up in anything, one of those women's shawls even. I'll just leave the basket and go, she decided. I shan't even wait for it to be emptied.

Then the door opened. A little woman in black showed in the gloom.

Laura said, "Are you Mrs. Scott?" But to her horror the woman answered, "Walk in please, miss," and she was shut in the passage.

"No," said Laura, "I don't want to come in. I only want to leave this basket. Mother sent—"

The little woman in the gloomy passage seemed not to have heard her. "Step this way, please, miss," she said in an oily voice, and Laura followed her.

She found herself in a wretched little low kitchen, lighted by a smoky. There was a woman sitting before the fire.

"Em," said the little creature who had let her in. "Em! It's a young lady." She turned to Laura. She said meaningly, "I'm her sister, Miss. You'll excuse'er, won't you?"

"Oh, but of course!" said Laura. "Please, please don't disturb her. I—I only want to leave—"

But at that moment the woman at the fire turned round. Her face, puffed up, red, with swollen eyes and swollen lips, looked terrible. She seemed as though she couldn't understand why Laura was there. What did it mean? Why was this stranger standing in the kitchen with a basket? What was it all about? And the poor face puckered up again.

"All right, my dear," said the other. "I'll thank the young lady."

And again she began, "You'll excuse her, miss, I'm sure," and her face, swollen too, tried an oily smile.

Laura only wanted to get out, to get away. She was back in the passage. The door opened. She walked straight through into the bedroom where the dead man was lying.

"You'd like a look at'im, wouldn't you?" said Em's sister, and she brushed past Laura over to the bed. "Don't be afraid, my lass,"—and now her voice sounded fond and sly, and fondly she drew down the sheet— "'e looks a picture. There's nothing to show. Come along, my dear."

Laura came.

There lay a young man, fast asleep—sleeping so soundly, so deeply, that he was far, far away from them both. Oh, so remote, so peaceful. He was dreaming. Never wake him up again. His head was sunk in the pillow, his eyes were closed; they were blind under the closed eyelids. He was given up to his dream. What did garden parties and baskets and lace frocks matter to him? He was far from all those things. He was wonderful, beautiful. While they were laughing and while the band was playing, this marvel had come to the lane. Happy ... happy ... All is well, said that sleeping face. This is just as it should be. I am content.

But all the same you had to cry, and she couldn't go out of the room without laying something to him. Laura gave a loud childish sob.

"Forgive my hat," she said.

And this time she didn't wait for Em's sister. She found her way out of the door, down the path, past all those dark people. At the corner of the lane she met Laurie.

He stepped out of the shadow. "Is that you, Laura?"

"Yes."

"Mother was getting anxious. Was it all right?"

"Yes, quite. Oh, Laurie!" She took his arm, she pressed up against him.

"I say, you're not crying, are you?" asked her brother.

Laura shook her head. She was.

Laurie put his arm round her shoulder. "Don't cry," he said in his warm, loving voice. "Was it awful?"

"No," sobbed Laura. "It was simply marvellous. But, Laurie—" She stopped, she looked at her brother. "Isn't life," she stammered, "isn't life—" But what life was she couldn't explain. No matter. He quite understood.

"Isn't it, darling?" said Laurie.

Study Questions:

1. How does Laura feel when she discovers that her mother and sister don't agree with her about the accident? When Laura tries on the new hat, why does she want her mother to be right about continuing with the party? How are Laura's thoughts conflicted?

2. Describe Laura's relationship with and attitude toward her mother both before and after Laura finds out about the accident.

3. What do we learn about Laura when she talks to the workmen about placement of the marquee? How sure of herself is she? How does she compare herself to her mother? How does she demonstrate confused feelings toward the workmen?

4. How important is Laura's brother, Laurie, in this story? How close is Laura to him? Why does she decide not to tell him about the accident after he compliments her new hat?

5. Describe Laura's thoughts and feelings when she visits the Scott family and views the corpse. Why are Mrs. Scott and her sister described in unflattering terms (Mrs. Scott's face is "puffed up, red, with swollen eyes and swollen lips", while her sister has "an oily smile")? Why does Laura think Scott's dead body is "wonderful, beautiful"?

6. What has Laura learned by the end of the story? Has she completely rejected her family's values? Does Laurie really understand his sister?

7. What does "The Garden Party" tell us about class relations?

[Reading Critically]

Stating the Theme

Finding the central theme of a story is only part of the challenge in reading about a work of fiction. It is also necessary to state the theme concisely and accurately in words. In a story we have read with understanding and enjoyment, and we often recognize the major theme intuitively. But how do we express that often slightly vague recognition in clear language?

One method is to do a bit of free writing. Rapidly jot down a list of everything you associate with the central point of the story. If you are discussing Stephen Crane's "The Open Boat", for example, you might write down a list like: "man against nature, life and death struggle, camaraderie of people in crisis, blindness of fate, courage in face of danger, bravery not enough". After completing your list, circle the two or three most important points and then try to combine them into a short sentence. For Crane, you might summarize the key point as: "The central theme of 'The Open Boat' is nature's indifference to the fate of even the most courageous individuals."

Once you have clearly and concisely stated the central theme, it will be easy to relate particular details of the story to it. If other elements do not demonstrate some connection to your theme, you might want to reevaluate your summation. Is there some important aspect you have missed? Or have you put some secondary idea into the theme? There is no shame in starting over. Recognizing our own mistakes is an important step in critical thinking.

8. Evaluating a Story

When we evaluate a story, we consider it and place a value on it. Perhaps we decide that it is a masterpiece, or a bit of trash, or a work of some value in between. No single method of judgment will work on every story. Still, there are things we can look for in a story—usually clear indications of its author's competence.

Good critics of literature have at least a working knowledge of some of its conventions. By conventions we mean usual devices and features of a literary work, by which we can recognize its kind. When in movies or on television we watch a yarn about a sinister old mansion full of horrors, we recognize the conventions of that long-lived species of fiction, the Gothic story. *The Castle of Otranto, A Gothic Story* (1764), by English author Horace Walpole, started the genre, supplied its name, and established its favorite trappings. In Walpole's short novel, Otranto is a cobwebbed ruin full of underground passages and massive doors that slam unexpectedly. There are awful objects: a statue that bleeds, a portrait that steps from its frame, a giant helmet that falls and leaves its victim "dashed to pieces". Atmosphere is essential to a Gothic story: dusty halls, shadowy landscapes, whispering servants seen at a distance imperfectly through the dusk. In Charlotte Bronte's *Jane Eyre* (1847), we find the model for a legion of heroines in the Gothic fiction of our own day. In the best-selling Gothic romances of

Victoria Holt, Phyllis A. Whitney, and others, young women similarly find love while working as governesses in ominous mansions. Lacking English castles, American authors of Gothic fiction have had to make do with dark old houses—like those in Nathaniel Hawthorne's novel *The House of the Seven Gables*, in Charlotte Perkins Gilman's "The Yellow Wallpaper", and in the short stories of Edgar Allan Poe, such as "The Tell-Tale Heart". William Faulkner, who brought the tradition to Mississippi, gives "A Rose for Emily" some familiar conventions: a rundown mansion, a mysterious servant, a madwoman, a hideous secret. But Faulkner's story, in its portrait of an aristocrat who refuses to admit that her world has vanished, goes far beyond Gothic conventions. When you set up court as a judge of stories, to recognize such conventions will be an advantage. Knowing a Gothic story for what it is, you won't condemn it for lacking "realism". And to be aware of the Gothic elements in "A Rose for Emily" may help you see how original Faulkner manages to be, in spite of employing some handed-down conventions.

Is the story a piece of commercial fiction tailored to a formula, or is it unique in its design? You can't demand the subtlety of Katherine Anne Porter for a writer of hard-boiled detective stories. Neither can you put down "The Jilting of Granny Weatherall" for lacking slam-bang action. Some stories are no more than light, entertaining bits of fluff—no point in damning them, unless you dislike fluff or find them written badly. Of course, you are within your rights to prefer solidity to fluff, or to prefer a Porter story to a typical paperback romance by a hack writer. Kurt Vonnegut's "Harrison Bergeron", though a simpler and briefer story than Franz Kafka's *The Metamorphosis* is no less finished, complete, and satisfactory as a work of art. Yet, considered in another light, Kafka's short novel may well seem a greater work than Vonnegut's. It reveals greater meaning and enfolds more life.

Masterpieces often have flaws; and so, whenever we can, we need to consider a story in its entirety. Some novels by Thomas Hardy and by Theodore Dreiser impress (on the whole), despite passages of stilted dialogue and other clumsy writing. If a story totally fails to enlist our sympathies, probably it suffers from some basic ineptitude: choice of an inappropriate point of view, a style ill suited to its theme, or possibly insufficient knowledge of human beings. In some ineffectual stories, things important to the writer (and to the story) remain private and unmentioned. In other stories, the writer's interests may be perfectly clear but they may not interest the readers, for they are not presented with sufficient art.

Some stories fail from sentimentality, a defect in a work whose writer seems to feel tremendous emotion and implies that we too should feel it, but does not provide us enough reason to share such feelings. Sentimentality is rampant in televised weekday afternoon soap operas, whose characters usually palpitate with passion for reasons not quite known, and who speak in melodramatic tones as if heralding the end of the world. In some fiction, conventional objects (locks of baby hair, posthumously awarded medals, pressed roses) frequently signal, "Let's have a good cry!" Revisiting home after her marriage, the character Amelia in William Makepeace Thackeray's *Vanity Fair* effuses about the bed she slept in when a virgin: "Dear little bed! how many a long night had she wept on its pillow."

Teary sentimentality is more common in 19th-century fiction than in ours. We have gone to the other extreme, some critics think, into a sentimentality of the violent and the hard-boiled. But in a grossly sentimental work of any kind, failure inheres in our refusal to go along with the author's implied attitudes. We laugh when we are expected to cry, feel delight when we are supposed to be horrified.

Besides knowing something about the conventions of stories, we need to know the evolvement of fiction. Generally, the writing of the fiction as a literary form reached its peak in the period of critical realism in the late 19th century, which could be represented from the works of Charles Dickens and William Makepeace Thackeray. They have established a pattern that everybody could imitate: a work should narrate a vivid and interesting story, portray one character or several characters, with these characters often falling into a kind of psychological or social contradictions and conflicts. Along with the development of the plot, the contradictions or conflicts could be solved in a certain way. Usually characters are taken as the core and the plot of the story can only unfold round the characters. The writer may portray these characters with details, such as their own looks, personalities, behavior and conduct, even their language is different from the common run, and they must live in given circumstances. In its narrative, the realistic fiction takes imitating or reproducing the objective reality as the basic principle, and the unfolding of plots and the development of events are arranged according to the time sequence of reality, being shown in linear narrative and causal logic. Of course, the circumstance in which the characters are and the description of their activities are confined in the conventional geometrical space. The realistic fiction has definite intentions and themes of writing. The stories that it narrates aim at showing a certain assured and concrete concept of value, moral principle or truth of life, trying to lead the readers to draw a specific moral conclusion and to realize the goal of moralization. The semantic meaning of this sort of fiction is onefold and transparent.

From the end of the 19th century, the concepts of values and aesthetics of realistic literature were challenged by the methods of modernist literature such as symbolism, expressionism, surrealism, stream-of-consciousness, etc. For modernist fictionist, the essential task of fiction is to represent man's innermost activities covered by the seeming phenomena of everyday life. Thus, in the modernist fiction, the description of outside circumstances and things that take place in it is reduced to the minimum limit and a majority of space is used to represent man's experience, reception and reflection of the outside, disorderly and absurd reality and goes deep into man's subconsciousness and unconsciousness, probing into man's innermost concealed secret and revealing man's despair and the sense of crisis, the absurdity of world and the meaninglessness of life, etc. Virginia Woolf's *To the Lighthouse* and James Joyce's *Ulysses* are typical examples for us to learn about modernist fiction in English literature.

Consequently, modernist fiction abandons the integrity and dramaticness of story plots and the protagonists and characters in it do not have vivid personalities any more. The characters are observed from different points of view and from different situations in which they are put. They appear to be dim and fragmented. To certain extent, modernist fiction overthrows the principles of representation and the mode of representation of realistic fiction and makes inside innovations in the structures, techniques, and languages of fiction. However, modernist fiction does not touch the totality, closeness, and oneness of fiction as a literary form. Instead, it reserves the outside boundary between it and other literary forms and genres, still pays much attention to the purity of its genre, and does its utmost to preserve the pureness and elegance of literary language and artistic artifices. Modernist fiction tries hard to express a certain metaphysical meaning or a suggestion that provides this meaning. Once they are extensively imitated and used, the techniques and forms of modernist fiction that are regarded as innovations quickly become new criteria and ossified modes that can no longer play any new designs. As a result, the assertion that "The fiction has died" is heard.

Postmodernist fiction restores the vitality of "the literature of exhaustion"[①] with new forms and techniques. Postmodernist fiction has destroyed the metaphysical conventions of modernist art, broken its close and self-contained aesthetic forms, and advocates thorough pluralism in thinking patterns, writing techniques, artistic genres, and language games. For postmodernist fiction, the narrative manner of traditional fiction, including realistic fiction and modernist fiction, is one of the makers of false reality, which leads the reader into the double falsehood, and then the task of fiction is to debunk this kind of beguilement and display the falsehood of reality and the falsehood of invented stories before the readers, thus urging them to think. Postmodernist fiction not only subverts the internal formation and structure of traditional fiction but also shows its doubts about the fictional form and narrative itself.

Postmodern metafiction, as presented in John Barth's *Chimera* and Donald

---

① Barth, John. "The Literature of Exhaustion". *The Friday Book: Essays and Other Nonfiction*. Baltimore: The John Hopkins University Press, 1997: 64.

Barthelme's *Snow White*, is the reflection, deconstruction and subversion of the fiction as a literary form and narrative itself. Metafiction is a fiction about a fiction. It overthrows the concept of pure fiction, destroys the narrative conventions of traditional fiction, blurs the dividing line between it and other literary genres, adopts a great deal of representational techniques of other literary genres. In metafiction, the time crosses the past, the present, and the future, and the names and identities of characters are all certain.

In the postmodernist fiction there is not any objective or transcendental meaning; the so-called meaning is only produced in the differences of man-made language signs, namely, the effect produced by the permutation and combination of signs. Therefore, the writing of invented texts is only a language game. Any text is open and incomplete. It depends on other texts (on its differentiation from and relation with them) and especially on the reader's interpretation. It is the reader's interpretation that gives a certain meaning to the combination and permutation of signs. Postmodernist fiction transcends the dividing lines between belles-letter and popular literature and between hight literature and light literature, thus turning the literature as the privilege of the high-browed intellectuals into the literature of the reading public and showing a tendency towards popularization.

In addition, in the postmodernist fiction, the artistic techniques of modernist fiction such as the interior monologue or stream-of-consciousness, symbolism, free association, the disorder of time and space, etc. have already dropped back to the secondary position though they have not yet been completely abandoned; the more frequently-used forms of expression are metafiction, language games, the tendency towards popularization, parody, collage, montage, labyrinth, black humor, etc. Such characteristics as the language subject, fragmented narrative, shifting signifiers, writing zeroes, etc. have also appeared in the postmodernist fiction.

In evaluating a story, we may usefully ask a few questions:
1. What is the tone of the story? By what means and how effectively is it communicated?
2. What is the point of view? Does it seem appropriate and effective in this story? Imagine the story told from a different point of view; would such a change be for the worse or for the better?
3. Does the story show us unique and individual scenes, events, and characters— or weary stereotypes?
4. Are any symbols evident? If so, do they direct us to the story's central theme, or do they distract us from it?
5. How appropriate to the theme of the story, and to its subject matter, are its tone

and style? Is it ever difficult or impossible to sympathize with the attitude of the author (insofar as we can tell what they are)?

6. Does our interest in the story mainly depend on following its plot, on finding out what will happen next? Or does the author go beyond the events to show us what they mean? Are the events (however fantastic) credible, or are they incredibly melodramatic? Does the plot greatly depend upon far-fetched coincidence?

7. Has the writer caused characters, events, and settings to come alive? Are they full of breath and motion, or simply told about in the abstract ("She was a lovable girl whose life had been highly exciting")? Unless the story is a fable or a tale, which needs no detailed description or deep portrayal of character, then we may well expect the story to contain enough vividly imagined detail to make us believe in it.

Eveline (1914)

James Joyce

She sat at the window watching the evening invade the avenue. Her head was leaned against the window curtains, and in her nostrils was the odour of dusty cretonne. She was tired.

Few people passed. The man out of the last house passed on his way home; she heard his footsteps clacking along the concrete pavement and afterwards crunching on the cinder path before the new red houses. One time there used to be a field there in which they used to play every evening with other people's children. Then a man from Belfast bought the field and built houses in it—not like their little brown houses, but bright brick houses with shining roofs. The children of the avenue used to play together in that field—the Devines, the Waters, the Dunns, little Keogh the cripple, she and her brothers and sisters. Ernest, however, never played: he was too grown up. Her father used often to hunt them in out of the field with his blackthorn stick; but usually little Keogh used to keep nix and call out when he saw her father coming. Still they seemed to have been rather happy then. Her father was not so bad then; and besides, her mother was alive. That was a long time ago; she and her brothers and sisters were all grown up; her mother was dead, Tizzie Dunn was dead, too, and the Waters had gone back to England. Everything changes. Now she was going to go away like the others, to leave her home.

Home! She looked round the room, reviewing all its familiar objects which she had dusted once a week for so many years, wondering where on earth all the dust came from. Perhaps she would never see again those familiar objects from which she had never dreamed of being divided. And yet during all those years she had never found out the name of the priest whose yellowing photograph hung on the wall above the broken harmonium beside the coloured print of the promises made to Blessed Margaret Mary Alacoque①. He had been a school friend of her father. Whenever he showed the photograph to a visitor her father used to pass it with a casual word:

"He is in Melbourne now."

She had consented to go away, to leave her home. Was that wise? She tried to weigh each side of the question. In her home anyway she had shelter and food; she had those whom she had known all her life about her. Of course she had to work hard, both in the house and at business. What would they say of her in the Stores when they found out that she had run away with a fellow? Say she was a fool, perhaps; and her place would be filled up by advertisement. Miss Gavan would be glad. She had always had an edge on her, especially whenever there were people listening.

"Miss Hill, don't you see these ladies are waiting?"

"Look lively, Miss Hill, please."

She would not cry many tears at leaving the Stores.

But in her new home, in a distant unknown country, it would not be like that. Then she would be married—she, Eveline. People would treat her with respect then. She would not be treated as her mother had been. Even now, though she was over nineteen, she sometimes felt herself in danger of her father's violence. She knew it was that that had given her the palpitations. When they were growing up he had never gone for her, like he used to go for Harry and Ernest, because she was a girl; but latterly he had begun to threaten her and say what he would do to her only for her dead mother's sake. And now she had nobody to protect her, Ernest was dead and Harry, who was in the church decorating business, was nearly always down somewhere in the country. Besides, the invariable squabble for money on Saturday nights had begun to weary her unspeakably. She always gave her entire wages—seven shillings—and Harry always sent up what he could, but the trouble was to get any money from her father. He said she used to squander the money, that she had no head, that he wasn't going to give her his hard-earned money to throw about the streets, and much more, for he was usually fairly bad on Saturday night. In the end he would give her the money and ask her had she any intention of buying Sunday's dinner. Then she had to rush out as quickly as she could and do her marketing, holding her black leather purse tightly in her hand as she elbowed her way through the crowds and returning home late under her load of provisions. She had hard work to keep the house together and to see that the two young children who had been left to her charge went to school regularly and got their meals regularly. It was hard work—a hard life—but now that she was about to leave it she did not find it a wholly undesirable life.

---

① Margaret Mary Alacoque: French nun (1647—1690). Jesus appeared to her in a vision and bade her to start devotion to *His Sacred Heart*. She was canonized in 1920.

She was about to explore another life with Frank. Frank was very kind, manly, open-hearted. She was to go away with him by the night-boat to be his wife and to live with him in Buenos Ayres, where he had a home waiting for her. How well she remembered the first time she had seen him; he was lodging in a house on the main road where she used to visit. It seemed a few weeks ago. He was standing at the gate, his peaked cap pushed back on his head and his hair tumbled forward over a face of bronze. Then they had come to know each other. He used to meet her outside the Stores every evening and see her home. He took her to see *The Bohemian Girl*① and she felt elated as she sat in an unaccustomed part of the theatre with him. He was awfully fond of music and sang a little. People knew that they were courting, and, when he sang about the lass that loves a sailor, she always felt pleasantly confused. He used to call her Poppens out of fun. First of all it had been an excitement for her to have a fellow and then she had begun to like him. He had tales of distant countries. He had started as a deck boy at a pound a month on a ship of the Allan Line going out to Canada. He told her the names of the ships he had been on and the names of the different services. He had sailed through the Straits of Magellan and he told her stories of the terrible Patagonians. He had fallen on his feet in Buenos Ayres, he said, and had come over to the old country just for a holiday. Of course, her father had found out the affair and had forbidden her to have anything to say to him.

"I know these sailor chaps," he said.

One day he had quarrelled with Frank, and after that she had to meet her lover secretly.

The evening deepened in the avenue. The white of two letters in her lap grew indistinct. One was to Harry; the other was to her father. Ernest had been her favourite, but she liked Harry too. Her father was becoming old lately, she noticed; he would miss her. Sometimes he could be very nice. Not long before when she had been laid up for a day, he had read her out a ghost story and made toast for her at the fire. Another day, when their mother was alive, they had all gone for a picnic to the Hill of Howth. She remembered her father putting on her mother's bonnet to make the children laugh.

Her time was running out, but she continued to sit by the window, leaning her head against the window curtain, inhaling the odour of dusty cretonne. Down far in the avenue she could hear a street organ playing. She knew the air. Strange that it should come that very night to remind her of the promise to her mother, her promise to keep the home together as long as she could. She remembered the last night of her mother's illness; she was again in the close, darkroom at the other side of the hall and outside she heard a melancholy air of Italy. The organ-player had been ordered to go away and given sixpence. She remembered her father strutting back into the sick-room saying:

"Damned Italians! Coming over here!"

---

① *The Bohemian Girl:* an opera composed by the Irish composer Michael William Balfe (1808—1870)

As she mused the pitiful vision of her mother's life laid its spell on the very quick of her being—that life of commonplace sacrifices closing in final craziness. She trembled as she heard again her mother's voice saying constantly with foolish insistence:

"*Derevaun Seraun*[①]! Derevaun Seraun!"

She stood up in a sudden impulse of terror. Escape! She must escape! Frank would save her. He would give her life, perhaps love, too. But she wanted to live. Why should she be unhappy? She had a right to happiness, Frank would take her in his arms, fold her in his arms. He would save her.

She stood among the swaying crowd in the station at the North Wall. He held her hand and she knew that he was speaking to her, saying something about the passage over and over again. The station was full of soldiers with brown baggages. Through the wide doors of the sheds she caught a glimpse of the black mass of the boat, lying in beside the quay wall, with illumined portholes. She answered nothing. She felt her cheek pale and cold and out of a maze of distress, she prayed to God to direct her, to show her what was her duty. The boat blew a long mournful whistle into the mist. If she went, tomorrow she would be on the sea with Frank, steaming towards Buenos Ayres. Their passage had been booked. Could she still draw back after all he had done for her? Her distress awoke a nausea in her body and she kept moving her lips in silent fervent prayer.

A bell clanged upon her heart. She felt him seize her hand: "Come?"

All the seas of the world tumbled about her heart. He was drawing her into them: he would drown her. She gripped with both hands at the iron railing.

"Come!"

No! No! No! It was impossible. Her hands clutched the iron in frenzy. Amid the seas she sent a cry of anguish.

"Eveline! Ewy!"

He rushed beyond the barrier and called to her to follow. He was shouted at to go on, but he still called to her. She set her white face to him, passive, like a helpless animal. Her eyes gave him no sign of love or farewell or recognition.

Study Questions:

1. What are the character traits of Eveline?
2. What does the author imply in mentioning the priest in Para. 3?
3. What do the odor of dusty cretonne and dust symbolize?
4. Why is Eveline in two minds on the question of leaving. or not leaving?
5. Why does Eveline pray to God to direct her (Para. 18)?
6. What are the symbolic meanings of the sea and the iron railing (Para. 20)?

---

① *Derevaun Seraun:* Gaelic for "the end of pleasure is pain"

7. What strikes you most about the story in language and style?
8. What is the narrative tone of the writing?
9. What does the author want to convey to the readers in this short story?

Catch-22 (1961)[①]
Joseph Heller

Chapter 41
SNOWDEN

"Cut," said a doctor.

"You cut," said another.

"No cuts," said Yossarian with a thick, unwieldy tongue.

"Now look who's butting in," complained one of the doctors. "Another county heard from. Are we going to operate or aren't we?"

"He doesn't need an operation," complained the other. "It's a small wound. All we have to do is stop the bleeding, clean it out and put a few stitches in."

"But I've never had a chance to operate before. Which one is the scalpel? Is this one the scalpel?"

"No, the other one is the scalpel. Well, go ahead and cut already if you're going to. Make the incision."

"Like this?"

"Not there, you dope!"

"No incisions," Yossarian said, perceiving through the lifting fog of insensibility that the two strangers were ready to begin cutting him.

"Another county heard from," complained the first doctor sarcastically. "Is he going to keep talking that way while I operate on him?"

"You can't operate on him until I admit him," said a clerk.

"You can't admit him until I clear him," said a fat, gruff colonel with a mustache and an enormous pink face that pressed down very close to Yossarian and radiated scorching heat like the bottom of a huge frying pan. "Where were you born?"

The fat, gruff colonel reminded Yossarian of the fat, gruff colonel who had interrogated the chaplain and found him guilty. Yossarian stared up at him through a glassy film. The cloying scents of formaldehyde and alcohol sweetened the air.

"On a battlefield," he answered.

---

① Heller's *Catch-22* holds a very important position in American literature history, and some critics assume that it is the output of World War II and its publication in 1961 brought black humor onto the literary stage, marking "the beginning of postmodernist novel of American literature" (Yang Renjing, 2004: 2).

"No, no. In what state were you born?"

"In a state of innocence."

"No, no, you don't understand."

"Let me handle him," urged a hatchet-faced man with sunken acrimonious eyes and a thin, malevolent mouth. "Are you a smart aleck or something?" he asked Yossarian.

"He's delirious," one of the doctors said. "Why don't you let us take him back inside and treat him?"

"Leave him right here if he's delirious. He might say something incriminating."

"But he's still bleeding profusely. Can't you see? He might even die."

"Good for him!"

"It would serve the finky bastard right," said the fat, gruff colonel. "All right, John, let's speak out. We want to get to the truth."

"Everyone calls me Yo-Yo."

"We want you to co-operate with us, Yo-Yo. We're your friends and we want you to trust us. We're here to help you. We're not going to hurt you."

"Let's jab our thumbs down inside his wound and gouge it," suggested the hatchet-faced man.

Yossarian let his eyes fall closed and hoped they would think he was unconscious.

"He's fainted," he heard a doctor say. "Can't we treat him now before it's too late? He really might die."

"All right, take him. I hope the bastard does die."

"You can't treat him until I admit him," the clerk said.

Yossarian played dead with his eyes shut while the clerk admitted him by shuffling some papers, and then he was rolled away slowly into a stuffy, dark room with searing spotlights overhead in which the cloying smell of formaldehyde and sweet alcohol was even stronger. The pleasant, permeating stink was intoxicating. He smelled ether too and heard glass tinkling. He listened with secret, egotistical mirth to the husky breathing of the two doctors. It delighted him that they thought he was unconscious and did not know he was listening. It all seemed very silly to him until one of the doctors said,

"Well, do you think we should save his life? They might be sore at us if we do."

"Let's operate," said the other doctor. "Let's cut him open and get to the inside of things once and for all. He keeps complaining about his liver. His liver looks pretty small on this X ray."

"That's his pancreas, you dope. This is his liver."

"No it isn't. That's his heart. I'll bet you a nickel this is his liver. I'm going to operate and find out. Should I wash my hands first?"

"No operations," Yossarian said, opening his eyes and trying to sit up.

"Another county heard from," scoffed one of the doctors indignantly. "Can't we make him shut up?"

"We could give him a total. The ether's right here."

"No totals," said Yossarian.

"Another county heard from," said a doctor.

"Let's give him a total and knock him out. Then we can do what we want with him."

They gave Yossarian total anesthesia and knocked him out. He woke up thirsty in a private room, drowning in ether fumes. Colonel Korn was there at his bedside, waiting calmly in a chair in his baggy, wool, olive-drab shirt and trousers. A bland, phlegmatic smile hung on his brown face with its heavy-bearded cheeks, and he was buffing the facets of his bald head gently with the palms of both hands. He bent forward chuckling when Yossarian awoke, and assured him in the friendliest tones that the deal they had made was still on if Yossarian didn't die. Yossarian vomited, and Colonel Korn shot to his feet at the first cough and fled in disgust, so it seemed indeed that there was a silver lining to every cloud, Yossarian reflected, as he drifted back into a suffocating daze. A hand with sharp fingers shook him awake roughly. He turned and opened his eyes and saw a strange man with a mean face who curled his lip at him in a spiteful scowl and bragged, "We've got your pal, buddy. We've got your pal."

Yossarian turned cold and faint and broke into a sweat.

"Who's my pal?" he asked when he saw the chaplain sitting where Colonel Korn had been sitting.

"Maybe I'm your pal," the chaplain answered.

But Yossarian couldn't hear him and closed his eyes. Someone gave him water to sip and tiptoed away. He slept and woke up feeling great until he turned his head to smile at the chaplain and saw Aarfy there instead. Yossarian moaned instinctively and screwed his face up with excruciating irritability when Aarfy chortled and asked how he was feeling. Aarfy looked puzzled when Yossarian inquired why he was not in jail. Yossarian shut his eyes to make him go away. When he opened them, Aarfy was gone and the chaplain was there. Yossarian broke into laughter when he spied the chaplain's cheerful grin and asked him what in the hell he was so happy about.

"I'm happy about you," the chaplain replied with excited candor and joy. "I heard at Group that you were very seriously injured and that you would have to be sent home if you lived. Colonel Korn said your condition was critical. But I've just learned from one of the doctors that your wound is really a very slight one and that you'll probably be able to leave in a day or two. You're in no danger. It isn't bad at all."

Yossarian listened to the chaplain's news with enormous relief. "That's good."

"Yes," said the chaplain, a pink flush of impish pleasure creeping into his cheeks. "Yes, that is good."

Yossarian laughed, recalling his first conversation with the chaplain. "You know, the first time I met you was in the hospital. And now I'm in the hospital again. Just about the only time

I see you lately is in the hospital. Where've you been keeping yourself?"

The chaplain shrugged. "I've been praying a lot," he confessed. "I try to stay in my tent as much as I can, and I pray every time Sergeant Whitcomb leaves the area, so that he won't catch me."

"Does it do any good?"

"It takes my mind off my troubles," the chaplain answered with another shrug. "And it gives me something to do."

"Well that's good, then, isn't it?"

"Yes," agreed the chaplain enthusiastically, as though the idea had not occurred to him before. "Yes, I guess that is good." He bent forward impulsively with awkward solicitude. "Yossarian, is there anything I can do for you while you're here, anything I can get you?"

Yossarian teased him jovially. "Like toys, or candy, or chewing gum?"

The chaplain blushed again, grinning self-consciously, and then turned very respectful. "Like books, perhaps, or anything at all. I wish there was something I could do to make you happy. You know, Yossarian, we're all very proud of you."

"Proud?"

"Yes, of course. For risking your life to stop that Nazi assassin. It was a very noble thing to do."

"What Nazi assassin?"

"The one that came here to murder Colonel Cathcart and Colonel Korn. And you saved them. He might have stabbed you to death as you grappled with him on the balcony. It's a lucky thing you're alive."

Yossarian snickered sardonically when he understood. "That was no Nazi assassin."

"Certainly it was. Colonel Korn said it was."

"That was Nately's girlfriend. And she was after me, not Colonel Cathcart and Colonel Korn. She's been trying to kill me ever since I broke the news to her that Nately was dead."

"But how could that be?" the chaplain protested in livid and resentful confusion. "Colonel Cathcart and Colonel Korn both saw him as he ran away. The official report says you stopped a Nazi assassin from killing them."

"Don't believe the official report," Yossarian advised dryly. "It's part of the deal."

"What deal?"

"The deal I made with Colonel Cathcart and Colonel Korn. They'll let me go home a big hero if I say nice things about them to everybody and never criticize them to anyone for making the rest of the men fly more missions."

The chaplain was appalled and rose halfway out of his chair. He bristled with bellicose dismay. "But that's terrible! That's a shameful, scandalous deal, isn't it?"

"Odious," Yossarian answered, staring up woodenly at the ceiling with just the back of his head resting on the pillow. "I think 'odious' is the word we decided on."

"Then how could you agree to it?"

"It's that or a court-martial, Chaplain."

"Oh," the chaplain exclaimed with a look of stark remorse, the back of his hand covering his mouth. He lowered himself into his chair uneasily. "I shouldn't have said anything."

"They'd lock me in prison with a bunch of criminals."

"Of course. You must do whatever you think is right, then." The chaplain nodded to himself as though deciding the argument and lapsed into embarrassed silence.

"Don't worry," Yossarian said with a sorrowful laugh after several moments had passed. "I'm not going to do it."

"But you must do it," the chaplain insisted, bending forward with concern. "Really, you must. I had no right to influence you. I really had no right to say anything."

"You didn't influence me." Yossarian hauled himself over onto his side and shook his head in solemn mockery. "Christ, Chaplain! Can you imagine that for a sin? Saving Colonel Cathcart's life! That's one crime I don't want on my record."

The chaplain returned to the subject with caution. "What will you do instead? You can't let them put you in prison."

"I'll fly more missions. Or maybe I really will desert and let them catch me. They probably would."

"And they'd put you in prison. You don't want to go to prison."

"Then I'll just keep flying missions until the war ends, I guess. Some of us have to survive."

"But you might get killed."

"Then I guess I won't fly any more missions."

"What will you do?"

"I don't know."

"Will you let them send you home?"

"I don't know. Is it hot out? It's very warm in here."

"It's very cold out," the chaplain said.

"You know," Yossarian remembered, "a very funny thing happened—maybe I dreamed it. I think a strange man came in here before and told me he's got my pal. I wonder if I imagined it."

"I don't think you did," the chaplain informed him. "You started to tell me about him when I dropped in earlier."

"Then he really did say it. 'We've got your pal, buddy,' he said. 'We've got your pal.' He had the most malignant manner I ever saw. I wonder who my pal is."

"I like to think that I'm your pal, Yossarian," the chaplain said with humble sincerity. "And they certainly have got me. They've got my number and they've got me under surveillance, and they've got me right where they want me. That's what they told me at my interrogation."

"No, I don't think it's you he meant," Yossarian decided. "I think it must be someone like Nately or Dunbar. You know, someone who was killed in the war, like Clevinger, Orr, Dobbs, Kid Sampson or McWatt." Yossarian emitted a startled gasp and shook his head. "I just realized it," he exclaimed. "They've got all my pals, haven't they? The only ones left are me and Hungry Joe." He tingled with dread as he saw the chaplain's face go pale. "Chaplain, what is it?"

"Hungry Joe was killed."

"God, no! On a mission?"

"He died in his sleep while having a dream. They found a cat on his face."

"Poor bastard," Yossarian said, and began to cry, hiding his tears in the crook of his shoulder. The chaplain left without saying goodbye. Yossarian ate something and went to sleep. A hand shook him awake in the middle of the night. He opened his eyes and saw a thin, mean man in a patient's bathrobe and pajamas who looked at him with a nasty smirk and jeered.

"We've got your pal, buddy. We've got your pal."

Yossarian was unnerved. "What the hell are you talking about?" he pleaded in incipient panic.

"You'll find out, buddy. You'll find out."

Yossarian lunged for his tormentor's throat with one hand, but the man glided out of reach effortlessly and vanished into the corridor with a malicious laugh. Yossarian lay there trembling with a pounding pulse. He was bathed in icy sweat. He wondered who his pal was. It was dark in the hospital and perfectly quiet. He had no watch to tell him the time. He was wide-awake, and he knew he was a prisoner in one of those sleepless, bedridden nights that would take an eternity to dissolve into dawn. A throbbing chill oozed up his legs. He was cold, and he thought of Snowden, who had never been his pal but was a vaguely familiar kid who was badly wounded and freezing to death in the puddle of harsh yellow sunlight splashing into his face through the side gunport when Yossarian crawled into the rear section of the plane over the bomb bay after Dobbs had beseeched him on the intercom to help the gunner, please help the gunner. Yossarian's stomach turned over when his eyes first beheld the macabre scene; he was absolutely revolted, and he paused in fright a few moments before descending, crouched on his hands and knees in the narrow tunnel over the bomb bay beside the sealed corrugated carton containing the first-aid kit. Snowden was lying on his back on the floor with his legs stretched out, still burdened cumbersomely by his flak suit, his flak helmet, his parachute harness and his Mae West. Not far away on the floor lay the small tail gunner in a dead faint. The wound Yossarian saw was in the outside of Snowden's thigh, as large and deep as a football, it seemed. It was impossible to tell where the shreds of his saturated coveralls ended and the ragged flesh began.

There was no morphine in the first-aid kit, no protection for Snowden against pain but the numbing shock of the gaping wound itself. The twelve syrettes of morphine had been stolen from their case and replaced by a cleanly lettered note that said: "What's good for M & M Enterprises is good for the country. Milo Minderbinder." Yossarian swore at Milo and held two aspirins out to ashen lips unable to receive them. But first he hastily drew a tourniquet around Snowden's thigh because he could not think what else to do in those first tumultuous moments when his senses were in turmoil, when he knew he must act competently at once and feared he might go to pieces completely. Snowden watched him steadily, saying nothing. No artery was spurting, but Yossarian pretended to absorb himself entirely into the fashioning of a tourniquet, because applying a tourniquet was something he did know how to do. He worked with simulated skill and composure, feeling Snowden's lackluster gaze resting upon him. He recovered possession of himself before the tourniquet was finished and loosened it immediately to lessen the danger of gangrene. His mind was clear now, and he knew how to proceed. He rummaged through the first-aid kit for scissors.

"I'm cold," Snowden said softly. "I'm cold."

"You're going to be all right, kid," Yossarian reassured him with a grin. "You're going to be all right."

"I'm cold," Snowden said again in a frail, childlike voice. "I'm cold."

"There, there," Yossarian said, because he did not know what else to say. "There, there."

"I'm cold," Snowden whimpered. "I'm cold."

"There, there. There, there."

Yossarian was frightened and moved more swiftly. He found a pair of scissors at last and began cutting carefully through Snowden's coveralls high up above the wound, just below the groin. He cut through the heavy gabardine cloth all the way around the thigh in a straight line. The tiny tail gunner woke up while Yossarian was cutting with the scissors, saw him, and fainted again. Snowden rolled his head to the other side of his neck in order to stare at Yossarian more directly. A dim, sunken light glowed in his weak and listless eyes. Yossarian, puzzled, tried not to look at him. He began cutting downward through the coveralls along the inside seam. The yawning wound—was that a tube of slimy bone he saw running deep inside the gory scarlet flow behind the twitching, startling fibers of weird muscle?—was dripping blood in several trickles, like snow melting on eaves, but viscous and red, already thickening as it dropped. Yossarian kept cutting through the coveralls to the bottom and peeled open the severed leg of the garment. It fell to the floor with a plop, exposing the hem of khaki undershorts that were soaking up blotches of blood on one side as though in thirst. Yossarian was stunned at how waxen and ghastly Snowden's bare leg looked, how loathsome, how lifeless and esoteric the downy, fine, curled blond hairs on his odd white shin and calf. The wound, he saw now, was not nearly as large as a football, but as long and wide as his hand and too raw and deep to see into clearly. The raw muscles inside twitched like live hamburger meat. A long sigh of relief escaped slowly through Yossarian's mouth when he saw that Snowden was not in danger of dying. The blood was already coagulating inside the wound, and it was simply a matter of bandaging him up and keeping him calm until the plane landed. He removed some packets of sulfanilamide from the first-aid kit. Snowden quivered when Yossarian pressed against him gently to turn him up slightly on his side.

"Did I hurt you?"

"I'm cold," Snowden whimpered. "I'm cold."

"There, there," Yossarian said. "There, there."

"I'm cold. I'm cold."

"There, there. There, there."

"It's starting to hurt me," Snowden cried out suddenly with a plaintive, urgent wince.

Yossarian scrambled frantically through the first-aid kit in search of morphine again and found only Milo's note and a bottle of aspirin. He cursed Milo and held two aspirin tablets out to Snowden. He had no water to offer. Snowden rejected the aspirin with an almost imperceptible shake of his head. His face was pale and pasty. Yossarian removed Snowden's flak helmet and lowered his head to the floor.

"I'm cold," Snowden moaned with half-closed eyes. "I'm cold."

The edges of his mouth were turning blue. Yossarian was petrified. He wondered whether to pull the rip cord of Snowden's parachute and cover him with the nylon folds. It was very warm in the plane. Glancing up unexpectedly, Snowden gave him a wan, co-operative smile and shifted the position of his hips a bit so that Yossarian could begin salting the wound with sulfanilamide. Yossarian worked with renewed confidence and optimism. The plane bounced hard inside an air pocket, and he remembered with a start that he had left his own parachute up front in the nose. There was nothing to be done about that. He poured envelope after envelope of the white crystalline powder into the bloody oval wound until nothing red could be seen and then drew a deep, apprehensive breath, steeling himself with gritted teeth as he touched his bare hand to the dangling shreds of drying flesh to tuck them up inside the wound. Quickly he covered the whole wound with a large cotton compress and jerked his hand away. He smiled nervously when his brief ordeal had ended. The actual contact with the dead flesh had not been nearly as repulsive as he had anticipated, and he found an excuse to caress the wound with his fingers again and again to convince himself of his own courage.

Next he began binding the compress in place with a roll of gauze. The second time around Snowden's thigh with the bandage, he spotted the small hole on the inside through which the piece of flak had entered, a round, crinkled wound the size of a quarter with blue edges and a black core inside where the blood had crusted. Yossarian sprinkled this one with sulfanilamide too and continued unwinding the gauze around Snowden's leg until the compress was secure.

Then he snipped off the roll with the scissors and slit the end down the center. He made the whole thing fast with a tidy square knot. It was a good bandage, he knew, and he sat back on his heels with pride, wiping the perspiration from his brow, and grinned at Snowden with spontaneous friendliness.

"I'm cold," Snowden moaned. "I'm cold."

"You'er going to be all right, kid," Yossarian assured him, patting his arm comfortably. "Everything's under control."

Snowden shook his head feebly. "I'm cold," he repeated, with eyes as dull and blind as stone. "I'm cold."

"There, there," said Yossarian, with growing doubt and trepidation. "There, there. In a little while we'll be back on the ground and Doc Daneeka will take care of you."

But Snowden kept shaking his head and pointed at last, with just the barest movement of his chin, down toward his armpit. Yossarian bent forward to peer and saw a strangely colored stain seeping through the coveralls just above the armhole of Snowden's flak suit. Yossarian felt his heart stop, then pound so violently he found it difficult to breathe. Snowden was wounded inside his flak suit. Yossarian ripped open the snaps of Snowden's flak suit and heard himself scream wildly as Snowden's insides slithered down to the floor in a soggy pile and just kept dripping out. A chunk of flak more than three inches big had shot into his other side just underneath the arm and blasted all the way through, drawing whole mottled quarts of Snowden along with it through the gigantic hole in his ribs it made as it blasted out. Yossarian screamed a second time and squeezed both hands over his eyes. His teeth were chattering in horror. He forced himself to look again. Here was God's plenty, all right, he thought bitterly as he stared—liver, lungs, kidneys, ribs, stomach and bits of the stewed tomatoes Snowden had eaten that day for lunch. Yossarian hated stewed tomatoes and turned away dizzily and began to vomit, clutching his burning throat. The tail gunner woke up while Yossarian was vomiting, saw him, and fainted again. Yossarian was limp with exhaustion, pain and despair when he finished. He turned back weakly to Snowden, whose breath had grown softer and more rapid, and whose face had grown paler. He wondered how in the world to begin to save him.

"I'm cold," Snowden whimpered. "I'm cold."

"There, there," Yossarian mumbled mechanically in a voice too low to be heard. "There, there."

Yossarian was cold, too, and shivering uncontrollably. He felt goose pimples clacking all over him as he gazed down despondently at the grim secret Snowden had spilled all over the messy floor. It was easy to read the message in his entrails. Man was matter, that was Snowden's secret. Drop him out a window and he'll fall. Set fire to him and he'll burn. Bury him and he'll rot, like other kinds of garbage. The spirit gone, man is garbage. That was Snowden's secret. Ripeness was all.

"I'm cold," Snowden said. "I'm cold."

"There, there," said Yossarian. "There, there." He pulled the rip cord of Snowden's parachute and covered his body with the white nylon sheets.

"I'm cold."

"There, there."

Study Questions:

1. In what way is the hospital scene related to Yossarian's reminiscence of Snowden?
2. How are we to understand the message Yossarian reads in Snowden's entrails?
3. What are the major sources of Heller's humor?
4. How do you think about this novel? Do you think that it is a traditional novel? If not, could you know which genre it belongs to?

Part Three Drama

Drama is life with the dull bits left out.

—Alfred Hitchcock

Unlike a short story or a novel, a **play** is a work of storytelling in which actors represent the characters. But to be essential, a play differs from a work of fiction: It is addressed not to readers but to spectators. To be part of an audience in a theater is an experience far different from reading a story in solitude. Expectant as the house lights dim and the curtain rises, we become members of a community. The responses of people around us affect our own responses. We, too, contribute to the community's response whenever we laugh, sigh, applaud, murmur in surprise, or catch our breath in excitement. In contrast, when we watch a movie alone by means of a videocassette recorder—say, a slapstick comedy—we probably laugh less often than if we were watching the same film in a theater, surrounded by a roaring crowd.

A theater of live actors has another advantage: a sensitive give-and-take between actors and audience. Such rapport, of course, depends on the actors being skilled and the audience being perceptive. Although professional actors may try to give a top-class performance on all occasions, it is natural for them to feel more keenly inspired by a lively, appreciative audience than by a dull, lethargic one.

In another sense, a play is more than actors and audience. Like a short story or a poem, a play is a work of art made of words. The playwright devoted thought and care and skill to the selection and arrangement of language. Watching a play, of course, we do not notice the playwright standing between us and the characters. If the play is absorbing, it flows before our eyes. In a silent reading, the usual play consists mainly of dialogue, exchanges of speech, punctuated by stage directions. In performance, though, stage directions vanish. And although the thoughtful efforts of perhaps a hundred people—actors, director, producer, stage designer, costumer, makeup artist, technicians—may have gone into a production, a successful play makes us forget its artifice. We may even forget that the play is literature, for its gestures, facial expressions, bodily stances, lighting, and special effects are as much a part of it as the playwright's written words. Even though words are not all there is to a living play, they are its bones. And the whole play, the finished production, is the total of whatever transpires on stage.

The sense of immediacy that derives from drama is suggested by the root of the word. Drama means "action" or "deed" (from the Greek *dran*, "to do"). We use drama as a synonym for plays, but the word has several meanings. Sometimes it refers to one play ("a stirring drama"); or to the work of a playwright, or dramatist ("Ibsen's drama"); or perhaps to a body of plays written in a particular time or place ("Elizabethan drama", "French drama of the 17th century"). In yet another familiar sense, drama often means events that elicit high excitement. In this sense, whatever is "dramatic" implies suspense, tension, or conflict. Plays, as we shall see, frequently contain such "dramatic" chains of events; and yet, if we expect all plays to be crackling with suspense or conflict, we may be disappointed. "Good drama," said critic George Jean Nathan, "is anything that interests an intelligently emotional group of persons assembled together in an illuminated hall".

In partaking of the nature of ritual—something to be repeated in front of an audience on a special occasion—drama is akin to a festival (whether a religious festival or a rock festival) or a church service. Twice in the history of Europe, drama has sprung forth as a part of worship: When in ancient Greece, plays were performed on feast days; and when in the Christian church of the Middle Ages, a play was introduced as an adjunct to the Easter mass with the enactment of the meeting between the three Marys and the angel at Jesus' empty tomb. Evidently, something in drama remains constant over the years— something as old, perhaps, as the deepest desires and highest aspirations of humanity.

1. Reading a Play

Most plays are written not to be read in books but to be performed. Finding plays in a literature anthology, the student may well ask: Isn't there anything wrong with the idea of reading plays on the printed page? Isn't that a perversion of their nature?

True, plays are meant to be seen on stage, but equally true, reading a play may afford advantages. One is that it is better to know some masterpieces by reading them than never to know them at all. Even if you live in a large city with many theaters, even if you attend a college with many theatrical productions, to succeed in your lifetime in witnessing, say, all the plays of Shakespeare might well be impossible. In print, they are as near to hand as a book on a shelf, ready to be enacted (if you like) on the stage of the mind.

After all, a play is literature before it comes alive in a theater, and it might be argued that when we read an unfamiliar play, we meet it in the same form in which it first appears to its actors and its director. If a play is rich and complex or if it dates from the remote past and contains difficulties of language and allusion, to read it on the page enables us to study it at our leisure and return to the parts that demand greater scrutiny.

Let us admit, by the way, that some plays, whatever the intentions of their authors, are destined to be read more often than they are acted. Such a play is sometimes called a **closet drama**—"closet" meaning "a small, private room". Percy Bysshe Shelley's neo-Shakespearean tragedy *The Cenci* (1819) has seldom escaped from its closet, even though Shelley tried without luck to have it performed on the London stage. Perhaps too rich in talk to please an audience or too sparse in opportunities for actors to use their bodies, such works nevertheless may lead long, respectable lives on their own, solely as literature.

But even if a play may be seen in a theater, sometimes to read it in print may be our way of knowing it as the author wrote it in its entirety. Far from regarding Shakespeare's words as holy writ, producers of *Hamlet*, *King Lear*, *Othello*, and other masterpieces often leave out whole speeches and scenes, or shorten them. Besides, the nature of the play, as far as you can tell from a stage production, may depend upon decisions of the director. Shall Othello dress as a Renaissance Moor or as a jet-setting contemporary? Every actor who plays Iago in *Othello* makes his own interpretation of this knotty character. Some see Iago as a figure of pure evil; others, as a madman; still others, as a suffering human being consumed by hatred, jealousy, and pride. What do you think Shakespeare meant? You can always read the play and decide for yourself. If every stage production of a play is a fresh interpretation, so, too, is every reader's reading of it.

Some readers, when silently reading a play to themselves, try to visualize a stage, imagining the characters in costume and under lights. If such a reader is an actor or a director and is reading the play with an eye toward staging it, then that reader may try to imagine every detail of a possible production, even shades of makeup and the loudness of sound effects. But the nonprofessional reader, who regards the play as literature, need not attempt such exhaustive imagining. Although some readers find it enjoyable to imagine the play taking place upon a stage, others prefer to imagine the people and events that the play brings vividly to mind. Sympathetically following the tangled life of Nora in *A Doll's House* by Henrik Ibsen, we forget that we are reading printed stage directions and instead find ourselves in the presence of human conflict. Thus regarded, a play becomes a form of storytelling, and the playwright's instructions to the actors and the director become a conventional mode of narrative that we accept much as we accept the methods of a novel or short story. If we read *A Doll's House* caring more about Nora's fate than the imagined appearance of an actress portraying her, we speed through an ordinary passage such as this (from a scene in which Nora's husband hears the approach of an unwanted caller, Dr. Rank):

> Helmer (*with quiet irritation*): Oh, what does he want now? (*Aloud.*) Hold on. (*Goes and opens the door.*) Oh, how nice that you didn't just pass us by!

We read the passage, if the story absorbs us, as though we were reading a novel whose author, employing the conventional devices for recording speech in fiction, might have written:

> "Oh, what does he want now?" said Helmer under his breath, in annoyance. Aloud, he called, "Hold on." Then he walked to the door and opened it and greeted Rank with all the cheer he could muster—"Oh, how nice that you didn't just pass us by!"

Such is the power of an excellent play to make us ignore the playwright's artistry that it becomes a window through which the reader's gaze, given focus, encompasses more than language and typography and beholds a scene of imagined life.

Most plays, whether seen in a theater or in print, employ some conventions: customary methods of presenting an action, usual and recognizable devices that an audience is willing to accept. In reading a great play from the past, such as *Oedipus the King* or *Othello*, it will help if we know some of the conventions of the classical Greek theater or the Elizabethan theater. When in *Oedipus the King* we encounter a character called the Chorus, it may be useful to be aware that this is a group of citizens who stand to one side of the action, conversing with the principal character and commenting. In *Othello*, when the sinister Iago, left on stage alone, begins to speak (at the end of Act II, Scene I), we recognize the conventional device of a soliloquy, a dramatic monologue in which we seem to overhear the character's inmost thoughts uttered aloud. Like conventions in poetry, such familiar methods of staging a story afford us a happy shock of recognition. Often, as in these examples, they are ways of making clear to us exactly what the playwright would have us know.

A Play in Its Elements

In most cases, the elements of drama are identical to those of fiction and poetry. Plays have plots, themes, characters, and settings and make use of many devices of poetic diction. Thus, many of the steps in the analysis of a play should parallel those used for a poem or a short story. At the same time, however, drama is a different literary genre and it imposes its own constraints on the playwright's use of certain elements of literature. These unique aspects of dramatic writing are our present concern.

Every play unfolds a story through the dialogue and actions of its characters. An understanding of these four elements—dialogue, story, character, and action—is therefore crucial to the appreciation of drama.

Dialogue

Dialogue in a play is what the actors speak on the stage. If a theatrical production does not have dialogue, it can be a mime or a ballet, but it is never a play. As Tom Stoppard puts it: A play can give you talk and characters without much action. And a play can give you talk and action without strong characters. But a play cannot give you characters and action without talk. It is all talk in drama.

Dramatic dialogue, however, is very different from the kind of dialogue that makes up so much of our ordinary lives. Actual conversation is full of hesitations, pauses, fragments, misunderstandings, and repetitions. The communication itself is often as much a product of inflections, gestures, and facial expressions as it is of the spoken word. It depends so much on innuendo and allusions to previous conversations that an outsider is often unable to determine the exact meaning of a discussion heard out of context. Usually a talk in real life is slow in tempo, and stylistically weak and grammatically inept, and maybe meanders along for several hours. But important conversations in drama slash past trivial details and strike the lure with vigor and directness. A play necessarily packs a story of significance into two or three hours of stage time. As a result, each sentence is hard and muscular—made up of concrete nouns and active verbs. The dialogue continuously and clearly builds toward its point, elimination irrelevancies and unnecessary repetitions. When trimmed to its dramatic core, a real conversation might be well cut by half.

Dramatic dialogue ordinarily carries with it still another burden: It must include sufficient background information to fix the time, place, and circumstances of the action firmly in the mind of the audience. The playwrights must introduce the characters and provide background information before the audience can really understand what is going on. Although some playwrights prefer to have a narrator set the scene in a formal prologue, most try to bring out the background information gradually during the play's first act. Generally speaking, dialogue in a play can be used to provide necessary factual information, to reminisce, to characterize, to speculate, and to foreshadow, and it may take the form of discussion, argument, or inquiry. It may accompany and clarify actions or simply reveal attitudes and opinions. In short, good dialogue is a very flexible narrative tool.

Dialogue is not, however, an easy tool to use. A playwright, unlike a novelist, cannot simply halt proceedings to introduce formal character sketches or to set a scene; nor can a playwright exert the same direct control over the "story". A fictional "yam" is spun out of a voice that the author, as narrator, can fully control. But the dramatist has no voice of his or her own. When the curtain rises, the fabric of the plot must emerge naturally from interwoven and independent threads of conversation. But the naturalness of dramatic dialogues does not mean that the dialogue itself must inevitably be "natural" or "realistic". In fact, the real words of real people often seem awkward and unnatural in transcript. Art is not life and it has a higher standard of probability, eloquence, and organization, therefore, nearly all dramatic dialogue is more rhetorical and more poetic than real dialogue.

In dramatic dialogue, there is also the matter of level of style. Dramatic theory during the classical and neoclassical periods held that tragedy should be written in the high style and that the colloquial, or low style was appropriate only to comedy. In practice, however, as the plays of Shakespeare amply demonstrate, such a distinction need not be rigidly observed, and in more modern times it has been all abandoned. Most drama is mixed in style, rising to eloquence or falling to informality according to the inherent demands of the dramatic situation.

Story

The purpose of staging a drama is not only to present a fine prescript or to give moral instruction, but also to entertain the audience by providing an engrossing story. An audience is, after all, a crowd, and the principal desire of a crowd is to find out "what happens next". Drama, however, would emphasize story even if it were not demanded by the audience, for the dramatic point of view necessitates a fundamentally chronological development of action. Reminiscences can be, and often are, used to precipitate the action, but once the play has begun, the events on the stage inevitably unfold according to the simple time sequence of a story.

Dramatic actions as they unfold upon the stage do not, of course, simply "happen": They are premeditated and artistically arranged by the playwright to yield a dramatic plot. The ability to understand the story (the "what happens") may satisfy our basic desire as theatergoers to be entertained, but as literary critics we also need to understand not only "what happens" but "why"—a question that invariably forces us to consider the dynamics of plot.

Like a typical short story, the plot of nearly every play contains five structural elements: exposition, complication, crisis, falling action, and resolution. The principal difference between fictional and dramatic plots is that the latter are more regular in their use of these five elements, as is illustrated in the following paragraphs.

The **exposition** provides essential background information, introduces the past, begins the characterization, and initiates the action. Some exposition is always provided in the first scene, and all of the essential background material is usually provided by the end of the first act. Sometimes, a formal prologue or introduction by a narrator helps to set the scene, but more often there is no sharp division between the exposition and the complication that follows. In fact, most plays begin in the middle of things, just after some event has taken place that will eventually lead to the crises.

The **complication** introduces and develops the conflict. It commences when one or more of the main characters first become aware of an impending difficulty or when their relationship first begin to change.

Crisis is the turning point of the play, occurring at the moment of peak emotional intensity and usually involves a decision, a decisive action, or an open conflict between the protagonist and antagonist. It is often called the obligatory scene because the audience demands to see such moments acted out on stage.

As the consequences of the crisis accumulate, events develop a momentum of their own. Especially in tragedy, the **falling action** of the play results from the protagonist's loss of control and a final catastrophe often appears inevitable. The plot of a comedy, however, frequently includes some unexpected twist. This twist cuts sharply through all difficulties and allows the play to end on a happy note.

In both tragedy and comedy, the **resolution** brings to an end the conflict that has been implicit (or explicit) since the play's opening scenes. When the curtain falls, the relationships among the characters have once more stabilized.

Although virtually all plays include an exposition, complication, crisis, falling action, and resolution, and most take approximately the same amount of time to perform, they differ drastically in the amount of fictional time covered by the action shown on stage. In some plays, the action begins just a few hours before the crisis. This allows the drama to unfold before the spectators' eyes, much as if they were looking in on real events. But because nearly any plot of significance builds to a crisis that caps a series of events dating back months or years, these unfolding plots necessarily make use of reminiscence introduced via the testimony of elderly step-parents, conversations between friends and servants, or other similar strategies. The manipulation of these reminiscences requires considerable ingenuity in order to avoid a sense of obvious contrivance. One alternative is to present the action episodically, skipping weeks, months, or years between scenes as the chief events leading up to the crisis are acted out on stage. Whether a plot is unfolding or episodic, it ought to be tightly structured and pruned of unnecessary characters, actions, speeches, and scenes.

Character

For many of us, an interest in literature is an outgrowth of our interest in people and in their personalities. Drama is particularly satisfying in this respect for plays are inevitably and immediately concerned with the human beings who are impersonated by live actors and actresses on the stage. The terms used to describe characters in drama are, for the most part, the same as those used for fiction. In fact, some of these terms were originally borrowed from drama to describe fictional qualities. The *dramatis personae* (or characters) of a play usually include a **protagonist** (the play's central character) and an opposing **antagonist** or an antagonistic force. In a tragedy, the protagonist is often called the **tragic hero**. A great many plays also include a **confidant** (confidante if female) to whom a major character "confides" his or her most private thoughts and feelings, a **foil**, a minor figure whose contrasting personality in some ways clarifies that of a major character, and a **caricature**, a character with a habit or trait that is carried to a ridiculous extreme.

This terminology underscores the obvious difference between major and minor characters. The parts of the protagonist and antagonist are major, whereas those of the confidant and foil are often (but not always) minor. Because it is only reasonable to assume that most of a playwright's attention will be focused on his major characters, one of our first steps in the analysis of a play is to identify the characters, who have leading roles. The most obvious clue is the number of lines spoken by each character: Major characters have many, and minor characters few. But more importantly, major characters are usually individualized and given both complex motives and a past, while minor characters often have no past at all and have few individual traits and serve primarily to convey information to the main characters and the audience.

In drama, characterizing details come to us from many different sources. We immediately learn something from the name and physical appearance of each character, although this information is often unreliable. A second method of characterization is through an individual's patterns of action over the course of the play. Much characterization, however, is accomplished through dialogue in one of four ways. A character can reveal his or her personality and motives through asides and soliloquies. There may also be self-revelation in the way a character speaks because dialect, word choice, and grammar all provide clues to a person's background and intelligence. Besides, the way a character responds to others is also important revelation of his or her personality. Finally, what others say about a character can help us to understand him or her. These characterizing details come at us in fragmentary glimpses during the normal ebb and flow of the conversation. Occasionally, however, an author may provide a more concentrated sketch of a character's actions or personality—usually in the form of a hidden narration.

The process of understanding drama is very closely linked to our ability to understand the personalities and motives of the major characters. As we read and study a play we inevitably raise a host of questions: Why doesn't the main character take action at last? What are his character traits that cause the hero's destruction? Is the heroine noble or is her character seriously flawed in some way? These questions and others like them are concerned with fundamental character traits and express our expectation that the actions of the characters should be plausible, consistent, and adequately motivated. In attempting to answer them, we continually compare what is said by or about a character with the way in which that character acts on stage, searching for the thread of unity that creates a convincing personality.

At the same time, however, characters who are too consistent generally seem unrealistic. Conventional wisdom tells us that real people are full of surprises and so, in literature, we tend to demand characters who are capable of surprising us in a convincing way. Their motives should be complex and even competing. Moreover, those characters who most interest us usually undergo a process of growth and change during the course of the play.

We must be careful, however, not to push too far the demand for growth and change in character. Many fine plays present personalities or dilemmas without even hinting at the possibility of moral improvement or permanent solutions. The value of such fine plays is not that they create characters just like our next-door neighbors, but rather that it shows how only slight distortions in personality can destabilize the whole structure of ordinary social relationships.

Action

The actions in a play may sometimes be indicated or suggested in the script, but they are just as often the inevitable by-products of the performance. The words of a play may be put into action by actors in different ways, and a director may also be free to present the actions as he wishes, and this presentation will affect both the characterization of the characters and the degree of dramatic emphasis given to their actions.

As readers of drama, we may attempt to be our own director, moving the characters about an imaginary stage and endowing them with gestures and expressions suitable to the dialogue. Most of us, however, are content to concentrate on the words in the play and leave the accompanying actions vague, except where they are demanded by the script. In either approach, however, we must be very sensitive to actions implied in the dialogue. This is especially true when we read plays written before the middle of the 19th century. Thereafter the techniques of the novel began to infiltrate drama and the playwright's stage directions became more frequent and more detailed. But early playwrights kept their stage directions to an absolute minimum, and actions are implicit in dialogue.

As readers we should realize that a script in any drama is only a partial guide to the dramatic action, as any glance at a director's prompt book would quickly prove. Both the formal stage directions and the creative contributions of the actors and director are designed either to emphasize the themes and character traits introduced in the dialogue or to stimulate further dialogue. The relationship between dialogue and dramatic action is like that between a diamond and its setting in a ring: In both cases the latter enhances and emphasizes the value and clarity of the former.

Here is a play by one of the greatest playwrights in the history of American literature, read and understand it.

Desire under the Elms (1924)
Eugene O'Neill

Scene IV (Excerpt)

(*About an hour later. Same as Scene III. Shows the kitchen and CABOT's bedroom. It is after dawn. The sky is brilliant with the sunrise. In the kitchen, ABBIE sits at the table, her body limp and exhausted, her head bowed down over her arms, her face hidden. Upstairs, CABOT is still asleep but awakens with a start. He looks toward the window and gives a snort of surprise and irritation—throws back the covers and begins hurriedly pulling on his clothes. Without looking behind him, he begins talking to ABBIE whom he supposes beside him.*) ①

CABOT② : Thunder 'n' lightin', Abbie! I hain't slept this late in fifty year! Looks's if the sun was full riz a'most. Must've been the dancin' an' liker. Must be gittin' old. I hope Eben's t' wuk. Ye might've tuk the trouble t' rouse me, Abbie. (*He turns—sees no one there—surprised.*) Waal—whar air she? Gittin' vittles, I calc'late. (*He tiptoes to*

---

① The italicized words in the brackets of the text are stage directions, which include speech tag, entrance, exit, character description and scene introduction.

② Characters in this play speak in the dialects in New England, e. g., in this passage spoken by Cabot, 'n = and; lightin' = lighting; hain't = haven't; 's = as; riz = arisen; a'most = almost; must've = must have; dancin' = dancing; likker = liquor; gittin' = getting; t' = to; wuk = work; ye = you; might've = might have; tuk = taken; waal = well; what ari = where is; vittle = victual; calc'late = calculate; mornin' = morning; purty = pretty; beller = bellow; o' = of; 'em = them; thar ye be = there you are.

the cradle and peers down—proudly.) Momin', sonny. Purty's a picture! Sleepin' sound. He don't beller all night like most o' 'em. (*He goes quietly out of the door in rear—a few moments later enters kitchen—sees ABBIE—with satisfaction.*) So, thar ye be. Ye got any vittles cooked?

ABBIE: (*without moving*) No.

CABOT: (*coming to her, almost sympathetically*) Ye feelin' sick?

ABBIE: No.

CABOT: (*pats her on shoulder. She shudders.*) Ye'd best lie down a spell. (*Half jocularly.*) Yer son'll be needin' ye soon. He'd ought t' wake up with a gnashin' appetite, the sound way he's sleepin'.

ABBIE: (*shudders—then in a dead voice*) He hain't never goin' t' wake up.

CABOT: (*jokingly*) Takes after me this mornin'. I hain't slept so late in ...

ABBIE: He's dead.

CABOT: (*stares at her—bewilderedly*) What ...

ABBIE: I killed him.

CABOT: (*stepping back from her—aghast*) Air ye drunk—'r crazy—'r ...!

ABBIE: (*suddenly lifts her head and turns on him—wildly*) I killed him, I tell ye! I smothered him. Go up an' see if ye don't b'lieve me! (*CABOT stares at her a second, then bolts out the rear door—can be heard bounding up the stairs—and rushes into the bedroom and over to the cradle. ABBIE has sunk back lifelessly, to her former position. CABOT puts his hand down on the body in the crib. An expression of fear and horror comes over his face.*)

CABOT: (*shrinking away—trembling*) God A'mighty! God A'mighty. (*He stumbles out the door—in a short while returns to the kitchen—comes to ABBIE, the stunned expression still on his face—hoarsely.*) Why did ye do it? Why? (*As she doesn't answer, he grabs her violently by the shoulder and shakes her.*) I ax ye why ye done it! Ye'd better tell me 'r①...!

ABBIE: (*gives him a furious push which sends him staggering back and springs to her feet— with wild rage and hatred*) Don't ye dare tech② me! What right hev ye t' question me 'bout him? He wa'n't yewr son! Think I'd have a son by yew? I'd die fust③! I hate the sight o' ye an' allus did! It's yew I should've murdered, if I'd had good sense! I hate ye! I love Eben. I did from the fust. An' he was Eben's son—mine an' Eben's—not your'n!

---

① 'r: or; otherwise
② tech: touch
③ fust: first

CABOT: (*stands looking at her dazedly—a pause—finding his words with an effort—dully*) That was it—what I felt—pokin' round the corners①—while ye lied—holdin' yerself from me—sayin' ye'd a'ready conceived②—(*He lapses into crushed silence—then with a strange emotion*) He's dead, sart'n③. I felt his heart. Pore little critter④! (*He blinks back one tear, wiping his sleeve across his nose.*)

ABBIE: (*hysterically*) Don't ye! Don't ye! (*She sobs unrestrainedly.*)

CABOT: (*with a concentrated effort that stiffens his body into a rigid line and hardens his face into a stony mask—through his teeth to himself.*) I got t' be—like a stone—a rock o' jedgment! (*A pause. He gets complete control over himself—harshly.*) If he was Eben's, I be glad he air gone! An' mebbe I suspicioned it all along. I felt they was somethin' onnateral⑤—somewhars—the house got so lonesome—an' cold—drivin' me down t' the barn—t' the beasts o' the field ... Ay-eh. I must've suspicioned—somethin'. Ye didn't fool me—not altogether, leastways—I'm too old a bird—growin' ripe on the bough ... (*He becomes aware he is wandering, straightens again, looks at ABBIE with a cruel grin.*) So ye'd like t' hev murdered me 'stead o' him, would ye? Waal, I'll live to a hundred! I'll live t' see ye hung! I'll deliver ye up t' the jedgment o' God an' the law! I'll git the Sheriff now. (*Starts for the door.*)

ABBIE: (*dully*) Ye needn't. Eben's gone fur him.

CABOT: (*amazed*) Eben—gone fur the Sheriff?

ABBIE: Ay-eh.

CABOT: T' inform agen ye⑥?

ABBIE: Ay-en.

CABOT: (*considers this—a pause—then in a hard voice*) Waal, I'm thankful fur him savin' me the trouble. I'll git t' wuk. (*He goes to the door—then turns—in a voice full of strange emotion.*) He'd ought t' been my son, Abbie. Ye'd ought t' loved me. I'm a man. If ye'd loved me, I'd I never told no Sheriff on ye no matter what ye did, if they was t' brile me alive!

ABBIE: (*defensively*) They's more to it nor yew know, makes him tell. ⑦

CABOT: (*dryly*) Fur yewr sake, I hope they be. (*He goes out—comes around to the gate—stares up at the sky. His control relaxes. For a moment he is old and weary. He murmurs*

---

① pokin' round the corners: speak in different ways to achieve one's aims
② conceived: been pregnant
③ sar'n: certain
④ critter: creature
⑤ onnateral: unnatural
⑥ T' inform agen ye: to inform against you, meaning to sue you in the court
⑦ They's more ... makes him tell: There is more to it than you know which makes him tell.

despairingly.) God A'mighty, I be lonesomer'n ever! (*He hears running footsteps from the left, immediately is himself again. EBEN runs in, panting exhaustedly, wild-eyed and mad looking. He lurches through the gate. CABOT grabs him by the shoulder, EBEN stares at him dumbly.*) Did ye tell the Sheriff?

EBEN: (*nodding stupidly*) Ay-eh.

CABOT: (*gives him a push away that sends him sprawling—laughing with withering contempt*) Good fur ye! A prime chip o' yer Maw ye be!①(*He goes toward the barn, laughing harshly. EBEN scrambles to his feet. Suddenly CABOT turns—grimly threatening.*) Git off this farm when the Sheriff takes her—or, by God, he'll have t' come back an' git me fur murder, too! (*He stalks off. EBEN does not appear to have heard him. He runs to the door and comes into the kitchen. ABBIE looks up with a cry of anguished joy. EBEN stumbles over and throws himself on his knees beside her—sobbing brokenly.*)

EBEN: Fergive me!

ABBIE: (*happily*) Eben! (*She kisses him and pulls his head over against her breast.*)

EBEN: I love ye! Fergive me!

ABBIE: (*ecstatically*) I'd fergive ye all the sins in hell fur sayin' that! (*She kisses his head, pressing it to her with a fierce passion of possession.*)

EBEN: (*brokenly*) But I told the Sherif. He's comin' fur ye!

ABBIE: I kin b'ar what happens t' me—now!

EBEN: I woke him up. I told him. He says, wait 'til I git dressed. I was waiting. I got to thinkin' o' yew. I got to thinkin' how I d' loved ye. It hurt like somethin' was bustin' in my chest an' head. I got t' cryin'. I knowed sudden I loved ye yet, an' allus would love ye!

ABBIE: (*caressing his hair—tenderly*) My boy, hain't ye?

EBEN: I begun t' run back. I cut across the fields an' through the woods. I thought you might have time t' run away—with me—an' …

ABBIE: (*shaking her head*) I got t' take my punishment—t' pay fur my sin.

EBEN: Then I want t' share it with ye.

ABBIE: Ye didn't do nothin'.

EBEN: I put it in yer head. I wisht he was dead! I as much as urged ye t' do it!

ABBIE: No. It was me alone!

EBEN: I'm as guilty as yew be! He was the child o' our sin.

ABBIE: (*lifting her head as if defying God*) I don't repent that sin! I hain't askin' God t' fergive that!

---

① A prime chip o' yer Maw ye be: Indeed you're the same as your mother, similar like "clip off the old block" (son looking alike father).

EBEN: Nor me—but it led up t' the other—an' the murder ye did, ye did 'count o' me①—an' it's my murder, too, I'll tell the Sheriff—an' if ye deny it, I'll say we planned it t'gether—an' they'll all b'lieve me, fur they suspicion everythin' we've done, an' it'll seem likely an' true to 'em. An' it is true—way down②. I did help ye—somehow.

ABBIE: (*laying her head on his—sobbing*) No! I don't want yew t' suffer!

EBEN: I got t' pay fur my part o' the sin. An' I'd suffer wust leavin' ye, goin' West, thinkin' o' ye day an' night, bein' out when yew was in—(*lowering his voice*) 'r bein' alive when yew was dead. (*A pause.*) I want t' share with ye, Abbie—prison 'r death 'r hell 'r anythin'! (*He looks into her eyes and forces a trembling smile.*) If I'm sharin' with ye, I won't feel lonesome, leastways.

ABBIE: (*weakly*) Eben! I won't let ye! I can't let ye!

EBEN: (*kissing her—tenderly*) Ye can't he'p yerself. I got ye beat fur once!

ABBIE: (*forcing a smile—adoringly*) I hain't beat—s'long's I got ye!

EBEN: (*hears the sound of feet outside*) Ssshh! Listen! They've come t' take us!

ABBIE: No, it's him. Don't give him no chance to fight ye, Eben. Don't say nothin'—no matter what he says. An' I won't neither. (*It is CABOT. He comes up from the barn in a great state of excitement and strides into the house and then into the kitchen. EBEN is kneeling beside ABBIE, his arm around her, hers around him. They stare straight ahead.*)

CABOT: (*stares at them, his face hard. A long pause—vindictively*) Ye make a slick pair o' murderin' turtle doves③! Ye'd ought t' be both hung on the same limb an' left thar t' swing in the breeze an' rot—a warnin' t' old fools like me t' b'ar their lonesomeness alone—an' fur young fools like ye t' hobble their lust. (*A pause. The excitement returns to his face, his eyes snap, he looks a bit crazy.*) I couldn't work today. I couldn't take no interest. T' hell with the farm! I'm leavin' it! I've turned the cows an' other stock loose! I've druv 'em into the woods whar they kin be free! By freein' 'em, I'm freein' myself! I'm quittin' here today! I'll set fire t' house an' barn an' watch 'em burn, an' I'll leave yer Maw t' haunt the ashes, an' I'll will the fields back t' God, so that nothin' human kin never touch 'em! I'll be a-goin' to Californi-a—t' jine Simeon an' Peter—true son o' mine if they be dumb fools—an' the Cabott'll find Solomon's Mines t'gether! (*He suddenly cuts a mad caper.*) Whoop! What was the song they sung? "Oh, Califomi-a! That's the land fur me." (*He sings this—then gets on his knees by the floor-board under which the money*

---

① ye did 'count o' me: you did on account of me
② way down: far down
③ turtle doves: a kind of bird, usu. referring to lovers

	was hid.) An' I'll sail thar on one o' the finest clippers I kin find! I've got the money! Pity ye didn't know whar this was hidden so's ye could steak. (*He has pulled up the board. He stares—feels—stares again. A pause of dead silence. He slowly turns, slumping into a sitting position on the floor, his eyes like those of a dead fish, his face the sickly green of an attack of nausea. He swallows painfully several times—forces a weak smile at last*) So ye did steal it!
EBEN:	(*emotionlessly*) I swapped it t' Sim an' Peter fur their share o' the farm—t' pay their passage t' California.
CABOT:	(*with one sardonic*) Ha! (*He begins to recover. Gets slowly to his feet—strangely*) I calc'late God give it to 'em—not yew! God's hard, not easy! Mebbe they's easy gold in the West but it hain't God's gold. It hain't fur me. I kin hear His voice warnin' me agen t' be hard an' stay on my farm. I kin see his hand usin' Eben t' steal t' keep me from weakness. I kin feel I be in the palm o'His hand, His fingers guidin' me. (*A pause—then he mutters sadly.*) It's a-goin't be lonesomer now than ever it war afore—an' I'm gettin' old, Lord—ripe on the bough … (*Then stiffening.*) Waal—what d'ye want? God's lonesome, hain't He? God's hard an'lonesome! (*A pause. The SHERIFF with two men comes up the road from the left. They move cautiously to the door. The SHERIFF knocks on it with the butt of his pistol.*)
SHERIFF:	Open in the name o' the law! (*They start.*)
CABOT:	They've come fur ye. (*He goes to the rear door.*) Come in, Jim! (*The three men enter. CABOT meets them in doorway.*) Jest a minit, Jim. I got 'em safe here. (*The Sheriff nods. He and his companions remain in the doorway.*)
EBEN:	(*suddenly calls*) I lied this mornin', Jim. I helped her to do it. Ye kin take me, too.
ABBIE:	(*brokenly*) No!
CABOT:	Take 'em both. (*He comes forward—stares at EBEN with a trace of grudging admiration.*) Purty good—fur yew! Waal, I got t' round up the stock. Good-by.
EBEN:	Good-by.
ABBIE:	Good-by. (*CABOT turns and strides past the men—comes out and around the corner of the house, his shoulders squared, his face stony, and stalks grimly toward the barn. In the meantime the Sheriff and men have come into the room.*)
SHERIFF:	(*embarrassedly*) Waal—we'd best start.
ABBIE:	Wait. (*Turns to EBEN.*) I love ye, Eben.
EBEN:	I love ye, Abbie. (*They kiss. The three men grin and shuffle embarrassedly. EBEN takes ABBIE's hand. They go out the door in rear, the men following, and come from the house, walking hand in hand to the gate. EBEN stops there and points to the sunrise sky.*) Sun's arizin'. Purty, hain't it?

ABBIE: Ay-eh. (*They both stand for a moment looking up raptly in attitudes strangely aloof and devout*)

SHERIFF: (*looking around at the farm enviously—to his companion*) It's a jim-dandy farm, no denyin'. Wished I owned it!

(*Curtain falls.*)

Study Questions:
1. What is Eben's response to the murder of the infant?
2. Why does Abbie forgive Eben for informing against her?
3. How is Cabot affected by the murder?
4. What tragic elements are there in the play?

[**Reading Critically**]

Conflict Resolution

A good play almost always presents a conflict. One or more characters want to accomplish something, but another person or thing stands in their way. The central action of the play is how those two opposing forces resolve the conflict.

Reading a play, you will understand it better if you can identify the central dramatic conflict. Who is the protagonist? What does he or she want? Who opposes the protagonist? If you can answer those basic questions, the overall design of the plot will usually become obvious. Remember that many full-length plays (or films) have a double plot (or subplot). In such a case, there will be a secondary set of characters with their own conflicts.

To begin reading about a play, you might start by listing the major characters. (It usually suffices to list only the three or four most important people.) Then after each name, write down what that character wants most at the beginning of the play. If you can't figure out a single, compelling motive for each character, write down several things that they want. You can decide later what motive is most important.

Now look at the list, and decide what character is the protagonist, or hero. What does he or she want, and who opposes that ambition? Then notice how the motivations of the other characters fit into the central conflict.

2. Dramatic Types

Tragedy

By tragedy, generally speaking, we mean a play that portrays a conflict between human beings and some superior, overwhelming force. It ends sorrowfully and disastrously, and this outcome seems inevitable. Few spectators of *Oedipus the King* wonder how the play will turn out or wish for a happy ending. "In a tragedy," French playwright Jean Anouilh has remarked, "nothing is in doubt and everyone's destiny is known ... Tragedy is restful, and the reason is that hope, that foul, deceitful thing, has no part in it. There isn't any hope. You're trapped. The whole sky has fallen on you, and all you can do about it is shout."①

Many of our ideas of tragedy go back to ancient Athens; the plays of the Greek dramatists Sophocles, Aeschylus, and Euripides exemplify the art of tragedy. Aristotle's famous definition of tragedy (Tragedy is an imitation of an action of high importance, complete and of some amplitude; in language enhanced by distinct and varying beauties; acted not narrated; by means of pity and fear effecting its purgation of these emotions.②), constructed in the 4th century B. C., is the testimony of one who probably saw many classical tragedies performed. Classical Greek tragedies generally involve a protagonist, or main character, who cuts a noble figure except for one tragic flaw that brings about his or her ruin. Usually the protagonist has one or more antagonists—rivals or opponents—and invariably there is a chorus, a group of players who narrate portions of the play and comment upon the action. According to this interpretation, every tragic hero has some fatal weakness, some moral Achilles' heel, which brings him to a bad end. In some classical tragedies, his transgression is a weakness that Greeks called hubris—extreme pride, leading to overconfidence.

Whatever Aristotle had in mind, however, many later critics find value in the idea of tragic flaw. In this view, the downfall of a hero follows from his very nature. Whatever view we take—whether we find the hero's sufferings due to a flaw of character or to an error of judgment—we will probably find that his downfall results from acts for which he himself is responsible in a Greek tragedy, the hero is a character amply

---

① Preface to *Antigonê*. Trans. by Louis Galantière. New York: Random, 1946.
② Aristotle. *Poetics*. Trans. by L. J. Potts. qt. from X. J. Kennedy & Dana Gioia (eds.) *Literature: An Introduction to Fiction, Poetry and Drama* (8th ed.). New York: Longman, 2002: 1457.

capable of making choices—capable, too, of accepting the consequences.

As a public art form, tragedy was not simply a stage for political propaganda to promote the status quo. Nor was it exclusively a celebration of idealized heroes nobly enduing the blows of harsh circumstances and misfortune. Tragedy often enabled its audience to reflect on personal values that might be in conflict with civic ideas, on the claims of minorities that it neglected or excluded from public life, on its own irrational prejudices toward the foreign or the unknown. Frequently a play challenged its audience to feel sympathy for a vanquished enemy, as in Euripides' *Trojan Women* dramatizing the horrible fate of captured women. Some plays explored the problems facing members of the politically powerless groups that made up nearly three fourths of the Athenian population: women, children, resident aliens, and slaves. A largely male audience also frequently watched make performers enact stories of the power and anger of women, like Euripides' *Medea*, which made their tragic violence understandable. Other plays such as Sophocles' *Oedipus the King* or Euripides' *Herakles* depicted powerful men reserved by misfortune, their own bad judgment, or hubris, and thrown into defeat and exile.

Such tragic stories required performers and audience to put themselves in the places of persons quite unlike themselves, in situations that might engulf any unlucky citizen like war, political upheaval, betrayal, and domestic crisis. The release of the powerful emotions of pity and fear through a carefully crafted plot in the orderly context of highly conventionalized accounts for the paradox of tragic drama—how a viewer takes aesthetic pleasure in witnessing the sufferings of others.

Such a notion about tragedy is still traced to Aristotle's definition of tragedy. By **purgation** (or **katharsis**), Aristotle probably means that after witnessing a tragedy we feel relief, having released our pent-up emotions, or he probably means that our feelings are purified, refined into something more ennobling. Scholars continue to argue. Whatever his exact meaning, clearly Aristotle implies that after witnessing a tragedy we feel better, not worse—not depressed, but somehow elated. We take a kind of pleasure in the spectacle of a noble man being abased, but surely this pleasure is a legitimate one.

In describing the workings of this inexorable force in *Oedipus the King*, Aristotle takes the term, recognition, or discovery that later critics have found helpful. It means the revelation of some fact not known before or some person's true identity. For Oedipus, he recognizes or discovers that he himself was the child whom his mother had given over to be destroyed. Modern critics take this term to mean also the terrible enlightenment that accomplishes such a recognition. Having made such a discovery, Oedipus suffers a reversal in his fortunes; he goes off into exile, blinded and dethroned. Such a fall from happiness seems intrinsic to tragedy, but we should know that Aristotle has a more particular meaning for his term, reversal. He means an action that turns out to have the opposite effect from the one its doer had intended. One of Aristotle's illustrations of such an ironic reversal is from *Oedipus the King*. The first messenger intends to cheer Oedipus with the partially good news that, contrary to prophecy that Oedipus would kill his father, his father has died of old age. The reversal is in the fact that, when the messenger further reveals that old Polybos was Oedipus's father only by adoption, the king, instead of having his fears allayed, is stirred to new dread.

So we are not sorry to see an arrogant man like Oedipus humbled, and yet it is difficult not to feel that the punishment of Oedipus is greater than he deserves. Possibly that feeling is what Aristotle meant in his observation that a tragedy arouses our pity and fear—our compassion for Oedipus and our terror as we sense the remorselessness of a universe in which a man is doomed. However, in the end of the play, Oedipus does not curse God and die. Although such a complex play is open to interpretations, it is safe to say that the play is not a bitter complaint against the universe. Finally, Oedipus accepts the divine will, prays for blessings upon his children, and prepares to endure his exile— fallen from high estate but uplifted in moral dignity.

Comedy

Comedy, from the Greek *komos*, "a revel", is thought to have originated in festivities to celebrate spring, ritual performances in praise of Dionysus, god of fertility and wine. In drama, comedy may be broadly defined as whatever makes us laugh. A comedy may be a name for one entire play, or we may say that there is comedy in only part of a play—as in a comic character or a comic situation.

Often, comedy shows people getting into trouble through error or weakness; in this respect it is akin to tragedy. An important difference between comedy and tragedy lies in the attitude toward human failing that is expected of us. When a main character in a comedy suffers from overweening pride, as does Oedipus, or if he fails to recognize that his bride-to-be is actually his mother, we laugh—something we would never do in watching a competent performance of *Oedipus the King*.

Lots of theories explain why we laugh. Some assume that laughter is a form of ridicule, implying a feeling of disinterested superiority, for all jokes are on somebody. French philosopher Henri Bergson suggests that laughter springs from situations in which we sense a conflict between some mechanical or rigid pattern of behavior and our sense of a more natural or "organic" kind of behavior that is possible. Other thinkers take laughter as our response to expectations fulfilled or to expectations set up but suddenly frustrated. Some view it as the expression of our delight in seeing our suppressed urge acted out and some hold it to be our defensive reaction to a painful and disturbing truth.

Derisive humor is basic to **satiric comedy**, in which human weakness or folly is ridiculed from a vantage point of supposedly enlightened superiority. Satiric comedy may be coolly malicious and gently biting, but it tends to be critical of people, their manners, and their morals. It is as old as the comedies of Aristophanes, who thrived in the 5th century B. C.

We usually divide comedy into two varieties—"high" and "low". **High comedy** relies more on wit and word play than on physical action for its humor. It tries to address the audience's intelligence by pointing out the pretension and hypocrisy of human behavior. High comedy also generally avoids derisive humor. Jokes about physical appearances would, for example, be avoided. One technique it employs to appeal to a sophisticated, verbal audience is use of the epigram, a brief and witty statement that memorably expresses some truth, large or small. Oscar Wilde's plays like *The Importance of Being Earnest* (1895) and *Lady Windermere's Fan* (1892) sparkle with such brilliant epigrams as: "I can resist everything except temptation"; "Experience is the name everyone gives to their mistakes"; "There is only one thing worse than being talked about, and that is not being talked about."

A type of high comedy is the **comedy of manners**, a witty satire set in elite or fashionable society. The comedy of manners was especially popular in the Restoration period (the period after 1660 when Charles II, restored to the English throne, reopened the London playhouse, which had been closed by the Puritans who considered theater immoral). The great Restoration playwrights like William Congreve and George Farquhar especially excelled at comedies of manners. In the 20th century splendid comedies of manners continue to be written. Bernard Shaw's *Pygmalion* (1913), which eventually became the musical *My Fair Lady*, contrasts life in the streets of London with that in aristocratic drawing rooms. Contemporary playwrights like Tom Stoppard, Michael Frayn, Tina Howe, and the late Joe Orton have all created memorable comedies of manners.

Low comedy explores the opposite extreme of humor. It places greater emphasis on physical action and visual gags, and its verbal jokes do not require much intellect to appreciate. Low comedy does not avoid derisive humor; rather it revels in making fun of whatever will get a good laugh. Drunkenness, stupidity, lust, senility, trickery, insult, and clumsiness are inexhaustible staples for this style of comedy. Although it is all too easy for critics to dismiss low comedy, it also serves a valuable purpose in satirizing human failings. Shakespeare indulged in coarse humor in some of his noblest plays. Low comedy is usually the preferred style of popular culture, and it has inspired many incisive satires on modern life.

Low comedy includes several distinct types. One is the **burlesque**, a broadly humorous parody or travesty of another play or kind of play. Another valuable type of low comedy is the **farce**, a broadly humorous play whose action is usually fast-moving and improbable. The farce is a descendant of the Italian *commedia dell'arte* ("artistic comedy") of the late Renaissance, a kind of theater developed by comedians who traveled from town to town, regaling crowds at country fairs and in marketplaces. Slapstick comedy is a kind of farce. Featuring pratfalls, pie throwing, fisticuffs, and other violent action, it takes its name from a circus clown's device—a bat with two boards that loudly clap together when one clown swats another.

Romantic comedy, another traditional sort of comedy, is subtler. Its main characters are generally lovers, and its plot unfolds their ultimately successful strivings to be united. Unlike satiric comedy, romantic comedy portrays its characters not with withering contempt but with kindly indulgence. It may take place in the everyday world, or perhaps in some never-never land, such as the forest of Arden in Shakespeare's *As You Like It*.

Tragicomedy and Theatre of the Absurd

One of the most prominent developments in the mid-20th century drama is the rise of **tragicomedies**, plays that stir us not only to pity and fear① but also to laughter. Although we think that tragicomedy is a kind of modern drama, it is by no means a new invention. The term was used by the Roman writer of comedy Plautus in about 185 B.C.

Since ancient times, playwrights have mingled laughter and tears, defying the neoclassical doctrine that required strict unity of action and tone② and decreed that a play must be entirely comic or entirely tragic. Shakespeare loves tragicomic mingling. For example, in *Hamlet*, the prince jokes with gravedigger and in *Antony and Cleopatra* the queen commits suicide with a poisonous asp brought to her by a wise-cracking clown. Likewise, Shakespeare's darker comedies like *Measure for Measure* and *The Merchant of Venice* deal with such stark themes as lust, greed, racism, revenge, and cruelty that they often seem like tragedies until their happy endings. In the tragedies of Shakespeare, passages of clownish humor are called comic relief, meaning that the

---

① Here is to echo Aristotle's description of the effect of tragedy, for Aristotle assumes that tragedy is acted not narrated; by means of pity and fear effecting its purgation of these emotions

② Unity refers to certain principles of good drama laid down by Italian literary critics in the 16th century. Interpreting the theories of Aristotle as binding laws, these critics set down three basic principles: A good play should display unity of action, unity of time, and unity of place. In practical terms, this theory maintained that a play must represent a single series of interrelated actions that take place within twenty-four hours in a single location. Furthermore, they maintained, to have true unity of action, a play had to be entirely serious or entirely funny. Mixing tragic and comic elements was not allowed.

section of comedy introduces a sharp contrast in mood. But such passage can do more than provide the relief. In *Othello*, the clown's banter with Desdemona for a moment makes the surrounding tragedy seem more poignant and intense.

No one doubts that *Othello* is a tragedy, yet some 20th-century plays leave us bemused and confused: Should we cry or laugh? One of the most discussed plays since World War II is Samuel Beckett's *Waiting for Godot*, which portrays two clownish tramps who make time in a wasteland, wistfully looking for a savior who never arrives. Contemporary drama, by the way, has often featured such antiheroes① (Obviously, there are antiheroines, too): ordinary, inglorious and inarticulate, conspicuously lacking in one or more of the usual attributes of a traditional hero like bravery, skill, idealism and sense of purpose. In *Waiting for Godot*, we cannot help laughing at the tramps' painful situation; while, turning the idea around, we also feel deeply moved by their ridiculous plight. Although a modern tragicomedy like *Waiting for Godot* does not show us great souls suffering greatly as we observe in a classical tragedy, nonetheless Beckett's play touches mysteriously on the universal sorrows of human existence. For such a kind of play, the spectators need take time to sink in. Perhaps we may be amused while watching a tragicomedy and then go home and feel deeply stirred by it.

Straddling the fence between tragedy and comedy, the plays of some modern playwrights portray people whose suffering seems ridiculous. These plays belong to the theatre of the absurd: a general name for a type of play first staged in Paris in the 1950s. Eugène Ionesco is one of the movement's leading playwrights. For him, nothing can be taken entirely seriously, nor entirely lightly. Behind the literary conventions of the theatre of the absurd stands the fear of existentialist philosophy that human existence has no meaning. Every person, such playwrights assume that, is a helpless waif alone in a universe full of ridiculous obstacles. In Ionesco's *Rhinoceros* (1958), the human race starts changing into rhinos, except for one man, who remains human and isolated. For the theatre of the absurd, a favorite theme is that communication of people is impossible and thus language is futile. Ionesco's *The Bald Soprano* (1948) accordingly pokes fun at polite social conversation in a scene whose dialogue consists entirely of illogical strings of catchphrases. In *Endgame* (1957) Samuel Beckett dramatizes his vision of mankind's present situation: The main character is blind and paralyzed, and his legless parents live inside two garbage cans. Oddly, the effect of the play is not total gloom; we leave the theatre both amused and bemused by it. Trends in drama change along with the convictions of playwrights, and during 1970s and 1980s the theatre of the absurd no longer seemed the dominant influence on new drama in America.

---

① The rise of the antiheroes in recent fiction is similar to that of antiheroes in contemporary drama.

Here are two plays (one tragedy, the other comedy) by the most ingenious British playwrights, appreciate them.

Hamlet (1601)
William Shakespeare
Act 3, Scene 1

A room in the castle.

(Enter KING, QUEEN, POLONIUS, OPHELIA, ROSENCRANTZ, GUILDENSTERN, Lords.)

KING:

And can you, by no drift of conference①,

Get from him why he puts on this confusion②.

Grating so harshly all his days of quiet

With turbulent and dangerous lunacy?

ROSENCRANTZ:

He does confess he feels himself distracted③;

But from what cause he will by no means speak.

GUILDENSTERN:

Nor do we find him forward to be sounded,

But, with a crafty madness, keeps aloof,

When we would bring him on to some confession

Of his true state.

QUEEN:

Did he receive you well?

ROSENCRANTZ:

Most like a gentleman.

GUILDENSTERN:

But with much forcing of his disposition④.

ROSENCRANTZ:

Niggard of question⑤, but, of our demands⑥.

Most free in his reply.

---

① no drift of conference: no device of conservation
② confusion: mental disorder
③ distracted: eager to be questioned
④ disposition: against his will
⑤ niggard of question: sparing of conversation
⑥ of our demands: to our question

QUEEN:

Did you assay him

To any pastime?①

ROSENCRANTZ:

Madam, it so fell out, that certain players

We o'er-raught② on the way: of these we told him;

And there did seem in him a kind of joy

To hear of it, they are here about the court,

And, as I think, they have already order

This night to play before him.

POLONIUS:

'Tis most true;

And he beseech'd me to entreat your majesties

To hear and see the matter③.

KING:

With all my heart, and it doth much content me

To hear him so inclin'd.

Good gentlemen, give him a further edge④.

And drive his purpose into these delights.

ROSENCRANTZ:

We shall, my lord.

(*Exeunt ROSENCRANTZ and GUIDENSTERN.*)

KING:

Sweet Gertrude, leave us too⑤;

For we have closely⑥ sent for Hamlet hither,

That he, as 'twere by accident, may here

Affront⑦ Ophelia:

Her father and myself, lawful espials⑧,

Will so bestow ourselves that, seeing, unseen,

We may of their encounter frankly judge,

---

① Did you assay him/To any pastime?: Did you try to interest him in any amusement?
② o'er-raught: overtook
③ matter: performance
④ a further edge: encouragement
⑤ too: so
⑥ closely: secretly
⑦ Affront: Confront
⑧ lawful espials: legitimate spies

And gather by him, as he is behav'd,
If' be th' affliction of his love or no
That thus he suffers for.
QUEEN:
I shall obey you.
And for your part, Ophelia, I do wish
That your good beauties be the happy cause
Of Hamlet's wildness①: so shall I hope your virtues
Will bring him to his wonted way② again,
To both your honours.
OPHELIA:
Madam, I wish it may. (*Exit QUEEN.*)
POLONIUS:
Ophelia, walk you here. Gracious③, so please you,
We will bestow ourselves. (*To OPHELIA*) Read on this book;
That show of such an exercise④ may colour⑤
Your loneliness. We are oft to blame in this—
'Tis too much prov'd—that with devotion's visage⑥
And pious action we do sugar o'er
The devil himself.
KING:
(*Aside*) O, 'is too true!
How smart a lash that speech doth give my conscience!
The harlot's cheek, beautied with plast'ring art⑦,
Is not more ugly to the thing that helps it⑧
Than is my deed to my most painted⑨ word:
O heavy burthen!
POLONIUS:
I hear him coming; let's withdraw, my lord.

---

① wildness: madness
② wonted way: normal state
③ Gracious: Your Majesty—addressed to the King
④ exercise: act of devotion
⑤ colour: give a plausible appearance to; explain
⑥ visage: an outward appearance of religion
⑦ beautied with plast'ring art: thickly painted
⑧ it: lust, which is the cause of its artificial beauty
⑨ painted: false

(*Exeunt* KING *and* POLONIUS.)
(*Enter* HAMLET.)
HAMLET:
To be, not to be—that is the question:
Whether 'tis nobler in the mind to suffer
The slings and arrows of outrageous① fortune
Or to take arms against a sea② of troubles,
And by opposing end them. To die—to sleep—
No more; and by a sleep to say we end
The heartache, and the thousand natural shocks
The flesh is heir to. 'Tis a consummation③,
Devoutly to be wish'd. To die—to sleep.
To sleep—perchance to dream: ay, there's the rub④!
For in that sleep of death what dreams may come
When we have shuffled⑤ off this mortal coil⑥,
Must give us pause. There's the respect⑦
That makes calamity of so long life⑧.
For who would bear the whips and scorns of time⑨,
Th' oppressor's wrong, the proud man's contumely⑩,
The pangs of despise'd⑪ love, the law's delay,
The insolence of office⑫, and the spurns⑬
That patient merit of th' unworthy takes⑭,
When he himself might his quietus make

---

① outrageous: cruel
② sea: an endless turmoil (a mixed metaphor)
③ consummation: completion
④ rub: impediment
⑤ shuffled: cast
⑥ mortal coil: turmoil, the fuss of life
⑦ respect: reason
⑧ That makes calamity of so long life: That makes it a calamity to have to live so long.
⑨ time: the world
⑩ contumely: insulting behavior
⑪ despis'd: rejected
⑫ office: office-holders
⑬ spurns: insults
⑭ That patient merit of th' unworthy takes: which men of merit have patiently to endure from the unworthy

With a bare bodkin①? Who would these fardels bear②,
To grunt and sweat under a weary life,
But that the dread of something after death—
The undiscover'd country, from whose bourn③
No travelers returns—puzzles the will,
And makes us rather bear those ills we have
Than fly to others that we know not of?
Thus conscience does make cowards of us all,
And thus the native hue④ of resolution
Is sicklied o'er⑤ with the pale cast⑥ of thought,
And enterprises of great pitch⑦ and moment⑧
With this regard⑨ their currents⑩ turn awry
And lose the name of action. —Soft you now!
The fair Ophelia! Nymph, in thy orisons⑪
Be all my sins rememb' red.

OPHELIA:

Good my lord,
How does your honour for this many a day?

HAMLET:

I humbly thank you; well, well, well.

OPHELIA:

My lord, I have remembrances of yours,
That I have longed long to re-deliver;
I pray you, now receive them.

HAMLET:

No, not I;
I never gave you aught.

---

① a bare bodkin: unsheathed dagger
② bear: burden
③ bourn: boundary
④ the native hue: the natural color
⑤ sicklied o'er: given a sickly tinge
⑥ cast: shade of color
⑦ pitch: height
⑧ moment: importance
⑨ regard: respect consideration
⑩ currents: courses
⑪ orisons: prayers

OPHELIA:
My honour'd lord, you know right well you did;
And, with them words of so sweet breath compos'd
As made the things more rich: their perfume lost,
Take these again; for to the noble mind
Rich gifts wax① poor when givers prove unkind.
There, my lord.
HAMLET: Ha, ha! are you honest?②
OPHELIA: My lord?
HAMLET: Are you fair③?
OPHELIA: What means your lordship?
HAMLET:
That if you be honest and fair, your honesty
should admit no discourse to your beauty④.
OPHELIA:
Could beauty, my lord, have better commerce⑤
than with honesty?
HAMLET:
Ay, truly; for the power of beauty will sooner
transform honesty from what it is to a bawd⑥ than
the force of honesty can translate beauty into his likeness:
this was sometime a paradox, but now the time⑦
gives it proof. I did love you once.
OPHELIA:
Indeed, my lord, you made me believe so.
HAMLET:
You should not have believed me; for virtue
cannot so inoculate⑧ our old stock

---

① wax: become
② honest: chaste and truthful
③ fair: just, honorable, and beautiful
④ if you be honest ... your beauty: If you are chaste and beautiful your chastity should have worthy to do with your beauty, because (so Hamlet thinks in hesitation) beautiful women are seldom chaste.
⑤ commerce: intercourse
⑥ bawd: brothel
⑦ the time: the present age
⑧ innoculate: graft (metaphorical)

but we shall relish of it① I loved you not.

OPHELIA:

I was the more deceived.

HAMLET:

Get thee to a nunnery②: why wouldst thou be

a breeder of sinners? I am myself indifferent honest③;

but yet I could accuse me of such things that it were

better my mother had not borne me: I am very proud,

revengeful, ambitious, with more offenses at my beck④

than I have thoughts to put them in, imagination to

give them shape, or time to act them in. What should

such fellows as I do crawling between earth and heaven?

We are arrant⑤ knaves, all; believe none of us.

Go thy ways to a nunnery. Where's your father?

OPHELIA: At home, my lord.

HAMLET:

Let the doors be shut upon him, that he may

play the fool no where but in's own house. Farewell.

OPHELIA:

O, help him, you sweet heavens!

HAMLET:

If thou dost marry, I'll give thee this plague

for thy dowry: be thou as chaste as ice, as pure as

snow, thou shalt not escape calumny.

Get thee to a nunnery, go: farewell. Or, if thou wilt needs marry,

marry a fool; for wise men know well enough what

monsters⑥ you make of them. To a nunnery, go, and

quickly too. Farewell.

OPHELIA:

O heavenly powers, restore him!

HAMLET:

---

① we shall relish of it: that we do not still have about us a taste of the old stock, i. e., retain our sinfulness

② nunnery: a place where she will be removed from temptation

③ honest: moderately virtuous

④ with more offenses at my beck: waiting to come when I beckon

⑤ arrant: thorough

⑥ monsters: an allusion to the horns of a cuckold

I have heard of your paintings too, well
enough; God hath given you one face, and you make
yourselves another: you jig①, you amble, and you lisp②;
you nick-name God's creatures, and make your
wantonness your ignorance③. Go to, I'll no more
on 't; it hath made me mad. I say, we will have no
more marriage: those that are married already, all
but one④, shall live; the rest shall keep as they are.
To a nunnery, go. (*Exit.*)
OPHELIA:
O, what a noble mind is here o'er-thrown!
The courtier's, soldier's, scholar's, eye, tongue, sword;
Th' expectancy and rose⑤ of the fair state,
The glass of fashion and the mould of form,⑥
Th' observ'd of all observers,⑦ quite, quite down!
And I, of ladies most deject and wretched,
That suck'd the honey of his music⑧ vows,
Now see that noble and most sovereign reason,
Like sweet bells jangled, out of time and harsh;
That unmatch'd form and feature of blown⑨ youth
Blasted with ecstasy⑩: O, woe is me,
T' have seen what I have seen, see what I see!
(*Enter KING and POLONIUS.*)
KING:
Love! his affections do not that way tend;
Nor what he spake, though it lack'd form a little,
Was not like madness. There's something in his soul,

---

① jig: move with jerky motion; probably allusion to the jig, or song and dance of the current stage
② lisp: walk and talk affectedly
③ wantonness your ignorance: excuse your wantonness on the ground of your ignorance
④ one: the King
⑤ rose: source of hope
⑥ The glass of fashion and the mould of form: the mirror of fashion and the pattern of courtly behavior
⑦ Th' observ'd of all observers: the center of attention in the court
⑧ music: musical
⑨ blown: blooming, perfect, like an open flower of its best
⑩ ecstasy: madness

O'er which his melancholy sits on brood①;
And I do doubt② the hatch and the disclose③
Will be some danger; which for to prevent,
I have in quick determination
Thus set it down; he shall with speed to England,
For the demand of our neglected tribute;
Haply the seas and countries different
With variable objects shall expel
This something—settled matter in his heart,
Whereon his brains still beating puts him thus
From fashion of himself④. What think you on 't?
POLONIUS:
It shall do well; but yet do I believe
The origin and commencement of his grief
Sprung from neglected love. How now, Ophelia!
You need not tell us what Lord Hamlet said;
We heard it all. My lord, do as you please;
But, if you hold it fit, after the play
Let his queen mother all alone entreat him
To show his grief; let her be round⑤ with him;
And I'll be placed, so please you, in the ear⑥
Of all their conference. If she find him not⑦,
To England send him, or confine him where
Your wisdom best shall think.
KING:
It shall be so:
Madness in great ones must not unwatch'd go.

Study Questions:

1. The act contains one of the famous soliloquies of Hamlet. Locate it and paraphrase it.
2. According to Hamlet, why is sleep so frightening, since it can "end" the heartache and the

---

① sits on brood: sits hatching like a hen
② doubt: fear
③ disclose: disclosure or revelation
④ puts him thus/From fashion of himself: separates him from his normal self
⑤ round: blunt
⑥ in the ear: hearing
⑦ find him not: not discover his problem

thousand natural shocks?

3. Why would people rather bear all the sufferings of the world instead of choosing death to get rid of them, according to Hamlet?

4. What, after all, makes people lose their determination to take action? Please explain in relation to the so-called hesitation of Hamlet.

5. What do you think of Hamlet's affection for Ophelia?

6. Read the whole excerpt carefully, then give a brief analysis of Hamlet's character.

The Importance of Being Earnest (1895)

Oscar Wilde

Act I (Excerpts)

Lane①: Mr. Ernest Worthing.

(*Enter Jack. Lane goes out.*)

Algernon: How are you, my dear Ernest? What brings you up to town?

Jack: Oh, pleasure, pleasure! What else should bring one anywhere? Eating as usual, I see, Algy!

Algernon: (*Stiffly.*) I believe it is customary in good society to take some slight refreshment at five o'clock. Where have you been since last Thursday?

Jack: (*Sitting down on the sofa.*) In the country.

Algernon: What on earth do you do there?

Jack: (*Pulling off his gloves.*) When one is in town one amuses oneself. When one is in the country one amuses other people. It is excessively boring.

Algernon: And who are the people you amuse?

Jack: (*Airily.*) Oh, neighbours, neighbours.

Algernon: Got nice neighbours in your part of Shropshire②?

Jack: Perfectly horrid! Never speak to one of them.

Algernon: How immensely you must amuse them! (*Goes over and takes sandwich.*) By the way, Shropshire is your county, is it not?

Jack: Eh? Shropshire? Yes, of course. Hallo! Why all these cups? Why cucumber sandwiches? Why such reckless extravagance in one so young? Who is coming to tea?

Algernon: Oh! Merely Aunt Augusta and Gwendolen.

Jack: How perfectly delightful!

Algernon: Yes, that is all very well; but I am afraid Aunt Augusta won't quite approve of your being here.

---

① Lane: Algernon's servant

② Shropshire: one shire in northwest of England

Jack: May I ask why?

Algernon: My dear fellow, the way you flirt with Gwendolen is perfectly disgraceful. It is almost as bad as the way Gwendolen flirts with you.

Jack: I am in love with Gwendolen. I have come up to town expressly to propose to her.

Algernon: I thought you had come up for pleasure? ... I call that business.

Jack: How utterly unromantic you are!

Algernon: I really don't see anything romantic about proposing. It is very romantic to be in love. But there is nothing romantic about a definite proposal. Why, one may be accepted. One usually is, I believe. Then the excitement is all over. The very essence of romance is uncertainty. If ever I get married, I'll certainly try to forget the fact.

Jack: I have no doubt about that, dear Algy. The Divorce Court was specially invented for people whose memories are so curiously constituted.

Algernon: Oh! There is no use speculating on that subject. Divorces are made in Heaven— (*Jack puts out his hand to take a sandwich. Algernon at once interferes.*) Please don't touch the cucumber sandwiches. They are ordered specially for Aunt Augusta. (*Takes one and eats it.*)

Jack: Well, you have been eating them all the time.

Algernon: That is quite a different matter. She is my aunt. (*Takes plate from below.*) Have some bread and butter. The bread and butter is for Gwendolen. Gwendolen is devoted to bread and butter.

Jack: (*Advancing to table and helping himself.*) And very good bread and butter it is too.

Algernon: Well, my dear fellow, you need not eat as if you were going to eat it all. You behave as if you were married to her already. You are not married to her already, and I don't think you ever will be.

Jack: Why on earth do you say that?

Algernon: Well, in the first place girls never marry the men they flirt with. Girls don't think it right.

Jack: Oh, that is nonsense!

Algernon: It isn't. It is a great truth. It accounts for the extraordinary number of bachelors that one sees all over the place. In the second place, I don't give my consent.

Jack: Your consent!

Algernon: My dear fellow, Gwendolen is my first cousin. And before I allow you to marry her, you will have to clear up the whole question of Cecily[①].
(*Rings bell.*)

---

① Cecily: granddaughter of Thomas Cadiu, who adopted Jack, the guardian of Cecily

Jack: Cecily! What on earth do you mean? What do you mean, Algy, by Cecily! I don't know anyone by the name of Cecily.

(*Enter Lane.*)

Algernon: Bring me that cigarette case Mr. Worthing left in the smoking-room the last time he dined here.

Lane: Yes, sir.

(*Lane goes out.*)

Jack: Do you mean to say you have had my cigarette case all this time? I wish to goodness you had let me know. I have been writing frantic letters to Scotland Yard[①] about it. I was very nearly offering a large reward.

Algernon: Well, I wish you would offer one. I happen to be more than usually hard up[②].

Jack: There is no good offering a large reward now that the thing is found.

(*Enter Lane with the cigarette case on a salve. Algernon takes it at once. Lane goes out.*)

Algernon: I think that is rather mean of you, Ernest, I must say. (*Opens case and examines it.*) However, it makes no matter, for, now that I look at the inscription inside, I find that the thing isn't yours after all.

Jack: Of course it's mine. (*Moving to him.*) You have seen me with it a hundred times, and you have no right whatsoever to read what is written inside. It is a very ungentlemanly thing to read a private cigarette case. Oh! It is absurd to have a hard-and-fast rule about what one should read and what one shouldn't. More than half of modern culture depends on what one shouldn't read.

Jack: I am quite aware of the fact, and I don't propose to discuss modern culture. It isn't the sort of thing one should talk of in private. I simply want my cigarette case back. Yes; but this isn't your cigarette case. This cigarette case is a present from someone of the name of Cecily, and you said you didn't know anyone of that name.

Jack: Well, if you want to know, Cecily happens to be my aunt.

Algernon: Your aunt!

Jack: Yes. Charming old lady she is, too. Lives at Tunbridge Wells[③]. Just give it back to Algy.

Algernon: (*Retreating to back of sofa.*) But why does she call herself Cecily if she is your aunt; and lives at Tunbridge Wells? (*Reading.*) From little Cecily with her fondest love.

Jack: (*Moving to sofa and kneeling upon it.*) My dear fellow, what on earth is there in that? Some aunts are tall, some aunts are not tall. That is a matter that surely an aunt may be allowed to decide for herself. You seem to think that every aunt should be

---

① Scotland Yard: London Police Office
② be more than usually hard up: be in need of money more than ever before
③ Turnbridge Wells: It is located in Kentshire, 30 miles south to London.

	exactly like your aunt! That is absurd! For Heaven's sake give me back my cigarette case. (*Follows Algernon round the room.*)
Algernon:	Yes. But why does your aunt call you her uncle? 'From little Cecily, with her for love to her dear Uncle Jack.' There is no objection, I admit, to an aunt being a small aunt, but why an aunt, no matter what her size may be, should call her own nephew her uncle, I can't quite make out. Besides, your name isn't Jack at all; it is Ernest.
Jack:	It isn't Ernest; it's Jack.
Algernon:	You have always told me it was Ernest. I have introduced you to everyone as Ernest. You answer to the name of Ernest. You look as if your name was Ernest. You are the most earnest looking person I ever saw in my life. It is perfectly absurd you say that your name isn't Ernest. It's on your cards. Here is one of them. (*Taking it from case.*) 'Mr. Ernest Worthing, B. 4, The Albany.' I'll keep this as a proof that your name is Ernest if ever you attempt to deny it to me, or to Gwendolen, or to anyone else. (*Puts the card in his pocket.*)
Jack:	Well, my name is Ernest in town and Jack in the country, and the cigarette case was given to me in the country.
Algernon:	Yes, but that does not account for the fact that your small Aunt Cecily, who lives at Tunbridge Wells, calls you her dear uncle. Come, old boy, You had much better have the thing out at once.
Jack:	My dear Algy, you talk exactly as if you were a dentist. It is very vulgar to talk a dentist when one isn't a dentist. It produces a false impression.
Algernon:	Well, that is exactly what dentists always do. Now, go on! Tell me the whole I may mention that I have always suspected you of being a confirmed and secret Bunburyist; and I am quite sure of it now.
Jack:	Bunburyist? What on earth do you mean by a Bunburyist?
Algernon:	I'll reveal to you the meaning of that incomparable expression as soon as you are kind enough to inform me why you are Ernest in town and Jack in the country.
Jack:	Well, produce my cigarette case first.
Algernon:	Here it is. (*Hands cigarette case.*) Now produce your explanation, and pray make it improbable.
	(*Sits on sofa.*)
Jack:	My dear fellow, there is nothing improbable about my explanation at all. In fact, it's perfectly ordinary. Old Mr. Thomas Cardew, who adopted me when I was a little boy, made me in his will guardian to his granddaughter, Miss Cecily Cardew. Cecily, who addresses me as her uncle from motives of respect that you could not possible appreciate, lives at my place in the country under the charge of her admirable governess, Miss Prism.

Algernon: Where is that place in the country, by the way?

Jack: That is nothing to you, dear boy. You are not going to be invited ... I may tell you candidly that the place is not in Shropshire.

Algernon: I suspected that, my dear fellow! I have Bunburyed all over Shropshire on two separate occasions. Now, go on. Why are you Ernest in town and Jack in the country?

Jack: My dear Algy, I don't know whether you will be able to understand my real motives. You are hardly serious enough. When one is placed in the position of guardian, one has to adopt a very high moral tone on all subjects. It's one's duty to do so. And as a high moral tone can hardly be said to conduce① very much to either one's health or one's happiness, in order to get up to town I have always pretended to have a younger brother of the name of Ernest, who lives in the Albany, and gets into the most dreadful scrapes②. That, my dear Algy, is the whole truth pure and simple.

Algernon: The truth is rarely pure and never simple. Modern life would be very tedious if it were either, and modern literature a complete impossibility!

Jack: That wouldn't be at all a bad thing.

Algernon: Literary criticism is not your forte③, my dear fellow. Don't try it. You should leave that to people who haven't been at a university. They do it so well in the daily papers. What you really are is a Bunburyist. I was quite right in saying you were a Bunburyist. You are one of the most advanced Bunburyists I know.

Jack: What on earth do you mean?

Algernon: You have invented a very useful younger brother called Ernest, in order that you may be able to come up to town as often as you like. I have invented an invaluable permanent invalid called Bunbury, in order that I may be able to go down into the country whenever I choose. Bunbury is perfectly invaluable. If it wasn't for Bunbury's extraordinary bad health, for instance, I wouldn't be able to dine with you at Willis's to-night, for I have been really engaged to Aunt Augusta for more than a week.

Jack: I haven't asked you to dine with me anywhere to-night.

Algernon: I know. You are absurdly careless about sending out invitations. It is very foolish of you. Nothing annoys people so much as not receiving invitations.

Jack: You had much better dine with your Aunt Augusta.

Algernon: I haven't the smallest intention of doing anything of the kind. To begin with, I

---

① conduce: help
② scrapes: perplexity
③ forte: expertise

	dined there on Monday, and once a week is quite enough to dine with one's own relations. In the second place, whenever I do dine there I am always treated as a member of the family, and sent down with either no woman at all, or two. In the third place, I know perfectly well whom she will place me next to, to-night. She will place me next Mary Farquhar, who always flirts with her own husband across the dinner-table. That is not very pleasant. Indeed, it is not even decent … and that sort of thing is enormously on the increase. The amount of women in London who flirt with their own husbands is perfectly scandalous. It looks so bad. It is simply washing one's clean linen in public. Besides, now that I know you to be a confirmed Bunburyist, I naturally want to talk to you about Bunburying. I want to tell you the rules.
Jack:	I'm not a Bunburyist at all. If Gwendolen accepts me, I am going to kill my brother, indeed I think I'll kill him in any case. Cecily is a little too much interested in him. It is rather a bore. So I am going to get rid of Ernest. And I strongly advise you to do the same with Mr … with your invalid friend who has the absurd name.
Algernon:	Nothing will induce me to part with Bunbury, and if you ever get married, which seems to me extremely problematic, you will be very glad to know Bunbury. A man who marries without knowing Bunbury has a very tedious time of it.
Jack:	That is nonsense. If I marry a charming girl like Gwendolen, and she is the only girl I ever saw in my life that I would marry, I certainly won't want to know Bunbury.
Algernon:	Then your wife will. You don't seem to realize, that in married life three is company and two is none.
Jack:	(*Sententiously*①) That, my dear young friend, is the theory that the corrupt French Drama has been propounding for the last fifty years.
Algernon:	Yes; and that the happy English home has proved in half the time.
Jack:	For heaven's sake, don't try to be cynical. It's perfectly easy to be cynical.
Algernon:	My dear fellow, it isn't easy to be anything nowadays. There's such a lot of beastly competition about. (*The sound of an electric bell is heard.*) Ah! that must be Aunt Augusta. Only relatives, or creditors, ever ring in that Wagnerian② manner. Now, if I get her out of the way for ten minutes, so that you can have an opportunity for proposing to Gwendolen, may I dine with you to-night at Willis's?
Jack:	I suppose so, if you want to.
Algernon:	Yes, but you must be serious about it. I hate people who are not serious about meals. It is so shallow of them.

---

① *Sententiously*: in a manner to teach a lesson
② Wagnerian: Wagner, a German composer (1813 — 1883). Here it refers to the style of Wagner.

Study Questions:
1. Who is Ernest? What is the relationship between Jack and Ernest?
2. Why does Jack finally agree to have dinner with Algernon tonight?
3. What do you think of Jack and Algernon? Do you like their witty words? Why or why not?

[Reading Critically]

Breaking the Language Barrier

From Peking to Berlin, Buenos Aires to Oslo, Shakespeare is almost universally acknowledged as the world's greatest playwright, a master entertainer as well as consummate artist. Literature holds few pleasures so consistently delectable. Shakespearean drama is a mountain nobody could go beyond, yet reading it is still a problem. For a modern reader, the basic problem he faces with Shakespeare is language. Shakespeare's English is more than four hundred years old, and it differs from contemporary English usage in innumerable small ways. Although his idiom may at first seem daunting, it is easily mastered if you make the effort. There is only one way to grow comfortable with Shakespeare's language: You must immerse yourself in it—a highly pleasurable undertaking.

There is no substitute for hearing Shakespeare's language in performance. He wrote the plays to be heard as spoken language rather than read silently on the page. Let your ears do the work. After reading the play, listen to a recording of it. This is also an invaluable and enjoyable way to review a play. Most school libraries have recordings of all the major plays of Shakespeare. Hearing *Othello* or *Hamlet* recited by an accomplished actor will almost always communicate its meaning to you, as well as familiarize you with the bard's Elizabethan idiom. It will also help to watch the play on videotape, although you will need to read it carefully as well since most films cut sections of the original text. The more time you spend listening, the more quickly you will master the nuances of the language.

Before you write about any Shakespearean play, read the text more than once. The first time through an Elizabethan-era text, you will almost certainly miss many things. As you grow more familiar with Shakespeare's language, you will be able to read it with more complete comprehension. If you choose to write about a particular episode or character, carefully study the speeches and dialogue in question (paying special attention to footnotes) so that you understand each word. You can't write about a text you don't know how to read. In your paper, don't hesitate to bring in what you have learned. Discuss how key words you quote had different meanings in Shakespeare's day. Enjoy yourself.

3. The Development of Drama

As a form of literature, drama dates back to the ancient Greeks and seems to have had its origin in religious ritual. The Greek philosopher Aristotle defined the principles of drama as he saw them, and his ideas were adopted and adapted by classical Roman playwrights and by the great dramatists of Elizabethan England in the 16th and early 17th centuries. Classical and Elizabethan dramas were generally written in verse, and the masterpieces of the great Elizabethan playwright, William Shakespeare (1564 –1616), are known as much for their powerful poetry as their perceptive insights into the human heart. Shakespeare's tragedies generally follow the pattern of Greek tragedies, but most of his comedies are lighthearted romances, quite different from the biting satires of Aristophanes.

The theater audience in Elizabethan times was a motley crew: Public theaters were open to people from all ranks of English society. However, by the end of the 17th century, the public theaters in London had all but disappeared, and plays were performed in private theaters attended chiefly by the wealthy classes. This period saw the birth of the comedy of manners, a realistic and often satirical look at life in sophisticated society. This kind of play owes much of its existence to the works of the French Playwright Molière (1622–1673). The comedy of manners remained a popular form throughout the 18th century, though English audiences of the period also enjoyed sentimental comedies, unrealistic tales that contain romance and tears and that usually offer a moral message.

With the rise of the Romantic Movement—a movement that spurred some of the world's greatest poetry and prose—drama declined, and a rather inferior form of play, the melodrama, was born. Melodramas are highly emotional plays with little concern for developing convincing motivation for their characters. They were extremely popular in the 19th century until the influence of Realism was felt upon the stage.

With realism came the great plays of Anton Chekhov (1860–1904), a Russian, and of Henrik Ibsen (1828–1906), a Norwegian, who explored social issues and gave audiences a "slice of life" as it was lived. Psychological realism came to the stage as expressionism, a movement in drama that is concerned with the inner realities of characters' minds. Early expressionist dramas are best exemplified in the plays of Sweden's Johan August Strindberg (1849–1912). The plays of Ibsen and Strindberg have had a profound impact on all subsequent drama worldwide, for the 20th-century drama often deals with external and internal realities. Also in the 20th-century drama we see an end to the classical distinctions between tragedy and comedy. To be sure, the terms are still used, but more and more the devices of each are blended within one work, and we refer to any serious modern play as a drama.

English Drama in the 20th Century

In England, the new age of English drama—designedly realistic, intellectual, and critical of the state of society—opened with the production of Bernard Shaw's first play, *Widowers' Houses*. Then English drama was headed by Shaw, John Galsworthy and J. M. Barrie until a new order appeared after World War I. In the post-war period London theaters fell into the maw of financiers with enough resources to bear inflated rents and crippling costs of production.

Before the war, the Abbey Theater, Dublin, the Gaiety Theater, Manchester and the Birmingham Repertory Theater under Barry Kackson had challenged the long monopoly of London. In Dublin, W. B. Yeats, J. M. Synge, Lady Gregory and others provided the Irish players with distinguished literary and acting material; Manchester produced a group of local dramatists, among whom Stanley Houghton (with *Hindle Wakes*, 1912) and Harold Brighouse (with *Hobson's choice*, 1916) reached a wider public; Birmingham's most acclaimed success was *Abraham Lincoln* (1918) by John Drinkwater, followed by Eden Phillpotts's unpretentious rural comedy, *The Farmer's Wife* (1916), and Rudolf Besier's *The Barretts of Wimpole Street* (1930).

In London Noel Coward first attracted attention with *The Vortex* (1923), a grim little play, and quickly went on to become the most prosperous playwright of his generation, with a skilled stage sense which disguised and triumphed over the frequent triviality of the dialogue. Thrillers, a kind of crime and detective plays, came to occupy much time and space in the theaters, among the most accomplished providers being Edgar Wallace and Agatha Christie.

Beginning with *French Without Tears* in 1936, Terence Rattigan had a series of successes. His defense in the preface to the second volume of his *Collected Plays*, of that ageless play-goer dubbed Aunt Edna, serves to uphold Dr Johnson's assertion that "the drama's laws the drama's patrons give", a view contested by the young "new wave" playwrights of the 1950s and after, who, as reformers "committed" to some philosophical or propagandist purpose, felt bound to register aggressive contempt of those who expected only to be entertained in the theater. History repeated itself in so far as the Court Theater in London became again the center of a new drama. There John Osborne's *Look Back in Anger*, performed in 1956, established the English Stage Company, and, in the year that followed, plays in the new manner were welcomed. A strong external influence on the drama of the period came from the stage work of Bertolt

Brecht (1898 – 1956), while Samuel Beckett's *Waiting for Godot* (1956), at first received with bewilderment, took its place in the Theater of the Absurd, a kind of theater developing from the existentialist philosophy and emphasizing the absurdity of human condition, which, with the Theater of the Cruelty, developed numerous offshoots.

In the next decade, with the addition of Harold Pinter, Arnold Wesker and John Arden to the roster of dramatists, more writers potentially competent in other literary fields chose the theater because of the greater hopes of finding a public and a subsidized outlet for their work. The number of tiny or temporary stages which gave writers their initial experience increased, and the opening of the National Theater in 1976 with its three stages, each supplying a different dramatic platform, went far towards making the reign of Elizabeth II notable for dramatic innovation. Non-realistic devices of staging and language entered into the dramatic conventions gradually accepted by audiences, while plays were again used as vehicles for moral, social and political comment. Among writers to be recognized since those already named may be listed Tom Stoppard, Edward Bond, Alan Bennett, Peter Shaffer, Christopher Hampton, Simon Gray, Peter Nichols, David Storey, originally a novelist of achievement, David Hare, Athol Fugard and Howard Brenton. Finally Alan Ayckboum whose popularity and productivity made him appear a whole theatrical industry in himself and who in a short time, like Neil Simon in the USA, has satisfied the widest audiences from the National Theater down to the provincial repertory playhouse. Drama again became an English art with the widest reputation abroad.

American Drama in the 20th Century

Up until the 20th century American drama made little impact on American literature as a whole. The reasons for the lack of American drama are understandable: Theaters such as the elitist European ones of the 18th century would not flourish in America, at that time an infant democracy, and the melodrama of the 19th century would not attract serious American writers. There were, of course, some American plays of literary interest written before 1900: Royall Tyler's *The Contrast* (1787), America's first comedy, and the 19th-century verse tragedies of George Henry Boker are considered to be of literary merit. However, it was not until Realism and Expressionism began to appear on the stage that serious American writers turned to drama.

At the beginning of the 20th century, so-called little theaters sprang up throughout the United States, theaters that encouraged serious playwrights because they were willing to produce original works by unknown talents. The first American dramatist to achieve an international reputation, Eugene O'Neill (1888–1953), began his career as a writer for the Provincetown Players, a "little theater" company begun in Provincetown, Massachusetts.

The plays of Eugene O'Neill reflect his New England background and Irish American heritage and display the Realism and interest in modern psychological characteristics of Ibsen and Strindberg. O'Neill's plays also reflect the Modernist experimentation of the early 20th century: In *Strange Interlude* (1928) characters' thoughts are heard by the audience, and in *The Great God Brown* (1926) characters don and remove masks while they are speaking. Among O'Neill's other famous plays are *Mourning Becomes Electro* (1931), *The Ice Man Cometh* (1946), and *Long Day's Journey into Night* (1956), a semi-autobiographical drama produced after the playwright's death.

Led by O'Neill, American drama flourished between the two world wars. Elmer Rice wrote a portrait of tenement life called *Street Scene* (1929); Clifford Odets explored serious social problems in *Awake and Sing!* (1935) and *Waiting for Lefty* (1935). Maxwell Anderson wrote plays in verse, and George S. Kaufman and Moss Hart entertained audiences with their witty satires.

The twenties and thirties also saw the development of a strictly American form, the musical comedy, which reached its peak after World War II in the works of Rodgers and Hammerstein, Lemer and Loewe, Leonard Bernstein, and Stephen Sondheim. Major American dramatists since World War II include Tennessee Williams (*The Glass Menagerie*, *A Streetcar Named Desire*), William Inge (*Picnic*, *The Dark at the Top of the Stairs*), Arthur Miller (*Death of a Salesman*, *The Crucible*).

In the late 1950s, the American theater was in a period of crisis. O'Neill was already dead. The golden age for Williams and Miller seemed to be over. It was not until 1958 that American drama made a big discovery in the Off Off Broadway. His name is Edward Albee, who is most closely connected with the Theater of the Absurd, developed mainly in Europe. Edward Albee is famous mainly for his plays *The sandbox* (1959), *The Death of Bessie Smith* (1960), *Who's Afraid of Virginia Woolf?* (1962), *The Delicate Balance* (1966), *A Play of Marriage* (1987) and *Finding the Sun* (1993).

Along with other protests of the 1960s, experimental theatre seemed to have spent its force and gradually exerted its influence on the creation of new drama in America. During the later period most of the critically celebrated new plays were neither absurd nor experimental. David Mamet's *American Buffalo* (1975) realistically portrays three thieves in a junk shop as they plot to steal a coin collection. Albert Innaurato's *Gemini* (1977) takes a realistic view of family life and sexual awakening in one of Philadelphia's Italian neighborhood. Beth Henley's Pulitzer-winning play, *Crimes of the Heart* (1979), presents an eccentric but still believable group of sisters in a small Southern town. In all three plays, the dialogue shows high fidelity to ordinary speech. Meanwhile, many of the most influential plays of feminist theatre, exploring the lives, problems, and occasional triumphs of contemporary women, were also written in a realistic style. Marsha Norman's *Night, Mother* (1983), Tina Howe's *Painting Churches* (1983), and Wendy Wasserstein's *The Heidi Chronicles* (1988) were greeted with notable success for both critics and the public.

Some critics, among them Richard Gilman, believed that the American theatre had entered an era of new naturalism. Indeed, many plays of this time subjected the lives of people, especially poor and unhappy ones, to a realistic, searing light, showing the forces that shaped them. Sam Sheppard's *Buried Child* (1978) explores violence and desperation in a family that dwells on the edge of poverty; while August Wilson, in *Joe Turner's Come and Gone* (1988), convincingly portrays life in a Pittsburgh ghetto lodging house. But we should note that both of the plays just mentioned contain rich and suggestive symbolism if these newly-established playwrights showed life as frankly as did the earlier naturalists.

However, experimental drama, greatly influenced by the theatre of the absurd, has made a comeback more recently. David Hwang's *The Sound of a Voice* (1983), in which two characters named Man and Woman act out a story reminiscent of a folk legend or a traditional Japanese Nōdrama①, combines realistic elements with overtly symbolic devices. Caryl Churchill's *Top Girls* (1982) presents a dinner party in which a contemporary woman invites legendary women from history to a restaurant dinner party. Although Churchill's play examines serious political issues, her straightforward treatment of an impossible premise owes much to Ionesco and Albee. Tony Kushner's *Angels in America* (1992) also mixes realism and fantasy to dramatize the plight of AIDS.

Seemingly, experimental theatre continues to exert a strong influence on contemporary drama. Tom Stoppard, probably the most influential living British playwright, in his comedy, *The Real Inspector Hound* (1968), takes certain principles from experimental drama, i. e. blurring the line between reality and fantasy, disruptions in chronology, and other absurdist ploys, and combines them with the most conventional and old-fashioned genre imaginable, the murder mystery play. The result is a play at once hilarious and aesthetically provocative. Milcha Sanchez-Scott, one of contemporary American dramatists, deftly assimilates several dramatic styles, such as symbolism, new naturalism, ethnic drama and theatre of the absurd in *The Cuban Swimmer* (1984), to create a brilliant original work. The work is simultaneously a family drama, a Latin comedy, a religious parable, and a critique of a media-obsessed American culture.

Here are two plays, read them and have a bird's-eye view of the modern theatre.

---

① Nōdrama is a type of symbolic aristocratic drama developed in the 14th-century Japan in which a ghost acts out the struggles of his or her life for a traveler.

Rosencrantz and Guildenstern Are Dead (1966)
Tom Stoppard

Act One

Two ELIZABETHANS *passing the time in a place without any visible character. They are well dressed—hats, cloaks, sticks and all. Each of them has a large leather money bag. GUILDENSTERN's bag is nearly empty. ROSENCRANTZ's bag is nearly full.*

The reason being: they are betting on the toss of a coin, in the following manner: GUILDENSTERN [hereafter " GUIL"] takes a coin out of his bag, spins it, letting it fall. ROSENCRANTZ [hereafter "ROS"] studies it, announces it as "heads" [as it happens] and puts it into his own bag. Then they repeat the process. They have apparently been doing this for some time.

The run of "heads" is impossible, yet ROS betrays no surprise at all—he feels none. However, he is nice enough to feel a little embarrassed at taking so much money off his friend. Let that be his character note.

GUIL is well alive to the oddity if it. He is not worried about the money, but he is worried by the implications; aware but not going to panic about it—his character note.

GUIL sits. ROS stands [he does the moving, retrieving coins].

GUIL spins. ROS studies coin.

ROS: Heads.

[*He picks it up and puts it in his bag. The process is repeated.*]

Heads.

[*Again.*]

Heads.

[*Again.*]

Heads.

[*Again.*]

Heads.

GUIL: [*Flipping a coin.*] There is an art to the building up of suspense.

ROS: Heads.

GUIL: [*Flipping another.*] Though it can be done by luck alone.

ROS: Heads.

GUIL: If that's the word I'm after.

ROS: [*Raises his head at GUIL.*] Seventy-six love[①].

[*GUIL gets up but has nowhere to go. He spins another coin over his shoulder without looking at it,*

[①] Seventy-six love: ROS wins seventy-six times, while GUIL wins none. "love" means "nought" in tennis match.

his attention being directed at his environment or lack of it.]

    Heads.

GUIL: A weaker man might be moved to re-examine his faith, if in nothing else at least in the law of probability.

[*He slips a coin over his shoulder as he goes to look upstage.*]

ROS: Heads.

[*GUIL, examining the confines of the stage, flips over two more coins as he does so, one by one of the course. ROS announces each of them as "heads".*]

GUIL: [*Musing*] The law of probability, it has been oddly asserted, is something to do with the proposition that if six monkeys [*He has surprised himself.*] ... if six monkeys were ...

ROS: Game?

GUIL: Were they?

ROS: Are you?

GUIL: [*Understanding.*] Game. [*Flips a coin.*] The law of averages. If I have got this right, means that if six monkeys were thrown up in the air for long enough they would land on their tails about as often as they would land on their—

ROS: Heads. [*He picks up the coin.*]

GUIL: Which even at first glance does not strike one as a particularly rewarding speculation, in either sense, even without the monkeys. I mean you wouldn't bet on it. I mean I would, but you wouldn't ... [*As he flips a coin.*]

ROS: Heads.

GUIL: Would you? [*Flips a coin.*]

ROS: Heads.

[*Repeat.*]

    Heads. [*He looks up at GUIL—embarrassed laugh.*] Getting a bit of a bore, isn't it?

GUIL: [*Coldly.*] A bore?

ROS: Well ...

GUIL: What about the suspense?

ROS: [*Innocently.*] What suspense?

[*Small pause.*]

GUIL: It must be the law of diminishing returns ... I feel the spell about to be broken.

[*Energizing himself somewhat.*] [*He takes out a coin, spins it high, catches it, turns it over on to the back of his other hand, studies the coin—and tosses it to ROS. His energy deflates and he sits.*]

    Well, it was an even chance ... if my calculations are correct.

ROS: Eighty-five in a row—beaten the record!

GUIL: Don't be absurd.

ROS: Easily!

GUIL: [*Angry.*] Is that it, then? Is that all?

ROS: What?

GUIL: A new record? Is that as far as you are prepared to go?

ROS: Well ...

GUIL: No questions? Not even a pause?

ROS: You spun them yourself.

GUIL: Not a flicker of doubt?

ROS: [*Aggrieved, aggressive.*] Well. I won—didn't I?

GUIL: [*Approaches him—quieter.*] And if you'd lost? if you'd come down against you, eighty-five times, one after another, just like that?

ROS: [*Dumbly.*] Eighty-five in a row? Tails?

GUIL: Yes! What would you think?

ROS: [*Doubtfully.*] Well ... [*Jocularly.*] Well, I'd have a good look at your coins for a start!

GUIL: [*Retiring.*] I'm relieved. At least we can still count on self-interest as a predictable factor ... I suppose it's the last to go. Your capacity for trust made me wonder if perhaps ... you, alone ... [*He turns on him suddenly, reaches out a hand.*] Touch. [*ROS clasps his hand. GUIL pulls, him up to him. More intensely.*] We have been spinning coins together since—[*He releases him almost as violently.*] This is not the first time we have spun coins!

ROS: Oh no—we've been spinning coins for as long as I remember.

GUIL: How long is that?

ROS: I forget. Mind you-eighty-five times!

GUIL: Yes?

ROS: It'll take some beating, I imagine.

GUIL: Is that what you imagine? Is that it? No fear?

ROS: Fear?

GUIL: [*In fury—flings a coin on the ground.*] Fear! The crack that might flood your brain with light!

ROS: Heads ... [*He puts it in his bag.*]

[*GUIL sits despondently. He takes a coin, spins it, lets it fall between his feet. He looks at it, throws it to ROS, who puts it in his bag.*]

GUIL: Takes another coin, spins it, catches it, turns it over on to his other hand, looks at it, and throws it to ROS who puts it in his bag.

GUIL: Takes a third coin, spins it, catches it in his right hand, turns it over on to his left wrist, labs it in the air, catches it with his left hand, raises his left leg, throws the coin up under it, catches it and turns it over on to the top of his head, where it sits. [*ROS comes, looks at it, puts it in his bag.*]

ROS: I'm afraid—

GUIL: So am I.

ROS: I'm afraid it isn't your day.

GUIL: I'm afraid it is.

    [*Small pause.*]

ROS: Eighty-nine.

GUIL: It must be indicative of something, besides the redistribution of wealth. [*He muses.*] List of possible explanations. One. I'm willing it. Inside where nothing shows, I am the essence of a man spinning double-headed coins, and betting against himself in private atonement for an unremembered past. [*He spins a coin at ROS.*]

ROS: Heads.

GUIL: Two. Time has stopped dead, and the single experience of one coin being spun once has been repeated ninety times ... [*He flips a coin, looks at it, tosses it to ROS.*] On the whole, doubtful. Three. Divine intervention, that is to say, a good turn from above concerning him, cf. children of Israel①, or retribution from above concerning me, cf. Lot's wife. Four. A spectacular vindication of the principle that each individual coin spun individual [*He spins one.*] is as likely to come down heads as tails and therefore should cause no surprise each individual time it does. [*It does. He tosses it to ROS.*]

ROS: I've never known anything like it!

GUIL: And a syllogism: One, he had never known anything like it. Two, he has never known anything to write home about. Three it is nothing to write home about ... Home ... What's the first thing you remember?

ROS: Oh, Let's see ... The first thing that comes into my head, you mean?

GUIL: No—the first thing you remember.

ROS: Ah. [*Pause.*] No, it's no good, it's gone. It was a long time ago.

GUIL: [*Patient but edged.*] You don't get my meaning. What is the first thing after all the things you've forgotten.

ROS: Oh I see. [*Pause.*] I've forgotten the question. [*GUIL leaps up and paces.*]

GUIL: Are you happy?

ROS: What?

GUIL: Content? At ease?

ROS: I suppose so.

GUIL: What are you going to do now?

---

    ① children of Israel: according to the Bible, they are led by God out of Egypt to the Promised Land.

ROS: I don't know. What do you want to do?

GUIL: I have no desires. None. [*He stops pacing dead.*] There was a messenger ... that's right. We were sent for. [*He wheels at ROS and raps out—*] Syllogism the second: one, probability is a factor which operates within natural forces. Two, probability is not operating as a factor. Three, we are now within un-, sub- or supernatural forces. Discuss. [*ROS is suitably startled—Acidly.*] Not too heatedly.

ROS: I'm sorry I—What's the matter with you?

GUIL: The scientific approach to the examination of phenomena is a defence against and pure emotion of fear. Keep tight hold and continue while there's time. Now—counter to the previous syllogism: tricky one, follow me carefully, it may prove a comfort. If we postulate, and we just have, that within un-, sub- or supernatural forces the probability is that the law of probability will not operate as a factor, then we must accept that the probability of the first part will not operate as a factor, in which case the law of probability will operate as a factor within un-, sub- or supernatural forces. And since it obviously hasn't been doing so, we can take it that we are not held within un-, sub- or supernatural forces after all; in all probability, that is. Which is a great relief to me personally. [*Small pause.*] Which is all very well, except that—[*He continues with tight hysteria, under control.*] We have been spinning coins together since I don't know when, and in all that time [if it is all that time] I don't suppose either of us was more than a couple of gold pieces up or down. I hope that doesn't sound surprising because its very unsurprisingness is something I am trying to keep hold of. The equanimity of your average tosser of coins depends upon the law, or rather a tendency, or let us say a probability, or at any rate a mathematically calculable chance, which ensures that he will not upset himself by losing too much nor upset his opponent by winning too often. This made for a kind of harmony and a kind of confidence. It related the fortuitous and the ordained into a reassuring union which we recognized as nature. The sun came up about as often as it went down, in the long run, and a coin showed heads about as often as it shows tails. Then a messenger arrived. We had been sent for. Nothing else happened. Ninety-two coins spun consecutively have come down heads ninety-two consecutive times ... and for the last three minutes on the wind of a windless day I have heard the sound of drums and flute ...

ROS: [*Cutting his fingernails.*] Another curious scientific phenomenon is the fact that the fingernails grow after death, as does the beard.

GUIL: What?

ROS: [*Loud.*] Beard!

GUIL: But you're not dead.

ROS: [*Irritated.*] I didn't say they started to grow after death!

[*Pause, calmer.*] The fingernails also grow before birth, though not the beard.

GUIL: *What?*

ROS: [*Shouts.*] Beard! What's the matter with you? [*Reflectively.*] The toenails, on the other hand, never grow at all.

GUIL: [*Bemused.*] The toenails on the other hand never grow at all?

ROS: Do they? It's a funny thing—I cut my fingernails all the time, and every time I think to cut them, they need cutting. Now, for instance. And yet, I never, to the best of my knowledge, cut my toenails. They ought to be curled under my feet by now, but it doesn't happen. I never think about them. Perhaps I cut them absent-mindedly, when I'm thinking if something else.

GUIL: [*Tensed up by this rambling.*] Do you remember the first thing that happened today?

ROS: [*Promptly.*] I woke up, I suppose. [*Triggered.*] Oh—I've got it now—that man, a foreigner, he woke us up—

GUIL: A messenger. [*He relaxes, sits.*]

ROS: That's it—pale sky before dawn, a man standing on his saddle to bang on the shutters—shouts—what's all the row about?! Clear off!—But then he called our names. You remember that—this man woke us up.

GUIL: Yes.

ROS: We were sent for.

GUIL: Yes.

ROS: That's why we're here. [*He looks round, seems doubtful, them the explanation.*] Travelling.

GUIL: Yes.

ROS: [*Dramatically.*] It was urgent—a matter of extreme urgency, a royal summons, his very words; official business and no questions asked—light in the stableyard, saddle up and off headlong and hotfoot across the land, our guides outstripped in breakneck pursuit of our duty! Fearful lest we come too late! [*Small pause.*]

GUIL: Too late for what?

ROS: How do I know? We haven't got there yet.

GUIL: Then what are we doing here, I ask myself.

ROS: You might well ask.

GUIL: We better get on.

ROS: You might well think.

GUIL: We better get on.

ROS: [*Actively.*] Right! [*Pause.*] On where?

GUIL: Forward.

ROS: [*Forward to footlights.*] Ah. [*Hesitates.*] Which way do we—[*He turns round.*] Which way did we—?

GUIL: Practically starting from scratch ... An awakening, a man standing on his saddle to bang on the shutters, our names shouted in a certain dawn, a message, a summons ... A new record for heads and tails. We have not been ... picked out ... simply to be abandoned ... set loose to find our own way ... We are entitled to some direction ... I would have taught.

ROS: [*Alert, listening.*] I say—! I say—!

GUIL: Yes?

ROS: I can hear—I thought I heard—music.

[*GUIL raises himself.*]

GUIL: Yes?

ROS: Like a band. [*He looks around, laughs embarrassedly, expiating himself.*] It sounded like—a band. Drums.

GUIL: Yes.

ROS: [*Relaxes.*] It couldn't have been real.

GUIL: "The colours red, blue and green are real. The colour yellow is a mystical experience shared by everybody"—demolish.

ROS: [*At edge of stage.*] It must have been thunder. Like drums ...

[*By the end of the next speech, the band is faintly audible.*]

GUIL: A man breaking his journey between one place and another at a third place of no name, character, population or significance, sees a unicorn cross his path and disappear. That in itself is startling, but there are precedents for mystical encounters of various kinds or, to be less extreme, a choice of persuasions to put it down to fancy; until—"My God," says a second man, "I must be dreaming, I thought I saw a unicorn." At which point, a dimension is added that makes the experience an alarming as it will ever be. A third witness, you understand, adds no further dimension but only spreads it thinner, and a fourth thinner still, and the more witnesses there are the thinner it gets and the more reasonable it becomes until it is as thin as reality, the name we give to the common experience ... "Look, look!" recites the crowd. "A horse with an arrow in its forehead! It must have been mistaken for a deer."

ROS: [*Eagerly.*] I knew all along it was a band.

GUIL: [*Tiredly.*] He knew all along it was a band.

ROS: Here they come!

GUIL: [*At the last moment before they enter—wistfully.*] I'm sorry it wasn't a unicorn. It would have been nice to have unicorns. [*The TRAGEDIANS are six in number, including a small BOY "ALFRED". Two pull and push a cart piled with props and belongings. There is also a DRUMMER, a HORN-PLAYER and a FLAUTIST. The SPOKESMAN "the*

PLAYER" has no instrument. He brings up the rear and is the first to notice them.]
PLAYER: Halt!
[The GROUP turns and halts.]
[Joyously] An audience!
[ROS and GUIL half rise.]
Don't move!
[They sink back. He regards them fondly.]
Perfect! A Jacky thing we came along.
ROS: For us?
PLAYER: Let us hope so. But to meet two gentlemen on the road—we would not hope to meet them off it.
ROS: No?
PLAYER: Well met, in fact, and just in time.
ROS: Why's that?
PLAYER: Why, we grow rusty and you catch us at the very point of decadence—by this time tomorrow we might have forgotten everything we ever knew. That's a thought, isn't it? [He laughs generously.] We'd be back where we started—improvising.
ROS: Tumblers, are you?
PLAYER: We can give you a tumble if that's your taste, and times being what they are … Otherwise, for a jingle of coin we can do you a selection of gory romance, full of fine cadence and corpses, pirated from the Italian; and it doesn't take much to make a jingle—even a single coin has music in it.
[They ALL flourish and bow, raggedly.]
Tragedians, at your command.
[ROS and GUIL have got to their feet.]
ROS: My name is Guildenstern, and this is Rosencrantz. [GUIL confers briefly with him.]
[Without embarrassment.]
I'm sorry—his name's Guildenstern, and I'm Rosencrantz.
PLAYER: A pleasure. We've played to bigger, of course, but quality counts for something. I recognized you at once—
ROS: And who are we?
PLAYER: —as fellow artists.
ROS: I thought we were gentlemen.
PLAYER: For some of us it is performance for others, patronage. They are two side of the same coin, or, let us say, being as there are so many of us, the same side of two coins. [Bows again.] Don't clap too loudly—it's a very old world.
ROS: What is your line?

PLAYER: Tragedy, sir. Deaths and disclosures, universal and particular, dénouements both unexpected and inexorable, transvestite① melodrama on all levels including the suggestive. We transport you into a world of intrigue and illusion ... clowns, if you like, murderers—we can do you ghosts and battles, on the skirmish level, heroes, villains, tormented lovers—set pieces in the poetic vein; we can do you rapiers or rape or both, by all means, faithless wives and ravished virgins—flagrante delicto at a price, but that comes under realism for which there are special terms. Getting warm, am I?

ROS: [*Doubtfully.*] Well, I don't know ...

PLAYER: It costs little to watch, and little more if you happen to get caught up in the action, if that's your taste and times being what they are.

ROS: What are they?

PLAYER: Indifferent.

ROS: Bad?

PLAYER: Wicked. Now what precisely is your pleasure? [*He turns to the TRAGEDIANS.*] Gentlemen, disport yourselves. [*The TRAGEDIANS shuffle into some kind of line.*] There! See anything you like?

ROS: [*Doubtful, innocent.*] What do they do?

PLAYER: Let your imagination run riot. They are beyond surprise.

ROS: And how much?

PLAYER: To take part?

ROS: To watch.

PLAYER: Watch what?

ROS: A private performance.

PLAYER: How private?

ROS: Well, there are only two of us. Is that enough?

PLAYER: For an audience, disappointing. For voyeurs, about average.

ROS: What's the difference?

PLAYER: Ten guilders.

ROS: [*Horrified.*] Ten guilders!

PLAYER: I mean eight.

ROS: Together?

PLAYER: Each. I don't think you understand—

ROS: What are you saying?

PLAYER: What am I saying—seven.

---

① transvestite: dressing and acting in a style traditionally associated with the opposite sex

ROS: Where have you *been*?

PLAYER: Roundabout. A nest of children carries the custom of the town. Juvenile companies, they are the fashion. But they cannot match our repertoire ... We'll stoop to anything if that's your bent ...

[*He regards ROS meaningfully but ROS returns the stare blankly.*]

ROS: They'll grow up.

PLAYER: [*Giving up.*] There's one born every minute. [*To TRAGEDIANS.*] On-ward!

[*The TRAGEDIANS start to resume their burdens and their journey, GUIL stirs himself at last.*]

GUIL: Where are you going?

PLAYER: Ha-alt!

[*They halt and turn.*]

Home, sir.

GUIL: Where from?

PLAYER: Home. We're travelling people. We take our chances where we find them.

GUIL: It was chance, then?

PLAYER: Chance?

GUIL: You found us.

PLAYER: Oh yes,

GUIL: You were looking?

PLAYER: Oh no.

GUIL: Chance, then.

PLAYER: Or fate.

GUIL: Yours or ours?

PLAYER: It could hardly be one without the other.

GUIL: Fate, then.

PLAYER: Oh yes. We have no control. Tonight we play to the court. Or the night after. Or to the tavern. Or not.

GUIL: Perhaps I can use my influence.

PLAYER: At the tavern?

GUIL: At the court. I would say I have some influence.

PLAYER: Would you say so?

GUIL: I have influence yet.

PLAYER: Yet what?

[*GUIL seizes the PLAYER violently.*]

GUIL: I have influence!

[*The PLAYER does not resist. GUIL loosen his hold. More calmly.*]

You said something—about getting caught up in the action—

PLAYER: [*Gaily freeing himself.*] I did!—I did!—You're quicker than your friend ... [*Confidingly.*] Now far a handful of guilders I happen to have a private and uncut performance of the Rape of the Sabine Women—or rather woman, or rather Alfred—[*Over his shoulder.*] Get your skit on, Alfred—

[*The BOY starts struggling into a female robe.*]

... and for eight you can participate.

[*GUIL backs, PLAYER follows.*]

... taking either part.

[*GUIL backs*]

... or both for ten.

[*GUIL tries to turn away. PLAYER holds his sleeve.*]

... with encores—

[*GUIL smashes the PLAYER across the face. The PLAYER recoils. GUIL stands trembling.*]
[*Resigned and quiet.*]

Get your skirt off, Alfred ...

[*ALFRED struggles out of his half—on robe.*]

GUIL: [*Shaking with rage and fright.*] It could have been—it didn't have to be obscene ... It could have been—a bird out of season, dropping bright-feathered on my shoulder ... It could have been a tongueless dwarf standing by the road to point the way ... I was prepared. But it's this, is it? No enigma, no dignity, nothing classical, portentous, only this—a comic pornographer and a rabble of prostitutes ...

PLAYER: [*Acknowledging the description with a sweep of his hat, bowing: sadly.*] Your should have caught us in better times. We were purists then. [*Straightens up.*] On-ward.

[*The PLAYER make to leave.*]

ROS: [*His voice has changed; he has caught on.*] Excuse me!

PLAYER: Ha-alt!

[*They halt.*]

A-al-l-fred!

[*ALFRED resumes the struggle. The PLAYER comes forward.*]

ROS: You're not—ah—exclusively players, then?

PLAYER: We're inclusively players, sir.

ROS: So you give—exhibitions?

PLAYER: Performances, sir.

ROS: Yes, of course. There's more money in that, is there?

PLAYER: There's more trade, sir.

ROS: Times being what they are.

PLAYER: Yes.

ROS: Indifferent.
PLAYER: Completely.
ROS: You know I'd no idea—
PLAYER: No.
ROS: I mean, I've heard of—but I've never actually—
PLAYER: No.
ROS: I mean, what exactly do you *do*?
PLAYER: We keep to our usual stuff, more or less, only inside out. We do on stage the things that are supposed to happen off. Which is a kind of integrity, if you look on every exit being an entrance somewhere else.
ROS: [*Nervy, loud.*] Well, I'm not really the type of man who—no, but don't hurry off—sit down and tell us about some of the things people ask you to do—[*The PLAYER turns away.*]
PLAYER: On-ward!
ROS: Just a minute!

[*They turn and look at him without expression.*]

Well, all right—I wouldn't mind seeing—just an idea of the kind of—[*Bravely.*] What will you do for what?

[*And tosses a single coin on the ground between them. The PLAYER spits at the coin, from where he stands. The TRAGDIANS demur①, trying to get at the coin. He kicks and cuffs them back.*]

PLAYER: On!

[*ALFRED is still half in and out of his robe. The PLAYER cuffs him. To ALFRED.*]

What are you playing at?

[*ROS is shamed into fury.*]

ROS: Filth! Disgusting—I'll report you to the authorities—perverts! I know your game all right, it's all fifth!

[*The PLAYERS are about to leave. GUIL has reminded detached.*]

GUIL: [*Casually.*] Do you like a bet?

[*The TRAGEDIANS turn and look interested. The PLAYER comes forward.*]

PLAYER: What kind of bet did you have in mind?

[*GUIL walks half the distance towards the PLAYER, stops with his foot over coin.*]

GUIL: Double or quits.
PLAYER: Well ... heads.

[*GUIL raises his foot. The PLAYER bends. The TRAGEDIANS crowd round. Relief and congratulations. The PLAYER picks up the coin. GUIL throws him a second coin.*]

---

① *demur*: to object

GUIL: Again?
[*Some of the TRAGEDIANS are for it, others against.*]
Evens.
[*The PLAYER nods and tosses the coin.*]
Heads.
[*It is. He picks it up.*]
Again.
[*GUIL spins coin.*]
PLAYER: Heads.
[*It is. The PLAYER picks up coin. He has two coins again. He spins one.*]
GUIL: Heads.
[*It is. GUIL picks it up. Then tosses it immediately.*]
PLAYER: [*Fractional hesitation.*] Tails.
[*But it's heads. GUIL picks it up. The PLAYER tosses down his last coin by way of paying up, and turns away. GUIL doesn't picks it up; he puts his foot on it.*]
GUIL: Heads.
PLAYER: No!
[*Pause. The TRAGEDIANS are against this. Apologetically.*]
They don't like the odds.
GUIL: [*Lifts his foot, squats; picks up the coin still squatting; looks up.*] You were right—heads. [*Spins it, slaps his hand on it, on the floor.*] Heads I win.
PLAYER: No.
GUIL: [*Uncovers coin.*] Right again. [*Repeat.*] Heads I win.
PLAYER: No.
GUIL: [*Uncovers coin.*] And right again. [*Repeat.*] Heads I win.
PLAYER: *No!*
[*He turns away, the TRAGEDIANS with him, GUIL stands up, comes close.*]
GUIL: Would you believe it? [*Stands back, relaxes, smiles.*] Bet me the year of my birth doubles is an odd number.
PLAYER: Your birth—!
GUIL: If you don't trust me don't bet with me.
PLAYER: Would you trust me?
GUIL: Bet me then.
PLAYER: My birth?
GUIL: Odd numbers you win,
PLAYER: You're on—
[*The TRAGEDIANS have come from forward, wide awake.*]

GUIL: Good. Year of your birth. Double it. Even numbers I win, odd numbers I lose.

[*Silence. An awful sigh as the TRAGEDIANS realize that any number doubled is even. Then a terrible row as they object. Then a terrible silence.*]

PLAYER: We have no money.

[*GUIL turns to him.*]

GUIL: Ah. Then what have you got?

[*The PLAYER silently brings ALFRED forward. GUIL regards ALFRED sadly.*]

Was it for this.

PLAYER: It is the best we've got.

GUIL: [*Looking up and around.*] Then the times are bad indeed. [*The PLAYER starts to speak, protestation, but GUIL turns on him viciously.*]

The very air stinks.

[*The PLAYER moves back. GUIL moves down to the footlights and turns.*]

Come here, Alfred.

[*ALFRED moves down and stands, frightened and small. Gently.*]

Do you lose often?

ALFRED: Yes, sir.

GUIL: Then what could you have left to lose?

ALFRED: Nothing, sir.

[*Pause. GUIL regards him.*]

GUIL: Do you like being ... an actor?

ALFRED: No, sir.

[*GUIL looks around, at the audience.*]

GUIL: You and I, Alfred—we could create a dramatic precedent here.

[*And ALFRED, who has been near to tears, starts to sniffle.*]

Come, come, Alfred, this is no way to fill the theatres of Europe.

[*The PLAYER has moved down, to remonstrate with ALFRED. GUIL cuts him off again. Viciously.*] Do you know any good plays?

PLAYER: Plays?

ROS: [*Coming forward, faltering shyly.*] Exhibitions ...

GUIL: I thought you said you were actors.

PLAYER: [*Dawning.*] Oh. Oh well, we are. We are. But there hasn't been much call—

GUIL: You lost. Well then—one of the Greeks, perhaps? You're familiar with the tragedies of antiquity, are you? The great homicidal① classics? Matri, patri, fratri, sorori, uxori and it goes without saying—

---

① homicidal: likely to murder

ROS: Saucy—

GUIL: —Suicidal—hm? Maidens aspiring to godheads—

ROS: And vice versa—

GUIL: Your kind of thing, is it?

PLAYER: Well, no, I can't say it is, really, We're more of the blood, love and rhetoric school.

GUIL: Well, I'll leave the choice to you, if there is anything to choose between them.

PLAYER: They're hardly divisible, sir—well, I can do you blood and love without the rhetoric, and I can do you blood and rhetoric without the love, and I can do you all three concurrent or consecutive, but I can't do you love and rhetoric without the blood. Blood is compulsory—they're all blood, you see.

GUIL: Is that what people want?

PLAYER: It's what we do. [*Small pause. He turns away. GUIL touches ALFRED on the shoulder.*]

GUIL: [*Wry, gentle.*] Thank you; we'll let you know.

[*The PLAYER has moved upstage. ALFRED follows.*]

PLAYER: [*To TRAGEDIANS.*] Thirty-eight!

ROS: [*Moving across, fascinated and hopeful.*] Position?

PLAYER: Sir?

ROS: One of your—tableaux?

PLAYER: No, sir.

ROS: Oh.

PLAYER: [*To the TRAGEDIANS, now departing with their cart, already taking various props off it.*] Entrances there and there [*Indicating upstage.*]

[*The PLAYER has not moved his position for his last four lines. He does not move now. GUIL waits.*]

GUIL: Well ... aren't you going to change into your costume?

PLAYER: I never change out of it, sir.

GUIL: Always in character.

PLAYER: That's it.

[*Pause.*]

GUIL: Aren't you going to—come on?

PLAYER: I am on.

GUIL: But if you are on, you can't come on. Can you?

PLAYER: I start on.

GUIL: But it hasn't started. Go on. We'll look out for you.

PLAYER: I'll give you a wave.

[*He does not move. His immobility is now pointed, and getting awkward. Pause. ROS walks up to him till they are face to face.*]

ROS: Excuse me.

[*Pause. The PLAYER lifts his downstage foot. It was covering Guil's coin. ROS puts his foot on the coin. Smiles.*]

Thank you.

[*The PLAYER turns and goes. ROS has bent for the coin.*]

GUIL: [*Moving out.*] Come on.

ROS: I say—that was lucky.

GUIL: [*Turning.*] What?

ROS: It was tails.

[*He tosses the coin to GUIL who catches it. Simultaneously—a lighting change sufficient to alter the exterior mood into interior, but nothing violent. And OPHELIA runs on in some alarm, holding up her skirts—followed by HAMLET.*]

*OPHELIA has been sewing and she holds the garment. They are both mute. HAMLET, with his doublet all unbraced, no hat upon his head, his stockings fouled, ungartered and down-gyved to his ankle, pale as his shirt, his knees knocking each other ... and with a look so piteous, he takes here by the wrist and holds her hard, then he goes to the length of his arm, and with his other hand over his brow, falls to such perusal*① *of her face as he would draw it ... At last, with a little shaking of his arm, and thrice his head waving up and down, he raises a sigh so piteous and profound that it does seem to shatter all his bulk and end his being. That done he lets her go, and with his head over his shoulder turned, he goes out backwards without taking his eyes off her ... she runs off in the opposite direction.*

ROS and GUIL have frozen. GUIL unfreezes first. He jumps at ROS.]

GUIL: Come on!

[*But a flourish—enter CLAUDIUS and GERTRUDE, attended.*]

CLAUDIUS: Welcome, dear Rosencrantz ... [*He raises a hand at GUIL while ROS bows—GUIL bows late and hurriedly.*] ... and Guildenstern.

[*He raises a hand at ROS while GUIL bows to him—ROS is still straightening up from his previous bow and half-way up he bows down again. With his head down, he twists to look at GUIL, who is on the way up.*]

   Moreover that we did much long to see you,
   the need we have to use you did provoke.
   our hasty sending.

[*ROS and GUIL still adjusting their clothing for CLAUDIUS's presence.*]

   Something have you heard

---

① *perusal*: reading carefully

Of Hamlet's transformation, so call it,
Sith nor th'exterior nor the inward man
Resembles that it was. What it should be,
More than his father's death, that thus hath put him,
So much from th'understanding of himself,
I cannot dream of. I entreat① you both
That, being of so young days brought up with him
And sith so neighboured to his youth and haviour
That you vouchsafe② your rest here in our court
Some little time, so by your companies
To draw him on to pleasures, and to gather
So much as from occasion you may glean,
Whether aught to us unknown afflicts him thus,
That opened lies within our remedy.

GERTRUDE: Good [*Fractional suspense.*] gentlemen ... [*They both bow.*]
He hath much talked of you,
And sure I am, two men there is not living
To whom he more adheres. If it will please you
To show us so much gentry and goodwill
As to expand your time with us awhile
For the supply and profit of our hope,
Your visitation shall receive such thanks
As fits a king's remembrance.

ROS: Both your majesties
Might, by the sovereign power you have of us, Put your dread pleasures more into command Then to entreaty.

GUIL: We both obey,
Ans here give up ourselves in the full bent
To lay our service freely at your feet,
To be commanded.

CLAUDIUS: Thanks, Rosencrantz [*Turning to ROS who is caught unprepared, while GUIL bows.*] and gentle Guildenstern [*Turning to GUIL who is bent double.*]

CERTRUDE: [*Correcting.*] Thanks, Guildenstern [*Turning to ROS, who bows as GUIL checks upward movement to bow too—both bent double, squinting at each other.*] ...

---

① entreat: to beg
② vouchsafe: to grant

and gentle

Rosencrantz.

[*Turning to GUIL, both straightening up—GUIL checks again and bows again.*]

And I beseech you instantly to visit

My too much changed son. Go, some of you,

And bring these gentlemen where Hamlet is.

[*Two ATTENDANTS exit backwards, indicating that ROS and GUIL should follow.*]

GUIL: Heaven make our presence and our practices pleasant and helpful to him.

GERTRUDE: Ay, amen!

[*ROS and GUIL move towards a downstage wing. Before they get there, POLONIUS enters. They stop and bow to him. He nods and hurries upstage to CLAUDIUS. They turn to look at him.*]

POLONIUS: The ambassadors from Norway, my good lord, are joyfully returned.

CLAUDIUS: Thou still hast been the father of good news,

POLONIUS: Have I, my lord? Assure you, my good liege①.

I hold my duty as I hold my soul,

Both to my God and to my gracious King;

And I do think, or else this brain of mine

Hunts not the trail of policy so sure

As it hath used to do, that I have found

The very cause of Hamlet's lunacy …

[*Exeunt—leaving ROS and GUIL.*]

ROS: I want to go home.

GUIL: Don't let them confuse you.

ROS: I'm out of my step here—

GUIL: We'll soon be home and high—dry and home—I'll—

ROS: It's all over my depth—

GUIL: —I'll hie you home and—

ROS: —out of my head—

GUIL: —dry you high and—

ROS: [*Cracking, high.*]—over my step over my head body!—I tell you it's all stopping to a death, it's boding to a depth, stepping to a head, it's all heading to a dead stop—

GUIL: [*The nursemaid.*] There! … and we'll soon be home and dry … and high and dry …

[*Rapidly.*] Has it ever happened to you that all of a sudden and for no reason at all you haven't the faintest idea how to spell the word— "wife"—or "house"—because when you write it down you just can't remember ever having seen those letters in that order

---

① liege: lord

before ... ?

ROS: I remember—

GUIL: Yes?

ROS: I remember when there were no questions.

GUIL: There were always questions. To exchange one set for another is no great matter.

ROS: Answers, yes. There were answers to everything.

GUIL: You've forgotten.

ROS: [*Flaring.*] I haven't forgotten—how I used to remember my own name—and yours, oh yes! There were answers everywhere you looked. There was no question about it—people knew who I was and if they didn't they asked and I hold them.

GUIL: You did, the trouble is, each of them is ... plausible, without being instinctive. All your life you live so close to truth, it becomes a permanent blur in the corner of your eye, and when something nudges it into outline it is like being ambushed① by a grotesque. A man standing in his saddle in the half—lit half-alive dawn banged on the shutters and called two names. He was just a hat and a clock levitating in the grey plume of his own breath, but when he called we came. That much is certain—we came.

ROS: Well I can tell you I'm sick to death of it. I don't care one way or another, so why don't you make up your mind.

GUIL: We can't afford anything quite so arbitrary. Nor did we come all this way for a christening. All that—preceded us. But we are comparatively fortunate; we might have been left to sift the whole field of human nomenclature, like two blind men looting a bazaar for their own portraits ... At least we are presented with alternatives.

ROS: Well as from now—

GUIL: —But not choice.

ROS: You made me look ridiculous in there.

GUIL: I looked just as ridiculous as you did.

ROS: [*An anguished cry.*] Consistency is all I ask!

GUIL: [*Low, wry rhetoric.*] Give us this day our daily mask.

ROS: [*A dying fall.*] I want to go home. [*Moves.*] Which way did we come in? I've lost mu sense of direction.

GUIL: The only beginning is birth and the only end is death—if you can't count on that, what can you count on?

   [*They connect again.*]

ROS: We don't owe anything to anyone.

---

① ambushed: attacked from a concealed position

GUIL: We've been caught up. Your smallest actions sets off another somewhere else, and is set off by it. Keep an eye open, an ear cocked. Tread warily, follow instructions. We'll be all right.

ROS: For how long?

GUIL: Till events have played themselves out. There's a logic at work—it's all done for you, don't worry. Enjoy it. Relax. To be taken in hand and led, like being a child again, even without the innocence, a child—It's like being given a prize, an extra slice of childhood when you least expect it, as a prize for being good, or compensation for never having had one ... Do I contradict myself?

ROS: I can't remember ... What have we got to go on?

GUIL: We have been briefed. Hamlet's transformation. What do you recollect?

ROS: Well, he's changed, hasn't he? The exterior and inward man fails to resemble—

GUIL: Draw him on to pleasures—glean what afflicts him.

ROS: Something more than his father's death—

GUIL: He's always talking about us—there aren't two people living whom he dotes on more than us.

ROS: We cheer him up—find out what's the matter—

GUIL: Exactly, it's a matter of asking the right questions and giving away as little as we can. It's a game.

ROS: And then we can go?

GUIL: And receive such thanks as fits a king's remembrance.

ROS: I like the sound of that. What do you think he means by remembrance?

GUIL: He doesn't forget his friends.

ROS: Would you care to estimate?

GUIL: Difficult to say, really—some kings tend to be amnesiac[①], others I suppose—the opposite, whatever that is ...

ROS: Yes—but—

GUIL: Elephantine ...?

ROS: Not how long—how much?

GUIL: Retentive[②]—he's a very retentive king, a royal retainer ...

ROS: What are you playing at?

GUIL: Words, words. They're all we have to go on.

[Pause.]

ROS: Shouldn't we be doing something—constructive?

---

① amnesiac: losing memory
② retentive: having good memory

GUIL: What did you have in mind? ... A short, blunt human pyramid ... ?
ROS: We could go.
GUIL: Where?
ROS: After him.
GUIL: Why? They've got us placed now—if we start moving around, we'll all be chasing each other all night.

[*Hiatus.*]

ROS: [*At footlights.*] How very intriguing! [*Turns.*] I feel like a spectator—an appalling prospect. The only thing that makes it bearable is the irrational belief that somebody interesting will come on in a minute ...
GUIL: See anyone?
ROS: No. You?
GUIL: No. [*At footlights.*] What a fine persecution—to be kept intrigued without ever quite being enlightened ... [*Pause.*] We've had no practice.
ROS: We could play at questions.
GUIL: What good would that do?
ROS: Practice!
GUIL: Statement? One-love.
ROS: Cheating!
GUIL: How?
ROS: I hadn't started yet.
GUIL: Statement. Two-love.
ROS: Are you counting that?
GUIL: What?
ROS: Are you counting that?
GUIL: Foul! No questions. Three-love. First game to ...
ROS: I'm not going to play if you're going to be like that.
GUIL: Whose serve?
ROS: Hah?
GUIL: Foul! No grunts. Love-one.
ROS: Whose go?
GUIL: Why?
ROS: Why not?
GUIL: What for?
ROS: Foul! No synonyms! One-all.
GUIL: What in God's name is going on?
ROS: Foul! No rhetoric. Two-one.

GUIL: What does it all add up to?
ROS: Can't you guess?
GUIL: Were you addressing me?
ROS: Is there anyone else?
GUIL: Who?
ROS: How would I know?
GUIL: Why do you ask?
ROS: Are you serious?
GUIL: Was that rhetoric?
ROS: No.
GUIL: Statement! Two-all. Game point.
ROS: What's the matter with you today?
GUIL: When?
ROS: What?
GUIL: Are you deaf?
ROS: Am I dead?
GUIL: Yes or no?
ROS: Is there a choice?
GUIL: Is there a God?
ROS: Foul! No non sequiturs, three-two, one game all.
GUIL: [Seriously.] What's your name?
ROS: What's yours?
GUIL: I asked first.
ROS: Statement. One-love.
GUIL: What's your name when you're at home?
ROS: What's yours?
GUIL: When I'm at home?
ROS: Is it different at home?
GUIL: What home?
ROS: Haven't you got one?
GUIL: Why do you ask?
ROS: What are you driving at?
GUIL: [With emphasis.] What's your name!
ROS: Repetition. Two-love. Match point to me.
GUIL: [Seizing him violently.] WHO DO YOU THINK YOU ARE?
ROS: Rhetoric! Game and match! [Pause.] Where's it going to end?
GUIL: That's the question.
ROS: It's all questions.

GUIL: Do you think it matters?

ROS: Doesn't it matter to you?

GUIL: Why should it matter?

ROS: What does it matter why?

GUIL: [*Teasing gently.*] Doesn't it matter why it matters?

ROS: [*Rounding on him.*] What's the matter with you?

[*Pause.*]

GUIL: It doesn't matter.

ROS: [*Voice in the wilderness.*] … What's the game?

GUIL: What are the rules?

[*Enter HAMLET behind, crossing the stage, reading a book—as he is about to disappear GUIL notices him.*]

GUIL: [*Sharply.*] Rosencrantz!

ROS: [*Jumps.*] What!

[*HAMLET goes. Triumph dawns on them, they smile.*]

GUIL: There! How was that?

ROS: Clever!

GUIL: Natural?

ROS: Instinctive.

GUIL: Got it in your head?

ROS: I take my hat off to you.

GUIL: Shake hands.

[*They do.*]

ROS: Now I'll try you—Guil—!

GUIL: —Not yet—catch me unawares.

ROS: Right. [*They separate. Pause. Aside to GUIL.*] Ready?

GUIL: [*Explodes.*] Don't be stupid.

ROS: Sorry.

[*Pause.*]

GUIL: [*Snaps.*] Guildenstern!

ROS: [*Jumps.*] What? [*He is immediately crestfallen, GUIL is disgusted.*]

GUIL: Consistency is all I ask!

ROS: [*Quietly.*] Immortality is all I seek …

GUIL: [*Dying fall.*] Give us this day our daily week …

[*Beat.*]

ROS: Who was that?

GUIL: Didn't you know him?

ROS: He didn't know me.
GUIL: He didn't see you.
ROS: I didn't see him.
GUIL: We shall see. I hardly knew him, he's changed.
ROS: You could see that?
GUIL: Transformed.
ROS: How do you know?
GUIL: Inside and out.
ROS: I see.
GUIL: He's not himself.
ROS: He's changed.
GUIL: I could see that. [*Beat.*] Glean what afflicts him.
ROS: Me?
GUIL: Him.
ROS: How?
GUIL: Question and answer. Old ways are the best ways.
ROS: He's afflicted.
GUIL: You question, I'll answer.
ROS: He's not himself, you know.
GUIL: I'm him, you see.

   [*Beat.*]

ROS: Who am I then?
GUIL: You're yourself.
ROS: And he's you?
GUIL: Not a bit of it.
ROS: Are you afflicted?
GUIL: That's the idea. Are you ready?
ROS: Let's go back a bit.
GUIL: I'm afflicted.
ROS: I see.
GUIL: Glean what afflicts me.
ROS: Right.
GUIL: Question and answer.
ROS: How should I begin?
GUIL: Address me.
ROS: My dear Guildenstern!
GUIL: [*Quietly.*] You've forgotten—haven't you?

ROS: My dear Rosencrantz!

GUIL: [*Great control.*] I don't think you quite understand. What we are attempting is a hypothesis in which I answer for him, while you ask me questions.

ROS: Ah! Ready?

GUIL: You know what to do?

ROS: What?

GUIL: Are you stupid?

ROS: Pardon?

GUIL: Are you deaf?

ROS: Did you speak?

GUIL: [*Admonishing.*] Not now—

ROS: Statement.

GUIL: [*Shouts.*] Not now! [*Pause.*] If I had any doubts, or rather hopes, they are dispelled. What could we possibly have in common except our situation? [*They separate and sit.*]

Perhaps he'll come back this way.

ROS: Should we go?

GUIL: Why?

[*Pause.*]

ROS: [*Starts up. Snaps fingers.*] Oh! You mean—you pretend to be him, and I ask you questions!

GUIL: [*Dry.*] Very good.

ROS: You had me confused.

GUIL: I could see I had.

ROS: How should I begin?

GUIL: Address me.

[*They stand and face each other, posing.*]

ROS: My honoured Lord!

GUIL: My dear Rosencrantz!

[*Pause.*]

ROS: Am I pretending to be you, then?

GUIL: Certainly not. If you like. Shall we continue?

ROS: Question and answer.

GUIL: Right.

ROS: Right. My honoured lord!

GUIL: My dear fellow!

ROS: How are you?

GUIL: Afflicted.

ROS: Really? In what way?

GUIL: Transformed.

ROS: Inside or out?

GUIL: Both.

ROS: I see. [*Pause.*] Not much new there.

GUIL: Go into details. Delve. Probe the background, establish the situation.

ROS: So—so your uncle is the king of Denmark?!

GUIL: And my father before him.

ROS: His father before him?

GUIL: No, my father before him.

ROS: But surely—

GUIL: You might well ask.

ROS: Let me get it straight. Your father was king. You were his only son. Your father dies. You are of age. Your uncle becomes king.

GUIL: Yes.

ROS: Unorthodox.

GUIL: Undid me.

ROS: Undeniable. Where were you?

GUIL: In Germany.

ROS: Usurpation①, then.

GUIL: He slipped in.

ROS: Which reminds me.

GUIL: Well, it would.

ROS: I don't want to be personal.

GUIL: It's common knowledge.

ROS: Your mother's marriage.

GUIL: He slipped in.

[*Beat.*]

ROS: [*Lugubriously.*] His body was still warm.

GUIL: So was hers.

ROS: Extraordinary.

GUIL: Indecent.

ROS: Hasty.

GUIL: Suspicious.

---

① Usurpation: the wrongful seizure of sovereignty

ROS: It makes you think.

GUIL: Don't think I haven't thought of it.

ROS: And with her husband's brother.

GUIL: They were close.

ROS: She went to him—

GUIL: —Too close—

ROS: —for comfort.

GUIL: It looks bad.

ROS: It adds up.

GUIL: Incest to adultery.

ROS: Would you go so far?

GUIL: Never.

ROS: To sum up; your father, whom you love, dies, you are his heir, you come back to find that hardly was the corpse cold before this young brother popped on to his throne and into his sheets, thereby offending both legal and natural practice. Now why exactly are you behaving in this extraordinary manner?

GUIL: I can't imagine! [*Pause.*] But all that is well known, common property. Yet he sent for us. And we did come.

ROS: [*Alert, ear cocked.*] I say! I heard music—

GUIL: We're here.

ROS: —Like a band—I thought I heard a band.

GUIL: Rosencrantz ...

ROS: [*Absently, still listening.*] What?

[*Pause, short.*]

GUIL: [*Gently wry.*] Guildenstern ...

ROS: [*Irritated by the repetition.*] What?

GUIL: Don't you discriminate at all?

ROS: [*Turning dumbly.*] Wha'?

[*Pause.*]

GUIL: Go and see if he's there.

ROS: Who?

GUIL: There.

[*ROS goes to an upstage wing, looks, returns, formally making his report.*]

ROS: Yes.

GUIL: What is he doing?

[*ROS repeats movement.*]

ROS: Talking.

GUIL: To himself?

    [*ROS starts to move. GUIL cuts in impatiently.*]

    Is he alone?

ROS: No.

GUIL: Then he's not talking to himself, is he?

ROS: Not by himself ... Coming this way, I think. [*Shiftily.*] Should we go?

GUIL: Why? We're marked now.

    [*HAMLET enters, backwards, talking, followed by POLONIUS, upstage. ROS and GUIL occupy the two downstage corners looking upstage.*]

HAMLET: ... for yourself, sir, should be as old as I am if like a crab you could go backward.

POLONIUS: [*Aside.*] Though this madness, yet there is method in it. Will you walk out of the air, my lord?

HAMLET: Into my grave.

POLONIUS: Indeed, that's out of the air.

    [*HAMLET crosses to upstage exit, POLONIUS asiding unintelligibly until—*]

    My lord, I will take my leave of you.

HAMLET: You cannot take from me anything that I will more willingly part withal—except my life, except my life, except my life ...

POLONIUS: [*Crossing downstage.*] Fare you well, my lord. [*To ROS.*] You go to seek Lord Hamlet? There he is.

ROS: [*To POLONIUS.*] God save you sir.

    [*POLONIUS goes.*]

GUIL: [*Calls upstage to HAMLET.*] My honoured lord!

ROS: My most dear lord!

[*HAMLET entred upstage, turns to them.*]

HAMLET: My excellent good friends! How does thou Guildenstern?

    [*Coming downstage with one arm raised to ROS, GUIL meanwhile bowing to no greeting. HAMLET corrects himself. Still to ROS.*] Ah Rosencrantz!

    [*They laugh good-naturedly at the mistake. They all meet midstage, turn upstage to walk, HAMLET in the middle, arm over each shoulder.*]

HAMLET: Good lads, how do you both?

Study Questions:

    1. How do you understand the opening scene of coin-tossing in the play?

    2. Stoppard is deeply influenced by Samuel Beckett in his writing. How do you relate *Rosencrantz and Guildenstern Are Dead* to Beckett's *Waiting for Godot*?

    3. How is the saying "all the world is a stage, and all the men and women are merely

players" embodied in the play?

4. In your opinion, what is the signification of using the plot structure of *Hamlet* in writing a new play?

The Death of a Salesman (1949)
Arthur Miller
Act II (Excerpt)

Stanley picks up a chair and follows them off. Knocking is heard off left. The Woman enters, laughing. Willy follows her. She is in a black slip; he is buttoning his shirt. Raw, sensuous music accompanies their speech.

Willy: Will you stop laughing? Will you stop?

The Woman: Aren't you going to answer the door? He'll wake the whole hotel.

Willy: I'm not expecting anybody.

The Woman: Whyn't you have another drink, honey, and stop being so damn self-centered?

Willy: I'm so lonely.

The Woman: You know you ruined me, Willy? From now on, whenever you come to the office, I'll see that you go right through to the buyers. No waiting at my desk any more, Willy. You ruined me.

Willy: That's nice of you to say that.

The Woman: Gee, you are self-centered! Why so sad? You are the saddest self-centeredest soul I ever did see-saw. (*She laughs. He kisses her.*) Come on inside, drummer boy. It's silly to be dressing in the middle of the night. (*As knocking is heard.*) Aren't you going to answer the door?

Willy: They're knocking on the wrong door.

The Woman: But I felt the knocking. And he heard us talking in here. Maybe the hotel's on fire!

Willy (*his tenor rising*): It's a mistake.

The Woman: Then tell him to go away!

Willy: There's nobody there.

The Woman: It's getting on my nerves, Willy. There's somebody standing out there and it's getting on my nerves!

Willy (*pushing her away from him*): All right, stay in the bathroom here, and don't come out. I think there's a law in Massachusetts about it, so don't come out. It may be that new room clerk. He looked very mean. So don't come out. It's a mistake, there's no fire.

The knocking is heard again. He takes a few steps away from her, and she vanishes into the wing.

The light follows him, and now he is facing Young Biff, who carries a suitcase. Biff steps toward him. The music is gone.

Biff: Why didn't you answer?

Willy: Biff! What are you doing in Boston!

Biff: Why didn't you answer? I've been knocking for five minutes, I called you on the phone—

Willy: I just heard you. I was in the bathroom and had the door shut. Did anything happen at home?

Biff: Dad—I let you down.

Willy: What do you mean?

Biff: Dad ...

Willy: Biff, what's this about? (*Putting his arm around Biff.*) Come on, let's go downstairs and get you a malted.

Biff: Dad, I flunked math.

Willy: Not for the term?

Biff: The term. I haven't got enough credits to graduate.

Willy: You mean to say Bernard wouldn't give you the answers?

Biff: He did, he tried, but I only got a sixty-one.

Willy: And they wouldn't give you four points?

Biff: Birnbaum refused absolutely. I begged him, Pop, but he won't give me those points. You gotta talk to him before they close the school. Because if he saw the kind of man you are, and you just talked to him in your way, I'm sure he'd come through for me. The class came right before practice, see, and I didn't go enough. Would you talk to him? He'd like you, Pop. You know the way you could talk.

Willy: You're on. We'll drive right back.

Biff: Oh, Dad, good work! I'm sure he'll change it for you!

Willy: Go downstairs and tell the clerk I'm checkin' out. Go right down.

Biff: Yes, Sir! See, the reason he hates me, Pop—one day he was late for class so I got up at the blackboard and imitated him. I crossed my eyes and talked with a lithp.

Willy (*laughing*): You did? The kids like it?

Biff: They nearly died laughing!

Willy: Yeah? What'd you do?

Biff: The thquare root of thixthy twee is ... (*Willy bursts out laughing; Biff joins him.*) And in the middle of it he walked in!

Willy laughs and the Woman joins in offstage.

Willy (*without hesitating*): Hurry downstairs and—

Biff: Somebody in there?

Willy: No, that was next door.

The Woman laughs offstage.

Biff: Somebody got in your bathroom!

Willy: No, it's the next room, there's a party—

> The Woman (*enters, laughing. She lisps this*): Can I come in? There's something in the bathtub, Willy, and it's moving!

> *Willy looks at Biff, who is staring open-mouthed and horrified at the Woman.*

Willy: Ah—you better go back to your room. They must be finished painting by now. They're painting her room so I let her take a shower here. Go back, go back ... (*He pushes her.*)

The Woman (*resisting*): But I've got to get dressed, Willy, I can't—

Willy: Get out of here! Go back, go back ... (*Suddenly striving for the ordinary.*) This is Miss Francis, Biff, she's a buyer. They're painting her room. Go back, Miss Francis, go back ...

The Woman: But my clothes, I can't go out naked in the hall!

Willy (*pushing her offstage*): Get outa here! Go back, go back!

> *Biff slowly sits down on his suitcase as the argument continues offstage.*

The Woman: Where's my stockings? You promised me stockings, Willy!

Willy: I have no stockings here!

The Woman: You had two boxes of size nine sheers for me, and I want them!

Willy: Here, for God's sake, will you get outa here!

The Woman (*enters holding a box of stockings*): I just hope there's nobody in the hall. That's all I hope. (*To Biff.*) Are you football or baseball?

Biff: Football.

The Woman (*angry, humiliated*): That's me too. G'night. (*She snatches her clothes from Willy, and walks out.*)

Willy (*after a pause*): Well, better get going. I want to get to the school first thing in the morning. Get my suits out of the closet. I'll get my valise. (*Biff doesn't move.*) What's the matter? (*Biff remains motionless, tears falling.*) She's a buyer. Buys for J. H. Simmons. She lives down the hall—they're painting. You don't imagine—(*He breaks off. After a pause.*) Now listen, pal, she's just a buyer. She sees merchandise in her room and they have to keep it looking just so ... (*Pause. Assuming command.*) All right, get my suits. (*Biff doesn't move.*) Now stop crying and do as I say. I gave you an order. Biff, I gave you an order! Is that what you do when I give you an order? How dare you cry! (*Putting his arm around*

Biff.) Now look, Biff, when you grow up you'll understand about these things. You mustn't—you mustn't overemphasize a thing like this. I'll see Birnbaum first thing in the morning.

Biff: Never mind.

Willy (*getting down beside Biff*) : Never mind! He's going to give you those points. I'll see to it.

Biff: He wouldn't listen to you.

Willy: He certainly will listen to me. You need those points for the U. of Virginia.

Biff: I'm not going there.

Willy: Heh? If I can't get him to change that mark you'll make it up in summer school. You've got all summer to—

Biff (*his weeping breaking from him*) : Dad …

Willy (*infected by it*) : Oh, my boy …

Biff: Dad …

Willy: She's nothing to me, Biff. I was lonely, I was terribly lonely.

Biff: You—you gave her Mama's stockings! (*His tears break through and he rises to go.*)

Willy (*grabbing for Biff*) : I gave you an order!

Biff: Don't touch me, you—liar!

Willy: Apologize for that!

Biff: You fake! You phony little fake! (*Overcome, he turns quickly and weeping fully goes out with his suitcase. Willy is left on the floor on his knees.*)

Willy: I gave you an order! Biff, come back here or I'll beat you! Come back here! I'll whip you!

   Stanley comes quickly in from the right and stands in front of Willy.

Willy (*shouts at Stanley*) : I gave you an order …

Stanley: Hey, let's pick it up, pick it up, Mr. Loman. (*He helps Willy to his feet.*) Your boys left with the chippies. They said they'll see you at home.

   A second waiter watches some distance away.

Willy: But we were supposed to have dinner together.

   Music is heard, Willy's theme.

Stanley: Can you make it?

Willy: I'll—sure, I can make it. (*Suddenly concerned about his clothes.*) Do I—I look all right?

Stanley: Sure, you look all right. (*He flicks a speck off Willy's lapel.*)

Willy: Here—here's a dollar.

Stanley: Oh, your son paid me. It's all right.

Witty (*putting it in Stanley's hand*) : No, take it. You're a good boy.

Stanley: Oh, no, you don't have to …

Willy: Here—here's some more, I don't need it any more. (*After a slight pause.*) Tell me—

is there a seed store in the neighborhood?

Stanley: Seeds? You mean like to plant?

As Willy turns, Stanley slips the money back into his jacket pocket.

Willy: Yes. Carrots, peas ...

Stanley: Well, there's hardware stores on Sixth Avenue, but it may be too late now.

Willy (*anxiously*): Oh, I'd better hurry. I've got to get some seeds. (*He starts off to the right.*) I've got to get some seeds, right away. Nothing's planted. I don't have a thing in the ground.

Willy hurries out as the light goes down. Stanley moves over to the right after him, watches him off. The other waiter has been staring at Willy.

Stanley (*to the waiter*): Well, whatta you looking at?

The waiter picks up the chairs and moves affright. Stanley takes the table and follows him. The light fades on this area. There is a long pause, the sound of the flute coming over. The light gradually rises on the kitchen, which is empty. Happy appears at the door of the house, followed by Biff. Happy is carrying a large bunch of long-stemmed roses. He enters the kitchen, looks around for Linda. Not seeing her, he turns to Biff, who is just outside the house door, and makes a gesture with his hands, indicating "Not here, I guess." He looks into the living room and freezes. Inside, Linda, unseen, is seated, Willy's coat on her lap. She rises ominously and quietly and moves toward Happy, who backs up into the kitchen, afraid.

Happy: Hey, what're you doing up? (*Linda says nothing but moves toward him implacably.*) Where's Pop? (*He keeps backing to the right, and now Linda is in full view in the doorway to the living room.*) Is he sleeping?

Linda: Where were you?

Happy (*trying to laugh it off*): We met two girls, Mom, very fine types. Here, we brought you some flowers. (*Offering them to her.*) Put them in your room, Ma.

She knocks them to the floor at Biff's feet. He has now come inside and closed the door behind him. She stares at Biff, silent.

Happy: Now what'd you do that for? Mom, I want you to have some flowers—

Linda (*cutting Happy off, violently to Biff*): Don't you care whether he lives or dies?

Happy (*going to the stairs*): Come upstairs, Biff.

Biff (*with a flare of disgust, to Happy*): Go away from me! (*To Linda.*) What do you mean, lives or dies? Nobody's dying around here, pal.

Linda: Get out of my sight! Get out of here!

Biff: I wanna see the boss.

Linda: You're not going near him!

Biff: Where is he? (*He moves into the living room and Linda follows.*)

Linda (*shouting after Biff*): You invite him for dinner. He looks forward to it all day—(*Biff appears in his parents' bedroom, looks ar'ound, and exits*)—and then you desert him there. There's no stranger you'd do that to!

Happy: Why? He had a swell time with us. Listen, when I—(*Linda comes back into the kitchen*)—desert him I hope I don't outlive the day!

Linda: Get out of here!

Happy: Now look, Mom.

Linda: Did you have to go to women tonight? You and your lousy rotten whores!

Biff re-enters the kitchen.

Happy: Mom, all we did was follow Biff around trying to cheer him up! (*To Biff.*) Boy, what a night you gave me!

Linda: Get out of here, both of you, and don't come back! I don't want you tormenting him anymore. Go on now, get your things together! (*To Biff.*) You can sleep in his apartment. (*She starts to pick up the flowers and stops herself.*) Pick up this stuff, I'm not your maid any more. Pick it up, you bum, you!

Happy turns his back to her in refusal. Biff slowly moves over and gets down on his knees, picking up the flowers.

Linda: You're a pair of animals! Not one, not another living soul would have had the cruelty to walk out on that man in a restaurant!

Biff (*not looking at her*): Is that what he said?

Linda: He didn't have to say anything. He was so humiliated he nearly limped when he came in.

Happy: But, Mom he had a great time with us—

Biff (*cutting him off violently*): Shut up!

Without another word, Happy goes upstairs.

Linda: You! You didn't even go in to see if he was all right!

Biff (*still on the floor in front of Linda, the flowers in his hand; with self-loathing*): No. Didn't. Didn't do a damned thing. How do you like that, heh? Left him babbling in a toilet.

Linda: You louse. You ...

Biff: Now you hit it on the nose! (*He gets up, throws the flowers in the waste-basket.*) The scum of the earth, and you're looking at him!

Linda: Get out of here!

Biff: I gotta talk to the boss, Mom. Where is he?

Linda: You're not going near him. Get out of this house!

Biff (*with absolute assurance, determination*): No. We're gonna have an abrupt conversation, him and me.

Linda: You're not talking to him!

Hammering is heard from, outside the house, affright. Biff turns toward the noise.

Linda (*suddenly pleading*): Will you please leave him alone?

Biff: What's he doing out there?

Linda: He's planting the garden!

Biff (*quietly*): Now? Oh, my God!

Biff moves outside, Linda following. The light dies down on them and comes up on the center of the apron as Willy walks into it. He is carrying a flashlight, a hoe and a handful of seed packets. He raps the top of the hoe sharply to fix it firmly, and then moves to the left, measuring off the distance with his foot. He holds the flash-light to look at the seed packets, reading off the instructions. He is in the blue of night.

Willy: Carrots ... quarter-inch apart. Rows ... one-foot rows. (*He measures it off.*) One foot. (*He puts down a package and measures off.*) Beets. (*He puts down another package and measures again.*) Lettuce. (*He reads the package, puts it down.*) One foot—(*He breaks off as Ben appears at the right and moves slowly down to him.*) What a proposition, ts, ts. Terrific, terrific. 'Cause she's suffered, Ben, the woman has suffered. You understand me? A man can't go out the way he came in, Ben, a man has got to add up to something. You can't, you can't—(*Ben moves toward him as though to interrupt.*) You gotta consider, now. Don't answer so quick. Remember, it's a guaranteed twenty-thousand-dollar proposition. Now look, Ben, I want you to go through the ins and outs of this thing with me. I've got nobody to talk to, Ben, and the woman has suffered, you hear me?

Ben (*standing still, considering*): What's the proposition?

Willy: It's twenty thousand dollars on the barrelhead. Guaranteed, gilt-edged, you understand?

Ben: You don't want to make a fool of yourself. They might not honor the policy.

Willy: How can they dare refuse? Didn't I work like a coolie to meet every premium on the nose? And now they don't pay off? Impossible!

Ben: It's called a cowardly thing, William.

Willy: Why? Does it take more guts to stand here the rest of my life ringing up a zero?

Ben (*yielding*): That's a point, William. (*He moves, thinking, turns.*) And twenty thousand—that is something one can feel with the hand, it is there.

Willy (*now assured, with rising power*): Oh, Ben, that's the whole beauty of it! I see it like a diamond, shining in the dark, hard and rough, that I can pick up and touch in my hand. Not like—like an appointment! This would not be another damned-fool appointment, Ben, and it changes all the aspects. Because he thinks I'm nothing, see, and so he spites me. But the funeral—(*Straightening up.*) Ben, that funeral will be massive! They'll come from Maine, Massachusetts, Vermont, New Hampshire! All the old-timers with the strange license plates—that boy will be thunder-struck, Ben, because he never realized—I am known! Rhode Island, New York, New Jersey—I am known, Ben, and he'll see it with his eyes once and for all. He'll see what I am, Ben! He's in for a shock, that boy!

Ben (*coming down to the edge of the garden*): He'll call you a coward.

Willy (*suddenly fearful*): No, that would be terrible.

Ben: Yes. And a damned fool.

Willy: No, no, he mustn't, I won't have that! (*He is broken and desperate.*)

Ben: He'll hate you, William.

The gay music of the boys is heard.

Willy: Oh, Ben, how do we get back to all the great times? Used to be so full of light, and comradeship, the sleigh-riding in winter, and the ruddiness on his cheeks. And always some kind of good news coming up, always something nice coming up ahead. And never even let me carry the valises in the house, and simonizing, simonizing that little red car! Why, why can't I give him something and not have him hate me?

Ben: Let me think about it. (*He glances at his watch.*) I still have a little time. Remarkable proposition, but you've got to be sure you're not making a fool of yourself.

Ben drifts off upstage and goes out of sight. Biff comes down from the left.

Willy (*suddenly conscious of Biff, turns and looks up at him, then begins picking up the packages of seeds in confusion*): Where the hell is that seed? (*Indignantly.*) You can't see nothing out here! They boxed in the whole goddam neighborhood!

Biff: There are people all around here. Don't you realize that?

Willy: I'm busy. Don't bother me.

Biff (*taking the hoe from Witty*): I'm saying good-by to you, Pop. (*Willy looks at him, silent, unable to move.*) I'm not coming back any more.

Willy: You're not going to see Oliver tomorrow?

Biff: I've got no appointment, Dad.

Willy: He put his arm around you, and you've got no appointment?

Biff: Pop, get this now, will you? Everytime I've left it's been a fight that sent me out of here. Today I realized something about myself and I tried to explain it to you and I—I think I'm just not smart enough to make any sense out of it for you. To hell with whose fault it is or anything like that. (*He takes Willy's arm.*) Let's just wrap it up, heh? Come on in, we'll tell Mom. (*He gently tries to pull Willy to the left.*)

Willy (*frozen, immobile, with guilt in his voice*): No, I don't want to see her.

Biff: Come on! (*He pulls again, and Willy tries to putt away.*)

Willy (*highly nervous*): No, no, I don't want to see her.

Biff (*tries to look into Willy's face, as if to find the answer there*): Why don't you want to see her?

Willy (*more harshly now*): Don't bother me, will you?

Biff: What do you mean, you don't want to see her? You don't want them calling you yellow, do you? This isn't your fault; it's me, I'm a bum. Now come inside! (*Willy strains to get away.*) Did you hear what I said to you?

Willy puts away and quickly goes by himself into the house. Biff follows.

Linda (*to Willy*): Did you plant, dear?

Biff (*at the door, to Linda*): All right, we had it out. I'm going and I'm not writing any more.

Linda (*going to Willy in the kitchen*): I think that's the best way, dear. 'Cause there's no use drawing it out, you'll just never get along.

Willy doesn't respond.

Biff: People ask where I am and what I'm doing, you don't know, and you don't care. That way it'll be off your mind and you can start brightening up again. All right? That clears it, doesn't it? (*Willy is silent, and Biff goes to him.*) You gonna wish me luck, scout? (*He extends his hand.*) What do you say?

Linda: Shake his hand, Willy.

Willy (*turning to her, seething with hurt*): There's no necessity to mention the pen at all, y'know.

Biff (*gently*): I've got no appointment, Dad.

Willy (*erupting fiercely*): He put his arm around ... ?

Biff: Dad, you're never going to see what I am, so what's the use of arguing? If I strike oil I'll send you a check. Meantime forget I'm alive.

Willy (*to Linda*): Spite, see?

Biff: Shake hands, Dad.

Willy: Not my hand.

Biff: I was hoping not to go this way.

Willy: Well, this is the way you're going. Good-by.

Biff looks at him a moment, then turns sharply and goes to the stairs.

Willy (*stops him with*): May you rot in hell if you leave this house!

Biff (*turning*): Exactly what is it that you want from me?

Willy: I want you to know, on the train, in the mountains, in the valleys, whereever you go, that you cut down your life for spite!

Biff: No. No.

Willy: Spite, spite, is the word of your undoing! And when you're down and out, remember what did it. When you're rotting somewhere beside the railroad tracks, remember, and don't you dare blame it on me!

Biff: I'm not blaming it on you!

Willy: I won't take the rap for this, you hear?

Happy comes down the stairs and stands on the bottom step, watching.

Biff: That's just what I'm telling you!

Willy (*sinking into a chair at the table, with full accusation*): You're trying to put a knife in me—don't think I don't know what you're doing!

Biff: All right, phony! Then let's lay it on the line. (*He whips the rubber tube out of his pocket and puts it on the table.*)

Happy: You crazy—

Linda: Biff! (*She moves to grab the hose, but Biff holds it down with his hand.*)

Biff: Leave it there! Don't move it!

Willy (*not looking at it*): What is that?

Biff: You know goddam well what that is.

Willy (*caged, wanting to escape*): I never saw that.

Biff: You saw it. The mice didn't bring it into the cellar! What is this supposed to do, make a hero out of you? This supposed to make me sorry for you?

Willy: Never heard of it.

Biff: There'll be no pity for you, you hear? No pity!

Willy (*to Linda*): You hear the spite!

Biff: No, you're going to hear the truth—what you are and what I am!

Linda: Stop it!

Willy: Spite!

Happy (*coming down toward Biff*): You cut it now!

Biff (*to Happy*): The man don't know who we are! The man is gonna know! (*To Willy.*) We never told the truth for ten minutes in this house!

Happy: We always told the truth!

Biff (*turning on him*): You big blow, are you the assistant buyer? You're one of the two assistants to the assistant, aren't you?

Happy: Well, I'm practically—

Biff: You're practically full of it! We all are! And I'm through with it. (*To Willy.*) Now hear this, Willy, this is me.

Willy: I know you!

Biff: You know why I had no address for three months? I stole a suit in Kansas City and I was in jail. (*To Linda, who is sobbing.*) Stop crying. I'm through with it.

Linda turns away from them, her hands covering her face.

Willy: I suppose that's my fault!

Biff: I stole myself out of every good job since high school!

Willy: And whose fault is that?

Biff: And I never got anywhere because you blew me so full of hot air I could never stand taking orders from anybody! That's whose fault it is!

Willy: I hear that!

Linda: Don't, Biff!

Biff: It's goddam time you heard that! I had to be boss big shot in two weeks, and I'm through with it!

Willy: Then hang yourself! For spite, hang yourself!

Biff: No! Nobody's hanging himself, Willy! I ran down eleven flights with a pen in my hand today. And suddenly I stopped, you hear me? And in the middle of that office building, do you hear this? I stopped in the middle of that building and I saw—the sky. I saw the things that I love in this world. The work and the food and time to sit and smoke. And I looked at the pen and said to myself, what the hell am I grabbing this for? Why am I trying to become what I don't want to be? What am I doing in an office, making a contemptuous, begging fool of myself, when all I want is out there, waiting for me the minute I say I know who I am! Why can't I say that, Willy? (*He tries to make Willy face him, but Witty pulls away and mows to the left.*)

Willy (*with hatred, threatening*): The door of your life is wide open!

Biff: Pop! I'm a dime a dozen, and so are you!

Willy (*turning on him now in an uncontrolled outburst*): I am not a dime a dozen! I'm Willy Loman, and you are Biff Loman!

Biff starts for Willy, but is blocked by Happy. In his fury, Biff seems on the verge of attacking his father.

Biff: I am not a leader of men, Willy, and neither are you. You were never anything but a hard-working drummer who landed in the ash can like all the rest of them! I'm one dollar an hour, Willy! I tried seven states and couldn't raise it. A buck an hour! Do you gather my meaning? I'm not bringing home any prizes any more, and you're going to stop waiting for me to bring them home!

Willy (*directly to Biff*): You vengeful, spiteful mutt!

Biff breaks from Happy. Willy, in fright, starts up the stairs. Biff grabs him.

Biff (*at the peak of his fury*): Pop, I'm nothing! I'm nothing, Pop. Can't you understand that? There's no spite in it any more. I'm just what I am, that's all.

Biff's fury has spent itself, and he breaks down, sobbing, holding on to Willy, who dumbly fumbles for Biff's face.

Willy (*astonished*): What're you doing? What're you doing? (*To Linda.*) Why is he crying?

Biff (*crying, broken*): Will you let me go, for Christ sake? Will you take that phony dream and burn it before something happens? (*Struggling to contain himself, he pulls away and moves to the stairs.*) I'll go in the morning. Put him—put him to bed. (*Exhausted, Biff moves up the stairs to his room.*)

Willy (*after a long pause, astonished, elevated*): Isn't that remarkable? Biff—he likes me!

Linda: He loves you, Willy!

Happy (*deeply moved*): Always did, Pop.

Willy: Oh, Biff! (*Staring wildly.*) He cried! Cried to me. (*He is choking with his love, and now cries out his promise.*) That boy—that boy is going to be magnificent!

Ben appears in the light just outside the kitchen.

Ben: Yes, outstanding, with twenty thousand behind him.

Linda (*sensing the racing of his mind, fearfully, carefully*): Now come to bed, Willy. It's all settled now.

Willy (*finding it difficult not to rush out of the house*): Yes, we'll sleep. Come on. Go to sleep, Hap.

Ben: And it does take a great kind of man to crack the jungle.

In accents of dread, Ben's idyllic music starts up.

Happy (*his arm around Linda*): I'm getting married, Pop, don't forget it. I'm changing everything. I'm gonna run that department before the year is up. You'll see, Mom. (*He kisses her.*)

Ben: The jungle is dark but full of diamonds, Willy.

Willy turns, moves, listening to Ben.

Linda: Be good. You're both good boys, just act that way, that's all.

Happy: 'Night, Pop. (*He goes upstairs.*)

Linda (*to Willy*): Come, dear.

Ben (*with greater force*): One must go in to fetch a diamond out.

Willy (*to Linda, as he moves slowly along the edge of the kitchen, toward the door*): I just want to get settled down, Linda. Let me sit alone for a little.

Linda (*almost uttering her fear*): I want you upstairs.

Willy (*taking her in his arms*): In a few minutes, Linda. I couldn't sleep right now. Go on, you look awful tired. (*He kisses her.*)

Ben: Not like an appointment at all. A diamond is rough and hard to the touch.

Willy: Go on now, I'll be right up.

Linda: I think this is the only way, Willy.

Willy: Sure, it's the best thing.

Ben: Best thing!

Willy: The only way. Everything is gonna be—go on, kid, get to bed. You look so tired.

Linda: Come right up.

Willy: Two minutes.

Linda goes into the living room, then reappears in her bedroom. Willy moves just outside the kitchen door.

Willy: Loves me. (*Wonderingly.*) Always loved me. Isn't that a remarkable thing? Ben, he'll worship me for it!

Ben (*with promise*): It's dark there, but full of diamonds.

Willy: Can you imagine that magnificence with twenty thousand dollars in his pocket?

Linda (*calling from her room*): Willy! Come up!

Willy (*calling from the kitchen*): Yes! Yes! Coming! It's very smart, you realize that, don't you, sweetheart? Even Ben sees it. I gotta go, baby. By! By! (*Going over to Ben, almost dancing.*) Imagine? When the mail comes he'll be ahead of Bernard again!

Ben: A perfect proposition all around.

Willy: Did you see how he cried to me? Oh, if I could kiss him, Ben!

Ben: Time, William, time!

Willy: Oh, Ben, I always knew one way or another we were gonna make it, Biff and I!

Ben (*looking at his watch*): The boat. We'll be late. (*He moves slowly off into the darkness.*)

Willy (*elegiacally, turning to the house*): Now when you kick off, boy, I want a seventy-yard boot, and get right down the field under the ball, and when you hit, hit low and hit hard, because it's important, boy. (*He swings around and faces the audience.*) There's all kinds of important people in the stands, and the first thing you know ... (*Suddenly realizing he is alone.*) Ben! Ben, where do I ... ? (*He makes a sudden movement of search.*) Ben, how do I ... ?

Linda (*calling*): Willy, you coming up?

Willy (*uttering a gasp of fear, whirling about as if to quiet her*): Sh! (*He turns around as if to find his way; sounds, faces, voices, seem to be swarming in upon him and he flicks at them, crying.*) Sh! Sh! (*Suddenly music, faint and high, stops him. It rises in intensity, almost to an unbearable scream. He goes up and down on his toes, and rushes off around the house.*) Shhh!

Linda: Willy?

There is no answer. Linda waits. Biff gets up off his bed. He is still in his clothes. Happy sits up. Biff stands listening.

Linda (*with real fear*): Willy, answer me! Willy!

There is the sound of a car starting and moving away at full speed.

Linda: No!

Biff (*rushing down the stairs*): Pop!

As the car speeds off, the music crashes down in a frenzy of sound, which becomes the soft pulsation of a single cello string. Biff slowly returns to his bedroom. He and Happy gravely don their jackets. Linda slowly walks out of her room. The music has developed into a dead march. The leaves of day are appearing over everything. Charley and Bernard, somberly dressed, appear and knock on the kitchen door. Biff and Happy slowly descend the stairs to the kitchen as Charley and Bernard enter. All stop a moment when Linda, in clothes of mourning, bearing a little bunch of roses, comes through the draped doorway into the kitchen. She goes to Charley and takes his arm. Now all move toward the audience, through the wall-line of the kitchen. At the limit of the apron, Linda lays down the flowers, kneels, and sits back on her heels. All stare down at the grave.

Study Questions:

1. Is Willy Loman tragic or pathetic? Is this play a tragedy in the classical sense of the word? Does it make any difference if this play is not a tragedy?

2. What is the function of the intermingling of present and past, and of illusion and reality in the play?

3. We do not know what Willy sells in the play and we do not know if the insurance money will be paid to his family. Why does the playwright leave these uncertainties for us?

[Reading Critically]

Critical Performance

Here are a few suggestions designed to help you tell the difference between an ordinary product and a work of drama that may offer high reward.

1. Discard any inexorable rules you may have collected that affirm what a drama ought to be. (Such a rule states that a tragedy is innately superior to a comedy, no matter how deep a truth a comedy may strike.) Don't expect all plays to observe the unities. (Shakespeare ignores such rules.) There is no sense in damning a play for lacking "realism". (What if it's an expressionist play or a fantasy?)

2. Instead, watch the play (or read it) alertly, with your mind and your senses open wide. Recall that theaters, such as the classic Greek theater of Sophocles impose conventions. Do not condemn *Oedipus the King* for the reason one spectator gave: "That damned chorus keeps sticking their noses in!" Do not complain that Hamlet utters soliloquies.

3. Ask yourself whether the characters are fully realized. Do their actions follow from the kinds of persons they are, or does the action seem to impose itself upon them, making the play seem falsely contrived? Does the resolution arrive (as in a satisfying play) because of the nature of the characters, or are the characters saved (or destroyed) merely by some nick-of-time arrival of the Marines?

4. Recognize drama that belongs to a family, for example a farce, a comedy of manners, or a melodrama (a play in which suspense and physical action are the prime ingredients). Recognizing such a familiar type of drama may help make some things clear to you and may save you from attacking a play for being what it is, in fact, supposed to be. After all, there can be satisfying melodramas, and excellent plays may have melodramatic elements. What is wrong with thrillers is not that they have suspense, but that suspense usually is all they have. Awhirl with furious action, they employ stick-figure characters.

5. If there are symbols, ask how well they belong to their surrounding worlds. Do they help to reveal meaning or merely decorate?

6. Test the play or film director for sentimentality, the failure of a dramatist, actor,

or director who expects from us a greater emotional response than we are given reason to feel.

7. Decide what it is that you admire or dislike and, for a play, whether it is the play or the production that you admire or dislike. (It is useful to draw this distinction if you are evaluating the play and not the production.)

8. Ask yourself what the theme is. What does the drama reveal? How far and how deeply does its statement go; how readily can we apply it beyond the play to the human world outside? Be slow, of course, to attribute to the playwright the opinions of the characters.

9. Don't be afraid of stating your own honest reaction (balanced, of course, by the careful considerations listed above). When the playwright Eugène Ionesco states that "a critic should describe, and not prescribe", he does not restrict the critic from trying accurately to describe his or her own response to the work in question. We cannot truthfully judge a work of art without somehow involving our own reactions—simple or complicated—to the experience of it.

Follow all these steps, and you may find that evaluating plays, movies, and television plays is a richly meaningful activity. It may reveal wisdom and pleasure that has previously bypassed you. It may even help you decide what to watch in the future, how to choose those works of drama that help you to fulfill—not merely to spend—your waking life.

Appendixes

Appendix 1

Writers Presented in This Book

Here are introductions to writers appearing in this book, and they are listed in the order in which they're presented in the book.

William Butler Yeats

William Butler Yeats (1865–1939), poet and playwright, an Irishman of English ancestry, was born in Dublin, the son of painter John Butler Yeats. For a time he studied art by himself and was irregularly schooled in Dublin and London. Early in life Yeats sought to transform Irish folklore and legend into mellifluous poems. He overcame shyness to take an active part in cataclysmic events. He became involved in the movement for an Irish nation (partly drawn into it by his unrequited love for Maud Gonne, a crusading nationalist) and in founding the Irish Literary Theatre (1898) and the Irish National Theatre, which in 1904 moved to the renowned Abbey Theatre in Dublin. Dublin audiences were difficult: In 1899 they jeered Yeats' first play, *The Countess Cathleen*, for portraying a woman who, defying the church, sells her soul to the devil to buy bread for starving peasants. Eventually Yeats retired from the fray, to write plays given in drawing rooms, like *Purgatory*. After the establishment of the Irish Free State, Yeats served as a senator (1922–1928). His lifelong interest in the occult culminated in his writing of *A Vision* (1937), a view of history as governed by the phases of the moon; Yeats believed the book inspired by spirit masters who dictated communications to his wife, Georgie Hyde-Lees. Had Yeats stopped writing in 1900, he would be remembered as an outstanding minor Victorian. Instead, he went on to become one of the most influential poets of the 20th century.

Robert Burns

Robert Burns (1759–1796), the greatest of the 18th century Scot poets, was born into a tenant farmer's family in Ayrshire, Scotland. Although poverty limited his formal education, yet he was encouraged in his self-education by his father, and his mother acquainted him with Scottish folk songs, legends, and proverbs. Burns did a great deal of reading in English literature and the Bible, and was familiar with major English writers like Shakespeare, Milton, Dryden, and Pope, and he read French writers including Racine. In common with other writers of his century, his art is eminently social: People in their relationships are his subject, not, as with the Romantics of whom he is often said to be a forerunner, man in his solitude with nature. On the other hand, thanks to the robust character of his Scots idiom, he drew on older traditions in which it was natural to write concretely of ordinary experience, as Chaucer did. His best work was written between 1785 and 1790, and most of it in 1785; these poems were published at Kilmarnock in *Poems Chiefly in the Scots Dialect* (1786), and they brought him fame. He has always been more popular, however, for his extremely musical sentimental pieces such as his songs—"Auld Lang Syne", "Ae Fond Kiss", "Highland Mary", etc., which, in the view of those who know his work are minor works compared to his satires: "To a Louse", "Holy Willie's Prayer", "The Holy Fair", "The Jolly Beggars," and so on.

Burns has become something of a national symbol for all Scotsmen all over the world, who celebrate "Burns Night" in January and can usually quote a great deal of his poetry. It is not possible to give a single reason for this. Burns had a profound sympathy for the down-trodden, whether man or mouse; his emotions, of fire or pathos, were deeply sincere; his vivid portrayal of country life was based on experience, not on mere observation; he was in all things an unashamed patriot.

Robert Frost

Robert Frost (1874 – 1963), though born in San Francisco, came to be popularly known as a spokesman of rural New England. In periods of farming, teaching school, and raising chickens and writing for poultry journals, Frost struggled until his late thirties to support his family and to publish his poems, with little success. Moving to England to write and farm between 1912 and 1915, he had his first book published in London: *A Boy's Will* (1913). Returning to America, he settled in New Hampshire, later teaching for many years (in a casual way) at Amherst College in Massachusetts. Audiences responded warmly to the poet's public readings; he was awarded four Pulitzer Prizes. In his later years the white-haired Frost became a sort of elder statesman and poet laureate of the John F. Kennedy administration: invited to read a poem at President Kennedy's inauguration, and dispatched to Russia as a cultural emissary. Frost is sometimes admired for putting colloquial Yankee speech into poetry—and he did, but more essentially he mastered the art of laying conversational America speech along a metrical line. In a three-volume biography (1966 – 1976), Lawrence Thompson made Frost out to be an overweening egotist who tormented his family, and we are only now coming around again to see him as more than that.

Robert Browning

Robert Browning (1812 – 1889), born in the suburb of London, was educated mainly in his father's six-thousand-volume library. With *Pauline* (1833), he began to print his poetry. After the death of his wife Elizabeth Barrett Browning, with whom he had lived in Italy, he returned to England to become (Henry James wrote) an "accomplished, saturated, sane, sound man of the London world". There, as he neared sixty, he enjoyed late but loud applause and the adulation of the Browning Society: faithful readers whose local groups met over their teacups to explicate him. Readers have most greatly favored Browning's story-poems in a form he perfected, the dramatic monologue, such as "My Last Duchess" and "Soliloquy of the Spanish Cloister", in which he brings to life persons from the past (some of them famous), has them speak their innermost thoughts and reveal their characters. His masterpiece, *The Ring and the Book* (1868 – 1869), is a long narrative poem in twelve monologues, based on a 12th-century Roman murder trial.

Browning also wrote several plays, among them *A Blot in the 'Scutcheon* (1842). Through the praise and emulation of his later admirers Ezra Pound and T. S. Eliot, Browning has profoundly affected modern poetry. A formal experimenter, he speaks to us in energetic, punchy words—and like many later poets he introduces learning into his poems without apology. More important, Browning is among the great yeasayers in English poetry: an affirmer and celebrant of life.

Walt Whitman

Walt Whitman (1819 – 1892) was born on Long Island, son of an impoverished farmer. He spent his early years as a schoolteacher, a temperance propagandist, a carpenter, a printer, and a newspaper editor on *The Brooklyn Eagle*. He began writing poetry in youth, sometimes declaiming his lines above the crash of waves on New York beaches. Apparently, he was also inspired to write wide, spacious, confident lines by attending performances of Italian opera. His self-published *Leaves of Grass* (1855) won praise from Ralph Waldo Emerson and gained Whitman readers in England. For the rest of his life, he kept revising and enlarging it, ceasing with a ninth or "deathbed edition" between 1891 and 1892. Americans at first were slow to accept Whitman's unconventionally open verse forms, his sexual frankness, and his gregarious egoism.

The poet of bondless faith in American democracy, Whitman tempered his vision by his experiences as a volunteer hospital nurse during the Civil War. After the war, he held secretarial jobs to support himself, and lost one such job when his employer's scandalized eye fell upon the *Leaves*. In old age, a semi-invalid after a stroke, Whitman made his home in Camden, New Jersey. Before he died he saw his work finally winning respect and worldwide acceptance. Whitman's influence on later American poetry has been profound, both by the example of his open forms and by his bold encompassing of subject matter that had formerly been considered unpoetic.

Emily Dickinson

Emily Dickinson (1830 – 1886) spent all her life in her family home in Amherst, Massachusetts. Her father, Edward Dickinson, was a prominent lawyer who ranked as Amherst's leading citizen. (He even served a term in the US Congress.) Dickinson attended one year of college at Mount Holyoke Female Seminary in South Hadley. She proved to be a good student, but suffering from homesickness and poor health, she did not return for the second year. This brief period of study and a few trips to Boston, Philadelphia, and Washington, D. C., were the only occasions she left home in her fifty-five-year life. As the years passed, Dickinson became more reclusive. She stopped attending church (and refused to endorse the orthodox Congregationalist creed). She also spent increasing time alone in her room—often writing poems. Dickinson never married, but she had a significant romantic relationship with at least one unidentified man. Although scholars have suggested several likely candidates, the historical objects of Dickinson's affections will never be known. What survives unmistakably, however, is the intensely passionate poetry written from these private circumstances. By the end of her life, Dickinson had become a locally famous recluse who rarely left home. She would greet visitors from her own upstairs room—clearly heard but never seen.

In 1886 she was buried, according to her own instructions, within sight of the family home. Although Dickinson composed 1,775 known poems, she published only seven in her lifetime.① She often, however, sent copies of poems to friends in letters, but only after her death would the full extent of her production become known when a cache of manuscripts was discovered in a trunk in the homestead attic—-handwritten little booklets of poems sewn together by the poet with needle and thread. From 1890 until the mid-20th century, nine posthumous collections of her poems were published by friends and relatives, some of whom rewrote her work and changed her idiosyncratic

---

① According to the latest studies from American scholars, Dickinson published ten poems in her lifetime.

punctuation to make it more conventional. Thomas H. Johnson's three-volume edition of *The Poems* (1955) established a better text. In relatively few and simple forms clearly indebted to the hymns she heard in church, Dickinson succeeded in being a true visionary and a poet of colossal originality.

Ted Hughes

Ted Hughes (1930–1998) was born in Yorkshire in 1930, and he attended Cambridge University after the Second World War. There he studied folklore and anthropology, which have a close relation to the manner and subject of his poetry later. In 1956 he married the anguished American poet, Sylvia Plath who at that time was studying at Cambridge. She remained with Hughes, mostly in England, until her suicide in 1963. Inevitably he was deeply moved by his wife's poetry and her pessimism as she helplessly approached her death. The poems of Ted Hughes and Sylvia Plath are closely linked, and in England Plath's work is considered to be part of English rather than American literature. Hughes edited and published her poems in three volumes after her death.

Hughes's first book of poetry, *Hawk in the Rain*, was published in 1957. The strong emotion and expressive vocabulary of the poems showed some of the influence of Dylan Thomas, and Hughes did not force them into stylistic neatness as the Movement poets at that time were doing. Two major themes concerned him: the dislocation evident in the mind of Europe since the First World War, and the violent, blind energy of nature demonstrated in both animals and man. His poems invited the reader to consider what could be the relation between the intelligent life of the mind and the wild, primitive forces of nature. Ted Hughes and Sylvia Plath visited America after the book was published and he was awarded a fellowship that left him free to write poetry when they returned to England.

His next book, *Lupercal* (1960), takes its title from Lupercus, the Roman god of flocks and herds. Theses poems concentrate on the turbulent world of predatory animals, primitive violence and moments of extreme human endurance, a harsh world ruled by impulse and instinct, containing no half-hatred human characteristics. The poems are fierce but highly organized and concentrated. They contained no sentimentality but rather the ruthlessness of animal energy and a precision of words that give him clarity and coherence. In 1961, he published *Selected Poems* with Thom Gunn. During the rest of the 1960s, he produced two more books of poetry, some short stories, a verse-play that was no successful, and several plays and poems for children. In 1970 he published "Crow", a long epic poem containing strong elements of folklore.

Ted Hughes's work was very influential; he was followed by a whole group of young poets who adopted his subjects, mannerism and vocabulary, known among poets as "The Tribe of Ted". In 1974, Ted Hughes was awarded the Queen's Gold Medal for Poetry.

William Wordsworth

William Wordsworth (1770–1850) was born in England's Lake District, whose landscapes and people were to inform many of his poems. As a young man he visited France, sympathized with the Revolution, and met a young Frenchwoman who bore him a child. The Reign of Terror prevented him from returning to France, and he and Annette Vallon never married. With his sister Dorothy (1771–1855), his lifelong intellectual companion and the author of remarkable journals, he settled in Dorsetshire. Later they moved to Grasmere, in the Lake District, where Wordsworth lived the rest of his life. In 1798 his friendship with Samuel Taylor Coleridge resulted in their joint publication of *Lyrical Ballads*, a book credited with introducing Romanticism to English poetry. To the second edition of 1800, Wordsworth supplied a preface calling for a poetry written "in the real language of men". Time brought him a small official job, a marriage, a swing from left to right in his political sentiments, and appointment as poet laureate. Although he kept on writing, readers have generally preferred his earlier poems. *The Prelude*, a long poem-memoir completed in 1805, did not appear until the poet's death. One of the most original of writers, Wordsworth, especially for his poems of nature and simple rustics, occupies a popular place in English poetry, much like that of Robert Frost in America.

William Blake

William Blake (1757–1827), poet, painter, and visionary, was born in the Soho district of London and early in life was apprenticed to an engraver. Becoming a skilled craftsman, he earned his living illustrating books, among them Dante's *Divine Comedy*, Milton's poems, and the *Book of Job*. A remarkable and original graphic artist whose only formal training came from a few months at the Royal Academy, Blake published his own poems, engraving them in a careful script embellished with hand-colored illustrations and decorations. His wife Catherine Boucher, whom he taught to read and write, shared his visions and helped him do the coloring. *Songs of Innocence* (1789) and *Songs of Experience* (1794), brief lyrics written from a child's point of view, are easy to enjoy; but anyone deeply interested in Blake copes also with the longer, more demanding "Prophetic Books", among them *The Book of Thel* (1789), *The Marriage of Heaven and Hell* (1790), and *Jerusalem* (1804–1820). In these later works, out of his readings in alchemy, the *Bible*, and the works of Plato and Swedenborg, Blake derived support for his lifelong hatred of scientific rationalism and created his own mythology, complete with devils and deities. A sympathizer with both American and French revolutions, Blake was once accused of sedition, but the charges were dismissed. In his lifetime, Wordsworth and Coleridge were among the few admirers of his short lyrics; his "Prophetic Books" have had to wait until our century for compassionate readers.

William Carlos Williams

William Carlos Williams (1883–1963) was born in Rutherford, New Jersey, where he remained in later life as a practicing pediatrician. While taking his MD degree at the University of Pennsylvania, he made friends with the poets Ezra Pound and H. D. (Hilda Doolittle). Surprisingly prolific for a busy doctor, Williams wrote (besides poetry) novels and short stories, plays, criticism, and essays in history (*The American Grain*, 1939). He kept a flip top desk in his office and between patients would haul out his typewriter and dash off poems. His encouragement of younger poets, among them Allen Ginsberg (whose doctor he was when Ginsberg was a baby), and the long-sustained example of his formally open poetry made him an appealing father figure to the generation of the Beat poets and the Black Mountain poets—Ginsberg, Gary Snyder, and Robert Creeley. But he also had great influence on Robert Lowell, and on a whole younger generation of American poets in our day. Williams believed in truth-telling about ordinary life, championed plain speech "out of the mouths of Polish mothers", and insisted that there can be "no ideas but in things". Combining poetry with prose (including documents and statistics), his long poem in five parts, *Paterson* (1946–1958) explores the past, present, and future of the New Jersey industrial city near which Williams lived for most of his days.

William Shakespeare

William Shakespeare (1590–1616) was born on April 23, 1564, in Stratford-on-Avon, a charming little town in Warwickshire. His father was a well-to-do trader in wool, hides and leathern articles. He got education in a local grammar school for a few years. There he picked up the "small Latin and less Greek". When Shakespeare was about fourteen years old, his father lost his little property and fell into debt, young William had to leave school to help support his family. His occupation perhaps was a country schoolmaster or a lawyer's clerk. In 1582, he married Anne Hathaway, the daughter of a peasant family, who was eight years older than her husband. A few years later, Shakespeare went to London, where he first did some odd jobs. It was said that he kept horses for the audience outside the playhouses. Then he became an actor and a writer. He worked very hard, and wrote for the theatre at the rate of two plays a year. In

1612, he retired from the stage and returned to his hometown, where he bought a considerable estate and lived until his death on April 23, 1616, which was his 52nd birthday.

During the twenty-two years of his literary career, he produced 37 plays, 154 sonnets and some long poems. His dramatic literary career can be divided into four periods. The first period (1590 – 1594) is his apprenticeship in play-writing, during which he made experiment in a number of dramatic forms: the historical play [Henry VI (Parts 1, 2, and 3) Richard III], varieties of comedies (The Comedy of Errors, The Taming of the Shrew, The Two Gentlemen of Verona, Love's Labour's Lost), the revenge tragedy (Titus Andronicus), and the romantic tragedy (Romeo and Juliet). In these years he also wrote two narrative poems, "Venus and Adonis" and "The Rape of Lucrece".

The Second Period (1595 – 1600) is Shakespeare's mature period, mainly a period of "great comedies" and mature historical plays. It includes 6 comedies (A Midsummer Night's Dream, The Merchant of Venice, The Merry Wives of Windsor, Much Ado about Nothing, As You Like It, Twelfth Night), 5 historical plays [Richard II, Henry IV (Parts 1 and 2) Henry V, King John], and a Roman tragedy (Julius Caesar). His sonnets are also thought to be written in this period.

The Third Period (1601 – 1607) is mainly the period of his "great tragedies" and "dark comedies". It includes 5 tragedies (Hamlet, Othello, King Lear, Macbeth, Timon of Athens), 3 comedies (Troilus and Cressida, All's Well That Ends Well, Measure for Measure) and 2 Roman tragedies (Antony and Cleopatra, Coriolanus).

The Fourth Period (1608 – 1612) is the period of romantic drama. It includes 4 romances or "reconciliation plays" (Pericles, Cymbeline, The Winter's Tale, Tempest) and a historical play (Henry VIII).

William Shakespeare is one of the most remarkable playwrights and poets the world has ever known. He was man of the late Renaissance who gave the fullest expression to humanist ideals. His works have been translated into every major language in the world. He has been given the highest praises by various scholars and critics in the world. His contemporary poet and dramatist Ben Johnson dedicates a poem in praise of him: "… he was not of an age, but for all time!" This is definitely true.

Henry Wadsworth Longfellow

Henry Wadsworth Longfellow (1807 – 1882) was born in Maine, and attended Bowdoin College, where one of his classmates was Nathaniel Hawthorne. He loved language and became so skilled in them that for most of his life, first at Bowdoin, later at Harvard, he taught a great variety of languages and literature, even writing his own language textbooks. As a result of his attachment to languages and his broad knowledge of European literature, and through his work as a teacher, anthologist, and poet, Longfellow did much to bring European culture to America.

Longfellow wrote poems on a wide range of subjects, contemporary and historical, and he used many different verse forms and meters with great technical skill. His most famous works, however, are those that bring to life stories from the American past: *Evangeline* (1847), *The Courtship of Miles Standish* (1858), and "Paul Revere's Ride" (1861). Later in life, grieving over his wife's death, Longfellow also translated *The Divine Comedy*, the 14th-century epic by the Italian poet Dante. Throughout his life Longfellow wrote noble and elevated verse built around romanticized characters and heroic sentiments. His versatility and enthusiasm won him a large audience, but, more important, he helped to popularize poetry itself in America.

Longfellow is the best-known of the fireside poets and the most successful American poet of his age. He was so revered that his seventy-fifth birthday was celebrated in schoolrooms across the country. When he died, a memorial bust was placed in the Poets' Corner of Westminster Abbey in England. He is still the only American so honored.

Robert Frost

Robert Frost (1874–1963) was the most popular American poet of this century. He won many prizes and the American government presented him a gold medal in 1960 for his contribution to American culture. At the age of 87, he was invited to read a poem at the inauguration of President Kennedy.

Frost was born in San Francisco, his father was a New Englander, a graduate of Harvard, who married a young Scottish woman and went west to become a newspaper reporter. When Frost was 10, his father died of TB (tubercle bacillus). The family took his body to New England to be buried; yet they were too poor to return to California, so Frost's mother became a schoolteacher in New England. Frost was a bad primary school student, but when he was in high school, he began to write poetry. His grandfather sent him to a good university, but after one term he ran away and went home to his mother. He worked at various jobs until he got married. Due to his ill health, on the advice of his doctor, his family moved to the countryside where he became a farmer.

He loved the farm, but he was a very inept farmer. No publisher would accept his poems, and the farm failed. Instead, he moved to England, there he met Ezra Pound, who appreciated his poetry and introduced him to British publishers. Two books of his poems were published and highly praised in England. He continued writing in his own style.

At the beginning of the First World War, he returned to America and was surprised to find a warm welcome from American publishers who heard his success in England. He lived to be almost 90, loved and honored not only in his native New England but also throughout America.

Frost did not experiment with form, as many poets did in the 1920s, but used conventional forms, plain language and a graceful style. His poems were very carefully constructed yet he made them seem effortless by using colloquial language and familiar, conventional rhythms. He used symbols from everyday country life to express his deep ideas. Frost's works have been published in many collections. Among his best-known poems are: "Stopping by Woods on a Snowy Evening", "Birches", "The Death of the Hired Man", "The Road Not Taken", and "Mending Wall".

Alfred, Lord Tennyson

Alfred, Lord Tennyson (1809–1892), was born Alfred Tennyson in Lincolnshire, England, the son of an alcoholic rural minister. When Queen Victoria made him a baron in 1883 (at seventy-five), he added the "lord" to his byline. A precocious poet, Tennyson began writing verse at five, and when still in his teens collaborated with his brother Charles on *Poems by Two Brothers* (1827). As a student at Cambridge, he was unusual: He kept a snake for a pet, won a medal for poetry, and went home without taking a degree. But in college he made influential friendships, especially that of Arthur Hallam, whose death in 1833 inspired Tennyson's *In Memoriam* (1850), the elegiac sequence that contains "Dark House by Which Once More I Stand." The year 1850 was a banner one for Tennyson in other ways: He at last felt prosperous enough to marry Emily Sellwood, who had remained engaged to him for fourteen years, and Queen Victoria named him poet laureate, in which capacity he served for four decades, writing poems for state occasions. Between 1859 and 1888 Tennyson completed *Idylls of the King*, a twelve-part narrative poem of King Arthur and his Round Table Knights. In his mid-sixties he wrote several plays. A spokesman for the Victorian age and its militant colonialism, Tennyson is still respected as a poet of varied assets, including an excellent ear.

Ezra Pound

Ezra Pound (1885–1872), among the most influential (and still controversial) modern poets, was born in Hailey, Idaho. He readied himself for a teaching career, but when in 1907 he lost his job at Wabash College for sheltering a penniless prostitute, he left America. Settling in England and later in Paris, he wielded influence on the work of T. S. Eliot, whose long poem *The Waste Land* he edited, W. B. Yeats, whom he served as a secretary and critic, and James Joyce. Pound was perpetually championing writers then unknown, like Robert Frost. In 1924 Pound settled permanently in Italy, where he came to admire Mussolini's economic policies. During World War II, he made broadcasts to America by Italian radio, deemed treasonous. When America armed forces arrested him in 1944, Pound spent three weeks in a cage in an army camp in Pisa. Flown to the United Stated to stand trial, he was declared incompetent and for twelve years was confined in St. Elizabeth's in Washington, a hospital for the criminally insane. In 1958, at the intervention of Robert Frost, Archibald MacLeish, and other old friends, he was pronounced incurable and allowed to return to Italy to spend his last, increasingly silent years. In his prime, Pound was a swaggeringly confident critic, a delectable humorist. Among his lasting books are *Personae* (enlarged edition, 1949), short poems; his *ABC of Reading* (1934), an introduction to poetry; and *literary Essays* (1954). His *Cantos*, a vast poem woven of historical themes published in installments over forty years, Pound never finished. He was a great translator of poetry from Italian, Provencal, Chinese, and other languages. Pare away his delusions, and a remarkable human being and splendid poet remains.

T. S. Eliot

T. S. Eliot (1888–1965) was born of a New England family who had moved to St. Louis. After studying at Harvard, Eliot emigrated to London, became a bank clerk and later an influential editor for the publishing house of Faber. In 1927 he became a British citizen and joined the Church of England. During the fire bombings of London in World War II, he served as an air raid warden. Although Eliot strove to keep his private, a recent biographer, Peter Ackroyd in *T. S. Eliot* (1984), throws light upon his troubled early marriage. Early poems such as "The Love Song of J. Alfred Prufrock" (1917) and *The Waste Land* (1922), an allusive and seemingly disconnected complaint about the sterility of contemporary city life, enormously influenced young poets. Eliot was mainly responsible for bringing French symbolism into English poetry, and as a critic he helped revive interest in John Donne and other Metaphysical poets. In an early essay, "Tradition and the Individual Talent" (1919), he finds a necessary continuity in Western civilization. *Four Quartets*, completed in 1943, was Eliot's last major work of poetry: an attempt to structure a long thematic poem like a work of music. In later years he devoted himself to writing verse plays for the London stage; the best received was *The Cocktail Party* (1950), in which Alec Guinness played a psychiatrist. In 1948, Eliot received the Nobel Prize in literature.

George Gordon Byron

George Gordon Byron (1788 – 1824), as an outstanding English romantic poet, ranks together with Shakespeare and Scott among the British writers who exert the greatest influence over the mainland of Europe. He was born of noble blood both on the paternal and maternal lines. He inherited the title of baron when he was ten years old upon the death of his great-uncle. He went to study at Harrow and then at Cambridge. In 1807 while a student at Cambridge, he was influenced by the enlightening ideas and published a collection of lyrical verse *Hours of Idleness*, which incurred the harsh criticism from *The Edinburgh Review*, a conservative magazine. Two years later, he wrote a satirical poem "English Bards and Scotch Reviewers", in which he satirically attacked Wordsworth, Coleridge, and Southey, and the Edinburgh critics.

From 1809 to 1811, he made a grand tour of the Continent. He visited Portugal, Spain, Albania, Greece, and other countries. He was deeply moved by these nations' brilliant culture, splendid civilization and historical achievements and also by the local people's struggle against all forms of oppression and their fight for national liberty and independence. In 1811, he took his seat in the House of Lords and made a vehement speech, attacking the reactionary policy of the English government and showing his great sympathy for the oppressed poor. The publication of the first two cantos of *Childe Harold's Pilgrimage* (1811), narrating his travel in Europe, won him great fame.

In the following two years, he had written a number of long verse-tales, generally known as the *Oriented Tales*, with similar kind of heroes. In 1815 he married an heiress but was soon separated from her. There arose a scandal, and Byron was to leave England forever. He first went to Switzerland, where he met Shelley. The two poets formed a close friendship, and under the influence of Shelley, he wrote *Prometheus*, *Sonnet on Chilian*, and *The Prisoner of Chilian*. Then he went to Italy and published the third and fourth cantos of *Childe Harold's Pilgrimage* (1816, 1818). They were followed by many other works, and the most famous is *Don Juan* (1818 – 1820). In Italy he met Shelley for the second time. In 1824 he equipped a troop of soldiers with his own money to support the Greeks in their struggle against the Turks. He died of fever in 1824 in Greece. The whole Greek nation mourned over his death.

Langston Hughes

Langston Hughes (1902 – 1967) was the most accomplished poet of the Harlem Renaissance in America. A true "Renaissance man", he wrote drama, fiction, popular songs and movie screenplays, however, he is best noted for his poetry. Hughes was born in Missouri and went to high school in Cleveland, Ohio, where he began writing poetry for a school magazine. He went on to Columbia University in New York City but a year later left to go to sea. After traveling as a merchant seaman to Africa and Europe, he returned to America and continued writing poetry. His work appeared in a number of prominent black journals and in the chief anthology of the Harlem Renaissance, *The New Negro* (1925). The poet Vachel Lindsay helped Hughes publish his first volume of poetry, *The Weary Blues* (1926). His literary reputation secure, Hughes decided to complete his formal education. After graduation from Lincoln University, he returned to New York City, where he continued to write and was active in the theatre. His later books of poems include *The Dream Keeper* (1932), *Fields of Wonder* (1947), and *Montage of a Dream Deferred* (1951). He wrote two autobiographical volumes, *The Big Sea* (1940) and *I Wonder as I Wander* (1956). Hughes embraced African-American jazz rhythms and incorporated blues, spirituals, colloquial speech, and folkways in his poetry.

Wallace Stevens

Wallace Stevens (1879–1955) was born in Reading, Pennsylvania; his father was a successful lawyer; his mother, a former schoolteacher. As a special student at Harvard, he became president of the student literary magazine, *The Harvard Advocate*, but he did not want a literal arts degree. Instead, he became a lawyer in New York City, and in 1916 joined the legal staff of the Hartford Accident and Indemnity Company. In 1936 he was elected a vice-president. Stevens, who would write poems in his head while walking to work and then dictate them to his secretary, was a leading expert on surety claims. Once asked how he was able to combine poetry and insurance, he replied that the two occupations had an element in common: "calculated risk". As a young man in New York, Stevens made lasting friendships with poets Marianne Moore and William Carlos Williams, but he did not seek literary society. Though his poems are full of references to Europe and remote place, his only travels were annual vacation trips to Key West. He printed his early poems in *Poetry* magazine, but did not publish a book until *Harmonium* appeared in 1923, when he was forty-four. Living quietly in Hartford, Connecticut, Stevens sought to discover order in a chaotic world with his subtle and exotic imagination. His critical essays, collected in *The Necessary Angel* (1951), and his *Letters* (1966), edited by his daughter Holly Stevens, reveal a penetrating, philosophic mind. His *Collected Poems* (1954), published on his seventy-fifth birthday, garnered major prizes and belated recognition for Stevens as a major American poet.

John Keats

John Keats (1795 – 1821) was a contemporary of Byron and Shelley, but of humbler social background. His father was a hostler and stable keeper and then married his employer's daughter. When he was eight, his father died, and his mother died of tuberculosis when he was fourteen. His guardian forced him to leave school at fifteen and apprenticed him to a surgeon. For five years he served his apprenticeship and then worked as the surgeon's helper for two more years. In 1817 he abandoned his profession and published his first collection of poems. In 1818 he published his long allegorical poem *Endymion*, which was about the love between a Greek shepherd and the moon goddess. Both collections were severely attacked by conservative critics. It is said that the attacks were the cause of his illness that took away his life. He went on writing, however, and his great year was 1819, during which he produced all the works on which his high reputation now rests: "The Eve of St. Agnes", "La Belle Dame sans Merci", "Lamia", "Eve of St. Mark", "Isabella", "Hyperion"; and the great odes—"To a Nightingale", "On a Grecian Urn", "On Melancholy", "To Psyche", "To Autumn". These were published in *Lamia and Other Poems* in 1820. In the same year Keats, very ill with tuberculosis, took ship for Rome, where he died.

John Donne

John Donne (1572–1631), English poet and divine, wrote his subtle, worldly love lyrics as a young man in the court of Queen Elizabeth I. At the time, he came to be known in London as (wrote his contemporary, Richard Baker) "a great visitor of ladies, a great frequenter of plays, a great writer of conceited verses". The poems of his *Songs and Sonnets* were first circulated in manuscript, for in his lifetime Donne printed little. When in 1601 he married without the consent of his bride's father, he was dismissed from his secretarial post at court. For several years he endured poverty. His longer poems, *The First Anniversary* (1611) and *The Second Anniversary* (1612), suffused with gloom, see the order of the universe shaken by science and doubt. In 1615 Donne—apparently with some reluctance, or he had been raised a Catholic—became a priest of the Anglican church. From 1621 until he died he was dean of St. Paul's Cathedral in London, where he preached sermons known for their eloquence. His "Holy Sonnets" date from later life. Almost forgotten for two centuries, Donne's work has had much influence in our time. H. J. C. Grierson brought out a great scholarly edition of it in 1912; shortly thereafter it was championed by T. S. Eliot.

Jane Austen

Jane Austen (1775–1817) was born in Hampshire, in southern England, of a country clergyman's family. Educated at home and unmarried, she led an uneventful life of forty-odd years at her native place and in the small towns nearby, paying only occasional visits to London. She started writing novels early in life and at first had difficulties in getting them published, but later became somewhat well-known so that the Prince Regent indirectly asked her to dedicate one of her novels to him. And in 1815 she dedicated one of her novels, *Emma*, to him, though previously she had privately expressed her antipathy toward him upon his attempt to divorce his wife. She wrote and completed six novels: *Sense and Sensibility* (1811), *Pride and Prejudice* (1813), *Mansfield Park* (1814), *Emma* (1815), *Northanger Abbey* and *Persuasion* (appearing posthumously in 1818); and she left behind three fragments *Lady Susan*, *The Watsons*, and *Sandition*. Her novels were not so well received in her lifetimes, being subject to non-too-favorable criticism from her contemporary reviewers, but have since had steadily growing popularity, especially in the 20th century, and she has sometimes been ranked among truly great English novelists by critics and literary historians.

The most striking thing about Jane Austen and her novels is her seeming obliviousness to the big social and political upheavals in the outside world of her time, as one would naturally surmise from her realistic pictures of the small circle of landed gentry in provincial England leading their apparently tranquil lives. In her novels, she depicted the everyday life of the families of bigger or smaller landlords and clergymen, with the interest centered chiefly upon the love and marriage of the younger and the not-so-young folk, describing in detail their ordinary conversations, walks, drives, teas, dances, visits, picnics, journeys and other common activities. The theme of the predominant money considerations in love and marriage is hinted at or indirectly suggested in her novels. And in these novels of the quiet and happy lives of the rural gentry, there is also expose of the egotism and hypocrisy and other vices of the respectable English men and women or less fixed incomes, as the author proceeds in her vivid and detailed narratives of the superficial but occasionally poisonous courtesies, the ambiguous compliments, the hypocritical poses toward one's relatives, the pretended friendly outpourings, and a hundred other mean and tricky little actions and speeches displayed by the apparently innocent and upright ladies and gentlemen, including the very heroes and heroines of these novels. It is this all-pervading though mild satire on her characters, usually conveyed with subtle irony though sometimes with forgiving humor, that makes Austen's novels still of interest to us today.

Thomas Hardy

Thomas Hardy (1840–1928) was the last important novelist of the Victorian age. In his Wessex novels, he vividly and truthfully described the tragic lives of the tenants in the last decade of the 19th century.

Hardy was born in Dorsetshire, a county in the south of England. His birthplace, later used as the setting of his novels, he gave the name Wessex, which suggests the mysterious past of England during the Anglo-Saxon period, for it was here the Wessex kingdom once prospered under King Alfred and the prehistorical Stonehenge is located. The place is rich in its legend, folk customs and superstitions— all these would play their roles in Hardy's Wessex' novels.

Born into an architect's family, he was expected to become an architect. He was an architect, but his real interest was in literature. His most famous novels are *Tess of the D'Urbervilles* (1891) and *Jude the Obscure* (1896).

Hardy was pessimistic in his view of life. His philosophy was that everything in the universe is determined by the Immanent Will, which is present in all parts of the universe and is impartially hostile towards human beings' desire for joy and happiness. The dominant theme of his novels is the futility of man's effort to struggle against cruel and unintelligible Fate, Chance, and Circumstances, which are all predestined by the Immanent Will. Although there is a humorous and attractive side to life, the prevailing mood in his novels is tragic. Since love is the most intense expression of human's desire for happiness, it is in love that the conflict between the efforts of human beings and the relentless force of the Immanent Will is most acute.

From 1896 Hardy turned to poetry writing. He wrote altogether 918 poems, published in eight collections. Besides, he also wrote a great epic-drama *The Dynasts*, which was published in three parts (1904, 1906, 1908).

Katherine Anne Porter

Katherine Anne Porter (1890–1980) was born in Indian Creek, Texas. Her mother died when she was two, and Porter was raised by a grandmother who surrounded the growing girl with books. At sixteen she ran away from school and soon married a railway clerk in Louisiana. Three years later, she divorced her husband and began supporting herself as a news reporter in Chicago, Denver, and Fort Worth, and sometimes as an actress and ballad singer traveling through the South. Sojourns in Europe and in Mexico supplied her with matter for some of her finest stories. Her brilliant, sensitive short fiction, first collected in *Flowering Judas* (1930), won her a high reputation. Her one novel, *Ship of Fools* (1962), with which she had struggled for twenty years, received harsh critical notices, but proved a commercial success. Made into a movie, it ended Porter's lifelong struggle to earn a living. In 1965 her *Collected Stories* received a Pulitzer Prize and a National Book Award.

Alice Walker

Alice Walker, a leading black writer and social activist, was born in 1944 in Eatonton, Georgia, the youngest of eight children. Her father, a sharecropper and dairy farmer, usually earned about $300 a year; her mother helped by working as a maid. Both entertained their children by telling stories. When Alice Walker was eight, she was accidentally struck by a pellet from a brother's BB gun. She lost the sight of one eye because the Walkers had no car to rush her to the hospital. Later she attended Spelman College in Atlanta and finished college at Sarah Lawrence College on a scholarship. While working for the civil rights movement in Mississippi, she met a young lawyer, Melvyn Leventhal. In 1967 they settled in Jackson, Mississippi, the first legally married interracial couple in town. They returned to New York in 1974 and were later divorced. First known as a poet, Walker has published four books of her verse. She also has edited a collection of the work of the neglected black writer Zora Neale Hurston, and has written a study of Langston Hughes. In her collected essays, *In Search of Our Mothers' Gardens: Womanist Prose* (1983), she recalls her mother and addresses her own daughter. (By womanist she means "black feminist".) But the largest part of Walker's reading audience know her fiction: two story collections, *In Love and Trouble* (1973), from which "Everyday Use" is taken, and *You Can't Keep a Good Woman Down* (1981); and her novels, *The Third Life of Grange Copeland* (1970), and *Meridian* (1976). Her best-known novel, *The Color Purple* (1982), won a Pulitzer Prize and was made into a film by Steven Spielberg in 1985. Her recent novels include *The Temple of My Familiar* (1989), *Possessing the Secret of Joy* (1992), and *By the Light of My Father's Smile* (1998). Walker now lives in Northern California.

Kate Chopin

Kate Chopin (1851–1904) was born Katherine O'Flaherty in St. Louis, daughter of an Irish immigrant grown wealthy in retailing. On her father's death, young Kate was raised by her mother's family: aristocratic Creoles, descendants of the French and Spaniards who had colonized Louisiana. Young Kate received a convent schooling, and at nineteen married Oscar Chopin, a Creole cotton broker from New Orleans. Later, the Chopins lived on a plantation near Cloutierville, Louisiana, a region whose varied people—Creoles, Cajuns, blacks—Kate Chopin was later to write about with loving care in *Bayou Folk* (1894) and *A Night in Arcadia* (1897). The shock of her husband's sudden death in 1883, which left her with the raising of six children, seems to have plunged Kate Chopin into writing. She read and admired fine women writers of her day, such as the Maine realist Sarah Orne Jewett. She also read Maupassant, Zola, and other new (and scandalous) French naturalist writers. She began to bring into American fiction some of their hard-eyed observation and their passion for telling unpleasant truths. Determined, in defiance of her times, frankly to show the sexual feelings of her characters, Chopin suffered from neglect and censorship. When her major novel, *The Awakening*, appeared in 1899, critics were outraged by her candid portrait of a woman who seeks sexual and professional independence. After causing such a literary scandal, Chopin was unable to get her later work published, and wrote little more before she died. *The Awakening* and many of her stories had to wait seven decades for a sympathetic audience.

Jack London

Jack London (1876–1916), born in San Francisco, won a large popular audience for his novels of the sea and the Yukon: *The Call of the Wild* (1903), *The Sea-Wolf* (1904), and *White Fang* (1906). Like Ernest Hemingway, he was a writer who lived a strenuous life. In 1893, he marched cross-country in Coxey's Army, an organized protest of the unemployed; in 1897, he took part in the Klondike gold rush; and later as a reporter he covered the Russo-Japanese War and the Mexican Revolution. Son of an unmarried mother and a father who denied his paternity, London grew up in poverty. At fourteen, he began holding hard jobs: working in a canning factory and a jute-mill, serving as a deck hand, pirating oysters in San Francisco Bay. These experiences persuaded him to join the Socialist Labor Party and crusade for workers' rights. In his political novel *The Iron Heel* (1908), London envisions a grim totalitarian America. Like himself, the hero of his novel *Martin Eden* (1909) is a man of brief schooling who gains fame as a writer, works for a cause, loses faith in it, and finds life without meaning. Though endowed with immense physical energy—he wrote 50 volumes—London drank hard, spent fast, and played out early. While his reputation as a novelist may have declined since his own day, some of his short stories have lasted triumphantly.

William Faulkner

William Faulkner (1897–1962) spent most of his days in Oxford, Mississippi, where he attended the University of Mississippi and where he sewed as postmaster until angry townspeople ejected him because they had failed to receive mail. During World War I he served with the Royal Canadian Air Force and afterward worked as a feature writer for the New Orleans Times-Picayune. Faulkner's private life was a long struggle to stay solvent; even after fame came to him, he had to write Hollywood scripts and teach at the University of Virginia to support himself. The violent comic novel *Sanctuary* (1931) caused a stir and turned a profit, but critics tend most to admire *The Sound and the Fury* (1929) (a tale partially told through the eyes of an idiot), *As I Lay Dying* (1930), *Light in August* (1932), *Absalom, Absalom* (1936), and *The Hamlet* (1940). Beginning with *Sartoris* (1929), Faulkner in his fiction imagines a Mississippi county named Yoknapatawpha and traces the fortunes of several of its families, including the aristocratic Compsons and Sartorises and the white-trash, dollar-grabbing Snopeses, from the Civil War to modern times. His influence on his fellow Southern writers (and others) has been profound. In 1950 he received the Nobel Prize for Literature. Although we think of Faulkner primarily as a novelist, he wrote nearly a hundred short stories. Forty-two of the best are available in his *Collected Stories* (1950).

Edgar Allan Poe

Edgar Allan Poe (1809–1849), orphaned child of traveling actors, was raised by well-off foster parents, John and Frances Allan, in Richmond, Virginia. At eighteen he published his first book of poems. When Poe ran up heavy gambling debts as a student at the University of Virginia, Allan called him home and eventually disowned him. After two years in the army and a brief stay at West Point, Poe became a successful editor in Richmond, Philadelphia, and New York and an industrious contributor to newspapers and magazines. Marriage in 1836 to his thirteen-year-old cousin Virginia Clemm increased his happiness but also his burdens; mercilessly, he drove his pen to support wife, self, and mother-in-law. Virginia, five years an invalid, died of tuberculosis in 1847. Poe, whose tolerance for alcohol was low, increased his drinking. He was found dead on a street in Baltimore.

As a writer, Poe was a true innovator. His bizarre, macabre tales have held generations spellbound, as have some of his highly musical poems ("The Raven," "Annabel Lee"). His tales ("The Murders in the Rue Morgue", "The Purloined Letter") have earned him the title of father of the modern detective story. Other tales and his novel *The Narrative of Arthur Gordon Pym* figure in the history of science fiction. His work has profoundly influenced not only American literature but also European literature through French translations by Charles Baudelaire.

Ernest Hemingway

Ernest Hemingway (1898–1961), born in Oak Park, Illinois, bypassed college to be a cub reporter. In World War I, as an eighteen-year-old volunteer ambulance driver in Italy, he was wounded in action. In 1922 he settled in Paris, then as warm with writers; he later recalled that time in *A Moveable Feast* (1964). Hemingway won swift acclaim for his early stories *In Our Time* (1925), and for his first, perhaps finest, novel, *The Sun Also Rises* (1926), portraying a "lost generation" of postwar American drifters in France and Spain. *For Whom the Bell Tolls* (1940) depicts the life during the Spanish Civil War. Hemingway became a celebrity, often photographed as a marlin fisherman or a lion hunter, and a fan of bullfighting. He wrote two nonfiction books on the subject: *Death in the Afternoon* (1932) and *The Dangerous Summer* (1985). After World War II, with his fourth wife, journalist Mary Welsh, he made his home in Cuba, where he wrote *The Old Man and the Sea* (1952). The Nobel Prize for Literature came to him in 1954. In 1961, mentally distressed and physically ailing, he shot himself. Hemingway brought a hard-bitten realism into American fiction. His heroes live dangerously, by personal codes of honor, courage, and endurance. Hemingway's distinctively crisp, unadorned style left American literature permanently changed.

John Steinbeck

John Steinbeck (1902 – 1968) was born in Salinas, California, where there was a fertile valley he remembered in "The Chrysanthemums". Off and on, he attended Stanford University, then sojourned in New York as a reporter and a bricklayer. After years of struggle to earn his living by fiction, Steinbeck reached a large audience with *Tortilla Flat* (1935), a loosely woven novel portraying Mexican-Americans in Monterey with fondness and sympathy. Great acclaim greeted *The Grapes of Wrath* (1939), the story of a family of Oklahoma farmers who, ruined by dust storms in the 1930s, join a mass migration to California. Like Ernest Hemingway and Stephen Crane, Steinbeck prided himself on his journalism: In World War II, he filed dispatches from battlefronts in Italy and Africa, and in 1966 he wrote a column from South Vietnam. Known widely behind the Iron Curtain, Steinbeck accepted an invitation to visit the Soviet Union, and reported his trip in *A Russian Journal* (1948). In 1962 he became the seventh American to win the Nobel Prize for Literature, but critics have never placed Steinbeck on the same high shelf with Faulkner and Hemingway. He wrote much, not all good, and yet his best work adds to an impressive total. Besides *The Grapes of Wrath*, it includes: *In Dubious Battle* (1936), a novel of an apple-pickers' strike; *Of Mice and Men*, a powerful short novel (also a play) of comradeship between a hobo and a retarded man; *The Log from the Sea of Cortez*, a nonfiction account of a marine biological expedition; and the short stories in *The Long Valley* (1938). Throughout the fiction he wrote in his prime, Steinbeck maintains an appealing sympathy for the poor and downtrodden, the lonely and dispossessed.

D. H. Lawrence

D. H. Lawrence (1885 – 1930) is one of the greatest English novelists of the 20th century, and perhaps, he is the greatest from England proper and from a working-class family. During his life-long literary career, he had written more than ten novels and several volumes of short stories. Besides being a great novelist, Lawrence is also a proficient poet, a combative essayist, an atmospheric travel-writer, and a prolific literary correspondent. Furthermore, he extends his talents to book-reviewing, translation, philosophical discourse and painting. But it is in the novels that his true greatness lies, and on them that his reputation rests.

Lawrence was born in Eastwood, Nottinghamshire, England. His father was a coal miner, his mother a former schoolteacher whose thwarted life and fierce ambition for her son pushed him to struggle up into the world of culture. The anguish of this effort amid family tensions is the subject of the novel *Sons and Lovers* (1913) which established him as a major literary figure. Before World War I he eloped to the Continent with the wife of a Nottingham professor, but spent the war years miserably in England, suspected of disloyalty because his wife was of German origin and oppressed by disgust at what was happening to his country. Through all the years of his maturity he was harassed by efforts to censor his books and paintings. His distaste for the industrialization and commercialism of English life in his time sent him wandering to Italy, Australia, Mexico, and the mountains of New Mexico in search of an alternative.

As he continued to outrage the guardians of public morals—and to reply to them in many of his works with polemic attacks and warnings of the disasters they were brewing—he attracted passionate disciples. His stature as prophet and critic of modern culture has always been a matter of controversy; his explorations of the dark strata of the unconsciousness, his shrewdly intuitive revisions of conventional notion of human motivation, and the vital energy of his style place him unarguably among the greatest poets and novelists of his age. His life has inspired a flood of biographies; his remarkable marriage and his death by tuberculosis in the south of France seem hardly distinguishable from his creations in prose and verse. Some of his best-known novels are *The Rainbow* (1915), *Women in Love* (1920), and *Lady Chatterley's Lover* (1928). His shorter works and poems are most easily found in *The Complete Stories* (1961), *Four Short Novels* (1965), and *The Complete Poems* (1970).

As an original writer, Lawrence tends to introduce psychology into his characterization, and by combining psychic exploration with social criticism he has made an important contribution to the advancement of the English psychological novel. Lawrence's early fiction deals mainly with such themes as the failure of contact, the lack of warmth between people and relationships between men and women, especially those of marriage. In the novels of his later period, Lawrence is deeply concerned with the themes of power, dominance, leadership and the relationships that men form with one another, rather than with women. His novels are characterized with symbolism and complex narrative. Irony, humor and wit are also the typical features of many of his stories.

Stephen Crane

Stephen Crane (1871 – 1900) was born in Newark, New Jersey, a Methodist minister's last and fourteenth child. After flunking out of both Lafayette College and Syracuse University, he became a journalist in New York, specializing in grim life among the down-and-out people in his early self-published novel *Maggie: A Girl of the Streets* (1893). Restlessly generating material for stories, Crane trekked to the Southwest, New Orleans, and Mexico. "The Open Boat" is based on experience. En route to Havana to report the Cuban revolution for the New York Press, Crane was shipwrecked when the SS Commodore sank in heavy seas east of New Smyrna, Florida, on January 2, 1897. He escaped in a ten-foot lifeboat with the captain and two members of the crew. Later that year, Crane moved into a stately home in England with Cora Taylor, former madam of a Florida brothel, hobnobbed with literary greats, and lived beyond his means. Hounded by creditors, afflicted by tuberculosis, he died in Germany at twenty-eight. Crane has been called the first writer of American realism. His famed novel *The Red Badge of Courage* (1895) gives an imagined but convincing account of a young Union soldier's initiation into battle. A handful of his short stories appear immortal. He was an original poet, too, writing terse, sardonic poems in open forms, at the time considered radical. In his short life, Crane greatly helped American literature to come of age.

Katherine Mansfield

Kathleen Mansfield Beauchamp (1888–1923) was born in Wellington, New Zealand, daughter of a respected businessman who was later knighted. In 1903 the family moved to London, where Kathleen and her sisters entered Queen's College, the first institution in England founded expressly for the higher education of women. The family returned to New Zealand, leaving the girls in London, but the Beauchamps brought their daughters home in 1906. By this time Kathleen had written a number of poems, sketches, and stories; and after experimenting with different pen names, she adopted that of Katherine Mansfield. She was restless and ambitious and chafed against the narrowness of middle-class life in New Zealand, at that time still very much a new country in the shadow of the British Empire.

In July 1908 Mansfield left again for London; she never returned to New Zealand. In 1909 she suddenly married G. C. Bowden, a teacher of singing and elocution, but left him the same evening. Shortly afterward she became pregnant by another man and went to Germany to await the birth, but she had a miscarriage there. Her experiences in Germany are told in carefully observed sketches full of ironic detail in her first published book, *In a German Pension* (1911).

In 1910 she briefly resumed life with Bowden, who put her in touch with A. R. Orage, editor of the avant-garde periodical *The New Age*. There she published a number of her stories and sketches. At the end of 1911 she met the critic John Middleton Murry, editor of the modernist magazine *Rhythm*, and eventually married him. She developed intense but conflicted friendships with D. H. Lawrence, Virginia Woolf, and other writers of the day. During all this time Mansfield experimented in technique and refined her art, attempting within the short story to illuminate the ambivalences and complexities of friendship and family, gender and class. The death in World War I in October 1915 of her much-loved younger brother sent her imagination back to their childhood days in New Zealand and in doing so gave a fresh change and significance to her writing. Using her newly developed style with an ever greater subtlety and sensitivity, she now produced her best stories, including "Prelude", "Daughters of the Late Colonel", "At the Bay", and "The Garden Party". With the publication of "The Garden Party" and "other stories" in February 1922, Mansfield's place as a master of the modern short story was ensured. But she was gravely ill with tuberculosis and dies suddenly at the age of thirty-four in Fontainebleau, France, where she had gone to try to find a cure by adopting the methods of the controversial mystic George Ivanovich Gurdjieff.

Mansfield produced her best and most characteristic work in her last years, when she combined incident, image, symbol, and structure in a way comparable with, yet different from, James Joyce's method in *Dubliners*, both writers sharing in the precise and understated art of the Russian writer Anton Chekhov. "Daughters of the Late Colonel", a story of two middle-aged sisters and their devotion to a tyrannical father, shows her working characteristically through suggestion rather than explicit development to illuminate a late-Victorian world, with the subdued elegiac sense of female lives wasted in the service of an outmoded patriarchal order, although the story's ironic surface is restrained comedy. The meaning is achieved through the atmosphere, built up by the accumulation of small strokes, none of which seems more than a shrewdly observed realistic detail. Mansfield also manipulates time masterfully: She makes particularly effective use of the unobtrusive flashback, where we find ourselves in an earlier phase of the action without quite knowing how we got there but fully aware of its relevance to the total action and atmosphere.

Joseph Heller

Joseph Heller (1923–1999), New York author who served in the air force in World War II. Later he received a B. A. from New York University, an M. A. from Columbia, studies at Oxford, and taught briefly before writing *Catch-22* (1961). This grotesquely comic tale of a madcap bombardier's resistance to his fanatic commander's ambition for promotion at the expense of his American squadron on a Mediterranean island satirizes military illogical glorification. It became enormously popular, particularly among younger readers during the Vietnam era, and its title became a catch phrase. More than that, *Catch-22* has come to be seen as a milestone in the history of the American novel: It marked the beginning of a new period, that of the Absurd or postmodernism. Heller's next novel, *Something Happened* (1974), is a dark view of the life of a business executive, disgusted with what he does and is. *Good as Gold* (1979) is a long novel more in the comic vein of his first in its farcical treatment of Jewish family life and of the Washington political scene. *God Knows* (1984) is a lively first-person novel of the Biblical David. *Picture This* (1988) is a novel treating Rembrandt's painting of Aristotle contemplating the bust of Homer that contrasts two eras. In 1994 appeared *Closing Time*, a sequel to *Catch-22*, with Yossarian, twice divorced, living alone in Manhattan with the knowledge that this time he can in no way outwit death. The novel's main character, however, is one Sammy Singer, whose life affirms marriage as the best of all possible worlds. He collaborated with Speed Vogel on *No Laughing Matter* (1986), a serious treatment, though sometimes humorous, of Heller's sudden paralytic sadness. Much earlier he wrote two plays, *We Bombed in New Haven* (1968) and *Clevinger's Trial* (1974).

James Joyce

James Joyce (1882–1941) is one of the most prominent English literary figures of the first half of the 20th century. In complicated artistic genius, Joyce has created a body of work worthy of comparison with the other masterpieces of English literature. Many critics feel that his virtuoso experiments in writing have recreated the form of modern novel. His mastery of the English language is also highly praised.

Joyce was born in Dublin, and though he fled the narrowness of Catholic Ireland for the broader cultural horizons of Europe, the Dublin of his experience and imagination was the setting for all his major work. In 1904 he went to live permanently on the Continent, supporting himself—badly—by teaching in language schools in Trieste and Zurich. The fear of censorship, coupled with the timidity of his publisher, delayed until

1914 the publication of his short stories in *Dubliners*. Soon after this, however, Joyce came to the attention of the energetic American poet Ezra Pound, who arranged for the first publication of *A Portrait of the Artist as a Young Man* (1916), Joyce's semi-autobiographical novel. Pound's support continued through the following years while Joyce was writing what is generally acknowledged as his masterpiece, the novel *Ulysses* (1922). When parts of it began to appear in a literary magazine, it touched off a storm of controversy that brought him both notoriety and lasting fame. On the one hand, this work experimented more boldly with language and devices of narration, including the use of the stream of consciousness, than any work in English that preceded it. On the other hand, some of the sexual passages were so candid that censors banned it from the United States until 1933. Joyce's experiments with language reached their height in *Finnegans Wake* (1939), which takes one step further the new type of language that Joyce was starting to create in *Ulysses*; here, not only the sentences are mixed up but also the forms of the words themselves. Again, Joyce uses references to ancient stories to express the themes of the nature of creation. The difficulty of the language, in which Joyce is forcing as many associations as possible into each word, gives many readers great problems of understanding.

Joyce is a self-conscious and self-prepared artist. When he was still in the college, he decided to devote his whole life to art. To enrich his knowledge, Joyce read widely in history, philosophy, aesthetics, mythology and popular sciences, especially medicine and psychology, as well as literature. His long search of his identity, his resolute fight for freedom and independence, his conscientious accumulation of knowledge all aimed to this direction. To be an artist, he absorbed the quintessence from the important thinkers in European history. He derived much of his aesthetic theory from Aristotle, Aquinas and Bergson; the elements of naturalism in his works came from Flaubert and Ibsen; and he was strongly influenced by Vico's theory of history, Nietzshe's atheism and nihilism, and Freud's psychoanalysis.

Joyce is concerned with the themes of the artist and the nature of the art of artistic creation, the humor and tragedy of human life, and also about the relationship between mind and body, especially when the author is attempting to show all the half-formed thoughts that go through the characters' minds. In his writings, Joyce likes to use references to ancient stories and adopts a completely new style of writing which allows the reader to move inside the minds of the characters, and presents their thoughts and feelings on a continuous dream. This style is known as "interior monologue" or "stream of consciousness" and it has had a powerful influence on the works of many other modernist writers.

Eugene O'Neill

Eugene O'Neill (1888–1953), unquestionably America's greatest playwright, and only one ever to receive the Nobel Prize, was the son of a celebrated romantic actor in a traveling theatre company, best-known for his role as the Count of Monte Cristo. Eugene happened to be born in New York while his father was performing there. He spent his childhood on trains, in hotels or backstage in theatres. While he got older, he was sent to Catholic boarding schools, which he hated. In 1906 he entered Princeton University, but he only stayed there for one year. He left there because he wanted to experience life, which he called "real education".

He became a seaman, and for five years he traveled all over the world, working at all sorts of hard jobs in many different countries. All the time, he observed and learned about the life of rough, uneducated workers, brooding about the various walks which fate played in their lives. In the winter of 1912, he entered a hospital in America with tuberculosis. During the five months of his recovery, he read a wide range of dramatic literature, especially Chekov, Ibsen and Strindberg. His illness forced him to reflect on his life's purpose. He decided to become a playwright with such conviction that he looked on this decision as a "rebirth".

He began by writing one-act plays, nearly all of them concerned with the life of seamen. In 1920 his first full-length play was produced on Broadway, where America's foremost plays are presented. During the next fifteen years he wrote almost 20 long plays and many short ones. In 1936, he was awarded the Nobel Prize for Literature. Then his energy flagged and he did not produce another play until 1946, one of his most pessimistic works.

O'Neill's own life was full of tragedy. He was married three times, the first two marriages ending in divorce and bitterness. His oldest son committed suicide. His younger son suffered from mental illness. His only, beloved daughter, Oona, incurred her father's everlasting anger in 1943 when, at the age of 18, she insisted on marrying Charlie Chaplin who was then 54 years old, and had been married three times before. O'Neill never spoke to his daughter again, from that time until his death ten years later. In the last years of his life he became ill with Parkinson's disease, which tortured him as to influence his writing a cycle of 11 plays. He finally died in 1953 in a hotel room.

In all his life, O'Neill was constantly experimenting with new styles and forms for his plays. About 20 of O'Neill's plays are considered as major works. The following are among the very best-known: *The Emperor Jones* (1920), *The Hairy Ape* (1922), *Desire under the Elms* (1924), *Mourning Becomes Electra* (1931), *The Iceman Cometh* (1946), *Long Day's Journey into Night* (1956).

Oscar Wilde

Oscar Wilde (1854–1900) was the representative of the aesthetic movement, which appeared on the literary scene of England in the late Victorian period. Wilde was an Irish dramatist, poet, novelist and essayist. He was born in Dublin and received education first at Trinity College, and later at Oxford University. At Oxford he was notorious for his style of life. He was a disciple of Walter Pater. He regarded capitalist society as some evil force which suffocated the talent of artists. He was a professed "socialist". In his essay "The Soul of Man under Socialism" (1891), he argues that only in "socialist" society where all property is held in common can every person fully develop his individualism and can art prosper. Claiming himself a "socialist", he is far from socialism, though in his essays and books he showed sympathy for the poor. From the eighties and nineties, Wilde wrote and published all his major works, which include two collections of fairy stories (*The Happy Prince and Other Tales*, 1888; *A House of Pomegranates*, 1891), a collection of short stories (*Lord Arthur Savile's Crime and Other Stories*), a series of critical essays (*Intentions*, 1891), his only novel *The Picture of Dorian Gray* (1891), his four comedies (*Lady Windermere's Fan*, 1893; *A Woman of No Importance*, 1894; *An Ideal Husband* and *The Importance of Being Earnest*, 1895), and one tragedy *Salome* (written originally in French and published in English translation with Aubrey Beardsley's illustrations in 1894). In May 1895, when Wilde rose to the summit of his fame, he was sentenced to two years' hard labor on a charge of immoral conduct. While in prison, he wrote a prose work, "De Profundis" (published in 1905). After release, he went to France, where he wrote his last work, "The Ballad of Reading Gaol" (1898) and then died suddenly in 1900.

Tom Stoppard

Tom Stoppard (1937–), dramatist, born in Czechoslovakia; his family moved to Singapore in 1939, where his father, Dr. Eugene Straussler, was killed, and he subsequently, on settling in England after the war, took his English stepfather's name. He left school at 17 and worked as a journalist before his first play, *A Walk on the Water*, was televised in 1963 (staged in London in 1968 as *Enter a Free Man*). He published a novel, *Lord Malquist and the Moon* (1965) and in 1966 his play *Rosencrantz and Guildenstern Are Dead* attracted much attention. This was followed by many witty and inventive plays: *The Real Inspector Hound* (1968, a play-within-a-play which parodies the conventions of the stage thriller), *Jumpers* (1972), *Travesties* (1974), *Dirty Linen* (1976, a satire of political life and parliamentary misdemeanours), *Every Good Boy Deserves Favour* (1977, about a political dissident in a Soviet psychiatric hospital), *Night and Day* (1978, about the dangers of the "closed shop" in journalism), *The Real Thing* (1982, a marital tragicomedy), *Arcadia* (1993, set in a country house in 1809) and *Indian Ink* (1995, an exploration of cultural identity). *The Invention of Love* (1997) presents, through the contrasted fates of A. E. Housman and Oscar Wilde, the sexual complexities of the Aesthetic movement, and the conflicts between art and scholarship.

Stoppard has also written many works for film, radio, and television, including *Professional Foul* (TV, 1977), set in Prague, which portrays the concurrent visits of an English philosopher and an English football team, and dramatizes the inner conflicts of the philosopher, caught between the abstraction of his own discipline and the realities of a regime which stifles free intellectual exchange. Stoppard's work displays a metaphysical wit, a strong theatrical sense and a talent for pastiche which enables him to move from mode to mode within the same scene with great flexibility and rapidity; yet the plays appear far from frivolous in intention, increasingly posing (though not always choosing to solve) considerable ethical problems.

Arthur Miller

Arthur Miller (1915–2005) was born into a lower-income Jewish family in New York's Harlem but grew up in Brooklyn. He studied play writing at the University of Michigan, later wrote radio scripts, and in World War II worked as a steamfitter. His first play, *Man Who Had All the Luck* (1944), treats an auto mechanic whose success in marriage and business is the result of work and care, and was followed by a nondramatic work of reportage, *Situation Normal* (1944), about military life at army bases, and *Focus* (1945), a novel about anti-Semitism. He returned to the drama with *All My Sons* (1947), about a manufacture whose defective airplane parts cause the death of his son and other aviators in wartime. His most impressive play is *Death of a Salesman* (1949, Pulitzer Prize), fusing realism and symbolism in reviewing the tragic life of a salesman victimized by his own false values and those of modern America. It was followed by *The Crucible* (1953), treating the Salem witch trials of 1692 as a parable for America during the era of McCarthyism, as the play probes into problems of individual conscience and guilt by association. *A View from the Bridge* (1953, Pulitzer Prize) presents two Italian longshoremen illegally in the US and *A Memory of Two Mondays*, another short play included with it in production and publication, presents varied views of workers in a Manhattan warehouse. *The Misfits* (1961), a so-called cinema-novel, that is, fiction based on what the camera can see, is actually the script of a motion picture for his wife Marilyn Monroe, which deals with a beautiful woman in Nevada for a divorce who falls in with three men who herd old horses for slaughter and

of her emotional relations with the men and feelings for the animals. *After the Fall* (1964) is a play in two long acts in which the quasi-autobiographical protagonist seeks self-knowledge, a sense of the meaning of his past and his meaning for his future as he reviews his marriages and other major experiences. *Incident at Vichy* (1965), a short play, concerns the Nazis in 1942. *The Price* (1968) is a play contrasting two brothers' views and ways of life as they meet after long separation to dispose of their parents' possessions. Later plays include: *The American Clock* (1980), dealing with the Great Depression; *Elegy for a Lady and Some Kind of Love*, two one-act plays both presented in 1982; *I Can't Remember Anything* and *Clara*, two more one-act plays that were produced together in 1987 as *Danger: Memory!* in 1990 a screenplay, *Everybody Wins*, was published. *The Last Yankee* was produced in 1993, a 70-minute one-acter set in a state mental institution that may be a metaphor for the USA in decline on all fronts—physical, moral, intellectual. In *Broken Glass* (1994), Miller attempts to connect the troubled lives of a middle-aged Brooklyn Jewish couple and the wife's mysterious paralysis to the hysteria sweeping over Germany in 1938. *I Don't Need You Anymore* (1967) collects nine stories, including "The Misfits"; *The Creation of the World and Other Business* (1972) is a serio-comic treatment of the book of Genesis; *Theater Essays* (1978) includes interviews. With his wife Inge Morath, a photographer, he has created books of text and pictures: *In Russia* (1969), *In the Country* (1977), set in rural Connecticut, and *Chinese Encounters* (1979). *Salesman in Beijing* (1984) is an account of producing his play in China in 1983. He made an adaption of Ibsen's *An Enemy of the People* (1951). In 1987 his full autobiography *Timebends*, was published.

Appendix 2

Reference Guide for Citations

Here is a summary of the types of citations students are likely to need for their writings of academic essays. The format follows the current MLA standards for Works Cited lists.

Books

No Author Listed

A Keepsake Anthology of the Fiftieth Anniversary Celebration of the Consultantship in Poetry. Washington: Library of Congress, 1987.

One Author

Middlebrook, Diane Wood. *Anne Sexton: A Biography.* Boston: Houghton, 1991.

Two or Three Authors

Jarman, Mark & Robert McDowell. *The Reaper Essays.* Brownsville, OR: Story Line, 1996.

Four or More Authors

Phillips, Rodney, et al. *The Hand of the Poet.* New York: Rizzoli, 1997.

Two Books by the Same Author

Bawer, Bruce. *The Aspect of Eternity.* St. Paul: Graywolf, 1993.

———. *Diminishing Fictions: Essays on the Modern American Novel and Its Critics.* St. Paul: Graywolf, 1988.

Corporate Author

Poets & Writers. *A Writer's Guide to Copyright.* New York: Poets & Writers, 1979.

Author and Editor

Shakespeare, William. *The Sonnets.* Ed. G. Blakemore Evans. Cambridge, Eng. : Cambridge UP, 1996.

One Editor

Monteiro, George (ed.) *Conversations with Elizabeth Bishop.* Jackson: UP of Mississippi, 1996.

Two Editors

Craig, David & Janet McCann (eds.) *Odd Angles of Heaven: Contemporary Poetry by People of Faith.* Wheaton, IL: Shaw, 1994.

Translation

Chekhov, Anton. *Selected Stories.* Trans. Ann Dunnigan. New York: Signet, 1960.

Introduction, Preface, Foreword, or Afterword

Thwaite, Anthony. Preface. *Contemporary Poets.* (6th ed.) Ed. Thomas Riggs. New York: St. James, 1996: vii – viii.

Lapham, Lewis. Introduction. *Understanding Media: The Extensions of Man.* By Marshall McLuhan. Cambridge: MIT P, 1994: vi – x.

Work in an Anthology

Alien, Dick. "The Emperor's New Clothes". *Poetry After Modernism.* Ed. Robert

McDowell. Brownsville, OR: Story Line, 1991: 71-99.

Translation in an Anthology

Neruda, Pablo. "We Are Many". Trans. Alastair Reid. *Literature: An Introduction to Fiction, Poetry, and Drama*. (8th ed.) Eds. X. J. Kennedy & Dana Gioia. New York: Longman, 2002: 1066.

Multivolume Work

Wellek, Rene. *A History of Modern Criticism, 1750-1950*. Vol. 7. New Haven: Yale UP, 1991. 8 vols. 1955-1992.

Book in a Series

Ross, William T. *Weldon Kees*. Twayne's US Authors Ser. 484. Boston: Twayne, 1985.

Republished Book

Ellison, Ralph. *Invisible Man*. New York: Vintage, 1995.

Revised or Subsequent Editions

Janouch, Gustav. *Conversations with Kafka*. Trans. Goronwy Rees. Revis ed. New York: New Directions, 1971.

Reference Books

Signed Article

McPhillips, Robert. "Timothy Steele". *The Oxford Companion to Twentieth-Century Poetry in English*. Ed. Ian Hamilton. Oxford: Oxford UP, 1994.

Unsigned Encyclopedia Article—Standard Reference Book

"James Dickey". *The New Encyclopaedia Britannica-Micropaedia* (15th ed.). 1987.

Dictionary Entry

"Design". *Merriam-Webster's Collegiate Dictionary* (10th ed.). 1993.

Periodicals

Journal with Continuous Paging

Balee, Susan. "Flannery O'Connor Resurrected". *Hudson Review*,1994,47: 377-393.

Journal with Pages Each Issue Separately

Salter, Mary Jo. "The Heart Is Slow to Learn". *New Criterion*, 1992,10(8): 23–29.

Signed Magazine Article

Gioia, Dana. "Studying with Miss Bishop". *New Yorker*, 5 Sept. 1986: 90–101.

Unsigned Magazine Article

"The Real Test". *New Republic*, 5 Feb. 2001: 7.

Newspaper Article

Lyall, Sarah. "In Poetry, Ted Hughes Breaks His Silence on Sylvia Plath". *New York Times*, 19 Jan. 1998.

Signed Book Review

Harper, John. "Well-Grafted Tales with Tabloid Titles". Rev. of *Tabloid Dreams*, by Robert Olen Butler. *Orlando Sentinel*, 15 Dec. 1996: D4.

Unsigned, Untitled Book Review

Rev. of *Otherwise: New and Selected Poems*, by Jane Kenyon. *Virginia Quarterly Review*, 1996, 72: 136.

CD-ROM Reference Works

Periodically Published Information, Collected on CD-ROM

Kakutani, Michiko. "Slogging Surreally in the Vietnamese Jungle". Rev of *The Things They Carried*, by Tim O'Brien. [*New York Times*, 6 Mar. 1990], late ed.: C 21. *New York Times on Disc*. CD-ROM. UMI-Proquest. Oct. 1993.

CD-ROM Publication

"Appall". *The Oxford English Dictionary* (2nd ed.). CD-ROM. Oxford: Oxford UP, 1992.

Online Databases

Online Scholarly Project

Voice of the Shuttle. Ed. Alan Liu. 1 Jan. 2001. U of California, Santa Barbara. 6 Feb. 2001. <http://vos.ucsb.edu/>.

Online Reference Database

Encyclopaedia Britannica Online. Vers. 99.1. Dec. 2000. Encyclopaedia Britannica. 15 Feb. 2001. <http://www.eb.com/>.

Online Professional Site

Wallace Stegner Environmental Center. San Francisco Public Library. 18 Feb. 2001. <http://sfpl.lib.ca.us/stegner/wallace.html>.

Online Book

Whitman, Walt. *Leaves of Grass*. [1892] 15 Mar. 2001. <http://www.bibliomania.com/Poetry/Whitman/Grass/>.

Article in Online Scholarly Journal

Hoffman, Tyler B. "Emily Dickinson and the Limit of War". *Emily Dickinson Journal* 3.2 (1994). 15 Mar. 2001. <http://www.colorado.edu/EDIS/journal/articles/III.2.Hoffman.html>.

Article in Online Newspaper

Koehler, Robert. "Latino Perspective Takes Center Stage". *Los Angeles Times Web Site* 31 July 1993. 15 Mar. 2001. <http://www.latimes.com/HOME/ARCHIVES/>.

Article Accessed via Computer Service

Bray, Rosemary L. "Renaissance for a Pioneer of Black Pride". *New York Times* 4 Feb. 1990, late ed., sec. 2: 7. *New York Times Online*. Nexis. 1 Mar. 1998.

Article in Online Magazine

Garner, Dwight. "The Salon Interview: Jamaica Kincaid". *Salon* 13 Jan. 1996. 1 Mar. 2001. <http://www.salonmagazine.com/05/features/kincaid.html>.

Review in Online Newspaper

Hollander, John. "The Fluent Mundo". Rev. of *Wallace Stevens: Collected Poetry and Prose*, by Wallace Stevens. *Los Angeles Times Web Site*. 16 Nov. 1997. 14 Mar. 1998. <http://www.latimes.com/HOME/ARCHIVES/>.

Online Posting

Grossenbacher, Laura. "Comments about the Ending Illustration". 4 Sept. 1996. Online posting. *The Yellow Wallpaper Site*. 14 Mar. 2001. <http://www:cwrl.utexas.edu/~daniel/amlit/wallpaper/readcomments.html>.

Audio Recordings

Roethke, Theodore. *Theodore Roethke Reads His Poetry*. Audiocassette. Caedmon, 1972.

Film

Hamlet. By William Shakespeare. Dir. Franco Zeffirelli. Perf. Mel Gibson, Glenn

Close, Helena Bonham Carter, Alan Bates, and Paul Scofield. Warner, 1991.

Television Program

Moby Dick. By Herman Melville. Dir. Franc Roddam. Perf. Patrick Stewart and Gregory Peck. 2 episodes. USA Network. 16–17 Mar. 1998.

Videocassette

Henry V. By William Shakespeare. Dir. Laurence Olivier. Perf. Laurence Olivier. 1944. Videocassette. Paramount, 1988.

Appendix 3

Glossary of Literary Terms

Allegory: A narrative in verse or prose in which the literal events (persons, places, and things) consistently point to a parallel sequence of symbolic ideas. This narrative strategy is often used to dramatize abstract ideas, historical events, religious systems, or political issues. An allegory has two levels of meaning: a literal level that tells a surface story and a symbolic level in which the abstract ideas unfold. The names of allegorical characters often hint at their symbolic roles.

Alliteration: The repetition of two or more consonant sounds in successive words in a line of verse or prose.

Allusion: A brief (and sometimes indirect) reference in a text to a person, place, or thing—fictitious or actual.

Anapest: A metrical foot in verse in which two unstressed syllables are followed by a stressed syllable.

Anecdote: A short narrative usually consisting of a single incident or episode. Often humorous, anecdotes can be real or fictional. When they appear within a larger narrative as a brief story told by one character to another, the author usually employs them to reveal something significant to the larger narrative.

Antagonist: The most significant character or force that opposes the protagonist in a narrative or drama. The antagonist may be another character, society itself, a force of nature, or even—in modern literature—conflicting impulses within the protagonist.

Anticlimax: An unsatisfying and trivial turn of events in a literary work that occurs in place of a genuine climax.

Antihero: A protagonist who is lacking in one or more of the conventional qualities attributed to a hero. Instead of being dignified, brave, idealistic, or purposeful, for instance, the antihero may be buffoonish, cowardly, self-interested, or weak. The antihero is often considered an essentially modern form of characterization, a satiric or frankly realistic commentary on traditional portrayals of idealized heroes or heroines.

Antithesis: Words, phrases, clauses, or sentences set in deliberate contrast to one another.

Apostrophe: A direct address to someone or something. In poetry an apostrophe often addresses something not ordinarily spoken to (e.g., "O mountain!").

Archetype: A recurring symbol, character, landscape, or event found in myth and literature across different cultures and eras. The idea of the archetype came into literary criticism from the Swiss psychologist Carl Jung who believed that all individuals share a "collective unconscious", a set of primal memories common to the human race that exists in our subconscious.

Aside: In drama a few words or short passage spoken in an undertone or to the audience. By convention, other characters onstage are deaf to the aside.

Assonance: The repetition of two or more vowel sounds in successive words, which creates a kind of rhyme.

Atmosphere: The dominant mood or feeling that pervades all or part of a literary work.

Auditory imagery: A word or sequence of words that refers to the sense of hearing.

Ballad: Traditionally, a song that tells a story. The ballad was originally an oral verse form—sung or recited and transmitted from performer to performer without being written down. Ballads are characteristically compressed, dramatic, and objective in their narrative style. There are many variations to the ballad form, most consisting of quatrains (made up of lines of three or four metrical feet) in a simple rhyme scheme. (*See also* Ballad stanza.)

Ballad stanza: The most common pattern of ballad makers consists of four lines rhymed *abcb*, in which the first and third lines have four metrical feet and the second and fourth lines have three feet (4, 3, 4, 3).

Bildungsroman: German for "novel of growth and development". Sometimes called an **apprenticeship novel**, this genre depicts a youth who struggles toward maturity, forming a worldview or philosophy of life. Dickens's *David Copperfield* and Joyce's *Portrait of the Artist as a Young Man* are classic examples of the genre.

Biography: A factual account of a person's life, examining all available information or texts relevant to the subject.

Blank verse: The most common and well-known meter of unrhymed poetry in English. Blank verse contains five iambic feet per line and is never rhymed.

Characterization: The techniques a writer uses to create, reveal, or develop the characters in a narrative.

Climax: The moment of greatest intensity in a story, which almost inevitably occurs toward the end of the work. The climax often takes the form of a decisive confrontation between the protagonist and antagonist. In a conventional story, the climax is followed by the resolution or denouement in which the effects and results of the climactic action are presented.

Closet drama: A play or dramatic poem designed to be read aloud rather than performed.

Comedy: A literary work aimed at amusing an audience. Comedy is one of the basic modes of storytelling and can be adapted to most literary forms—from poetry to film.

Conceit: A poetic device using elaborate comparisons, such as equating a loved one with the graces and beauties of the world.

Connotation: An association or additional meaning that a word, image, or phrase may carry, apart from its literal denotation or dictionary definition. A word picks up connotations from all the uses to which it has been put in the past. For example, an owl in literature is not merely the literal bird. It also carries the many associations (connotations, that is) attached to it.

Consonance: Also called **Slant rhyme**. A kind of rhyme in which the linked words share similar consonant sounds but different vowel sounds, as in *reason* and *raisin*, *mink* and *monk*. Sometimes only the final consonant sound is identical, as in *fame* and *room*, *crack* and *truck*. Used mostly by modern poets, consonance often registers more subtly than exact rhyme, lending itself to special poetic effects.

Convention: Any established feature or technique in literature that is commonly understood by both authors and readers.

Couplet: A two-line stanza in poetry, usually rhymed, which tends to have lines of equal length.

Crisis: The point in a drama when the crucial action, decision, or realization must be made, marking the turning point or reversal of the protagonist's fortunes.

Dialogue: The direct representation of the conversation between two or more characters.

Drama: Derived from the Greek *dran*, "to do", *drama* means "action" or "deed". Drama is the form of literary composition designed for performance in the theater, in which actors take the roles of the characters, perform the indicated action, and speak the written dialogue.

Dramatic irony: A special kind of suspenseful expectation, when the audience or reader understands the implication and meaning of a situation onstage and foresees the oncoming disaster (in tragedy) or triumph (in comedy) but the character does not. The irony forms between the contrasting levels of knowledge of the character and the audience.

Dramatic monologue: A poem written as a speech made by a character at some decisive moment.

Elegy: A lament or a sadly meditative poem, often written on the occasion of a death or other solemn theme.

English sonnet: Also called **Shakespearean sonnet**. The English sonnet has a rhyme scheme organized into three quatrains with a final couplet: *abab cdcd efef gg*. The poem may turn, that is, shift in mood or tone, between any of the quatrains (although it usually occurs on the ninth line).

Envoy: A short, often summarizing stanza that appears at the end of certain poetic forms.

Epic: A long narrative poem usually composed in an elevated style tracing the adventures of a legendary or mythic hero. Epics are usually written in a consistent form and meter throughout.

Epigram: A very short poem, often comic, usually ending with some sharp turn of wit or meaning.

Epigraph: A brief quotation preceding a story or other literary works. An epigraph usually suggests the subject, theme, or atmosphere the story will explore.

Epiphany: A moment of insight, discovery, or revelation by which a character's life is greatly altered. An epiphany generally occurs near the end of a story. The term, which means "showing forth" in Greek, was first used in Christian theology to signify the manifestation of God's presence in the world. This theological idea was first borrowed by James Joyce to refer to a heightened moment of secular revelation.

Episode: An incident in a large narrative that has unity in itself. An episode may bear close relation to the central narrative, but it can also be a digression.

Episodic plot/structure: A form of plotting where the individual scenes and events are presented chronologically without any profound sense of cause-and-effect relationship. In an episodic narrative the placement of many scenes could be changed without greatly altering the overall effect of the work.

Epistolary novel: Novel in which the story is told by way of letters written by one or more of the characters. This form often lends an authenticity to the story, a sense that the author may have discovered these letters; but in fact they are a product of the author's invention.

Euphony: The harmonious effect when the sounds of the words connect with the meaning in a way pleasing to the ear and mind.

Explication: Literally, an "unfolding". In an explication an entire poem is explained in detail, addressing every element and unraveling any complexities as a means of analysis.

Exposition: The opening portion of a narrative or drama. In the exposition, the scene is set, the protagonist is introduced, and the author discloses any other background information necessary to allow the reader to understand and relate to the events that are to follow.

Expressionism: A dramatic style developed between 1910 and 1924 in Germany in reaction against realism's focus on surface details and external reality. To draw an audience into a dreamlike subjective realm, expressionistic artistic styles used episodic plots, distorted lines, exaggerated shapes, abnormally intense coloring, mechanical physical movement, and telegraphic speech (the broken syntax of a disordered psyche). Staging the contents of the unconscious, expressionist plays ranged from Utopian visions of a fallen, materialistic world redeemed by the spirituality of "new men" to pessimistic nightmare visions of universal catastrophe.

Eye rhyme: Rhyme in which the spelling of the words appears alike, but the pronunciations differ, as in *laughter* and *daughter*, *idea* and *flea*.

Fable: A brief, often humorous narrative told to illustrate a moral. The characters in fables are traditionally animals whose personality traits symbolize human traits. Particular animals have conventionally come to represent specific human qualities or values. For example, the ant represents industry, the fox craftiness, and the lion nobility. A fable often concludes by summarizing its moral message in abstract terms.

Fairy tale: A traditional form of short narrative folklore, originally transmitted orally, which features supernatural characters such as witches, giants, fairies, or animals with human personality traits. Fairy tales often feature a hero or heroine who seems destined to achieve some desirable fate—such as marrying a prince or princess, becoming wealthy, or destroying an enemy.

Falling action: The events in a narrative that follow the climax and bring the story to its conclusion, or denouement.

Fantasy: A narrative that depicts events, characters, or places that could not exist in the real world. Fantasy has limited interest in portraying experience realistically. Instead, it freely pursues the possibilities of the imagination. Fantasy usually includes elements of magic or the supernatural. Sometimes it is used to illustrate a moral message as in fables. Fantasy is a type of romance that emphasizes wish fulfillment (or nightmare fulfillment) instead of verisimilitude.

Farce: A type of comedy featuring exaggerated character types in ludicrous and improbable situations, provoking belly laughs with sexual mix-ups, crude verbal jokes, pratfalls, and knockabout horseplay.

Fiction: From the Latin *ficio*, "act of fashioning, a shaping, a making". Fiction refers to any literary work that—although it might contain factual information—is not bound by factual accuracy, but creates a narrative shaped or made up by the author's imagination. Nonfiction, as the name suggests, is a category conventionally separate from fiction.

Figure of speech: An expression or comparison that relies not on its literal meaning, but rather on its connotations and suggestions.

First-person narrator: A story in which the narrator is a participant in the action. Such a narrator refers to himself or herself as "I" and may be a major or minor character in the story. His or her attitude and understanding of characters and events shapes the reader's perception of the story being told.

Flashback: A scene relived in a character's memory. Flashbacks can be related by the narrator in a summary or they can be experienced by the characters themselves. Flashbacks allow the author to include events that occurred before the opening of the story, which may show the reader something significant that happened in the character's past or give an indication of what kind of person the character used to be.

Flat character: A term coined by English novelist E. M. Forster to describe a character with only one outstanding trait. Flat characters are rarely the central characters in a narrative and are often based on stock characters. Flat characters stay the same throughout a story.

Folklore: The body of traditional wisdom and customs—including songs, stories, myths, and proverbs—of a people as collected and continued through oral tradition.

Folktale: A short narrative drawn from folklore that has been passed down through an oral tradition.

Foot: The unit of measurement in metrical poetry. Different meters are identified by the pattern and order of stressed and unstressed syllables in their foot, usually containing two or three syllables, with one syllable accented.

Foreshadowing: In plot construction, the technique of arranging events and information in such a way that later events are prepared for, or shadowed, beforehand. The author may introduce specific words, images, or actions in order to suggest significant later events. The effective use of foreshadowing by an author may prevent a story's outcome from seeming haphazard or contrived.

Free verse: From the French *vers libre*. Free verse describes poetry that organizes its lines without meter. It may be rhymed (as in some poems by H. D.), but it usually is not.

Genre: A conventional combination of literary form and subject matter, usually aimed at creating certain effects. A genre implies a preexisting understanding between the artist and the reader about the purpose and rules of the work. A horror story, for example, combines the form of the short story with certain conventional subjects, style, and theme with the expectation of frightening the reader. Major short story genres include science fiction, gothic, horror, and detective tales.

Gothic fiction: A genre that creates terror and suspense, usually set in an isolated castle, mansion, or monastery populated by mysterious or threatening individuals. The Gothic form, invented by Horace Walpole in *The Castle of Otranto* (1764), has flourished in one form or another ever since. The term *Gothic* is also applied to medieval architecture, and Gothic fiction almost inevitably exploits claustrophobic interior architecture in its plotting—often featuring dungeons, crypts, torture chambers, locked rooms, and secret passageways. In the 19th century, writers such as Nathaniel Hawthorne, Edgar Allan Poe, and Charlotte Perkins Gilman brought the genre into the mainstream of American fiction.

Hero: The central character in a narrative.

Heroic couplet: A pair of lines in iambic pentameter that rhyme.

Hexameter: A verse meter consisting of six metrical feet, or six primary stresses, per line.

Iamb: A metrical foot in verse in which an unaccented syllable is followed by an accented one. The iambic measure is the most common meter used in English poetry.

Iambic meter: A verse meter consisting of a specific recurring number of iambic feet per line.

Iambic pentameter: The most common meter in English verse—five iambic feet per line. Many fixed forms, such as the sonnet and heroic couplets, are written in iambic pentameter. Unrhymed iambic pentameter is called **blank verse.**

Image: A word or series of words that refers to any sensory experience (usually sight, although also sound, smell, touch, or taste). An image is a direct or literal recreation of physical experience and adds immediacy to literary language.

Imagery: The collective set of images in a poem or other literary works.

Impartial omniscience: Refers to an omniscient narrator who, although he or she presents the thoughts and actions of the characters, does not judge them or comment on them.

Implied metaphor: A metaphor that uses neither connectives nor the verb to be.

Impressionism: In fiction, a style of writing that emphasizes external events less than the impression those events make on the narrator or protagonist.

Interior monologue: An extended presentation of a character's thoughts in a narrative. Usually written in the present tense and printed without quotation marks, an interior monologue reads as if the character was speaking aloud to himself or herself, for the readers to overhear.

Irony: A literary device in which a discrepancy of meaning is masked beneath the surface of the language. Irony is present when a writer says one thing but means something quite the opposite. There are many kinds of irony, but the two major varieties are verbal irony (in which the discrepancy is contained in words) and situational irony (in which the discrepancy exists when something is about to happen to a character or characters who expect the opposite outcome).

Italian sonnet: Also called **Petrarchan sonnet**, a sonnet with the following rhyme pattern for the first eight lines (the octave): *abba, abba*; the final six lines (the **sestet**) may follow any pattern of rhymes, as long as it does not end in a couplet. The poem traditionally turns, or shifts in mood or tone, after the octave.

Katharsis, catharsis: Often translated as purgation or purification, the term is drawn from the last element of Aristotle's definition of tragedy, relating to the final cause or purpose of tragic art. Catharsis generally refers to the feeling of emotional release or calm the spectator feels at the end of tragedy. In Aristotle katharsis is the final effect of the playwright's skillful use of plotting, character, and poetry to elicit pity and fear from the audience. Through katharsis, drama taught the audience compassion for the vulnerabilities of others and schooled it in justice and other civic virtues.

Legend: A traditional narrative handed down through popular oral tradition to illustrate and celebrate a remarkable character, an important event, or to explain the unexplainable. Legends, unlike other folktales, claim to be true and usually take place in real locations, often with genuine historical figures.

Limited omniscience: Also called third-person limited point of view. A type of point of view in which the narrator sees into the minds of some but not all of the characters. Most typically, limited omniscience sees through the eyes of one major or minor character. In limited omniscience, the author can compromise between the immediacy of first-person narration and the mobility of third person.

Literary ballad: Ballad not meant for singing, written for literate readers by sophisticated poets rather than arising from the anonymous oral tradition.

Literary epic: A crafted imitation of the oral folk epic written by an author living in a society where writing has been invented. Examples of the literary epic are *The Aeneid* by Virgil and *The Divine Comedy* by Dante Alighieri.

Local color: The use of specific regional material—unique customs, dress, habits, and speech patterns of ordinary people—to create atmosphere or realism in a literary work.

Locale: The location where a story takes place.

Low comedy: A comic style arousing laughter through jokes, slapstick humor, sight gags, and boisterous clowning. Unlike high comedy, it has little intellectual appeal. (*See also* Comedy.)

Lyric: A short poem expressing the thoughts and feelings of a single speaker. Often written in the first person, lyric poetry traditionally has a songlike immediacy and emotional force.

Magic Realism: Also called **Magical Realism**. A type of contemporary narrative in which the magical and the mundane are mixed in an overall context of realistic storytelling. The term was coined by Cuban novelist Alejo Carpentier in 1949 to describe the matter-of-fact combination of the fantastic and every day in Latin American fiction. Magic Realism has become the standard name for an international trend in contemporary fiction such as Gabriel Garcia Marquez's *One Hundred Years of Solitude.*

Masks: In Latin, *personae.* In classical Greek theater, full facial masks made of leather, linen, or light wood, with headdress, allowed male actors to embody the conventionalized characters (or *dramatis personae*) of the tragic and comic stage. Later, in the 17th and 18th centuries, stock characters of the ***commedia dell' arte*** wore characteristic half masks made of leather.

Melodrama: Originally a stage play featuring background music and sometimes songs to underscore the emotional mood of each scene. Melodramas were notoriously weak in characterization and motivation but famously strong on action, suspense, and passion. Melodramatic characters were stereotyped villains, heroes, and young lovers. When the term *melodrama* is applied to fiction, it is almost inevitably a negative criticism implying that the author has sacrificed psychological depth and credibility for emotional excitement and adventurous plotting.

Metafiction: Fiction that consciously explores its own nature as a literary creation. The Greek word *meta* means "upon"; metafiction consequently is a mode of narrative that does not try to create the illusion of verisimilitude but delights in its own fictional nature, often by speculating on the story it is telling. The term is usually associated with late-20th-century writers like John Barth, Italo Calvino, and Jorge Luis Borges.

Metaphor: A statement that one thing is something else, which, in a literal sense, it is not. By asserting that a thing is something else, a metaphor creates a close association between the two entities and usually underscores some important similarity between them.

Meter: A recurrent, regular, rhythmic pattern in verse. When stresses recur at fixed intervals, the result is meter.

Metonymy: Figure of speech in which the name of a thing is substituted for that of another closely associated with it.

Microcosm: The small world as created by a poem, play, or story that reflects the tensions of the larger world beyond. In some sense, most successful literary works offer a microcosm that illuminates the greater world around it.

Mime: Either a play or sketch without words, or the performer.

Minimalist fiction: Contemporary fiction written in a deliberately flat, unemotional tone and an appropriately unadorned style.

Monologue: An extended speech by a single character. The term originated in drama, where it describes a solo speech that has listeners (as opposed to a soliloquy, where the character speaks only to himself or herself). A short story or even a novel can be written in monologue form if it is an unbroken speech by one character to another silent character or characters.

Myth: A traditional narrative of anonymous authorship that arises out of a culture's oral tradition. The characters in traditional myths are usually gods or heroic figures. Myths characteristically explain the origins of things—gods, people, places, plants, animals, and natural events—usually from a cosmic view. A culture's values and belief systems are traditionally passed from generation to generation in myth. In literature, myth may also refer to boldly imagined narratives that embody primal truths about life. Myth is usually differentiated from legend, which has a specific historical base.

Narrative poem: A poem that tells a story. Narrative is one of the four traditional modes of poetry, along with lyric, dramatic, and didactic. Ballads and epics are two common forms of narrative poetry.

Naturalism: A type of fiction or drama in which the characters are presented as products or victims of environment and heredity. Naturalism, considered an extreme form of realism, customarily depicts the social, psychological, and economic milieu of the primary characters. Naturalism was first formally developed by French novelist Emile Zola in the 1870s. In promoting naturalism as a theory of animal behaviour, Zola urged the modeling of naturalist literature and drama on the scientific case study. The writer, like the scientist, was to record objective reality with detachment; events onstage should be reproduced with sufficient exactness to demonstrate the strict laws of material causality. Important American Naturalists include Jack London, Theodore Dreiser, and Stephen Crane.

Nonfiction novel: A genre in which actual events are presented as a novel-length story, using the techniques of fiction (flashback, interior monologues, etc.).

Novel: An extended work of fictional prose narrative. The term *novel* usually implies a book-length narrative (as compared to more compact forms of prose fiction like the short story). Because of its extended length, a novel usually has more characters, more varied scenes, and a broader coverage of time than a short story.

Novella: In modern terms, a prose narrative longer than a short story but shorter than a novel (approximately 30,000 to 50,000 words). Unlike a short story, a novella is long enough to be published independently as a brief book. Classic modern novellas include Franz Kafka's *The Metamorphosis*, Joseph Conrad's *Heart of Darkness*, and Thomas Mann's *Death in Venice*. During the Renaissance, however, the term *novella* originally referred to short prose narratives such as those found in Giovanni Boccaccio's *Decameron*.

Octameter: A verse meter consisting of eight metrical feet, or eight primary stresses, per line.

Octave: A stanza of eight lines. *Octave* is a term usually used when speaking of sonnets to indicate the first eight-line section of the poem, as distinct from the *sestet* (the final six lines).

Omniscient narrator: Also called all-knowing narrator. A narrator who has the ability to move freely through the consciousness of any character. The omniscient narrator also has complete knowledge of all of the external events in a story.

Onomatopoeia: A literary device that attempts to represent a thing or action by the word that imitates the sound associated with it (e.g., crash, bang, pitter-patter).

Open denouement: One of the two conventional types of denouement or resolution. In open denouement, the author ends a narrative with a few loose ends, or unresolved matters, on which the reader is left to speculate.

Open form: Verse that has no set formal scheme—no meter, rhyme, or even set stanzaic pattern. Open form is always in free verse.

Overstatement : Also called **hyperbole**. Exaggeration used to emphasize a point.

Pantomime: Acting on the stage without speech, using only posture, gesture, movement, and exaggerated facial expressions to mimic a character's actions and express feelings. Originally, in ancient Rome, a pantomime was a performance all the parts played single-handedly.

Parable: A brief, usually allegorical narrative that teaches a moral.

Paradox: A statement that at first strikes one as self-contradictory, but that on reflection reveals some deeper sense. Paradox is often achieved by a play on words.

Parallelism: An arrangement of words, phrases, clauses, or sentences side-by-side in similar grammatical or structural way. Parallelism organizes ideas in a way that demonstrates their co-ordination to the reader.

Parody: A mocking imitation of a literary work or individual author's style, usually for comic effect. A parody typically exaggerates distinctive features of the original for humorous purposes.

Pentameter: A verse meter consisting of five metrical feet, or five primary stresses, per line. In English, the most common form of pentameter is iambic.

Persona: Latin for "mask". A fictitious character created by an author to be the speaker of a poem, story, or novel. A persona is always the narrator of the work and not merely a character in it.

Personification: A figure of speech in which a thing, an animal, or an abstract term is endowed with human characteristics. Personification allows an author to dramatize the nonhuman world in tangibly human terms.

Petrarchan sonnet: See **Italian sonnet**.

Picaresque: A type of narrative, usually a novel, that presents the life of a likable scoundrel who is at odds with respectable society.

Plot: The particular arrangement of actions, events, and situations that unfold in a narrative. A plot is not merely the general story of a narrative but the author's artistic pattern made from the parts of the narrative, including the exposition, complications, climax, and denouement.

Point of view: The perspective from which a story is told. There are many types of point of view, including first-person narrator (a story in which the narrator is a participant in the action) and third-person narrator (a type of narration in which the narrator is a non-participant).

Prosody: The study of metrical structures in poetry.

Protagonist: The central character in a literary work. The protagonist usually initiates the main action of the story, often in conflict with the antagonist.

Psalms: Sacred songs, usually referring to the 150 Hebrew poems collected in the Old Testament.

Pun: A play on words in which one word is substituted for another similar or identical sound, but of very different meaning.

Purgation: See **Katharsis**.

Quatrain: A stanza consisting of four lines. Quatrains are the most common stanza used in English-language poetry.

Realism: An attempt to reproduce faithfully the surface appearance of life, especially that of ordinary people in everyday situations. As a literary term, realism has two meanings—one general, the other historical. In a general sense, realism refers to the representation of characters, events, and settings in ways that the spectator will consider plausible, based on consistency and likeness to type. This sort of realism does not necessarily depend on elaborate factual description or documentation but more on the author's ability to draft plots and characters within a conventional framework of social, economic, and psychological reality. In a historical sense, Realism (usually capitalized) refers to a movement in the 19th-century European literature and theater that rejected the idealism, elitism, and romanticism of earlier verse dramas and prose fiction in an attempt to represent life truthfully. Realist literature customarily focused on the middle class (and occasionally the working class) rather than the aristocracy, and it used social and economic detail to create an accurate account of human behavior. Realism began in France with Honoré de Balzac, Gustave Flaubert, and Guy de Maupassant and then moved internationally. Other major realists include Leo Tolstoy, Henry James, Anton Chekhov, and Edith Wharton.

Refrain: A word, phrase, line, or stanza repeated at intervals in a song or poem. The repeated chorus of a song is a refrain.

Regionalism: The literary representation of a specific locale that consciously uses the particulars of geography, custom, history, folklore, or speech. In regional narratives, the locale plays a crucial role in the presentation and progression of a story that could not be moved to another setting without artistic loss. Usually, regional narratives take place at some distance from the literary capital of a culture, often in small towns or rural areas. Examples of American regionalism can be found in the writing of Willa Gather, Kate Chopin, William Faulkner, and Eudora Welty.

Resolution: The final part of a narrative, the concluding action or actions that follow the climax.

Restoration period: In England, the period following the restoration of Charles II to the throne in 1660, extending to 1700. King Charles reopened the theaters that had been closed by the Puritans as sinful institutions. The Restoration period reintroduced a strong secular and urbane element back into English literature.

Rhyme, Rime: Two or more words that contain an identical or similar vowel sound, usually accented, with following consonant sounds (if any) identical as well: queue and stew, prairie schooner and piano tuner.

Rhyme/Rime scheme: Any recurrent pattern of rhyme within an individual poem or fixed form. A rhyme scheme is usually described by using small letters to represent each end rhyme—*a* for the first rhyme, *b* for the second, and so on. The rhyme scheme of a stanza of common meter or hymn meter, for example, would be notated as *abab.*

Rhythm: The pattern of stresses and pauses in a poem. A fixed and recurring rhythm in a poem is called meter.

Rising action: That part of the play or narrative, including the exposition, in which events start moving toward a climax. In the rising action the protagonist usually faces the complications of the plot to reach his or her goal.

Romance: In general terms, romance is a narrative mode that employs exotic adventure and idealized emotion rather than realistic depiction of character and action; in the romantic mode—out of which most popular genre fictions develop—people, actions, and events are depicted more as we wish them to be (heroes are very brave, villains are very bad) rather than the complex ways they usually are. Medieval romances (in both prose and verse) presented chivalric tales of kings, knights, and aristocratic ladies. Modern romances, emerging in the 19th century, represented by adventure novels like Sir Walter Scott's *Ivanhoe* or Nathaniel Hawthorne's *The House of the Seven Gables*, which embodied the symbolic quests and idealized characters of earlier, chivalric tales in slightly more realistic terms, a tradition carried on in contemporary popular works like the *Star Wars* and James Bond films.

Romantic comedy: A form of comic drama in which the plot focuses on one or more pairs of young lovers who overcome difficulties to achieve a happy ending (usually marriage).

Round character: A term coined by English novelist E. M. Forster to describe a complex character who is presented in depth and detail in a narrative. Round characters are those who change significantly during the course of a narrative. Most often, round characters are the central characters in a narrative.

Run-on line: A line of verse that does not end in punctuation, but carries on grammatically to the next line. Such lines are read aloud with only a slight pause at the end. A run-on line is also called **enjambment.**

Sarcasm: A conspicuously bitter form of irony in which the ironic statement is designed to hurt or mock its target.

Satiric comedy: A genre using derisive humor to ridicule human weakness and folly or attack political injustices and incompetence. Satiric comedy often focuses on ridiculing characters or killjoys, who resist the festive mood of comedy. Such characters, called humors, are often characterized by one dominant personality trait or ruling obsession.

Satiric poetry: Poetry that blends criticism with humor to convey a message. Satire characteristically uses irony to make its points. Usually its tone is one of detached amusement, withering contempt, and implied superiority.

Scene: In drama, the scene is a division of the action in an act of the play. There is no universal convention as to what constitutes a scene, and the practice differs by playwright and period. Usually a scene represents a single dramatic action that builds to a climax (often ending in the entrance or exit of a major character). In this last sense of a vivid and unified action, the term can be applied to fiction.

Selective omniscience: The point of view that sees the events of a narrative through the eyes of a single character. The selectively omniscient narrator is usually a non-participant narrator.

Sentimentality: A usually pejorative description of the quality of a literary work that tries to convey great emotion but fails to give the reader sufficient grounds for sharing it.

Sestet: A poem or stanza of six lines. *Sestet* is a term usually used when speaking of sonnets, to indicate the final six-line section of the poem, as distinct from the octave (the first eight lines).

Setting: The time and place of a literary work. The setting may also include the climate and even the social, psychological, or spiritual state of the participants.

Simile: A comparison of two things, indicated by some connectives, usually *like*, *as*, *than*, or a verb such as *resemble*. A simile usually compares two things that initially seem unlike but are shown to have a significant resemblance. "Cool as a cucumber" and "My love is like a red, red rose" are examples of similes.

Slack syllable: An unstressed syllable in a line of verse.

Slant rhyme: A rhyme in which the final consonant sounds are the same but the vowel sounds are different, as in letter and litter, bone and bean. Slant rhyme may also be called **near rhyme**, **off rhyme**, or **imperfect rhyme**.

Soliloquy: In drama, a speech by a character alone onstage in which he or she utters his or her thoughts aloud. The soliloquy is important in drama because it gives the audience insight into a character's inner life, private motivations, and uncertainties.

Sonnet: From the Italian *sonnetto*: "little song". A traditional and widely used verse form, especially popular for love poetry. The sonnet is a fixed form of fourteen lines, traditionally written in iambic pentameter, usually made up of an **octave** (the first eight lines) and a concluding **sestet** (six lines). There are, however, several variations, most conspicuously the Shakespearean, or English sonnet, which consists of three quatrains and a concluding couplet. Most sonnets turn, or shift in tone or focus, after the eight lines, although the placement may vary.

Spondee: A metrical foot of verse containing two stressed syllables often substituted into a meter to create extra emphasis.

Stanza: From the Italian, meaning "stopping-place" or "room". A recurring pattern of two or more lines of verse, poetry's equivalent to the paragraph in prose. The stanza is the basic organizational principle of most formal poetry.

Static character: See **Flat character**.

Stock character: A common or stereotypical character that occurs frequently in literature.

Stream of consciousness: Not a specific technique, but a type of modern narration that uses various literary devices, especially interior monologue, in an attempt to duplicate the subjective and associative nature of human consciousness. Stream of consciousness often focuses on imagistic perception in order to capture the pre-verbal level of consciousness.

Stress: An emphasis or accent placed on a syllable in speech. Clear pronunciation of polysyllabic words almost always depends on correct placement of their stress. Stress is the basic principle of most English-language meter.

Style: All the distinctive ways in which an author, genre, movement, or historical period uses language to create a literary work. An author's style depends on his or her characteristic use of diction, imagery, tone, syntax, and figurative language. Even sentence structure and punctuation can play a role in an author's style.

Surrealism: A modernist movement in art and literature that tries to organize art according to the irrational dictates of the unconscious mind. Founded by the French poet André Breton, surrealism sought to reach a higher plane of reality by abandoning logic for the seemingly absurd connections made in dreams and other unconscious mental activities.

Suspense: Enjoyable anxiety created in the reader by the author's handling of plot. When the outcome of events is unclear, the author's suspension of resolution intensifies the reader's interest—particularly if the plot involves characters to whom the reader or audience is sympathetic. Suspense is also created when the fate of a character is clear to the audience, but not to the character. The suspense results from the audience's anticipation of how and when the character will meet his or her inevitable fate.

Symbol: A person, place, or thing in a narrative that suggests meanings beyond its literal sense. Symbol is related to allegory, but it works more complexly. In an allegory an object has a single additional significance. By contrast, a symbol usually contains multiple meanings and associations.

Symbolic act: An action whose significance goes well beyond its literal meaning. In literature, symbolic acts usually involve some conscious or unconscious ritual element like rebirth, purification, forgiveness, vengeance, or initiation.

Symbolist movement: An international literary movement that originated with the 19th-century French poets such as Charles Baudelaire, Arthur Rimbaud, and Paul Verlaine. Symbolists aspired to make literature resemble music. They avoided direct statement and exposition for powerful evocation and suggestion. Symbolists also considered the poet as a seer who could look beyond the mundane aspects of the everyday world to capture visions of a higher reality.

Synecdoche: The use of a significant part of a thing to stand for the whole of it or vice versa.

Tactile imagery: A word or sequence of words that refers to the sense of touch.

Tale: A short narrative without a complex plot, the word originating from the Old English *talu*, or "speech". Tales are an ancient form of narrative found in folklore, and traditional tales often contain supernatural elements. A tale differs from a short story by its tendency toward lesser developed characters and linear plotting. British writer A. E. Coppard characterized the underlying difference by claiming that a story is something that is written and a tale is something that is told. The ambition of a tale is usually similar to that of a yarn; revelation of the marvelous rather than illumination of the everyday world.

Tall tale: A humorous short narrative that provides a wildly exaggerated version of events. Originally an oral form, the tall tale assumes that its audience knows the narrator is distorting the events. The form is often associated with the American frontier.

Tetrameter: A verse meter consisting of four metrical feet, or four primary stresses, per line.

Theater of the absurd: Postwar European genre depicting the grotesquely comic plight of human beings thrown by accident into an irrational and meaningless world. The critic Martin Esslin coined the term to characterize plays by writers such as Samuel Beckett, Jean Genet, and Eugene Ionesco. Samuel Beckett's *Waiting for Godot* (1955), considered to be the greatest example of the absurd, features in two nearly identical acts two tramps waiting almost without hope on a country road for an unidentified person, Godot. "Nothing happens, nobody comes, nobody goes, it's awful," one of them cries, perhaps echoing the unspoken thoughts of an audience confronted by a play that refuses to do anything.

Theme: A generally recurring subject or idea conspicuously evident in a literary work.

Third-person narrator: A type of narration in which the narrator is a non-participant. In a third-person narrative the characters are referred to as "he", "she", or "they". Third-person narrators are most commonly omniscient, but the level of their knowledge we may vary from total omniscience (the narrator knows everything about the characters and their lives) to limited omniscience (the narrator is limited to the perceptions of a single character).

Tone: The attitude toward a subject conveyed in a literary work.

Total omniscience: A type of point of view in which the narrator knows everything about all of the characters and events in a story. A narrator with total omniscience can also move freely from one character to another. Generally, a totally omniscient narrative is written in the third person.

Tragedy: The representation of serious and important actions that lead to a disastrous end for the protagonist. The final purpose of tragedy in Aristotle's formulation is to evoke catharsis by means of events involving pity and fear. A unified tragic action, from beginning to end, brings a morally good but not perfect tragic hero from happiness to unhappiness because of a mistaken act, to which he or she is led by a **hamartia**, an error in judgment. Tragic heroes move us to pity because their misfortunes are greater than they deserve, because they are not evil, having committed the fateful deed or deeds unwittingly and involuntarily. They also move us to fear, because we recognize in ourselves similar possibilities of error. We share with the tragic hero a common world of mischance.

Tragic flaw: A fatal weakness or moral flaw in the protagonist that brings him or her to a bad end.

Tragicomedy: A type of drama that combines elements of both tragedy and comedy.

Transferred epithet: A figure of speech in which the poet attributes some characteristic of a thing to another thing closely associated with it. Transferred epithet is a kind of metonymy. It usually places an adjective next to a noun in which the connection is not strictly logical but has expressive power.

Trimeter: A verse meter consisting of three metrical feet, or three primary stresses, per line.

Trochaic, trochee: A metrical foot in which a stressed syllable is followed by an unstressed syllable as in the words *sum-mer* and *chor-us*. The trochaic meter is often associated with songs, chants, and magic spells in English.

Understatement: An ironic figure of speech that deliberately describes something in a way that is less than the true case.

Unities: The three formal qualities recommended by Italian Renaissance literary critics to unify a plot in order to give it a cohesive and complete integrity. Traditionally, good plots honored the three unities—of action, time, and place. The action in neoclassical drama, therefore, was patterned by cause and effect to occur within a 24-hour period. The setting took place in one unchanging locale. In *The Poetics*, Aristotle urged only the requirement of unity of plot, with events patterned in a cause-and-effect relationship from beginning through middle to the end of the single action imitated.

Unreliable narrator: A narrator who—intentionally or unintentionally—relates events in a subjective or distorted manner. The author usually provides some indication early on in such stories that the narrator is not to be completely trusted.

Verbal irony: A statement in which the speaker or writer says the opposite of what is really meant.

Verisimilitude: The quality in a literary work of appearing true to life. In fiction, verisimilitude is usually achieved by careful use of realistic detail in description, characterization, and dialogue.

Verse: From the Latin *versum*, "to turn". Verse has two major meanings. First, it refers to any single line of poetry. Second, it refers to any composition in lines of more or less regular rhythm—in contrast to prose.

Visual imagery: A word or sequence of words that refers to the sense of sight or presents something one may see.

Appendix 4

Critical Approaches to Literature

Formalist Criticism

Formalist Criticism regards literature as a unique form of human knowledge that needs to be examined on its own terms. To a formalist, a poem or story is not primarily a social, historical, or biographical document; it is a literary work that can be understood only by reference to its intrinsic literary features, that is, those elements found in the text itself. To analyze a poem or story, therefore, the formalist critic focuses on the words of the text rather than facts about the author's life or the historical milieu in which it was written. The critic would pay special attention to the formal features of the text—the style, structure, imagery, tone, and genre. These features, however, are usually not examined in isolation, because formalist critics believe that what gives a literary text its special status as art is how all of its elements work together to create the reader's total experience.

A key method that formalists use to explore the intense relationships within a poem is **close reading**, a careful step-by-step analysis and explication of a text. The purpose of close reading is to understand how various elements in a literary text work together to shape its effects on the reader. Since formalists believe that the various stylistic and thematic elements of literary work influence each other, these critics insist that form and content cannot be meaningfully separated. The complete interdependence of form and content is what makes a text literary. When we extract a work's theme or paraphrase its meaning, we destroy the aesthetic experience of the work.

Biographical Criticism

Biographical Criticism begins with the simple but central insight that literature is written by actual people and that understanding an author's life can help readers more thoroughly comprehend the work. Anyone who reads the biography of a writer quickly sees how much an author's experience shapes—both directly and indirectly—what he or she creates. A formalist critic might complain that we would also have noticed those things through careful textual analysis, but biographical information provides the practical assistance of underscoring subtle but important meanings in the poems. Though many literary theorists have assailed biographical criticism on philosophical grounds, the biographical approach to literature has never disappeared because of its obvious practical advancing advantage in illuminating literary texts.

It may be helpful here to make a distinction between biography and biographical criticism. **Biography** is, strictly speaking, a branch of history; it provides a written account of a person's life. To establish and interpret the facts of a poet's life, for instance, a biographer would use all the available information—not just personal documents such as letters and diaries but also the poems for the possible light they might shed on the subject's life. A biographical critic, however, is not concerned with recreating the record of an author's life. Biographical criticism focuses on explicating the literary work by using the insight provided by knowledge of the author's life. Quite often, biographical critics will examine the drafts of a poem or story to see both how the work came into being and how it might have been changed from its autobiographical origins.

A reader, however, must use biographical interpretations cautiously. Writers are notorious for revising the facts of their own lives; they often delete embarrassments and invent accomplishments while changing the details of real episodes to improve their literary impact. A savvy biographical critic always remembers to base an interpretation on what is in the text itself; biographical data should amplify the meaning of the text, not drown it out with irrelevant material.

Historical Criticism

Historical Criticism seeks to understand a literary work by investigating the social, cultural, and intellectual context that produced it—a context that necessarily includes the artist's biography and milieu. Historical critics are less concerned with explaining a work's literary significance for today's readers than with helping us understand the work by re-creating, as nearly as possible, the exact meaning and impact it had on its original audience. A historical reading of a literary work begins by exploring the possible ways in which the meaning of the text has changed over time.

Psychological Criticism

Psychological Criticism is a diverse category, but it often employs three approaches. First, it investigates the creative process of the arts: What is the nature of literary genius, and how does it relate to normal mental functions? Such analysis may also focus on literature's effects on the reader. How does a particular work register its impact on the reader's mental and sensory faculties? The second approach involves the psychological study of a particular artist. The third common approach is the analysis of fictional characters. Freud's study of *Oedipus* is the prototype to this approach, which tries to bring modern insights about human behavior into the study of how fictional people act. While, psychological criticism carefully examines the surface of the literary work, it customarily speculates on what lies underneath the text—the unspoken or perhaps even unspeakable memories, motives, and fears that covertly shape the work, especially in fictional characterization.

Mythological Criticism

Mythological Criticism is an interdisciplinary approach that combines the insights of anthropology, psychology, history, and comparative religion. If psychological criticism examines the artist as an individual, mythological criticism explores the artist's common humanity by tracing how the individual imagination uses symbols and situations—consciously or unconsciously—in ways that transcend its own historical milieu and resemble the mythology of other cultures or epochs.

A central concept in mythological criticism is the archetype, a symbol, character, situation, or image that evokes a deep universal response. The idea of the archetype came into literary criticism from the Swiss psychologist Carl Jung, a lifetime student of myth and religion. Jung believed that all individuals share a "collective unconscious", a set of primal memories common to the human race, existing below each person's conscious mind. Archetypal images (which often relate to experiencing primordial phenomena like the sun, moon, fire, night, and blood), Jung believed, trigger the collective unconscious. We do not need to accept the literal truth of the collective unconscious, however, to endorse the archetype as a helpful critical concept. The late Northrop Frye defined the archetype in considerably less occult terms as "a symbol, usually an image, which recurs often enough in literature to be recognizable as an element of one's literary experience as a whole".

Sociological Criticism

Sociological Criticism examines literature in the cultural, economic, and political context in which it is written or received. "Art is not created in a vacuum," critic Wilbur Scott observed, "it is the work not simply of a person, but of an author fixed in time and space, answering a community of which he is an important, because articulate part." Sociological criticism explores the relationships between the artist and society. Sometimes it looks at the sociological status of the author to evaluate how the profession of the writer in a particular milieu affected what was written; sociological criticism also analyzes the social content of literary works—what cultural, economic or political values a particular text implicitly or explicitly promotes. Finally, sociological criticism examines the role the audience has in shaping literature.

An influential type of sociological criticism has been **Marxist Criticism**, which focuses on the economic and political elements of art. Marxist criticism often explores the ideological content of literature. It is frequently evaluative and judges some literary work better than others on an ideological basis. There is always a danger in sociological criticism—Marxist or otherwise—of imposing the critic's personal politics on the work in question and then evaluating it according to how closely it endorses that ideology. As an analytical tool, however, Marxist criticism and sociological methods can illuminate political and economic dimensions of literature that other approaches overlook.

Gender Criticism

Gender Criticism examines how sexual identity influences the creation and reception of literary works. Gender studies began with the feminist movement and influenced by such works as Simone de Beauvoir's *The Second Sex* (1949) and Kate Millett's *Sexual Politics* (1970) as well as sociology, psychology, and anthropology. Feminist critics believe that culture has been so completely dominated by men that literature is full of unexamined "male-produced" assumptions. They see their criticism correcting this imbalance by analyzing and combating patriarchal attitudes. Feminist criticism has explored how an author's gender influences—consciously or unconsciously—his or her writing. Another important theme in feminist criticism is analyzing how sexual identity influences the reader of a text. Finally, feminist critics carefully examine how the images of men and women in imaginative literature reflect or reject the social forces that have historically kept the sexes from achieving total equality.

Recently, gender criticism has expanded beyond its original feminist perspective. Critics have explored the impact of different sexual orientations on literary creation and reception. A men's movement has also emerged in response to feminism, seeking not to reject feminism but to rediscover masculine identity in an authentic, contemporary way. Led by poet Robert Bly, the men's movement has paid special attention to interpreting poetry and fables as myths of psychic growth and sexual identity.

Reader-Response Criticism

Reader-Response Criticism attempts to describe what happens in the reader's mind while interpreting a text. If traditional criticism assumes that imaginative writing is a creative act, reader-response theory recognizes that reading is also a creative process. Reader-response critics believe that no text provides self-contained meaning; literary texts do not exist independently of readers' interpretations. A text, according to this critical school, is not finished until it is read and interpreted. Reader-response criticism explores how the different individuals (or classes of individuals) see the same text differently. It emphasizes how religious, cultural and social values affect readings; it also overlaps with gender criticism in exploring how men and women read the same text with different assumptions.

Deconstructionist Criticism

Deconstructionist Criticism rejects the traditional assumption that language can accurately represent reality. Language, according to deconstructionists, is a fundamentally unstable medium; consequently, literary texts, which are made up of words, have no fixed, single meaning. Deconstructionists insist, according to critic Paul de Man, on "the impossibility of making the actual expression coincide with what has to be expressed, of making the actual signs coincide with what is signified". Since they believe that literature cannot definitively express its subject matter, deconstructionists tend to shift their attention away from what is being said to how language is being used in a text.

Paradoxically, deconstructionist criticism often resembles formalist criticism; both methods usually involve close reading. But while a formalist usually tries to demonstrate how the diverse elements of a text cohere into meaning, the deconstructionist approach attempts to show how the text "deconstructs", that is, how it can be broken down—by a skeptical critic—into mutually irreconcilable positions. A biographical or historical critic might seek to establish the author's intention as a means to interpreting a literary work, but deconstructionists reject the notion that the critic should endorse the myth of authorial control over language. Deconstructionist critics like Roland Barthes and Michel Foucault have therefore called for "the death of the author", that is, the rejection of the assumption that the author, no matter how ingenious, can fully control the meaning of a text. They have also announced the death of literature as a special category of writing. In their view, poems and novels are merely words on a page that deserve no privileged status as art; all texts are created equal—equally untrustworthy, that is.

Deconstructionists focus on how language is used to achieve power. They try to understand how some "interpretations" come to be regarded as truth. A major goal of deconstruction is to demonstrate how those supposed truths are at best provisional and at worst contradictory. Deconstruction calls for intellectual subtlety and skill. It may strike you as a negative, even destructive, critical approach, and yet its best practitioners are adept at exposing the inadequacy of much conventional criticism. By patient analysis, they can sometimes open up the most familiar text and find unexpected significance.

Cultural Studies

Cultural Studies refers to a relatively recent interdisciplinary field of academic inquiry. This field borrows methodologies from other approaches to analyze a wide range of cultural products and practice. From the start, this interdisciplinary field relied heavily on literary theory, especially Marxist and feminist criticism. It also employed the documentary techniques of historical criticism combined with political analysis focused on issues of social class, race, and gender. (This approach flourished in the United where it is called New Historicism.) Cultural studies is also deeply anti-formalist, since the field concerns itself with investigating the complex relationship among history, politics, and literature. Cultural studies rejects the notion that literature exists in an aesthetic realm separate from ethical and political categories.

A chief goal of cultural studies is to understand the nature of social power as reflected in "texts". The relevant mission of cultural studies is to identify both the overt and covert values reflected in a cultural practice. The cultural studies critic also tries to trace out and understand the structures of meaning that hold those assumptions in place and give them the appearance of objective representation. Any analytical technique that helps illuminate these issues is employed.

In theory, a cultural studies critic might employ any methodology. In practice, however, he or she will most often borrow concepts from deconstruction, Marxist analysis, gender criticism, race theory, and psychology. Each of these earlier methodologies provides particular analytical tools that cultural critics find useful. What cultural studies borrows from deconstructionism is its emphasis on uncovering conflict, dissent, and contradiction in the works under analysis. Whereas traditional critical approaches often sought to demonstrate the unity of a literary work, cultural studies often seeks to portray social, political, and psychological conflicts it masks. What cultural studies borrows from Marxist analysis is an attention to the ongoing struggle between social classes, each seeking economic (and therefore political) advantage. Cultural studies often asks questions about what social class created a work of art and what class (or classes) served as its audience. Among the many things that cultural studies borrowed from gender criticism and race theory is a concern with social inequality between the sexes and races. It seeks to investigate how these inequities have been reflected in the texts of a historical period or a society. Cultural studies is, above all, a political enterprise that views literary analysis as a means of furthering social justice.

Bibliography

Abrams, M. H. (ed.). *The Norton Anthology of English Literature*. (7th ed. 2 vols.) London and New York: W. W. Norton & Company, 2003.

Baldick, C. *Oxford Concise Dictionary of Literary Terms*. Oxford: Oxford University Press, 2000.

Barth, John. "The literature of exhaustion". *The Friday Book: Essays and Other Nonfiction*. Baltimore: The John Hopkins University Press, 1997.

Baym, Nina, et al (eds.). *The Norton Anthology of American Literature*. (6th ed.) New York: W. W. Norton and Company, 2003.

Bigsby, C. W. E. *Modern American Drama: 1945-2000*. Cambridge: Cambridge University Press, 2000.

Booz, Elizabeth B. *A Brief Introduction to Modern American Literature*. Shanghai: Shanghai Foreign Language Education Press, 1982.

Booz, Elizabeth B. *A Brief Introduction to Modern English Literature*. Shanghai: Shanghai Foreign Language Education Press, 1984.

Chang, Yaoxin. *A History of American Literature*. Tianjin: Nankai University Press, 2008.

Chen, Jia (ed.). *Selected Readings in English Literature* (3 vols.) Beijing: The Commercial Press, 1986.

Chen, Shidan. *A Study of American Postmodernist Fiction*. Tianjin: Nankai University Press, 2010.

Drabble, Margaret (ed.). *The Oxford Companion to English Literature* (6th ed.). Oxford: Oxford University Press, 2005.

Elliott, Emory. *The Columbia History of the American Novel*. Beijing: Foreign Language Teaching and Research Press, 2005.

Greenblatt, Stephen, et al (eds.). *The Norton Anthology of English Literature* (8th ed.). New York: W. W. Norton and Company, 2006.

Harmon, William & C. Hugh Holman. *A Handbook to Literature* (7th ed.). Upper Saddle River, New Jersey: Prentice Hall, 1996.

Hayman, Ronald. *British Theatre Since 1955: A Reassessment*. Oxford: Oxford University Press, 1979.

Hart, James D. *The Oxford Companion to American Literature* (6th ed.). Oxford: Oxford University Press & Beijing: Foreign Language Teaching and Research Press, 2005.

Hu, Jialuan (ed.). *Annotated English Poetry, an Anthology*. Beijing: Foreign Language Teaching and Research Press, 2003.

Kennedy, X. J. & Dana Gioia. *Literature: An Introduction to Fiction, Poetry, and Drama* (8th ed.). New York: Longman, 2002.

Liu, Bingshan (ed.). *The Concise History of British Literature*. Kaifeng: Henan People's Press, 2005.

Liu, Bingshan & Luo Yimin (eds.). *An Annotated Anthology of English Literature*. Kaifeng: Henan People's Press, 2005.

Millard, Kenneth. *Contemporary American Fiction: An Introduction to American Fiction Since 1970*. Beijing: Foreign Language Teaching and Research Press & Oxford: Oxford University Press, 2006.

Miller, Ruth & A. Greensberg Robert. *Poetry: An Introduction*. New York: St. Martin's Press, 1981.

Nelson, Carry (ed.). *Anthology of Modern American Poetry*. Oxford: Oxford University Press, 2000.

Rabey, David Ian. *English Drama Since 1940*. Essex: Peason Education Ltd., 2003.

Richetti, John (ed.). *The Columbia History of the British Novel*. Beijing: Foreign Language Teaching and Research Press, 2005.

Selden, Raman. *Practicing Theory and Reading Literature: An Introduction*. New York: Harvester Wheatsheaf, 1989.

Stoppard, Tom. *Rosencrantz and Guildenstern Are Dead*. London: Faber and Faber Ltd., 1967.

陈世丹. 美国文学史. 北京:中国人民大学出版社,2013.

戴桂玉. 新编英美文学欣赏教程. 北京:中国社会科学出版社,2001.

侯维瑞. 英国文学通史. 上海:上海外语教育出版社,1999.

刘海平,王守仁. 新编美国文学史(四卷本). 上海:上海外语教育出版社,2000.

金李俪. 英美戏剧选读. 武汉:武汉大学出版社,2007.

钱青. 美国文学名著精选. 北京:商务印书馆,1994.

秦秀白. 文体学概论. 长沙:湖南教育出版社,1986.

陶洁. 美国文学选读. 北京:高等教育出版社,2005.

王守仁. 英国文学选读. 北京:高等教育出版社,2005.

杨岂深. 美国文学选读. 上海:上海译文出版社,1987.

杨岂深. 英国文学选读. 上海:上海译文出版社,1981.

杨仁敬. 美国后现代派小说论. 青岛:青岛出版社,2004.

杨仁敬. 简明美国文学史. 上海:复旦大学出版社,2014.

张定铨,吴刚. 新编英国文学史. 上海:上海外语教育出版社,2002.